# BIG GAME HUNTER'S DIGEST

## By Tom Brakefield

DBI BOOKS, INC. NORTHFIELD, ILLINOIS

**STAFF**

EDITOR
**TOM BRAKEFIELD**

COVER AND EDITORIAL PHOTOGRAPHY
**TOM BRAKEFIELD**

CONTRIBUTING PHOTOGRAPHERS
**JACK JONAS**
**JACK ATCHESON**
**ELGIN GATES**

PRODUCTION MANAGER
**PAMELA J. JOHNSON**

ASSOCIATE PUBLISHER
**SHELDON L. FACTOR**

## Dedication

*For Johnny Holmes —*
*The Cassiar Mountains outfitter who is a keen*
*student of both hunting and hunters . . . and a*
*darn fine guy to share a spotting scope with!*

# TABLE OF CONTENTS

**CHAPTER 1:**
How To Get Your Whitetail Deer ........................ 5

**CHAPTER 2:**
How To Get Your Mule Deer ......................... 20

**CHAPTER 3:**
How To Get Your Pronghorn ......................... 33

**CHAPTER 4:**
How To Get Your Elk ............................. 43

**CHAPTER 5:**
How To Get Your Caribou ......................... 56

**CHAPTER 6:**
How To Get Your Moose .......................... 71

**CHAPTER 7:**
How To Get Your Mountain Game:
The Sheep And Goats ........................... 88

**CHAPTER 8:**
How To Get Your Black Bear ..................... 105

**CHAPTER 9:**
How To Get Your Alaskan Brown And Grizzly Bear ........ 116

**CHAPTER 10:**
What Is Killing Power? ......................... 130

**CHAPTER 11:**
How To Spot Game ............................ 140

**CHAPTER 12:**
How To Choose Your Hunting Optics ................. 150

**CHAPTER 13:**
The Big Game Hunter's Knife ..................... 162

**CHAPTER 14:**
Choosing And Using The Right Clothing And Duffle ........ 170

**CHAPTER 15:**
Getting The Most Out Of Your Trophies And Meat ........ 193

**CHAPTER 16:**
How To Book A Hunt With A Professional Outfitter ....... 208

**CHAPTER 17:**
Tips On How To Save Money ...................... 222

**CHAPTER 18:**
Big Game Hunting In Alaska ..................... 234

**CHAPTER 19:**
Recommended First Big Hunt: Late Season Moose/Caribou ... 248

**CHAPTER 20:**
Using A Hunting Consultant Or Booking Agent ........... 256

**CHAPTER 21:**
Take Care Of Those Leather Goods! ................. 267

**CHAPTER 22:**
A Planning Primer For Your Hunt Of A Lifetime .......... 271

**APPENDIX**
Where To Get Your Deer
(Whitetail, Mule, and Blacktail Deer) .................. 286

# INTRODUCTION

MAN has evolved over countless millenia as an eyes-front, binocular-visioned, weapons-fashioning and weapons-using hunter. And he *will* hunt. Whether at the office, at the cocktail party or business social or even out on the golf course. Quite simply: he is a predator.

And though a few thousand years of surface acculturation have taught him how to partially control and channel these primordial instincts so that he can function in a complex and interdependent human society, the process has been incomplete at best. When these hunting instincts are denied and sublimated past a certain point, the person in question becomes vulnerable to all sorts of negative and even neurotic impulses. And, certainly in this era, this applies to women as well as men. For those instincts are there and they will be heard from. To deny man's hunting heritage — his *need* to hunt — is as naive as to believe that a single coat of paint can transform the character of a worn out, useless automobile.

There are the cosmetics and there are the realities of life. To confuse the two can be more than dangerous. In this era of mass production and mass application, it can be cataclysmic.

This is a book about hunting in the most direct and, many of us feel, most constructive sense. The book is directed at the beginning-to-intermediate hunter with — hopefully — enough insight and substance to also interest the veteran. The aim is to better acquaint the reader with the craft of big game hunting — not so that he can kill more efficiently, but so that he can hunt more enjoyably.

Today's big game hunting is not a narrow and parochial sport primarily concerning itself with the act of killing. No. It is far more than that. For many urbanized people who become ever more removed from the natural world each year, it furnishes one of the best ways known to apply those natural hunting instincts in a constructive fashion. Hunting is a *process* which enables many to familiarize themselves with and function within the natural world in a fashion that is simply not possible in any other way.

Throughout years past some grievous excesses were committed in the name of hunting. However, today sport hunters furnish the hard dollars that finance practically all of the vitally needed work in the areas of both scientific research and practical game management. For big game is a dynamic, renewable, changeable resource that must be managed. It can not be "stockpiled" as the total-preservationist would have one believe.

In fact, to confuse the terms "preservationist" and "conservationist" will eventually spell disaster — for the animals and for man himself. The well-informed hunter is one of the most influential and effective conservationists in the land. The total-preservationist, however well intentioned, is not.

Special thanks must go to DBI Books, Inc., for granting the necessary time extension when personal affairs delayed the completion of this book. It is their understanding and generosity that have allowed me to share with you my continuing fascination with this never-ending education process that some call big game hunting.

# CHAPTER 1

# How To Get Your Whitetail Deer

**THICK MIST** oozed slowly upward from the damp south Alabama bottomlands. A small boy crouched near the end of a thick fence row, dividing a pasture from a thick stubble field. It was the random ears of corn scattered throughout the stubble field that had made the boy decide to take his stand there. The deer liked corn and often came, as the tracks showed, to do some corn stealing. It had been spooky walking down the narrow, two-rutted country road in the moonless night to get there. The gentle rain had pattered down, not enough to drench the boy but enough to add to the overall dampness that now seeped into the marrow of his bones as he sat motionless by his fence row. The darkness of the moonless night and the intermittent rain made the boy believe that the deer would not be out feeding then but would wait for the warmth and dryness of dawn to eat breakfast. If his logic were right, then he might well get his first shot at a deer.

The east bloomed from orange to yellow as the cold sun made its way over the pines, gaining in warmth and light as it rose higher. The brighter light began shredding the mist into ever smaller swatches, and now the lad could make out the dim outline of undergrowth

A big whitetail buck like this fellow is a magnificently honed survival machine. To take him, you must gun the game fields, know where and how your quarry lives and what his weak spots are.

# WHITETAIL DEER RANGE

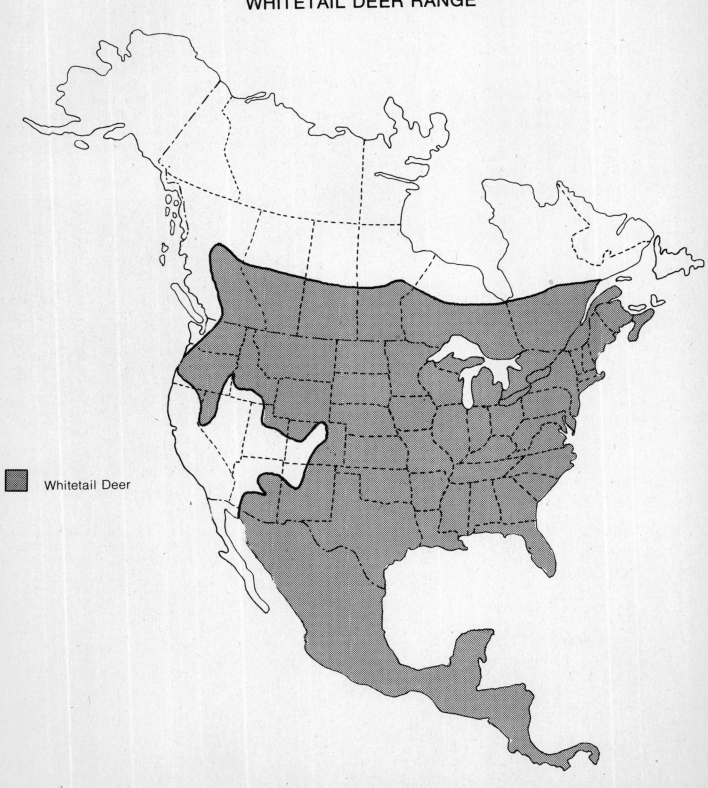

Whitetail Deer

bordering the tree line on the other side of the stubble field. A thousand needles began piercing his feet where they had gone to sleep. But still he dared not move. He had read how sharp-eyed and wary the deer were. And now, at first light, was the time he had dreamed of so often. The time when he would get his first buck. The time when he would become a *big game hunter*.

His eyes constantly roved back and forth searching the fence row and the edge of the other side of the field. He had to blink them furiously to clear them every once in a while when they teared up due to the strain he was putting on them by staring so intensely. A hint of movement caught his attention out of the left. Was it real or imagined? Was he just seeing his own eye blink and getting excited for nothing? (That had happened several times before.) He strained his eyes so hard he found himself squinting. There it was again. Just a twitch. And again. Now he could tell what it was as the side of a deer's head and neck slowly resolved themselves among the hanging vines and honeysuckle tangle. A flicking ear as the deer nervously surveyed the scene, nose in the air to test the wind. The gentle breeze blew straight into the young hunter's face, and the boy silently thanked whatever providence was responsible for such good works.

The deer, a large, round-barreled doe, moved tentatively out to the edge of the trees. As she flitted along daintily beside the undergrowth, several more shapes materialized behind her. Two smaller does and a fawn of the year followed her out into the field, nosing their way along after corn. The boy bit his lip and muttered to himself, but still he stood silent and unmoving. Time dragged. The four deer had fanned well out into the field, and if the young hunter moved, he was sure to be seen now.

And then he was there. A second before there was nothing but emptiness. Then a proud little six-point buck stood at the field's edge looking out toward the

does with a hunger for more than the corn. This was what the boy had been counting on. The little buck stamped his foot, almost impatiently it seemed, and moved toward the does with a twitch of his tail. The buck stopped, still about 40 yards out and partially obscured by the other deer. This was a bit further than the boy wanted to shoot with his "double aught" loaded 12 gauge shotgun, so he waited. The buck nosed up to the tail of the largest doe just as the boy felt a wayward eddy of wind against the back of his neck. Suddenly, as if on the same string, all four deer threw their heads up and darted off toward the sheltering trees. Up came the battered old 12 gauge Browning to the boy's shoulder and it settled in, bead on the buck, just as he reached the last row of knee-high stubble stalks.

A running whitetail buck is a tough target to hit.

A typical deer hunting sight — a startled whitetail buck the instant before it whirls away through the trees. Quick reflexes and sure gun handling are called for here.

The long gun belched just as the buck gave one final lunge and was lost in the trees. The boy stood there, numb and frozen to the spot. His first deer and he had missed! Then he noticed a rustling in the brush. There it came again, spasmodically as the young buck kicked out his life. The boy ran toward the brush, heart up in his mouth, and gingerly parted the creepers and branches. There he was. A fine young buck, laying in a bower of honeysuckle with his eyes already glazing. A clean kill on his first shot ever at "big" game.

Of course, as you've guessed by now, I was that skinny long-legged boy, and the thrill of that magic morning has never worn off to this day, a generation later in time. In fact the thrill of all whitetail deer hunting remains as exciting and engrossing as ever it was on that trip and the many youthful ramblings (most of them fruitless, I might add) that were to follow. Because, over the years as I've come to know my quarry better, I've found that the whitetail deer, in every region of the country and in every season of the year, always had something new to teach me. He's a lifetime course in natural history, this marvelous whitetail deer of ours, and we're fortunate indeed to have him in this country and in such good numbers.

## The Quarry

Once I heard a rather wealthy and well traveled hunter disparaging deer hunting, saying that it was "only" whitetail that the people he was talking about were after. It was obvious that this hunter had, somewhere along the way, lost sight of his hunting basics. Though the whitetail isn't the largest of big game animals, the most ferocious of adversaries, or even the prettiest of trophies, there are many that feel he can claim to be king of all the world's many fabulous big

The moment of truth. A deer hunter about to take his buck that has just wandered into sight over the ridge.

This hunter has just taken his buck from a stand in the mists of early dawn on opening day.

A hunter's sight of a lifetime — two magnificent trophy bucks each with a spread of better than 20 inches, fighting furiously during the annual rut. This is the one period when even the cagiest old bucks can get a little careless.

game species. A contradictory statement you say? Not really. If the ultimate test of an animal's challenge as a game species is his wariness, cunning and adaptability — his *survival quotient* — then the whitetail deer must surely rank right up at the top.

He's the most populous large game animal in the world with his North American totals running well over 11 million. Only the African wildebeest or gnu with possibly 8 million or 9 million head and the African zebra with perhaps a herd of 5 million to 7 million could even begin to challenge him. And yet the situation for these three animals is in no way comparable. Though Africa is rapidly becoming overpopulated and "development" of the land is proceeding apace, it is still a far cry from the most industrialized nation on earth, as is our own country where the whitetail lives and thrives. To make the picture even more intriguing though the whitetail exists in one fashion or another in just about all 48 of the contiguous U. S. states, *his highest populations are still found in the heavily populated, highly*

A real trophy. Very large buck alert in snowy woods and about to line it out. Many hunters never see a buck this nice in the hard hunted eastern woods where most bucks are taken before they can reach the age of 6 or 7 — the number of years it takes to grow antlers this size.

*industrialized eastern section of the country!*

Though various taxonomists may disagree a hair, it is commonly agreed that there are approximately 30 different subspecies of the whitetail deer in North America and that about 17 of these range throughout the southern 48 states and eight Canadian provinces. (The remaining 13 subspecies live further to the south in Mexico and Central America.) These range upward in size from the tiny key deer which stand an elfin 24 to 26 inches at the shoulder and weigh between 45 and 65 pounds. There are only about 300 of these miniature deer left within their restricted range, so they are of interest to the hunter only as a charming little curiosity. The largest of the whitetails are found in the northeastern U. S. and southeastern and southcentral Canada. Some of these enormous deer have been verified as weighing 400 pounds and more (live weight).

However, the average buck will weigh some 120 to 160 pounds and stand between 36 and 40 inches at the shoulder with an occasional large-average specimen standing 42 inches and weighing upwards of 200 pounds. Most beginning hunters tend to greatly overestimate the size of what they are looking for when they first take to the deer woods. For some reason, perhaps the feeling conveyed by the term "big game" itself, many beginners tend to look for animals that are chest to shoulder height on a man rather than animals that are belt buckle high plus a couple of inches. Or, to put it another way, many novices take off unconsciously looking for yearling-elk-sized game rather than for game about the size of a very large dog.

It's a common saying that "whitetail deer are more common nowadays than before the coming of Columbus." This is actually true for very basic and easily understandable reasons. The whitetail is a "succession species" meaning that it thrives on the bushy shrubs and lower branches of young trees in immature forests. When a forest is a mature or "climax" forest, the deer don't do so well as the lower branches of the trees are too high for them to feed on and the taller trees with larger, bushier crowns tend to choke off the sunlight and prevent it from reaching the ground where it would encourage the growth of shrubs, brush and undergrowth that the deer could browse on.

Prior to the coming of the white man, the eastern part of the country was practically a single, uninterrupted climax forest. Though fire, both from natural causes like lightning and due to some burning by Indians, interrupted this here and there with succession forest, the vast majority of the land was filled with tall climax forests that supported only a thin density of deer at best. With the advent of the white man and his land clearing, many succession species such as whitetail deer and cottontail rabbits literally exploded in population (more similarities between these two species will be noted as we go along). That is not so surprising, given a knowledge of the basic conditions. What *is*

In Texas hunters often "rattle up" bucks by rattling together another pair of antlers to simulate a rutty buck horning the brush or two other bucks jousting for a doe. Here veteran Texas woodsman Bob Ramsey demonstrates just how effectively this technique can be.

amazing is that the deer have been able to largely maintain their high densities in the face of ever denser human populations and ever more intensive land exploitation especially since the turn of the 20th century.

They have done this through their supreme adaptability. More specifically, they have learned, especially in densely populated areas, to become largely nocturnal animals, seldom venturing very far during the daylight hours. Many people in farming, exurbia and even densely packed suburban areas would be astounded if they knew how many deer were living in proximity to them. And yet, with the exception of seeing an occasional deer reflected in the headlights of their car as the animal crosses the highway or noting an occasional fresh track in the mud of a recent rain, the deer remain practically invisible.

Another advantage that the deer have going for them is their sensitivity in all the physical senses. Deer hear well, see well and have a marvelous sense of smell. All of these acute senses are constantly on the alert, and a whitetail deer, especially in heavily human-inhabited areas, literally never "relaxes." Like the cottontail rabbit, wariness and caution are engraved into the deepest core of their being. They don't get careless, to put it another way.

Perhaps their biggest advantage, the one that has done them the most good, is behavioral. The whitetail is not a wide ranging, easily flushed quarry. He has learned to skulk, to hide and, above all, to play it cool. When he sees man invade his home area, his first impulse isn't to charge away in wild abandon thus telegraphing his presence to possible enemies all around him. This is contrary to the behavior of practically all other North American big game species, incidentally.

No, when he spots his enemy, the whitetail usually freezes on the spot and lets him pass by. Most every deer hunter (and rabbit hunter) has had the experience of practically stepping on his game before suddenly flushing it out. Usually the hunter is so shocked and surprised that he either doesn't get a shot off or, at best, manages a rather hasty and poorly aimed shot at the rapidly bounding target. This emphasizes what should be the Number One Axiom for the whitetail deer hunter: *ALWAYS* STAY ALERT.

## How to Hunt for Whitetail Deer

Most every deer hunter with much experience knows that whitetails are just overgrown cottontail rabbits with antlers. By that sacrilege I mean that they're homebodies who grow up and often live and die within the same square mile. They survive by knowing "their" mile or so of turf as intimately as the rabbit knows his 1 or 2 acres of ground. They know every covert, fold of ground or thicket that they can hide in. They know every trail as intimately as a hunting dog knows his kennel run. They can bound off at flank

speed on any trail with complete safety. Put them in strange and unknown territory and they have accidents rushing through thick cover that is laced with unknown hidden holes, overhangs or other booby traps.

Yet I'm surprised at how few hunters realize just *how much* of a stay-at-home the whitetail is and — more to the point — how to put that habit to their advantage when hunting him without the benefit of dogs or other buddies to help drive the deer. The jumped whitetail who bounds off like a guy on the way to a date with Raquel Welch is actually going to stop just as soon as he has put some cover between himself and the hunter. This cover can be as substantial as a small hill or bluff or as skimpy as a small thicket or swamp. Anything that lets the deer put the brakes on unobserved and *without forcing him off his own beloved little home range.* A flushed out, wildly bounding deer will usually stop within 300 or 400 yards when not pressed too hard by a single hunter on foot.

Now that you know this, you can put it to good use. The deer invariably travels upwind, always questing with that laser-like nose for advance knowledge of what lies ahead of him. When the deer stops, his first reaction is to swing back in arcs to let whatever is trailing him catch up and pass him by while he watches, safely hidden off to the side. This way he has everything going

Though a whitetail looks like he's heading for the next state when you jump him up, don't be fooled. He'll stop just as soon as he puts a couple of obstructions between you and himself and then he'll probably circle around to cut your back trail and get downwind of you. Don't give up on a deer after you flush him out. Often you can intercept him on the back trail skulking arc and take him the second time around!

his way — he's safely hidden with the hunter upwind of him where the deer can keep tabs on the hunter, and the deer never had to leave the safety afforded by that precious homeland.

The seasoned deer hunter takes all this into account when he follows up a spooked deer. The hunter does *not* trail the deer directly but follows up roughly parallel to and downwind of the deer's trail, swinging in wide gentle arcs himself so as to intercept the crafty old buck as he starts arcing back himself. The knowing hunter pussyfoots along s-l-o-w-l-y ever so s—l—o—w—l—y. Time is strictly a man-made concept with no meaning to nature's creatures and least of all to a patient skulker like the whitetail. That old buck has all the time in the world — he's not meeting anyone anywhere, and he has no chores to do elsewhere. He's concentrating on one thing and one thing only — staying alive. And he's not going anywhere. He's already home. What he's going to do is very predictable and the hunter doesn't have to be in any kind of hurry himself. The hunter must see the buck before the buck sees him. Otherwise the game begins all over again, but this time the hunter has lost the critical element of initial surprise and thus is at a bigger disadvantage.

Here's a bird's-eye view of how the scene I've just described looks:

A big smart whitetail buck will practically let you step on him before flushing up in front of you. Just one of many things they have in common with that other animal which has adapted superlatively to civilization — the cottontail rabbit.

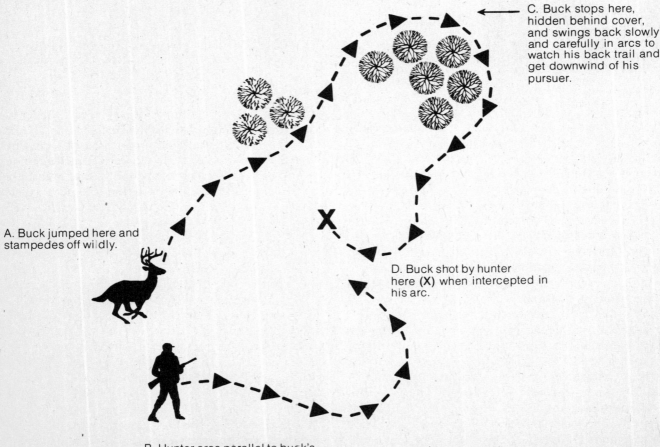

C. Buck stops here, hidden behind cover, and swings back slowly and carefully in arcs to watch his back trail and get downwind of his pursuer.

A. Buck jumped here and stampedes off wildly.

D. Buck shot by hunter here (X) when intercepted in his arc.

B. Hunter arcs parallel to buck's trail to intercept him after jumping him.

(Above) Good whitetail cover means thick cover, especially where those cagey old trophy bucks dwell. A deer was shot where the hunter is standing from where the camera is placed. Note that the hunter is almost hidden though he is hardly 30 feet from the camera.

(Left) Stand hunting is, by and large, probably the most effective way to take whitetail across the country under a variety of circumstances. But it takes patience.

The primary mistake that most hunters make when "still hunting" (moving through the woods trying to locate deer) is that they move far too fast and too noisily. Remember: deer are rather densely populated in good deer territory, and they're "homebodies." If you are on good deer ground, you don't have to move around much to come in contact with them. The best bet is to work your way through the woods slowly, taking three or four slow motion steps at a time and then pausing to look carefully ahead at all likely looking spots that might hide a deer. Place each foot carefully to avoid all the dry twigs, leaves and other natural noisemakers. If you spend all morning moving a mile or so, fine. If you walked several miles up and down hill and dale, you were moving too much and too fast. One thing that keeps the deer population high and the hunter success ratio low is that hunters get bored, and they begin to equate *movement* with *hunting*. Unfortunately, the two terms usually are anything but synonymous. If the hunter has done his homework properly, he shouldn't have to tramp around mile upon mile in the woods to locate his deer.

By homework, I mean that the hunter should have spent some research time and scouting time verifying that the area he is hunting is a good area for deer to begin with. Once he has established this, he should have spent additional time in pre-season scouting through the woods to locate the deer trails leading to and from the bedding areas and the feeding areas. He should never, if at all possible, enter the deer woods "blind" on opening day. He should know where to go and why.

Deer strategy varies during the season. In many states, especially the urbanized eastern "incubator" states with their densely populated herds of man-wise animals, more than half of the deer taken during the 2- to 3-week seasons are taken on opening day. To carry this further often more than half of *those* deer (or, more than a quarter of the total season's kill) are taken in the first hour or two that the season is open.

During this critical opening morning period, stand hunting is often the best bet. In fact, it's usually a good idea to do some stand hunting at dawn anytime throughout the season. Chances are better that the deer will still be moving around on their own at this time and, on a stand, you are much less likely to be seen by them before you can spot them. Elevated stands (where legal) are by far the most effective. Be sure to check

In much of the sparsely settled backcountry South, especially along the Gulf Coast, 4WD vehicles are every bit as necessary for deer hunters as they are out in the rough country West. Especially when the seasonal rains hit in their monsoon-like intensity.

your current state regulations about the height that stands may be and any other restrictions or limitations placed upon these elevated hiding places. Deer don't often look up so these "hides" are extremely effective. They don't have to be terribly high, either. Eight or 10 feet off the ground will often do fine. If, for one reason or another, elevated stands aren't a possibility, try to locate a good well-traveled deer trail leading from bedding grounds to feeding areas and then post yourself in some cover that will overlook a relatively open spot and still break up your own outline.

Once on stand it is necessary to move as little as possible. More and more hunters are turning to the use of strong scents, many of them man-made and approximating apples or other natural smells, to mask the human odor. The handiest of these come in small cloth bags that may be conveniently pinned to the lapel or collar of the hunting coat.

Perhaps a word about the feeding and movement habits of deer would help to clarify the situation. The average adult buck deer needs between 10 and 12 pounds of browse per day, depending upon the size and condition of the deer, the quality of the food and the coldness of the weather. Though he can temporarily get by with much less, over a long period a deer needs this much food to stay healthy. It will take a deer 1 to 2 hours of feeding to gather this much food, depending upon how often the deer is disturbed while feeding and how far he must travel to feed.

This food is compressed into cuds (about the size of lemons) in the deer's stomach. Later the deer will regurgitate these cuds and chew them while bedding down. How long he spends chewing these cuds also varies depending upon how often he is disturbed and how much food he took in. It takes about 60 seconds on the average to chew and re-swallow each cud. Though it may vary considerably, I would estimate that a deer spends roughly 2 to 3 hours a day, often in many separate sessions, chewing its cud.

Deer often feed at night or during the dawn hours. If the deer are bedded down at night chewing their cuds, they usually like to bed at the lower elevations during these cool hours. The colder nighttime temperatures mean that most air currents are flowing downwards and the deer can better use their noses to locate danger at these lower elevations. Conversely, during the day as the temperature gradually rises, the slightest bit of sunlight starts the thermals rising and wafting the scent *upwards*. Thus the deer move up toward the tops of the ridges (not necessarily on the very crests, though) to take advantage of these thermals as early warning signals and also because it is a bit more difficult for the hunters to climb up to them without being heard.

Pre-season scouting should tell you where the main trails are between these higher elevation bedding areas and the lower level bedding and feeding/watering spots. Deer, like most wild creatures, are creatures of habit and will use the same trails over and over and will bed in the same general area time after time. When scouting these trails for possible stand locations, look for natural gullies and gaps in the ridges and heavy brushy areas between the upper and lower bedding areas. Immediately after opening day the deer abandon the open trails and start skulking through these gaps and coverts to take advantage of all possible cover when crossing from one ridge to another or moving back and forth between the different elevations.

The whitetail, for all his acute vision, is (like all other mammals except man and the great apes) color blind. He sees everything in varying shades of gray. Though this is no handicap when spotting moving objects, it is a great disadvantage when trying to resolve stationary ones. Also, being an eyes-side prey species rather than an eyes-front predatory species (like man), his field of good depth perception — where the vision of both eyes overlaps significantly thus offering good "binocular" vision — is much narrower than man's. However, again due to his eyes-side vision, his wide angle or peripheral vision is much wider than man. Thus, overall he can see moving objects over a much wider span of view than

(Above) These deer hunters are slogging into the wet late winter woods to drop off standers along the way and then set up a deer drive with several drivers working a pattern back through the standers.

(Left) Here the leader of a deer drive is positioning the standers in a classic button hook drive pattern before setting the drivers to work back through them, hopefully driving several bucks in front of them as they do so.

man, but he has much more trouble fully resolving stationary objects when he does see them. Most all deer hunters have had does and fawns practically walk right over them when the wind was right and the hunter remained completely motionless. I have had deer come from hundreds of feet away and nonchalantly dawdle by within 6 feet of me. Inevitably they would notice me and become a bit quizzical and nervous, but if I didn't make any movements whatsoever (including blinking my eyes!), they would walk calmly by me. So, stand hunting is tremendously effective if:

1. The deer are moving around.
2. The stand is located in a good traffic area.
3. The hunter remains completely motionless.

Later in the day when the deer are bedded down, the hunter can either hunt by "still hunting" (moving through the woods slowly by himself to spot bedded deer) or by "driving" in conjunction with several other hunters and/or dogs. The ideal day for still hunting is when the conditions are drizzly, windy and generally a bit "sour" outside. The woods are damp and soundless, and the patient hunter can pussyfoot through them as silently as the deer themselves. The gusting, eddying wind constantly changes direction making it hard for the

deer to work his normal into-the-wind pattern in order to get a solid fix on disturbing odors up ahead of him.

If the wind is strong enough to whip the branches and limbs around making all sorts of odd and unpredictable noises, that's better yet as it keeps the deer on edge and makes it hard for him to identify the sounds of the hunter. The deer knows this is the most dangerous time as well as you do. Thus he seeks shelter in the heaviest, most inaccessible cover on his range during this kind of day. This is the day when the good hunter has a more reasonable chance at a midday deer and no one should go back to camp for a midday siesta as some do on clear, dry deer-advantage days.

The other midday option, especially on dry and windless days, is to drive the deer. This can be done with all hunters (as in the East) or with dogs or dogs and hunters (as in the South). A number of different driving patterns may be used but basically they all attempt to take advantage of the natural topographical features as well as the driver's movements in order to funnel the deer along predictable routes which will take them by standers that have been spotted along the way with ambush in mind.

Though many drivers take along all sorts of

(Above) A happy young deer hunter with his nice eight-point Pennsylvania (eastern count) buck.

(Right) These deer hunters enjoy a welcome break at mid-day with hot mulligan stew (made of venison, of course) back in deer camp.

noisemakers and whoop and holler it up, I have long felt that most hunters penalize themselves unnecessarily when they make a lot of noise on a deer drive (excepting southern dog hunters, that is). I prefer to just walk along normally. The deer will hear you anyway under these conditions, even if it's moist underfoot. But, unlike the situation where you are shouting, whistling and using noisemakers, the deer will have a more difficult time identifying just exactly where you are and how you are moving.

It is almost impossible to truly "drive" a deer who knows exactly where you are. His every instinct is to skulk back through the driver line and let them pass while he relaxes downwind and behind the danger. And a deer can slip between drivers who are amazingly close together. Especially those canny, coolheaded old bucks that we are all gunning for. But, if the deer knows there's trouble behind him in several spots, but he's not exactly sure where all the drivers are and how they are moving, he'll tend to keep dawdling along up ahead of the driver line (thus moving along where you want him, toward your standers) until he can get a better fix on their locations. He will not commit himself to the close encounter involved with slipping between drivers unless he knows for sure where all of them are.

Hunting or driving with dogs is a bit of a different proposition. Hunting deer with dogs is probably the most misunderstood type of relatively widespread hunting that exists in this country. The popular conception among many Easterners and Westerners who have never hunted this way, is to visualize a pack of evil-eyed, ravenous curs snapping at the very heels of the deer and finally running the poor exhausted creature to earth. Nothing could be further from the truth.

Although this isn't particularly a favorite hunting method of mine, for the country and conditions where it's used, it makes very good (and sporting) sense. Without the dogs, and the drivers who accompany them, there simply would not be enough hunting pressure from other hunters to keep the deer stirring. These southern states are, compared to the eastern states, thinly populated, and they don't field the legions of hunters that the latter do.

Also, the cover and undergrowth is much thicker here, making the deer almost impossible to spot or surprise. Dogs are almost a necessity in order to keep the deer moving, and even then they are difficult targets at best in this jungle-like underbrush.

The concept of the lean, ferocious deer hound is also far from the truth. Deer dogs come in all shapes, shades and sizes. All the good ones that I have ever seen were mixed breeds or mongrels, usually with a bit of hound of

This small but high quality Gerber folding knife is just about ideal for dressing out whitetails. (Photo courtesy of Gerber Legendary Blades)

(Left) This hunter is skinning an exceptionally fat young whitetail buck. Someone is going to have some outstanding winter eating off this fellow!

(Below) At the end of a successful deer hunt it's time to celebrate. This party involved some beer, several bushels of fresh oysters and lots of tall tales!

one type or another nesting in the family tree back along the way. Actually a good deer dog is one that is about worthless for anything else. You don't want him to be too cold nosed (keen nosed) or he'll spend far too much time unraveling a single old trail where the deer went many hours ago. You don't want him to be too persistent so that he won't spend too much time on any single trail unless it's smoking hot. Your good deer dog should be a bit adenoidal to the point of only smelling slightly better than a dedicated non-smoker. That way the mutt only picks up and works the warm trails and then promptly loses each of them as it cools and he hops onto another and then yet another. The idea is to stir up as many deer as possible, not to trail and track any single deer.

Furthermore, your good deer dog should *not* have a good set of legs and lots of "bottom" so that, like a prime Walker foxhound, he can strike a trail and then run it at high-cruise for hours on end. That would merely spook a single deer all the way out of the country (deer will temporarily leave that precious home range if

Here Jacqueline Parker, wife of noted big game hunter George Parker, shows the very fine Coues deer (a smaller southwestern race of whitetail) that she took in southern Arizona.

pressed hard enough) and well past all the standers. Again, the idea is to stir up many different deer and do it within gun range of the stander formation.

To cap it off, it's better still if the dog does not have a lot of heart and will to hunt. If he does, then not only will he push the deer too hard and run them out of the country rather than just keeping them stirred up, but he'll also tire himself out so that he can only run a single race every day or two rather than running the preferred two races a day. Also, at the end of the race he'll be much more difficult to round up (if he has a lot of will to hunt, that is) and that'll tire *you* out trying to catch him.

So, as I said before, the best deer dog is generally about the biggest four-legged bum you can find. Usually an overaged, overweight canine that has failed at most everything else. No special training is necessary, most any dog that can breathe would rather run deer than anything else if given even the mildest bit of encouragement.

The best deer dog that I ever personally saw work was an elderly and somewhat portly part basset/part God-knows-what. He was slow and lazy and a complete loser as far as possessing the normal magnificent basset nose. He worked close to the drivers, seldom getting out of their sight as he jumped from one deer trail to another with all the fickleness of a high school prom queen. He only opened up on the hottest of trails, and he soon lost them. Slow as cold molasses, he let each deer loaf along a comfortable 300 to 400 yards ahead of him, and he has never yet run a deer out of the country. He usually tired of all this activity after an hour or two and came in of his own accord. No one ever stayed out after dark looking for him, and he was so lazy that you could usually squeeze a modest afternoon race

out of him after running him in the morning unless the weather was too hot. He was one fine deer dog.

## Guns for Whitetail Deer

Whitetail are not very large animals, and being rather highly strung animals, they are somewhat susceptible to shock and thus relatively easy to lay down. No great amount of power or penetration is needed to dispatch

This whitetail buck is very large and would almost make the Boone and Crockett Record Book. The whitetail is by far the hardest species to "make the book" with.

18

The Winchester 94 carbine in .30-30 caliber is the all time best selling centerfire rifle and cartridge. Though losing some popularity in today's eastern deer woods, it is still a classic "close-in" deer hunting combination. (Photo courtesy Winchester-Western)

This 1.5-4.5x Swift Variable Power riflescope is just about ideal for all types of close-in to medium range whitetail hunting whether in the South, the East or the Midwest and far West.

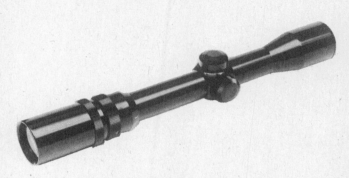

them neatly, and the types of guns and cartridges historically used on them in different regions of the country have reflected differences in cover and in the way the animal is hunted in that area rather than peculiarities of the animal itself.

In the East and the Southeast from the early 1900's through the late 1950's the classic "deer gun" was the fast talking lever action such as the Winchester Model 94 or the Marlin 336 in the time-tested .30/30, .32 special (a .30/30 by another name) and the .35 Remington. These guns fired fast and the "thutty-thutty" was felt to be a rather romanticized and "special" deer caliber. Though the .30/30 lever guns are still immensely popular, more and more hunters are switching to other guns and other cartridges. For those men desiring raw firepower, the advent of the modern autoloading centerfire rifle, shooting considerably more potent cartridges than those just mentioned, has been given the nod more and more in the last 20 years.

Also, as far more hunters have journeyed westward to try for mule deer and elk with flatter shooting and more accurate bolt action rifles, they have tended to also use these guns in the thick coverts at home. This makes sense not only for purposes of economy but also because the more familiar the hunter is with his gun, whether hunting in the East or the West, the better he is going to hit with it. Thus many hunters, especially the younger ones, now take to the woods east of the big river with various bolt actioned .243's, and .270's as well as all manner of heavier duty cartridges which really aren't needed for whitetail killing but serve nicely if the hunter can stand the extra recoil and doesn't mind carrying the extra weight.

Another legacy of the changing times is that far more southern and eastern hunters now use low powered scopes or vari-powered scopes rather than the old standby peep sight or the notoriously inaccurate full buckhorn open sights of another era. Actually, any gun that you feel comfortable with and can shoot accurately and that meets the legal minimums for your state's whitetail deer hunting regulations makes a fine deer rifle. The problem with whitetail is to find them and hit them, not to kill them.

# CHAPTER 2

# How To Get Your Mule Deer

**IN THE EARLY** 1960's I saw and missed the largest mule deer buck I have ever seen or probably ever will see. Great sweeping beams, thick as a woman's forearm and rivaling those of the average six-point bull elk in inside spread, insure that I will never forget my brush with that fellow. Quite possibly I will never see another mule deer of that size, and I *know* I'll never miss another really big one in quite the same fashion.

I was hunting in Wyoming's southeastern corner hard by the Colorado border on a combo hunt for both mule deer and pronghorn. Opening day of pronghorn season had seen me get lucky and collect on the near record book buck that I had spotted and been glassing for 2 days prior to the season. Now I was out after an equally impressive muley, and right at sunup I spotted a well qualified candidate peering out at me with some interest from a bit over 500 yards out. He was bedded down in some rocks on the rim of a small canyon with only his head showing. Those massive antlers, stained a rich mahogany, looked like a gnarled old bush they were so massive.

I had been glassing the open lands a half-mile and more behind the big deer for some good while before I

A nice mule deer buck pauses for a moment while working his way through the woods. In recent years muleys, especially shootable bucks like this fellow, have become less open country animals.

# MULE AND BLACKTAIL DEER RANGE/S

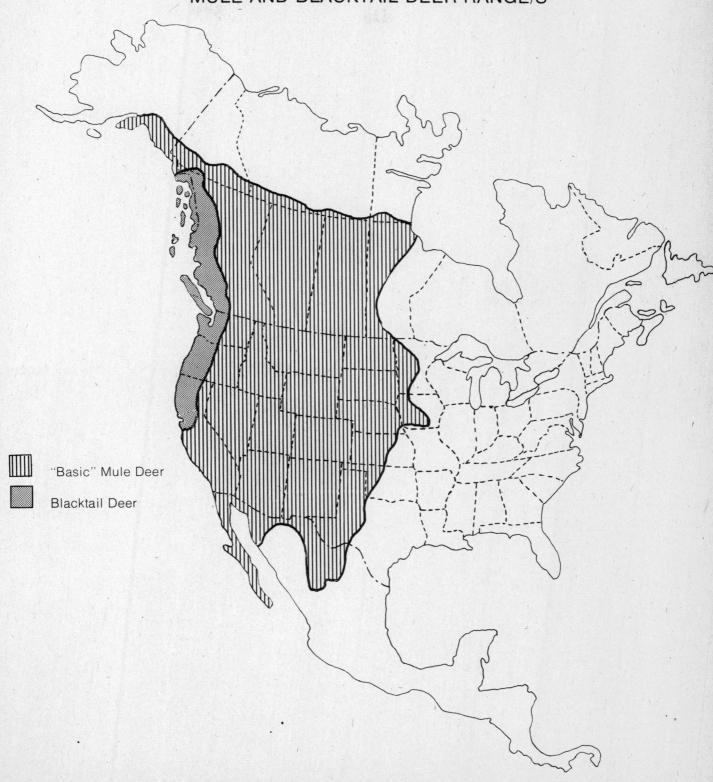

- ||||| "Basic" Mule Deer
- ▨ Blacktail Deer

This very large Montana mule deer buck has an unusually heavy and massive non-typical rack. Truly a trophy of a lifetime for the confirmed muley hunter.

A pair of miniature binoculars such as these Swift 7x-25's are effective in most mule deer hunting situations, and they are light and convenient to carry.

spotted him. Doubtless he had been eyeballing me all the while. Just as I was about to hop back into the beat up old pickup and move on, I idly swung the glasses by the rockpile where he was bedded down and I picked up the small highlight thrown up by the watery early morning sun glinting off that magnificent hatrack. It was just blind luck that I spotted him at all, and it certainly shows that outdoor writers are fallible creatures as I had been violating one of the most basic maxims of spotting game — ALWAYS SCAN THE FOREGROUND FIRST! There's a very lamentable but human tendency to glass the far areas first and then work in closer visually. I suppose this is due to the unconscious and erroneous assumption that no game will be nearby or, that if it is, you can either spot it casually with your naked eye or that it will spook too fast to shoot anyway. This old fellow had never read such sage outdoor writing so, instead of spooking, he had merely lain there and calmly counted the threads in my shirt while I energetically (and futilely) glassed half of Wyoming over his back.

We stared at each other with some interest for several moments. All he had to do was to duck his head a few inches and then drop down off the canyon wall behind him and he would be safely away. He was as safe as any Yellowstone Park mule buck dying of old age, and he knew it as well as I did. I stood there lusting after those big antlers and trying to figure out how in the dickens to stalk him in that situation.

Hopeless. The truck was completely out in the open with the nearest cover on either side being over a hundred yards away. I leaned over the hood studying him through the glasses. By now he knew not only how many teeth I had but where the fillings were — if I made the slightest suspicious move he'd be gone in a twinkling. Better to leave him in peace, mark the spot and try again later. Moving as if mired in molasses, I e-a-s-e-d open the offside door of the pickup, slid slowly across the seat to the steering wheel and cranked up the motor. As I drove slowly off, I could tell that my friend was still sitting there watching, no doubt chuckling to himself.

After a large circle of several miles I was on the big flat a mile or so behind where I had last seen him. About 1½ hours had gone by, and I figured he'd still be hanging around, probably moving up-canyon a bit to shift position to where the sun would be warming the rocks on this blustery cold day.

The little canyon was a pocket-sized mule deer Eden with food and water in abundance and offering all sorts of hiding places on its rocky walls, many with multiple and blind escape routes. Like a cagey old whitetail buck

A nice mule buck almost hidden by the high sage. The hunter must glass patiently and carefully in order not to miss trophies like this that are seemingly "out in the open."

Another mule deer buck that has learned to wait, look and listen before sneaking away in safety. His father and grandfather would have probably taken off running at first alert (and thus been out in plain sight for the hunter).

who knows every square centimeter of his rather small range intimately and depends upon this knowledge as his basic line of defense, why should this muley move from his natural haven at all? No wonder he had lived long enough to grow those neck-cricking antlers.

Switching off the engine, I quietly closed the door and snicked a round into the chamber of the .270. Off I started across the gently undulating sagebrush speckled flat. It was quite open and most of the sage clumps ran knee to chest high but looked hardly large enough to completely conceal a large deer. I wasn't even hunting yet, but was just making tracks for the back side of the rough little canyon where I was sure I would find my trophy from earlier in the morning. That was boner #2 for that day, and it taught me something else I've never forgotten: WHENEVER YOU ARE HUNTING, *STAY* ALERT!

I was only 400 yards from the truck when a huge, rolling fat deer magically conjured himself up from out of a sage clump that looked hardly large enough to hide a big jackrabbit. I goggled at him. Sure enough, he had to be my big buck, there just couldn't be two bucks that size in that immediate area. By the time I recovered my wits, he was about 200 yards out and moving away at top speed on that offbeat, pogo-stick bounce peculiar to muleys.

I snapped the gun up to my shoulder, swung through the running buck and as the cross hairs passed in front of his bobbing muzzle, touched off a shot. Dust mushroomed up in an ocher cloud about 2 feet behind his black tipped tail. He was moving faster than I thought, and the near miss inspired him to switch on the afterburner and really make tracks for the Colorado border.

Up until the late 1960's a mule deer buck about to disappear over a ridge as this one is about to do could often be halted for a last standing shot by a loud yell. No more. These deer have become much more sophisticated as they have been hunted harder in the intervening years.

Fuming and muttering, I frantically racked the bolt back, and in keeping with the conventional wisdom of those times, I let out a piercing yell just as the deer was about to go over a fold in the rolling flat and be lost to me forever.

Two things happened immediately. Sure enough, the big deer halted momentarily on the small crest and peered back my way, giving me a hurried opportunity to shoot at a standing target. Simultaneous with that the bolt jammed on me. The gun maker had just seen fit to change his basic bolt gun in a major fashion that year even though it had been the leader in the field for nearly 30 years. This "improved engineering" (which was mostly thinly disguised cost cutting that negatively affected the quality of the gun in certain respects) had resulted in a bolt that tended to jam when racked back hard. Anti-bind rails helped to correct that particular defect a year or so later, but that didn't help me with this deer. The big deer stood there for several agonizing seconds giving me plenty of time for an aimed shot —*if* I could have gotten that blasted gun to work.

Too late. I almost whimpered as a trophy of a lifetime finally turned and disappeared out of my life while I

A trotting mule deer buck, even one moving relatively slowly such as this fellow, makes a deceptively tough target due to their peculiar, pogo stick gait.

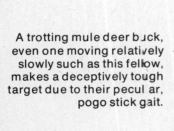

On a shot like this the mule deer hunter should place his bullet immediately behind the front leg and about one-third of the way up from the brisket or bottom of the deer's chest.

fussed with that cursed gun. Perhaps, between my own mistakes and that gun, the Almighty just didn't mean for me to get my venison that day. Aside from the jammed gun this story is fairly typical for the period that I call the "golden era" of mule deer hunting. This time span peaked in the mid-1960's but persisted as late as 1970-72 in some areas. It is far from typical today.

## The Game

Mule deer stand 40-42 inches at the shoulder, and the average adult will be substantially larger than a comparable whitetail doe or buck, though the very largest members of both deer tribes are, surprisingly, just about identical in size. A nice, average mule deer buck will run 175 to 200 plus pounds (live weight) while a comparable whitetail buck, depending upon which of the 30 or so subspecies are involved, will run around 135 to 175 pounds. The mule deer buck will measure 6½ feet in body length (again, for a good average buck) which is about 6 to 10 inches longer than a comparable whitetail buck. The tail of the muley is smaller than the whitetail's and black-tipped rather than all white, while

the ears and, more importantly, the antlers are considerably larger. The mule deer's antlers are, in addition to being larger, shaped entirely differently. Whereas on the whitetail's antlers all points rise from the same main beam, the mule deer's antlers are forked or "bifurcated." The mule deer has a prominent black forehead patch which is missing on the whitetail, and he is basically more of an open country animal while the whitetail prefers heavier brush and denser woodlands. While whitetails abound in goodly numbers both east and west of the Mississippi and have, in the last 50 years, been extending their range, mule deer have never existed east of the big river and their range as a species is basically stable or shrinking a bit rather than expanding.

Mule deer have been noted for being somewhat stupid (compared to the cannier, skulking whitetail), but this is incorrect. It is true that, especially in earlier years when they weren't hunted so hard, mule deer were considerably more *naive* than whitetail (which is considerably different than being stupid). Mule deer preferred higher, more open country and were easier to spot. They flushed more easily than whitetail and would not lie around and let a hunter practically walk over them, thus adding to their visibility. More times than not a big mule deer, one of the most curious of animals, could be halted momentarily by a shrill yell or other unusual noise or commotion. This could be done in full flight as occurred in the situation I described at the beginning of this chapter. Whitetail always tended to "hang tough" and not spook so easily, but when they did go, nothing could make them hang around that extra fatal instant as was often the case with the muley.

That has changed. As any wild creature becomes more acquainted with man, he tends to become more sophisticated. The ruffed grouse of New England that is hotly pursued by legions of devoted hunters each fall is a spooky, canny bird that can easily drive hunters to

none of the hesitation that characterized the flight of his ancestors. I'm quite certain that I'll never again see a situation when I can halt a very large (thus older and wiser) mule deer buck by yelling as I did with the one mentioned earlier. For better or for worse, mule deer have come of age and become a far cagier and more challenging game animal. Still not the equal of the whitetail in coolness, they are trending more and more that way, and given several more generations of intimate exposure to man, who knows but that they may end up equaling the whitetail in wiliness and sophistication.

## Changing Trends in Mule Deer Hunting

With continent-wide numbers hovering around the 3

Mule deer, in common with whitetails, have become skulkers and sneakers as they have been hunted more intensively in recent years. Note this big buck sneaking through sage rather than running.

the brink of distraction. Yet the same bird in many western areas where it is seldom hunted hard can appear downright foolish. Some Easterners think that I'm pulling their leg when I tell them that I have seen areas where their beloved "partridge" can be killed with rocks! Same species but entirely different birds due to differences in exposure to man.

Thus it is with the mule deer. As he has become much more hotly pursued in the last 10 to 15 years, he has changed a good bit. Now he tends to haunt heavier cover, to feed more at night or during very early and later hours. He doesn't spook so easily and foolishly anymore, and when he does, he usually lines out with

million mark, the mule deer is still one of the half-dozen or so most populous large game animals on earth. There are a lot of mule deer around, and there is still a lot of good mule deer hunting. But the numbers have declined a bit over the peak era in the 50's and 60's, especially in certain areas. Reasons for this decline are complex and not yet fully understood. Part of it can most certainly be blamed on habitat loss due to more intensive farming, grazing, damming, highway construction and the like. Increased hunting pressure has had some effect but that has affected the average size of the trophies now being taken (fewer older, thus larger bucks nowadays) more than the total species populations.

This young mule deer buck with his doe is not as wary as he would be before or after the "moon of madness" as the annual rut is sometimes called.

Greatly increased coyote populations have certainly had a significant effect on mule deer populations in some areas. The wily little brush wolf is an interesting, even fascinating, predator who has taken about everything that man could throw at him and not only survived but, with the decline of larger competitive species like the cougar and timber wolves, even prospered. With the ban on poisoning and some other types of coyote control programs in recent years, the extremely intelligent little "yodel" dogs have undergone what amounts to a population explosion in many western and northern areas.

I'm not "anti-coyote" by any means. He's an exciting game animal in his own right, and he adds charm and excitement to the country he inhabits merely by being there. But, as his numbers have increased, so has his impact on the mule deer herds on which he preys heavily in many areas. Anyone who says coyotes don't kill adult mule deer as well as fawns doesn't know his natural history.

Coyotes, like the larger gray wolves, like to hunt around rivers and lakes, especially in the winter. Any hoofed animals that they catch crossing the ice or that they can haze out onto the ice are virtually helpless and can be easily killed, even by a single coyote. Hoofed animals simply can not maneuver on ice since they can hardly stand on the slick surface. In a recent winter, estimates ran as high as 1,400 deer killed by coyotes on eastern Montana's giant Fort Peck reservoir alone.

However, ice isn't necessary. Several coyotes working together can take the largest mule deer or even cow or calf elk if the latter are weakened by the rigors of the winter. I know of one instance where several coyotes hazed a cow elk into knee deep water in a Montana river and held her there for several days until she weakened, and when she did try to break out, they killed her relatively easily. They are smart animals, and they frequently hunt co-operatively to vastly increase their effectiveness against large prey.

## Increased Costs of Quality Mule Deer Hunting

Though total herd numbers are still good, they are down a bit. But the real change has come in the number of older, trophy-sized adult bucks. In any unhunted deer herd, the ratio of large, outsized bucks is rather small, running around 5 percent to 6 percent of total herd. When hunted these numbers decrease because these are, of course, the animals that most hunters (especially visiting out-of-state hunters from the East) are concentrating on. In addition mule deer are being much more heavily hunted now than just 5 to 10 years ago. Every year there are 10 percent or more additional hunters in the field and rather obviously the deer herd cannot continue to increase to match this growth so the result is increased pressure on the deer that are available.

Many areas that used to allow the taking of two or even three animals each season now allow only one or, in some cases, are closed entirely. Seasons have continued to shrink in length, and more and more areas now require the visiting Easterner to buy the complete big game license for elk, black bear and deer (which gener-

Mule deer hunters plan their hunting strategy in camp before dawn of opening day. (Photo courtesy Browning Arms Co.)

Typical hunting camp for a large group of hunters planning to hunt for a week or more.

ally runs around $200 to $250 these days) even if all the hunter wants is a deer tag. The deer-only license, for out-of-staters anyway, appears to be a rapidly dying option.

As demand for big mule deer bucks has gone up while supply has dwindled, prices for mule deer hunts — especially good trophy hunts — have exploded. To illustrate this point properly we'll compare the cost changes that a trophy mule deer hunt has undergone in recent years. We need to make a few arbitrary assumptions to flesh out our example. We'll assume that our visiting hunter is an Easterner who is an experienced, average-to-good deer hunter and that he has done a thorough job of selecting a good outfitter and area. He is going on a 5-day trophy hunt, and he wants a nice set of antlers which means he is not going to lower the boom on the first muley he sees whose rack exceeds that of any whitetail he has ever taken in Pennsylvania or Michigan or wherever he hails from.

Our hunter is sharing a guide with another hunter on his 5-day outing, and he is hunting a prime area with a first class outfitter. In this little exercise we are going to compare the costs of hunts that would give him a 75 percent chance of securing a decent trophy, assuming he does his part by being able to walk, climb and shoot straight. Here's how this hunt would have stacked up throughout the last few years:

|  | 1965 | 1970 | Today |
|---|---|---|---|
| Cost per day/ per hunter (*sharing* a guide) | $35 | $75 | $125-$150 and up (Sometimes added trophy fee charged for an unusually big head.) |
| 75% chance of taking trophy (including bad weather, etc.) | 26″ spread buck | 24″ | 20″-22″ |

These figures are worth pondering at some length. Since the mid-60's inflation has affected the general value of money to the extent of about 75 percent. Hunting, sadly, has been rising faster in cost than the general inflation rate of all mixed goods and services. Quality hunting, depending upon the area and the species of game animal, has probably risen in the neighborhood of 100 percent to 150 percent for most species. Some have skyrocketed even faster. My preceeding example indicates a price increase of over 250 percent for the comparable mule deer hunt over a period of somewhat more than a decade. Many mule deer hunting outfitters also charge an added trophy fee on the taking of a particularly good head, this often being scaled to the size of the rack. If you should happen to take a near record book head, expect to part with some coin!

There are other, subtler cost increases (or equivalents). For instance on the very same hunt, even quality outfitters now tend to hunt more men from the same camp than might have been the case back in 1965. Although vehicles are now often used to get hunters to and from the hunting area, thus vastly expanding the hunter's radius of action when compared to the all-horseback or all-backpack type of hunt, it's still not a good idea to hunt too many men out of the same camp. There are only so many good spots to hunt in a given area and only so many nice bucks to take. The same operator who might have hunted four men out of camp in 1965 will more than likely hunt six or perhaps even eight today.

This is a particularly important point to check before confirming your hunt. Sharing a guide with only one other hunter rather than two or three others loses much of its significance if the outfitter is hunting 10 or 12 men out of the same camp in a fairly restricted area. The size of an outfitter's area and the way he hunts it will govern how many hunters the outfitter can legitimately hunt from one camp at the same time. I prefer to hunt with no more than three other hunters in camp and with never more than five other hunters if I am after anything but meat for the larder.

This example illustrates graphically that quality mule deer hunting has zoomed in cost faster than most other hunting (partially because it used to be so cheap and thus for years was one of the best bargains around). Yet many hunters don't realize this and are not willing to pay the tab to get into a good area, well off the road with a good outfitter. As a consequence they fall prey to those few unscrupulous fast buck artists offering "trophy hunts" at ludicrously low prices. Except in special cases, the days of good cheap mule deer trophies are gone forever, my friends. A good mule deer hunt today rivals the same quality elk hunt in cost on a per diem basis; the main difference being that the mule deer hunt runs 5 to 7 days while the elk equivalent is usually a larger scale expedition taking 10 to 14 days thus costing more overall.

However, there's nothing inherently wrong with this situation. Mule deer are marvelous trophies. Frankly, up until rather recently, big mule deer bucks were underappreciated by many hunters simply due to the fact that they were — in relation to comparable trophies of other species — often available far more easily and cheaply. No more.

## Blacktail Hunting

Though taxonomically there is only one species of mule deer, blacktails or coastal muleys which inhabit a range running up the Pacific coast from northern California to Alaska have long enjoyed a bit of a separate status. These sub-variants of the basic mule deer usually run a bit smaller (about the size of the average eastern whitetail or perhaps 20 percent lighter than a comparable Rocky Mountain mule deer buck), and their racks are substantially smaller and lighter.

These are generally rain forest animals, inhabiting

The classic wool stag shirt is a good bet for late fall and early winter western mule deer hunting.

Taxidermist shows a nice mule deer head in the process of being mounted.

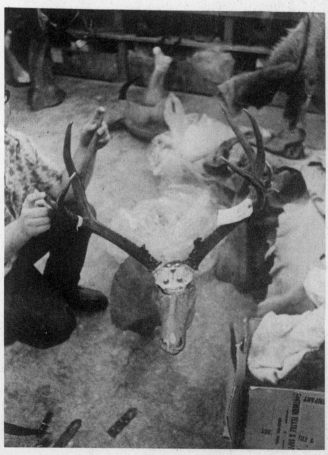

the thick matted cover of the coastal areas and often clinging to precipitous slopes that would give a mountain sheep pause. Hunting them is a tough proposition physically, and they are often considerably more elusive than the more open country muleys to the east of them. Dedicated blacktail stalkers delight in this difficult, arduous type hunting and prefer it to the dryer, more open mule deer hunting in the interior. The further north the blacktail ranges the smaller he runs in body size (thus providing a mild exception to the basic rule of nature postulating that the members of any given mammalian species ranging furthest from the equator are generally larger than their southern cousins). The elfin Sitka blacktails of the Alaskan coastal range offer difficult and challenging hunting for an elegant little trophy in some of the world's most beautiful and most difficult terrain. These little deer range right up with the mountain goats and can climb in an inspired fashion.

### Where to Go

Some of the best mule deer hunting for the "basic" animal occurs in Wyoming, Montana, Idaho and Colorado, all of which boast average annual kills running around 40,000 and herds running from a bit over 250,000 to about half a million. There is also quite good hunting for large muleys in selected areas of Arizona, New Mexico, and Utah, though the guiding and outfitting facilities for out-of-staters in these states are not as well developed as those in the first four mentioned states.

British Columbia boasts a large and healthy mule deer herd of some 500,000, and with the exception of areas close to the U. S. border, these animals are generally not nearly as hotly pursued as their southern counterparts due to the emphasis on other and larger

big game. A hunter in good condition and looking for a good mule deer trophy could do worse than hunt here.

Washington and Oregon probably boast the best overall blacktail hunting though good hunting is also found in British Columbia and Alaska. Since blacktail hunting is usually a bit more specialized, uncomfortable and arduous than general mule deer hunting, far fewer out-of-staters pursue these animals, and the services

Two nice mule deer bucks—the one on the left from Wyoming and the one on the right from Alberta in the trophy room of John McCartt of Warrior, Alabama.

This magnificent non-typical mule deer buck was shot by Elgin Gates, the well-known trophy hunter from Needles, California.

Another magnificent mule deer trophy taken by Elgin Gates. This one was shot in Arizona's Kaibab forest which for many years yielded outsized muley trophies.

far more on both the competence and *attitude* of his guide.

It is still relatively easy to get a "guide's" license in some western states to the extent that some of these "guides" are not the most competent around. The fly-by-night outfitter may be using youngsters from nearby ranches who know the country but may not be the best of hunters or who may be good hunters but who have little or no knowledge of how to best work with visiting out-of-state hunters who come from substantially different backgrounds and whose hunting experiences are considerably different from their own. Or, our cost-cutting outfitter who is mass manufacturing mule deer hunting may employ strangers who don't know much more about the area and the location of the game than do the out-of-state hunters.

The ability to properly size-up the visitor, get along with him so that he enjoys the hunting experience, as well as get the game and yet avoid communications problems along the way is definitely a knack that takes a bit of study and learning and one that is usually under-emphasized in outdoor writings of this type.

Good guides are always in short supply, and these other less reputable types are easier to find and cheaper to pay. So check out the guides as carefully as is reasonable when checking the outfitter's references. Find out how many hunters the outfitter will work from each camp, and if you are in good physical shape (and you should be, especially if you're out after a bragging-sized trophy), see if he has an area that is high, rough and must be hunted largely afoot.

Many mule deer outfitters hunt from comfortable ranches down in the valley, driving their hunters to the tops of the mountains in 4WD's and letting them out to hunt their way downhill back to the ranch or to a previously agreed upon pickup point. This is a reasonably comfortable way to do things, and it saves the outfitter the bother of setting up and maintaining semi-permanent high camps. It also implies that the area is hard combed by hunters of most any age or physical condition. Though it's a bit of a truism, it's still "oh, so true" that the best hunting for the big bucks is well

catering to nonresident hunters are much less well developed than those for hunters out after mule deer. However, a request for information from the Fish and Game Department of the state or province which you are interested in can provide some leads.

### Tips on How to Best Set Up a Successful Mule Deer Hunt

If I were an Easterner, Midwesterner or Southerner with designs on a nice trophy mule deer buck, I would spend a considerable amount of time checking references and arranging my hunt. I would be at least as interested in *who* I hunted with as I was in *where* I hunted. I would want to share a guide with no more than one other hunter (unless it was strictly a meat hunt), and I would be interested in knowing something about my outfitter's guiding staff. (How long have they been guiding, how long have they been with him, do *they* have any references, etc?) Due to the nature of most mule deer hunting, the outfitter is oftentimes less important (relatively) and the guides more important than other types of deep wilderness hunts for other species. On many mule deer hunts the visiting hunter may hardly meet the outfitter except at the hunt's beginning and end, and the success or failure of the outing may hinge

The Savage 99 is a classic lever action design that has been in use for over half a century, and it offers somewhat hotter, flatter shooting cartridges for open country muley hunting than do most other lever models. (Photo courtesy Savage Arms Co.)

The model 670 Winchester rifle (shown here with 4x Weaver scope) is a fine all-around big game rifle that comes in a variety of calibers. It is an ideal choice for the economy minded mule deer hunter. (Photo courtesy of Winchester-Western)

areas as I have previously described. A flat shooting rifle is called for, and if you are doing a lot of high country climbing, rifle weight and bulk become important factors.

If bigger game isn't also on the menu, rifles of the .243/6mm Remington/.257 Roberts class are fine and dandy. Recoil is light, so they are comfortable shooters even for ladies, youngsters and hunters who don't shoot much. Few people flinch when shooting one of these mild rounds. The .270 offers a bit more power and wind bucking ability, and it is probably the classic mule deer cartridge of them all. For the hunter who enjoys shooting it (and that should be the great majority of us), the .270 can hardly be beat. The rifle can still be kept rather light and short (with a 22-inch or 21-inch barrel), and muzzle blast and recoil will be tolerable. The .30/06 with spitzer pointed 150-grain bullets and the classic old 7mm mauser with sharp pointed 139-grain bullets are both mule deer killers that have performed well over a span of many years. The multitude of .270 look-alikes such as the .280 Remington, the .284 Winchester, the 6.5mm Remington Magnum and the .264 Winchester Magnum also work well though there is a bit more muzzle blast involved with the latter round.

The larger and more potent .284 and .308 Magnums aren't at all necessary for mule deer unless the hunter just happens to prefer his all-around gun in one of these calibers and thus wants to use it on muleys as well as thicker skinned game. Extremely heavily constructed bullets should be avoided as mule deer aren't massively built and any decently constructed controlled expansion bullet will penetrate to their vitals. A bullet designed to do a first class job of breaking the shoulders on a big moose or grizzly may well penetrate all the way through a mule deer, especially on a long range shot, thus wasting most of its precious energy on the landscape behind him.

away from the road up in the higher and rougher country where the average hunter can't drive or ride to get to them. If you want to go on a road hunt or modified road hunt, better plan on being out for meat more than antlers.

Book a 5- to 7-day hunt. The 3-day mule deer hunt doesn't work as well as it did a generation ago. If bad weather or a vehicle or horse type accident knocks you out of a day's hunting or if your hunting partner scores first and the necessary chore of field dressing his buck and getting it back to camp chews up most of a day (which it most often does), you're cutting your odds pretty thin on a 3-day hunt. Better to pay a bit extra and be successful. The longer hunt is usually a bit cheaper per day, and a hunt that was one big rush and thus isn't enjoyable isn't a bargain at any price.

### Guns for Mule Deer

Mule deer aren't particularly hard to lay down and keep down, so enormous power isn't necessary in your choice of rifle. Muleys are still basically an open country animal though they have taken to doing considerably more skulking around various ''edge'' and cover

# CHAPTER 3

# How To Get Your Pronghorn

**THE FALL WIND** had already sharpened, and the Wyoming hillsides glittered with reds and golds as the quaking aspens began turning color in their annual signal that winter was not far behind. It was a natural spectacle, and even though I had driven straight through from New York to Wyoming with only a wadded-up nap in the front seat of my station wagon in the pre-dawn stillness of western Nebraska. I felt myself quickening. Suddenly the cobwebs were gone, and whereas an hour ago I was exhausted, I now felt rejuvenated and began whistling some meaningless ditty to myself.

The road was wide and straight, and I drove slowly so I could ogle first one vista and then another as the wind made the hills sparkle and shimmer in an ever changing panorama as the leaves fluttered this way and that. A good time and a good place to be alive in. When I rounded one of the few curves in the road, I saw a gorgeous hillside, literally bathed in flickering gold, looming to my left. After several months of nothing more scenic than the Long Island Expressway, I drank it in as greedily as a thirsty man suddenly confronting a trickling alpine stream of purest snow melt.

And then I saw them. It was just as I had read in so many of those stories about hunting pronghorn out West. In the wide flat leading from the road up to that gorgeous golden ridge, I counted nine of them — all standing there watching me every bit as intently as I was looking at them. If I had not spotted a couple of

# PRONGHORN RANGE

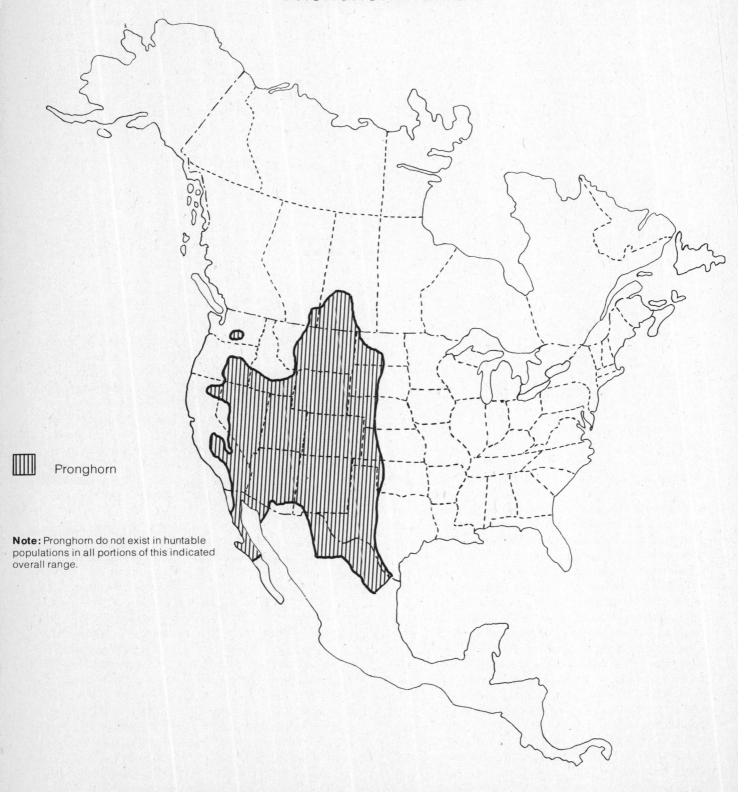

Pronghorn

**Note:** Pronghorn do not exist in huntable populations in all portions of this indicated overall range.

specks of white (the prominent white rump patches), I might have missed them altogether. Even in the 7x glasses they were still a bit small since they were well over 500 yards out. I coasted the wagon to a stop on the shoulder of the road but remained inside watching them. They stood their ground and watched me, alertly but with no panic, in fact seemingly without a care in the world.

I fumbled for the 20x spotting scope that I kept unpacked in the backseat for just such an occasion. The sill of the car window provided a steady rest, and

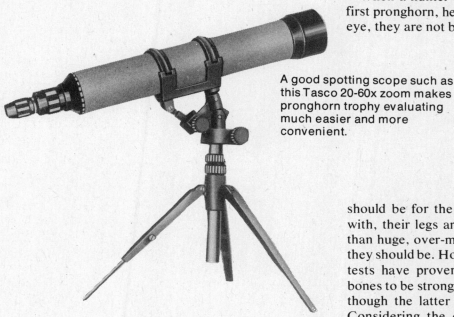

A good spotting scope such as this Tasco 20-60x zoom makes pronghorn trophy evaluating much easier and more convenient.

through the clear cool air of the high plains with no heat waves to interfere, the scope seemed to bring us practically nose to nose. What handsome, delicately beautiful little animals they were. Standing about 3 feet at the shoulder, they resembled a rather small, lightly limbed but round barreled little deer. But in general appearance they resembled no other animal because they are very unique, in both physiology and habit.

As an exercise I once spent some time trying to come up with the most appropriate one word description for each major North American big game species. With some of them I had to debate among several names, but there was never any doubt about the pronghorn. He has to be *UNIQUE*. He's the fastest animal in North America and, many believe, in the world. His closest competitors appear to be the cheetah and the Indian blackbuck. Some experienced Texans who have had plenty of opportunity to see both the pronghorn and the blackbuck run it with everything pushed to the firewall claim the pronghorn gets the nod. (A number of east Texas ranches have stocked the small Indian antelope both for their own enjoyment and for fee hunting.) The cheetah might be faster (though it's not certain by any

stretch), but like all cats with their miniature lungs, he's strictly limited to a few hundred yards at burst speed.

The fact that the pronghorn can, for short stretches, actually hit speeds in excess of 60 miles an hour is phenomenal. The fact that he can run for miles in excess of 40 mph is, to my mind, even more fantastic. The strength and power, the specialized adaptation of everything from organs such as the lungs and heart to the bone structure, that enable him to do this, simply boggles the mind. I would not believe that flesh and blood were capable of it were it not for the fact that the pronghorn is living proof that it is.

When a hunter kills and inspects at close range his first pronghorn, he is often surprised. To the untutored eye, they are not built the way one might suppose they should be for the world's fastest mammal. To begin with, their legs are tiny little pipe stem affairs rather than huge, over-muscled limbs one might assume that they should be. However, carefully organized scientific tests have proven these honeycombed, semi-hollow bones to be stronger than the bones of adult cattle even though the latter animals weigh ten times as much. Considering the enormous stresses placed on their bones by such high speed running over rough ground, there is undoubtedly more pressure applied to the bone structures of pronghorns than to those of the considerably heavier livestock.

The real secret of the pronghorn's blinding speed is not his legs but the secondary or support systems that enable him to drive these legs. He runs with his mouth gaping open and his tongue lolling out in an almost grotesque looking posture. This enables him to gulp a maximum amount of air through the mouth. His windpipe, lungs and heart are all enormously overdeveloped for an animal his size thus allowing him to take in and process or "burn" a phenomenal amount of oxygen. I'll never forget my reaction to my first pronghorn. Up close he was a highly attractive little trophy but not the svelte speedster I had quite imagined.

The cheetah is the perfect embodiment of the lithe, sinewy speedster built for a blinding single burst of speed. My pronghorn on the other hand had an enlarged barrel of a body supported by tiny, paperstraw-thin legs. He looked, as a buddy of mine once observed, something like a nice round potato jacked up on four toothpicks. Since then I have come to recognize the pronghorn's conformation for what it is: one of the most

Though pronghorn does also have horns, they are usually short and uninteresting and not worth taking as trophies.

A nice pronghorn head makes an unusual and relatively inexpensive addition to the trophy room.

marvelous engineering masterpieces in nature, allowing this rather tiny and fragile animal to run with power and endurance unmatched anywhere else in the animal kingdom.

The pronghorn abounds with other unique characteristics. Horns, as opposed to antlers, are never shed but are retained and continue to grow throughout the life of the animal. Horns are never branched, antlers always are. The pronghorn is the single exception anywhere in the world to these two "rules" of nature. His horns are true horns and not antlers. Yet they are shed (the bony core underneath them isn't however) and regrown each year. They are also branched thus the "prong" in pronghorn. He also is the only deer or antelope type ruminant that does not have dewclaws (the outer first and fourth toes) on either front or hind legs. Actually the pronghorn is neither antelope, deer nor goat, even though (largely due to his often heavy and musky odor) many residents of pronghorn country call them "goats."

The pronghorn is the sole remaining member of what was once a large and varied family of *Antilocapridae* (or, to oversimplify, antelope-goats). He and his family have always resided in North America and never in Asia. This is quite the contrary of most all other species of North American big game which had their origins in Asia. Another distinction is that he is our only surviving true plains game animal, although one might qualify the caribou in some areas and at some times of the year in that group. The elk and grizzly have been converted from plains animals to purely mountain game, and the buffalo, which once thundered over our plains in numbers of 70 or 80 million — undoubtedly more than the population of any other single large animal in history — has for all practical purposes been done away with as far as a generally available big game animal. Hunting the buffalo has been reduced to certain limited and highly restricted situations. That leaves only the pronghorn as our sole surviving year-around plains game animal.

### Hunting the Pronghorn

The fact that he is a plains animal makes hunting the pronghorn as unique as the animal itself. Earlier in this chapter I mentioned my surprise and delight at seeing a small band of pronghorn standing out in the open calmly surveying me. For any eastern hunter who has grown up and cut his hunting teeth on the furtive, skulking whitetail to actually *see* all manner of game standing out in the open ogling back at you is a strange and curious experience.

However, this is not at all an uncommon experience, especially before opening day of the hunting season. The pronghorn is one of the most curious beasts (along with the caribou) in North America. He wants to see you and see what you are up to, and he quickly learns what his zone of safety is. Most pronghorns, unless hard pressed during the hunting season itself, are rather deliberate and calm about maintaining a 500-yard or so interval between themselves and those weird looking two legged apparitions that periodically show up on their beloved high plains. Also, the pronghorn knows quite well that, as a fast moving object while running from here to there, he is highly visible to other potential predators, both two-legged and four-legged, up ahead. Furthermore, he himself can't see nearly as well when in full flight as when standing or moving off more slowly and deliberately. So, unless pressed repeatedly and hard, he'd just as soon not run but would rather stand around and look, thank you.

And how he can see! It's been said that he has the equivalent of 8x binocular vision. I believe this to be an understatement, particularly on moving objects. It has been proven in tests that pronghorns can successfully resolve *small* moving objects at *more than* 4 miles distance. That's being gimlet-eyed and then some. Pronghorns are usually ranked with mountain goats and sheep as being our sharpest-eyed game, but it has been my experience that they see better than the two high country animals.

Not only do they see acutely, but they also have a unique (that word again) insect-like capability of seeing all around and partly behind themselves. This is because their large, lustrous eyes are set very high up on the head and are more than a bit "popeyed" they bulge outward so much. Thousands of otherwise flawless pronghorn stalks have been blown because the hunter was slinking in from the rear quarter — a blind spot on any other big game — when the pronghorn had his head up. Although he can't see directly behind him, it's a good idea when exposed to only move forward when the beasts have their heads down and there is some obstruction between that head and your own carcass.

Hunting pronghorn is often both highly frustrating and highly rewarding. I know of no other game where the hunting of the animal, after it has been spotted, is so important. With most game animals the trick is to find them and then, given reasonable care and skill on the hunter's part, the game is more than half over before the stalk starts. With the pronghorn all this turns over and comes up backwards. Spotting the animals is frequently no problem and even spotting them before they see you is not necessarily as difficult as it is with some game. What *is* difficult is to stalk them within fair shooting range — across an area that has far more cover for the enterprising hunter than one might initially suspect but is still much more open than most other game fields — without the pronghorn seeing you.

These two pronghorn hunters are looking over the high plains from a higher vantage point in order to spot stalkable herds of pronghorn.

Due to the long distance involved, 10x roof prism binoculars such as these Bushnell 10x40's are an ideal choice for the pronghorn hunter.

For the patient hunter, the man who has a sense of hunting as well as of killing, stalking pronghorn can be quite exciting. Planning the stalk, which may often cover a mile or so of extra ground in order to take advantage of the maximum cover available, and then executing it with speed and yet patience takes a knack that most non-pronghorn hunters aren't used to. To be able to go for long periods without peering above or around the cover to satisfy that pronghorn-losing curiosity about "whether they're still there" takes discipline. To spend the time and energy worming your way over the rough ground takes commitment. But the feeling of taking your game through superior hunting and stalking is very rewarding.

Sadly, all too many hunters approach pronghorn as if they were in a shooting gallery rather than stalking and taking a superb little trophy. These chaps tend to drive around in 4WD's, and when they scare up a batch of the little beasts, which are always decamping at top speed by then, they start banging away at ranges of 500 yards and better at animals running 40, 50 or even 60 miles an hour. Sometimes they do this from the moving vehicle, not even bothering to dismount. Sure, they often hit an animal. But it's most always the wrong animal (generally three or four animals behind the one they had hoped to hit), and it's practically always a bad hit in the leg, flank or belly. *No one can properly aim at and hit animals traveling at these speeds a quarter of a mile to a half a mile out!*

Thus, one is treated to the sad spectacle of all too many of these little fellows wandering around with a leg shot off or humped up in agony due to being gut shot. This is because the "hunter" then approached the animal and found it was a doe or an immature buck. Not wanting to waste his precious permit taking that animal, he pulls up stakes and leaves it there to suffer. I've finished off more than one of these plucky little fellows in those kinds of desperate straits. I realize these are harsh words, painting a gruesome picture. That was my intent in order to try to discourage this kind of heinous practice and to hold up to disgrace and scorn those who insist on continuing the practice. There is more abuse in pronghorn hunting than in any other major big game hunting on this continent, and unless we hunters begin doing more self-policing by reporting such miscreants, things will probably get worse not better. The old line "it's none of my business" simply won't wash. It *is* your business, both as a citizen and as a sportsman. Your license dollars and Pittman-Robinson excise tax dollars (levied on firearms and ammunition) are helping to support the management of that animal, and your sporting privilege (not right) is being jeopardized by this kind of armed juvenile delinquent. He's stealing from you just as surely as if he entered your car and lifted your favorite firearm. He's wrong, and he knows it. Get his license number and automobile make and model and report him. You owe it to yourself and to the rest of us who are playing the game fairly.

Though vehicles are most often used in pronghorn country, horses can come in particularly handy when covering the rougher country.

## Where to Hunt for Pronghorn

Fossils indicate that many thousands of years ago the pronghorn existed as far east as Illinois, but for all practical purposes they have always been a western animal. During the heyday of the buffalo it has been estimated that there were as many as 15 to 20 million pronghorn. The buffalo kept much of the grass eaten down so that the sage and other plants that the pronghorn relishes could flourish. (He's basically not a grass eater and thus doesn't compete directly with livestock.) And thus the pronghorn himself flourished. With the near extermination of the buffalo in the latter part of the 19th century, much of the pronghorn's food was choked out due to the growth of the tall grasses. It has been reliably estimated that shortly after the turn of the century there were fewer than 20,000 pronghorn left on earth. Since that time, due to enlightened game management, aggressive transplanting and changing land use patterns, the pronghorn has staged a miraculous comeback. There are now something over 300,000 of them existing in varying numbers in about 15 U.S. states and a couple of Canadian provinces. Between 50,000 and 60,000 of them are harvested each year on a limited permit basis.

**Wyoming,** the pronghorn hunter's Mecca with around 180,000 animals, boasts more than half the world's population in its herd. About 40,000 are harvested annually and any sportsman who really wants a

Pronghorn make attractive and decorative trophies as this grouping of 13-inch class Wyoming heads indicates.

Though pronghorn are still relatively easy to take (once the necessary permit is secured), nice trophies, such as this 15 as this 15 3/4-inch head taken author in 1967 in southeastern Wyoming, are becoming considerably scarcer.

Any pronghorn over 16 inches is a marvelous trophy, and one over 17 inches is a trophy of several lifetimes. This huge 17 5/8-inch buck taken by hunting consultant Jack Atcheson in eastern Montana is literally "one in 10,000!"

Pronghorn hunting is one of the few practical big game hunting uses that the extremely high-powered zoom riflescopes, such as this Tasco 4-12x, 40mm variable, can be put to. (Photo courtesy Tasco Sales Inc.)

pronghorn trophy and has the patience to apply for a permit several years running if necessary, is eventually sure to get one.

Hunter success is remarkable, ranging from 90 percent to 95 percent most years and approaching 100 percent for nonresidents who have a bit of guiding help. The trick is to get the permit and then to be able to shoot accurately and to have a bit of patience while hunting.

**South Dakota** (herd estimate: 42,000) and **Oregon** (herd estimate: 14,000) both have decent pronghorn availability, but they usually restrict these animals to resident hunting only. **Colorado** has about 30,000 with a healthy kill of a bit over 3,000, and nonresidents are welcome to try for their permits. **Montana,** especially the flat eastern part of the state, has an unestimated herd that yields about 1,300 kills a year and probably totals about 15,000 - 20,000 animals. The hunting is good here with a high ratio of big bucks (over 13 inches in horn length). Other states and provinces offer some limited nonresident pronghorn hunting but Wyoming, Colorado and Montana are the three best areas to try your luck in.

### Costs of Pronghorn Hunting

One of the more agreeable aspects of pronghorn hunting is that, as quality big game hunting goes, it is relatively modest in price. There are a variety of hunts

available, depending upon the hunter's pocketbook and inclination.

Many ranchers in pronghorn country allow nonresident hunters to either stay with them in their homes, or in an out-cabin, or to camp on their land while hunting there for rather reasonable rates. Generally the rancher himself can be employed as a "guide" for some or all of the time you're there. (Really he's more valuable in being able to take you around for a day and show you the "lay of the land.") You may be able to rent a 4WD vehicle from him separately. Usually these stripped down services (often including some delicious eating at the ranch house) are very modest in cost. Three days should do it if you've picked a relatively good area and if you've taken the all-important precaution of arriving in the area a day or so before hunting season opens in order to scout it and plan your strategy thoroughly *before* opening day. Opening day is far and away the best pronghorn hunting before the herds have been stirred up so much. It's reasonable to figure a decent little hunt like this, excluding license cost and travel to

A good pronghorn hunt, due to its nature (open terrain with animals often in sight and high degree of vehicle use on some types of hunts) is a good way to start very young hunters out on their big game hunting career. This young fellow has shot himself a fine 14-inch class buck.

and from your home to the hunting area, at around $200-$300.

The next step up is the outfitted and guided hunt, usually sharing a full-time guide with one other hunter. These usually run about $100 - $200 per day depending upon the duration of the hunt and the number of amenities in camp and the type of transportation while hunting (horses, vehicles or both in combination).

A 3-day hunt will usually run about $400 to $600 while a 5-day trip will run about $750. These hunts are a marvelous way to introduce a youngster or wife to big game hunting by the way. The weather is usually salubrious, the country interesting and unusual if not spectacular, and the fact that game is frequently in sight keeps people who otherwise might have a short attention span rather keyed up and involved. The lightweight, easy-to-live-with guns used on pronghorn hunts are also comfortable for youngsters and ladies to use. Nor are these hunts especially physically taxing.

### Tips for a Successful Pronghorn Hunt

Get there a couple of days before the season's opening and plot your strategy. Opening day is when the best hunting occurs. Write to the Fish and Game Department well in advance of the season. Pronghorn permits often must be applied for many months in advance and sometimes, depending upon the timing of the pronghorn drawings in various states and your own schedule, it may pay you to apply simultaneously to more than one state.

Ask the Fish and Game Department for a list of ranchers catering informal pronghorn hunts as well as the formal list of hunting outfitters. These ranch hunts usually save you money, and the comfortable, homey atmosphere is a plus that many of us appreciate. Ask for a list of all the pronghorn areas showing number of permits available by area and number of animals taken in the previous pronghorn season. This gives you hunter success ratios, *by area.*

If you are particularly interested in taking a trophy-sized pronghorn, you might also want to ask for their comments on the areas where the biggest heads have been taken in the last few seasons. These areas generally are not the spots with the largest overall number of kills or the highest hunter success ratio. Also, ask for the name, address and phone number of the resident (or closest) Fish and Game Department biologist in the area(s) that interest you most. A follow-up phone call to the biologist on the spot will get you the most timely, accurate information available. You can also check various Chambers of Commerce and motels in towns catering to visiting hunters. Often they can furnish some good information but, of course, they are obviously going to present data that makes the best impression for their area.

About trophy pronghorn. Here are my purely personal thoughts on what constitutes a "trophy:" No does should ever be shot, even if legal. Though does wear horns, they are practically always underdeveloped, spindly little affairs. I personally would never shoot a buck with horns under 12 inches and would hold out for 13 inches if at all possible. For a first pronghorn, anything over 13 inches should probably be taken unless there seems to be a superabundance of big heads in the area you are hunting. Anything over 14 inches should always be taken unless you already have taken record book class pronghorn heads. Over 15 inches should be taken no matter who you are. As you approach 16 inches in horn length, the head becomes a potential record book qualifier.

Carry good optics on any pronghorn hunt. Binoculars should be of best quality and at least 8x with 10x preferred in the lighter, more compact models. Riflescopes of the vari-power breed get the nod over the fixed 4x and 6x models. Due to the relatively smaller, lighter rifles used for this type of hunting, I prefer the 2x to 7x variables to the 3x to 9x models. The latter are so heavy and bulky as to almost overwhelm the lighter slimmer rifles used here, while the former offer all the power generally needed. Good spotting scopes are a must for sizing-up their horns at long ranges in order to decide whether to commit yourself to a stalk that may take up to several hours. Either best quality variables (15x to 40x or 20x to 60x) may be used or a good fixed power model with interchangeable eyepieces of perhaps 20x, 30x and 40x for differing situations.

### Guns for Pronghorn

Pronghorn are stout little animals, but they are also quite small and rather high strung in temperament thus somewhat extra-susceptible to the shocking effect of a rifle cartridge. They are not particularly hard to put down, and any sort of decent hit, in most of the open situations where they are found, will afford the hunter a good follow-up shot. The best pronghorn cartridges are the .24's and .25's. The .243 and 6mm Remington are fine, with the .257 Weatherby and the .25/06 offering a bit flatter trajectory but also coughing up extra power, recoil and muzzle blast — none of which is really necessary here.

The .270 offers more power than is needed, but if that's your main gun and one you feel comfortable with, then use it by all means. Its flat trajectory and still relatively mild recoil and muzzle blast make it a good weapon. There really is no need whatsoever for any of the hotter .284 or .308 magnums in this type of hunting and, if one is used, care should be taken in bullet selection to insure that heavily constructed bullets which might punch right through the animal without adequate expansion are avoided.

Our pronghorn is a marvelous little "all American." An almost exotically handsome fellow whose jet black horns and rich tan color set off by two brown bands across his white throat give him a dapper, "dressed" look. He deserves to be honestly hunted and fairly won.

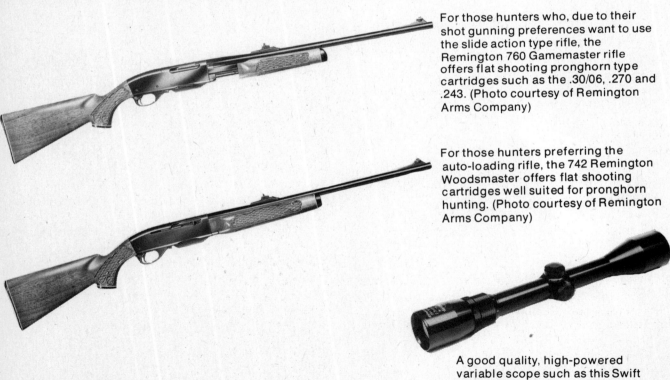

For those hunters who, due to their shot gunning preferences want to use the slide action type rifle, the Remington 760 Gamemaster rifle offers flat shooting pronghorn type cartridges such as the .30/06, .270 and .243. (Photo courtesy of Remington Arms Company)

For those hunters preferring the auto-loading rifle, the 742 Remington Woodsmaster offers flat shooting cartridges well suited for pronghorn hunting. (Photo courtesy of Remington Arms Company)

A good quality, high-powered variable scope such as this Swift 3-9x, 40mm wide angle model is an almost ideal riflescope for pronghorn hunting. (Photo courtesy of Swift Instruments, Inc.)

An extremely sharply pointed bullet, such as this Remington Bronze Point, that shoots with a very flat trajectory is a good choice for those often necessary long-range pronghorn shots. (Photo courtesy of Remington Arms Company)

# CHAPTER 4

# How To Get Your Elk

**GHOSTLY SHAPES** flitted silently, almost daintily, down the icy sidehill some 400 yards in front and to the right of me. It was so cold my ears burned and my eyes teared. I shivered. Not so much from the below zero cold as from the roller-coaster nervousness I felt, for those shapes were elk. They were the first I had ever seen in the wild, and they looked absolutely huge to my whitetail deer orientated eyes.

The shadowy forms moved single file across a small stream bed in front of me. There were seven of them led by a big, sway-backed cream colored cow. Two more cows followed her, then came a young spike bull followed by two more flat heads. Trailing along in the rear was a decent young four-point bull. The flat crack of my .270 and the accompanying *splat* of the 130-grain Corelokt striking home surprised me almost as much as it did him. He spun madly away and melted from sight as if he had simply been erased. I stood there flat-footed and shaking for a moment before I came to myself and took off to trail him up.

No need. He was piled up about 75 yards away, killed cleanly with a broken back. I stood there and marvelled at him. Though hardly 400 pounds and no "trophy" by any stretch, he looked simply enormous to me.

Bugling season means that elk can often be located, if not called in, by some artful bugling on the part of the hunter.

# ELK RANGE

Elk

Elk country usually means rough country. The author has found trophy elk hunting to be, by and large, tougher than sheep hunting.

Later, in another time and another place, I got my first big bull elk. The cold was piercing, and snow was deep. Even though this was a hard combed area and most of the big bulls had learned long since to do little or no bugling, this fellow was so big and ardent he couldn't restrain himself. Though we didn't call him in, he squealed so much that he pulled us right in to him. Just as he was about to disappear over a small snowy fold in the mountainside ahead, I drilled a single shot into him. Another .270 and another broken back. He thrashed and whirled madly down the steep slope in a cascade of snow that hung and shimmered in the clear Canadian air, but he was dead before he came to rest 100 feet below the spot where I hit him.

Since then I have killed other, larger elk but never have I forgotten or recovered from the thrill of those first few magic mornings when I got my first elk. These magnificent big game animals still rouse that same kind of excitement in me, and they always will.

### The Game

Elk or wapiti (Shawnee Indian name meaning "white rump") are the second largest deer in the world and the largest round antlered deer in the world. Only the larger subspecies of moose exceed them in shoulder height and body weight. Some would say that no large animal anywhere exceeds them in beauty and grandeur. A big bull elk will stand 5 feet at the shoulder and weigh on the average from 600 to 800 pounds though there are authenticated examples of certain bulls, under unusual conditions, weighing 1,200 pounds and more on the hoof.

A nice 700-pound bull elk will run about 9 feet in body length and sport what is possibly the most magnificent set of antlers in the world. These may well approach 5 feet in tip to tip spread and when measured around the outside curve of each main beam. Actually elk have a rather squarish, blocky build. Moose are much more long legged and the caribou, a considerably smaller animal that will usually weigh only about half as much as an elk, stands almost as tall at the shoulder.

However, the conformation of the elk is such that this heavy, square body does not convey a feeling of clumsiness or unattractiveness. Far from it. The elk is a majestic animal with an attractive face and body build that conveys a feeling of regal power and vigor.

The way a big bull elk stands and moves is lordly and impressive. He's an intelligent animal, and he's gifted

(Left) Any bull elk, large or small, has a way of looking enormous to hunters whose previous experience has been limited to deer and pronghorn.

(Below) A nice six-point bull elk is one of the most impressive trophies in the world.

with a balanced mix of rather keen senses. He hears, sees and smells well, and he does an excellent job of translating these visual stimuli into warning signals when such is the case. Furthermore, a big bull is a stout hearted chap who is difficult to lay down and even more difficult to keep down. It has been my experience that a 700-pound bull elk is considerably harder to knock down and keep down than a 1,400 pound bull moose. Once an elk is wounded, he will carry on until the end, running the proverbial 20 miles if possible. Most other ruminants, especially moose, don't do so and will wander off and ''lay up'' if allowed to do so before being pressed too hard by the following hunter.

After wounding a moose or caribou it is often a good idea to take a break for a couple of minutes (if the animal is hard hit) and allow it to slow down and lay down. The animal will invariably do this and stiffen up so that it either dies on the spot or is not able to regain its feet and continue on when the hunter approaches. This is not a good strategy for the robust, decisive elk. Once he makes up his mind to change counties, there is no hesitation, no indecision. He will not stop until he drops, whether pressed by the hunter or not. Thus, a wounded elk should always be trailed up as quickly and relentlessly as possible.

Elk originally lived in most of the eastern states ex-

(Above) Here Jack Atcheson, the Butte, Montana hunting consultant and taxidermist, shows two nice bulls taken by him and his oldest son.

(Left) Tom Brakefield shows nice six-point bull elk taken on late season elk hunt in western Alberta.

(Below) This Pennsylvania hunter looks over two yearling "meat bulls" taken on a successful Montana meat hunt. There is about 175 pounds of finished butchered meat in each of these fellows.

cept for New England, but they had largely been extirpated by 1800. They were eliminated in the midwestern areas in various stages throughout the mid-1800's with a few scattered remnants hanging on in North Dakota until near the turn of the century and in Minnesota until 1908. Elk originally were plains animals in the West, and though they were slaughtered ruthlessly by commercial hunters and, due to land use conflicts, by the increasing waves of settlers, they did fare considerably better than the larger and more truculent buffalo. This was partially because they were more intelligent and wary and partially because they tended to inhabit somewhat rougher and more remote country.

Within the last century man has transformed the elk into a mountain animal, and his most densely populated stronghold is now the Rocky Mountains stretching from southwestern Canada to northern New Mexico though he does exist elsewhere, too. However, nowhere is he found in any significant numbers except in mountain country. The scattered herds found in Arkansas, Virginia, Pennsylvania and other spots are very small, totally protected "curiousities" rather than viable herds that can stand reasonable sport hunting. The elk has adapted well to his new home. Though a large animal, he can climb slopes that one has to see to believe, and he has learned, over the years, to lay his head back and carry those sweeping antlers back along his body in order to charge through the dense spruce tangles at high speed (if necessary) with little or no commotion and contact.

**Where to Hunt**

Elk are available in good, huntable populations in several western U. S. states and Canadian provinces. As is the case with most big game hunting, the places for the best "chance at an elk" usually are not the places for the best chance at a *big* elk. Those "incubator" type areas where a maximum elk herd is raised and killed usually do not see many bulls living the requisite 6 to 8 years to grow real trophy-sized antlers. Conversely, those areas with a fair share of big bulls usually are not heavily populated with elk (which is one reason why they are not so intensively hunted) and are usually much higher, rougher and more difficult areas to reach (which is the other reason why they aren't hunted so heavily).

Colorado (100,000 elk) and Oregon (100,000 + elk) probably have the largest elk herds. Colorado offers good nonresident guiding and outfitting services for the visitor, and though the chances of taking a really big bull here are not as high as in some other areas, there's good general elk hunting. Some good bulls are taken each year, but when that number is compared with the total elk kill and with the total man hours spent afield hunting elk in this very intensively hunted state, then it must be seen that the big bulls are few and far between.

Oregon boasts an even larger herd than Colorado

services. They field a respectable herd of some 60,000 elk with a kill that is equally respectable, running around 10,000 per year. Wyoming is a fine elk hunting ground with a nice herd of about 75,000 animals, gorgeous countryside, well developed guide and outfitting services and a good kill of around 15,000 to 18,000 per year. Wyoming's usual hunter success ratio of 30 percent to 38 percent (of those buying elk licenses) is the highest in the nation.

Idaho and Montana do not release estimates of their elk herd sizes but both are substantial. The kills average about the same in both states (around 9,000), and I would figure that there are probably between 35,000 and 50,000 elk in each. Both offer very efficient and well developed guiding and outfitting services and the hunting is good. Idaho in particular features some very

Bull elk fighting during the annual rut is one of nature's most impressive spectacles.

though the kill (around 14,000) is considerably less than Colorado's (which is about 23,000 to 24,000 for a very respectable success ratio in elk hunting terms). This is because much of the Oregon hunting is along the precipitous, rain forest areas of the coast that are difficult to climb, move around in and hunt. This is blacktail deer country, and the elk hunted here are the heavier, darker bodied and shorter antlered Roosevelt elk not the longer antlered, lighter and somewhat more spectacular Rocky Mountain elk located further to the east. Both types of elk are found in Oregon but much of the herd is of the Roosevelt type. The facilities catering to out-of-state hunters are not nearly as well developed as in Colorado, Montana, Wyoming or Idaho, nor does Oregon exactly encourage out-of-state hunters to come stalk their elk.

Washington State elk hunting is very similar to Oregon's in most all respects from the type of hunting to the absence of well developed guide and outfitting

rough country, and while elk hunting for big racks is always a tough physical proposition, the hunter going to Idaho should be in doubly good shape. The old saw about "if you ironed all the mountains out flat in Idaho, the state would be larger than Texas" isn't too far from the truth.

Arizona has a rather modest herd of about 10,000 with an equally modest kill of some 800 to 1,200 per year. Nonresident opportunities for elk permits are limited as are the services catering to nonresident hunters, but some very big bull elk are taken in Arizona each year. New Mexico has about twice as many elk and kills about 2,000 per year with good big bulls showing up in relative abundance. There are some quite good ranch hunts available in New Mexico, and they are generally well worth the $1,200 to $1,800 price tags if one has his heart set on a big six- or seven-point bull elk. This is very high country with much of the hunting running at 10,000 to 12,000 feet, so lose weight and stop

(Above) Dragging in a bull elk is quite a job as these three hunters, headed for the valley far below, are finding out.

(Below) A typical wilderness base camp for elk hunting.

smoking if you decide New Mexico elk hunting is on your agenda.

Actually, for a chance at a trophy bull elk, I would probably recommend northern New Mexico and northern British Columbia, which happen to be the most northerly and southerly limits of the elk range in North America. British Columbia has a rather unimposing herd of about 15,000 elk, but they appear to be expanding their range in the north and can now be hunted as far up as Mile 400 and farther on the Alaska Highway. This area is primarily mixed game country for people out after sheep, moose, caribou and grizzly. To hunt elk generally would require trekking to a new corner of the outfitter's territory and spending extra time in the field on what is already a very expensive hunt running $200 to $250 per day. Most hunters figure, quite understandably, that they'll wait and try for elk on another hunt further south in a year or two and that they'll concentrate on the far north species while up on this far north hunt.

That's a reasonable and logical approach, and it's also the reason why more big elk are probably dying of old age in this general area than anywhere else on the continent. If a trophy bull elk is your number one priority, this might well be the place to look. Alberta has a nice herd about the size of British Columbia's but concentrated in considerably less area. Historically these grounds have produced some of the best bighorn sheep and biggest bull elk racks. Elk have occupied a decreased priority in recent years here in order to up the priority management of bighorns (an approach which I heartily agree with, incidentally), but it is still a good area to hunt for the big deer.

## Elk Hunting Costs

Elk are big, free ranging animals not homebodies limiting themselves to a small and intimately known area, like whitetails. Elk are also deep wilderness animals. Logging roads or even just bare slopes that lend themselves to 4WD's and all-terrain vehicles usually signal the end of good trophy hunting for elk and a definite decrease even in meat hunting success.

All of these factors tend to drive up the costs for *quality* elk hunting. Getting "back in" well away from all roads and open trails usually involves a fair amount of expense and/or time. A bush plane can get you and your gear in quickly, but this kind of flying doesn't come cheaply. It is also necessary to either freight in considerable amounts of tentage, food and duffle or pay for a camp which has been set up by someone else. Once "outside," horses are a good idea in order to cover large swaths of the rough wilderness country that elk inhabit. All of these factors add up to higher costs as compared with deer hunting, pronghorn hunting and even goat or caribou and moose hunting in some situations.

A quality trophy elk hunt will usually set the hunter

back about $150 to $250 per day depending upon the area (how prime), the accomodations (how plush), the transportation (how convenient) and the guide service (shared with other hunters or not). Anyone paying less than $100 per day these days usually isn't going on a decent trophy hunt in anything but name only.

Actually, elk hunting has been "packaged" in more variations than any other type of North American big game hunting. At the bottom of the heap are the drop hunts wherein the rancher or outfitter signs on basically to pack the hunters and their gear in by horseback, to drop them off and then to return in several days and bring them, their gear and their game out. This type of hunt comes in several sub-variants. The operator can merely furnish the horses and hired help to take the hunters and their gear in, and the hunters can furnish all of their own food, camping gear and duffle, setting up their own camp once back in. For this simple, straightforward service the charge is usually a flat fee of about $100 to $250 per hunter depending upon whether the ride in takes 1, 2 or 3 days each way, how many horses are required, and whether the camp is to be erected on the rancher's land or on hunting consignment or whether it is to be on open, public lands.

In some more complex variations on this theme, the outfitter may furnish some or all of the tentage and camp gear, and he may provide some help in erecting and breaking camp (or he may just trail the hunters into a preset camp which he is providing and then leave them there to hunt on their own). The fee for this service can run from $250 to $400 per man depending upon whether the outfitter is furnishing the groceries

Getting "back in" to good elk country via the classic Rocky Mountain packstring means an unforgettable experience for any hunter.

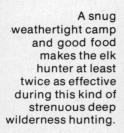

A snug weathertight camp and good food makes the elk hunter at least twice as effective during this kind of strenuous deep wilderness hunting.

(Above) Often the best elk hunting is during the extreme cold of late season hunts when the bigger bulls have been forced down off the peaks.

(Left) Late season mid-winter hunts, when many of the biggest trophy bulls are taken, demand the best in camp accommodations to keep the hunters functioning effectively.

(Below) The packstring hunt is not only a good way to get back into good elk country, but it also means that the hunters will have saddle horses to use so they can cover more ground while hunting the big, free ranging animals.

(and, if so, how fancy the grub is) and other variables.

The next step up is the gang group hunt, usually strictly a meat hunt. Here the outfitter trails in a number of hunters to an already set up camp and then hunts them out of it for anywhere from 5 to 10 days. There are practically always too many hunters sharing the same guide and too many hunters sharing the same camp for this to qualify as any sort of trophy hunt. At the bottom end the "outfitter" has his camps located too close together and he shoehorns far too many hunters into the same camp (10 or 12 or even more) and too many hunters to the guide (4, 6 or even more). These "hunts" are little more than an excuse for some fellowship in the woods and some good all-night poker games. Costs for these kinds of hunts may run around $50 per day per hunter.

A bit further up the scale where the outfitter is hunting only 6 or 7 men out of the same camp, the camps are more than one ridge apart, and there are no more than three hunters per guide, the chances and the costs go up a bit. Figure on these hunts running anywhere from $60 to $100 per day depending upon the length of the hunt, the desirability of the game area and the other specifics. However, these are still more of a good solid meat hunt with an off chance at an occasional trophy rather than what one could literally call a full-fledged trophy hunt.

Next up the line is the modified trophy hunt with four to six hunters in camp and no more than two hunters sharing a guide. This hunt usually sees a full-time wrangler as well as a cook in camp to help with the horses, packing and general scut work. This allows the guides and hunters to leave earlier and return later, thus capitalizing to the fullest on those precious dawn and dusk hours when so much game is actually taken. These hunts don't come cheap. Expect to part with $125 to $200 per day depending upon the length of the hunt and the other variables. (Longer hunts cost less per day,

Most good quality elk hunting, especially trophy hunting for the big six- and seven-point bulls, involves packing in by horseback well away from the roads or areas readily traveled by 4WD vehicles.

Getting a bull elk, even a young spike like this one, out of the wilderness and back to a vehicle without the help of a horse can be an imposing task.

Keeping both yourself and your clothing and gear clean is very important in wilderness elk hunting.

Elk hunting in steep mountain country without a horse demands that the hunter be in the best possible physical condition.

other things being equal.)

The crème-de-la-crème of trophy elk hunting is the one-hunter-per-guide, two to four hunters per camp foray. If the guides know their business and have done their homework to locate and keep up with the game in the area and if it's a good area, then the chances for a nice bull elk begin to blossom. This should be a 10- to 14-day hunt, never less than one week. On a 12-day hunt of this type where the hunter is willing to work hard and can hit the game put in front of him, chances at a nice bull can reasonably run from 50 percent to 75 percent perhaps even higher if the weather gods smile. Bring money. This hunt will usually set you back around $1,500 to $2,500, but a good one is well worth it.

## Basic Elk Hunting Tips

Elk hunting is usually demanding hunting. Though these things can vary considerably, I would rate the average *trophy* elk hunt as being more physically demanding than the average Stone or Dall sheep hunt and almost as tough as the average goat hunt. Lose weight. Every ounce you have to climb with weighs a ton by the time you lug it to the crest of the ridge. You simply can't be too skinny (within the terms of reasonable good health) for this kind of work. Stop smoking. Take up jogging to condition yourself.

Be disciplined in your own mind. If you are serious about a trophy elk hunt, be prepared to pay the freight. Don't expect a six-point bull at meat hunt costs. You might get him — but then again you might win the Irish Sweepstakes. Do your homework. Write a number of outfitters in different areas and then follow up and contact the references they give you. *Getting a good bull elk, even on an expensive trophy hunt is at least twice as tough as taking a comparable sized moose or caribou bull on a comparable quality hunt.* Up your odds as much as possible by choosing the right outfitter and an area that best matches up with your resources, time available and preferred way of hunting.

### Guns for Elk

As I have indicated, elk are sturdy citizens that take considerable killing. I have never lost one yet, but I've usually hit them well, and I've been downright lucky a couple of times. For years one of the most "animated discussions" in outdoor writing was whether the .270, the .30/06 and cartridges of similar disposition were "adequate" as elk killers. The battle of the typewriters waxed and waned and, in the process, more than one gun pundit's house note was paid and kids were packed

them — even under the best of circumstances. While the .270 brand of cartridge may have worked reasonably well on them in years gone by, and even though I took my first two with that shell (one shot on one and three shots, of which the last two weren't needed, on the other), I would not recommend it now unless the shooter has a severe recoil problem.

Under good conditions the .270 will certainly perform well on the big deer and many hundreds have been killed with it over the years, not to mention those legions of elk taken with "thutty-thuttys" and old black powder standbys of even milder persuasion back before the turn of the century. But "good" conditions are sometimes hard to come by in today's elk stalking. Even "reasonable" or "barely adequate" conditions may not occur during the precious 10-day outing that the sportsman has saved for and trained for perhaps as long as 3 or 4 years. It's difficult to tell a man, who has worked hard for 10 or 12 days and spent enough money on the hunt to buy a good used car or a new subcompact, that he should pass up a semi-desperation last day shot and wait another 5 years to try again.

Certainly there are some shots that should never be taken by the decent sportsman; especially those at

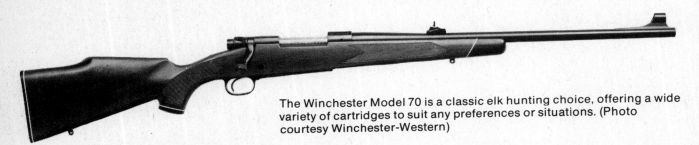

The Winchester Model 70 is a classic elk hunting choice, offering a wide variety of cartridges to suit any preferences or situations. (Photo courtesy Winchester-Western)

off to college. Though it was never truly settled (these things never are), the consensus among the *cognoscenti* was that they are adequate. That is — that under most conditions and if the hunter does his reasonable share, cartridges building between 2,700 and 3,000 pounds of muzzle energy with bullets in the 130-grain to 160- or 180-grain class are fine for elk hunting.

*Tempus fugit* my friends. Time passes and things change. Elk hunting has changed considerably in the last generation. There are more hunters and far fewer elk relative to demand, and trophy elk have become downright scarce while hunting costs have zoomed faster than most anything around except good medical care, good plumbing and good coffee. One particular hunt that I made a bit more than a decade ago has exactly *quadrupled* in cost! And the hunting isn't as good in that area now as it was then.

Elk have taken to hanging in much thicker cover and feeding more at night or by first and last light. The upshot of all this is that elk are far more expensive to hunt and far more difficult to take when you do hunt

ridiculously long ranges where any hit is a matter of luck. But there are all sorts of other gray area, borderline shots where the hunter, if he's quick and decisive, has a snap shot at a close range elk fast decamping through thick brush that is almost certain to yield a hit. But, the question is, will it *stop* the big adrenaline pumping animal? Killing him 10 miles away isn't enough. That usually means a lost trophy and several hundred pounds of tasty meat squandered. He has to be stopped and *now*. A gun that has the authority to either knock him down right now or at least slow him down enough for a more measured follow-up shot is what is called for in these times.

The 7mm Remington Magnum with a heavily constructed 175-grain bullet is a better bet than the old faithfuls of yesteryear. Ditto for the wide variety of .308 class magnum shells with bullets weighing from 200 to 250 grains punching out an extra 800 to 1,500 pounds of muzzle energy over the fine old .270. If the hunter can handle one, the .338 and the various .350 class magnums are extra good. It takes consistent range practice for a man to accustom himself properly to the punishing recoil and blast of these big guns, and they are going to weigh on the order of 10 pounds rather than 8 to 8½, so they are going to be a bit more tiring to carry afield. But, in a clinch, they have the extra sauce to get the job done.

Before hordes of angry .270/.30/06 partisans descend upon my head, let me state unequivocally that I have the greatest respect for both of these classic rounds. As I write this, two of the former and one of the latter are nestling in the three gun cabinets sitting across the room. I have used and continue to use both cartridges regularly. But, the era of giving them a blanket endorsement for elk hunting is long gone.

Well constructed bullets that can penetrate that chunky, muscular build and get to the vitals under all sorts of conditions and at ranges varying from 25 feet to 300 yards are a must. Noslers, Bitteroots, Remington Core-Lokts and Winchester Silvertips will all do a good job of it. Take care to avoid more lightly constructed ''deer bullets'' especially if you are handloading and running them out of the muzzle a bit hotter than factory loads.

Elk are magnificent animals. There is no finer trophy, and they are superb on the table, far exceeding any venison that I have ever eaten and equaling the best moose and sheep meat. To hunt them is a joy and to take a big one is an honor.

Here Elgin Gates shows an extremely massive elk head he shot some years ago in Wyoming.

# CHAPTER 5

# How To Get Your Caribou

**IN THE PRE-DAWN** morning of my sixth day in Alaska there was a tang in the air as tangible as a fresh Bermuda onion and the stars were seemingly close enough to pluck out of the sky. Though still early September, the skim ice in the wash basin took more than a gentle finger poke to break, and the water underneath was cold enough to guarantee that you entered the new day feet first and wide awake. Breakfast was a steaming mound of fluffly pancakes slathered in real butter with a big side helping of homemade Alaskan rose hip jelly. A moment to relish in the happening and to savor in the memory. Good hunts are never really over.

An hour later we were 3 miles up the rubble strewn Kuskokwim river course as the watery sun slowly rose over the horizon and began painting the surrounding ridges with those lovely cool pastels of dawn. Though this was one of the best Barren Ground caribou areas on earth (the limit was three bulls at the time), I had only seen one indifferent young bull in nearly a week.

As we picked our way through the boulders lining the twisting, cloudy stream of glacial water, I caught a flicker of movement over on the far tree line across the river. The 8x Leitz glasses put the big bull and his three cows almost in my lap even though they were over a

Shoot quick! A bull caribou on the alert and about to charge off across the tundra.

# CARIBOU RANGE

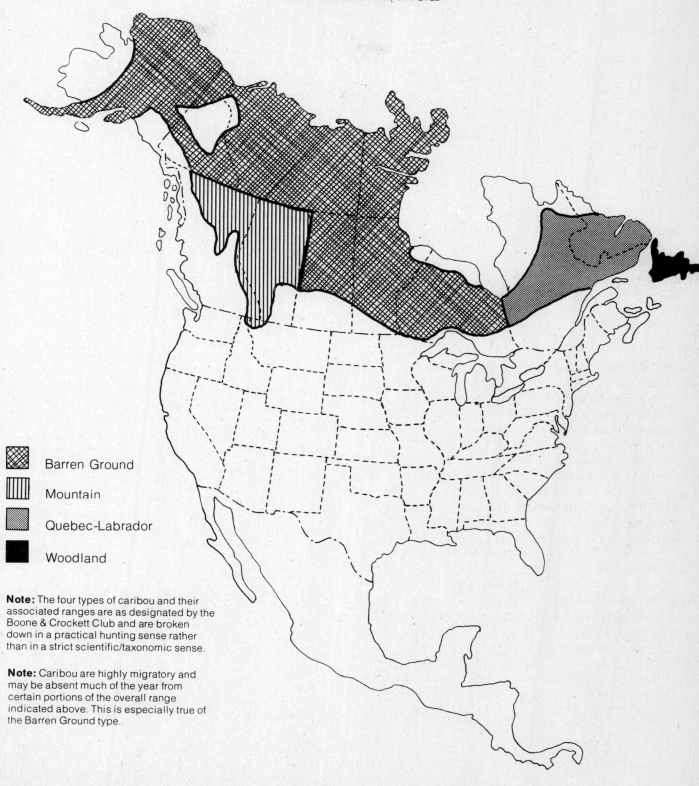

Barren Ground

Mountain

Quebec-Labrador

Woodland

**Note:** The four types of caribou and their associated ranges are as designated by the Boone & Crockett Club and are broken down in a practical hunting sense rather than in a strict scientific/taxonomic sense.

**Note:** Caribou are highly migratory and may be absent much of the year from certain portions of the overall range indicated above. This is especially true of the Barren Ground type.

Though caribou cows (front and right) are the only female deer in the world to regularly grow antlers, they are basically small and spindly affairs and of no interest to the trophy hunter.

A big double-shovel bull caribou can hide himself surprisingly easy among ground willows and other underbrush in the Arctic.

quarter-mile away. I whistled at Phillip as he trudged along ahead of me and directed his attention over toward the four caribou across the way. He knelt and as he glassed them whistled a quick exclamation to himself.

I had set a caribou with 50-inch main beams and a 40-inch spread as my goal before ever leaving for the hunt. "I think he'll make it and maybe then some," I whispered.

"Yup. Him look pretty good alright," Phillip grunted.

"How do you want to work the stalk," I asked. It was wide open with no cover between the animals and us, and short of making a 2-mile detour, I saw no way of making a blind approach. The caribou were shuffling along in that deceptive ground eating walk of theirs, and they'd be long gone before we could work any sort of long-distance flanking movement on them. It looked like I might have to chance a very long shot on him and I didn't like that. They weren't moving too fast, and I felt I could hit him, but the three cows kept weaving to and fro in front of him and I was afraid of wounding the wrong animal.

"No stalk him," Phillip whispered. "We get-um come over here to us."

With that he took off his stocking cap and extended his arm full length, waving it slowly back and forth in a 180-degree arc above his head. We were both kneeling on the rocky plain, not so much to try and hide as that was impossible, but to lower our silhouette and disguise our man shape. Caribou are notorious as not having the best eyesight among the ungulates.

I had heard of waving or "tolling" with both pronghorns and caribou but had never thought I'd see it done. Though this technique had worked well with these two species and even with some of the other, less curious species, it had been used mostly in the 19th century when all of these animals had been a good bit less sophisticated and man-wise. Now, here we were, pulling a Buffalo Bill type move on these fellows and, due to the rather inflexible situation at hand, I was hoping fervently that it worked.

The big bull cocked his head quizzically and started loping slowly our way, sweeping in a big semi-circle to pick up our wind. Fortunately the light breeze was dead in our faces. Gradually he worked his way toward us, sweeping back and forth in front of us in large arcs. I marveled at him as he came. What a magnificent creature he was with the now brighter sun glinting off of his sweeping brown antlers and setting off the flowing white beard and mane against his gray-brown body color.

Like those of his kind he moved with the high stepping, airy grace of a Tennessee walking horse. As he tossed his head this way and that, I could see that his single shovel was a beauty, going well over the 12-inch mark, and from his shiny black hooves and white stockinged feet to the tips of those breathtaking top points on his rack, he was 400 pounds of animated beauty.

Closer and closer he came, and I followed him in with my variable scope set on 4 power. As he approached within 175 yards, the silly spavined looking cows, who were as unattractive as he was comely, began milling tightly around him. For the next 50 yards they stayed right on top of him, obscuring him from me even though he was working his way practically into my lap. I cursed myself mentally for being so wrapped up in the spectacle that I hadn't gone ahead and put him away when he had offered so many easy broadside shots out around 200 yards. The closer he got, the more impressive he looked, and the more I feared those silly cows might, in some fashion, conspire to rob me of my prize.

Now I followed him with the scope locked on him in a more than casual fashion. Barely a hundred yards out the cows parted magically, and I glimpsed an unobstructed front shoulder. The rifle seemed to take over automatically, and I was surprised when I heard the wicked flat crack of the hotted-up 130-grain .270 handload. Instantly the flat *splat* of a solid hit came back, and the big bull desperately whirled away and began to flee.

I stood up, jacked another shell into the chamber and, without thinking, swung through on him offhand. This *splat* had an even sharper sound signaling a hit on the left ham. That spun the bull around, and he was going down even as I fed another shell into the gun and

A big bull caribou, feeding out in the open on his beloved tundra, is a marvelous sight to see and one that quickens the heart of any hunter.

Excited hunter approaches just downed caribou bull.

prepared to shoot again. But, this time, he was down for good. The second shot hadn't been necessary but I had been so single-mindedly interested in getting that particular big bull that I wasn't taking any chances at all.

At that time I still smoked, and I found myself gazing at him over a lingering cigarette before we even took any pictures or began field dressing. It was all there; the gray-brown of the Alaskan talus that pocks his beloved Alaska Range mountains was reflected in his basic body color, and this was pointed up by the snowy mane and beard that reflected the snow patches he sought out in order to escape the heat of fall and spring. He looks across the room at me now as I write this, and a pause to glance at that magnificent rack and head brings it all back to me as fresh and alive as if it had happened the day before yesterday rather than many years ago. Since then I have stalked and killed caribou in more than one Canadian province and territory, and I have returned to Alaska for other bulls equally beautiful and impressive. But never has the excitement and wonder of caribou hunting worn thin. The country they live in is so beautiful and wild, and the beasts themselves, though not overly brainy, are so unpredictable and so magnificently *stylish* that I could happily spend the rest of my life watching them, photographing them and hunting them without getting bored by it all.

## The Game

Caribou present one of the more complex, poten-tially confusing situations among the varied cast of North American big game. The caribou is basically a circumpolar animal occurring only in the northern part of the northern hemisphere but stretching in a wide belt from northern Norway and Sweden through northern Eurasia and Asia on across northern Alaska and Canada to the islands of Newfoundland and Greenland. The European and Eurasian animal is called the reindeer though somewhere in Siberia this gives way to the American term of "caribou." Whether called reindeer or caribou most taxonomists now classify these many subspecies as being all the same animal, a single species known as *Rangifer tarandus*.

The American caribou is a somewhat larger, better antlered and more robust animal than are his European and Asian counterparts. A big bull can weigh from 350 to 450 pounds though in some extraordinary (and rather artificial) instances they have scaled as much as 700 pounds. The North American caribou clan can be and has been broken down any number of ways. The broadest umbrella has been the approach of breaking all 12 to 20 or so subspecies (depending upon which authority one wants to cite) into two basic types: the Barren Ground and the woodland.

An intermediate and eminently sound approach has been the one set up and followed by the Boone & Crockett Club, the arbiter of North American trophy hunting standards. This approach — a reasonable combination of the "pure" (scientific) and the "practical"

The Peary's caribou is an interesting dwarf race that ranges from off white to white in color, and though of no interest to hunters (due to his small size and inaccessibility), he's a fascinating and elegant little fellow to observe.

(hunting) — divides all the *huntable* caribou populations into four different types. These types are based on general body and antler size and conformation and their physical location and separation from each other. The four types are:

| Type | Location | General Characteristics |
|---|---|---|
| 1. Barren Ground | Alaska, Yukon, Northwest Territories, Manitoba, Saskatchewan, Ontario | Medium body size (bulls 350-400 lbs.); longer beamed and tined, somewhat lighter antlers; longer top tines but fewer top points; fewer double shovel bulls; lighter body color (relatively). |
| 2. Mountain | British Columbia, Alberta | Heavier bodied (400 lbs. and heavier); shorter heavier racks with more points and more palmation (flattening of beams at top); darker body color; higher ratio of double shovel bulls. |
| 3. Quebec-Labrador | Quebec, Labrador | Actually very similar to above Barren Ground type. Separate status accorded due more to wide physical separation of the two than due to significant anatomical differences. However, tend to be even longer beamed, lighter racked and approximately same body size and color as "basic" Barren Ground. |
| 4. Woodland | Newfoundland | Heaviest bodied and darkest colored of all. Short, compressed but heavy beamed racks that are considerably less impressive than other three types. |

There are overlappings and exceptions to all of the above generalizations but such would be the case with any single system, of a practical nature, that tried to

Caribou have huge, snowshoe-sized feet for negotiating vast distances over the often wet, marshy tundra. Note the fact that the caribou foot (right) from a 400-pound animal has almost the surface area of the moose foot (left) which came from a far larger animal weighing about 1,200 pounds.

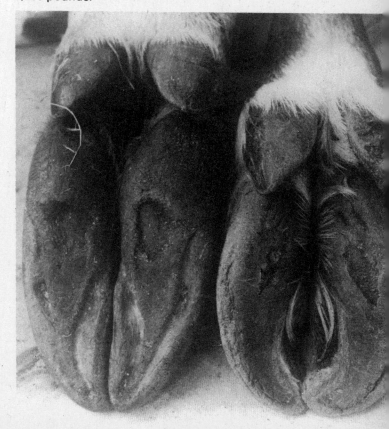

A magnificent record book caribou head taken by Elgin Gates of Needles, California.

Tom Brakefield with big Osborn bull that sported main beams in excess of 4 feet and that almost made the record book.

encompass this widespread and complex animal. This approach has the advantage of being basically valid and logical and yet being rather easy to understand and apply as far as trophy identification scoring.

### Trophy Value

The caribou makes one of the most impressive physical trophies imaginable. Though hardly half the weight of a comparable bull elk, his antlers will often be every bit as long and have perhaps even more spread not to mention more points and the somewhat exotic fillip provided by a large single or double shovel on the "lower story" of the rack. Caribou racks follow several types. All have the flattened, out-thrust lower point that is called a shovel. This peculiar conformation has no known practical value; it certainly is not used to shovel aside snow from buried food as some have speculated in the past. The most common situation is to see a single shovel (hopefully over 6 inches in depth for trophy purposes) paralleled by a single round tine of approximately the same length and branching off from near the base of the other main beam, directly across from the shovel.

Working up the main beam of the antler, the next formation is the bez which also juts out toward the front and can either be of the cupped hand variety with the individual points extending out of the base as more or less equal length "fingers," or it can be of the branched type with two or three secondary branches coming off the main beam, each of these bearing several points. Above the bez there are generally backpoints, single points sticking straight out the back of each main beam not quite halfway up the main beams. These are missing on one or both beams of a fair number of heads.

At the top is (no pun intended) the crowning glory of the caribou rack. There is practically always some palmation or flattening of the main beam present, but this is usually far more pronounced in the mountain and woodland racks than in the Barren Ground and Quebec-Labrador types. The main beam can sweep either forward or backward when it reaches the top, but the former is more common. On forward sweep heads the points always come off the single main beam more or less like a whitetail deer rack. On the backward sweeping tops this can be the case or they can "Y" with the main beam primarily continuing backwards but also sending out a strong secondary beam to the front and points branching off both. One of the exciting aspects of caribou racks as trophies is that it is quite possible to have three, four or five racks on the wall and yet have no duplicates. There is enormous variation in type among these sweeping and dramatic racks.

### Where to Hunt Caribou

**Alaska:** Alaska still offers some of the finest caribou hunting on earth though the herds have seen a radical decline from about 1970 through 1976. As recently as 1969 the total statewide population was estimated at approximately 650,000 animals, and by the fall of 1976 that had been reduced to about 230,000. Caribou are herd animals with cyclical population swings and a variety of factors are contributing to this trend, but by far the two most prominent are overkilling by natives (especially in the far north — north of the Brooks Range) and by wolves which have multiplied greatly since the elimination of practically all wolf control programs.

Historically the harvest of caribou in Alaska has exceeded that of all other big game animals combined. This is changing. Areas that used to offer a limit of three bulls in a season that was months long are now restricted to a single animal (or in some cases closed entirely) in a season that is only weeks long. North of the Yukon River there has historically been no limit on caribou; a person could literally shoot as many as he pleased of any sex, year-around. In the mid-70's this was changed to a limit of one bull.

Most Alaskan hunting is done by bush plane fly-in and then walking, though there is some horseback hunting available, especially in areas further south. Caribou are migratory animals and are constantly on the move. An area that may be empty of animals for a week may suddenly fill up when the animals literally move in "overnight." Hunting them on foot is tricky since a bull caribou, walking along at his leisure nipping at some grass here and some browse there, will soon outdistance a running man. It is almost impossible to keep up with them on foot if they are on the move at all.

Caribou hunting is generally rather expensive. This is not because they have yet become rather rare as is the case with the grizzly and some of the sheep in many areas. This is more because they are deep wilderness animals and one must usually get well back into the wilderness for good caribou hunting. More to the point: it may be necessary to move around a good bit once "back in" in order to locate these constantly shifting nomads. All this trucking around in the deep woods usually adds up to a fair amount of coin or an awful lot of time spent afield. Once located, caribou are generally rather easy to stalk and take, though their unpredictability always adds spice to the game. Alaskan costs generally run from $150 to $250 per day, depending upon whether it is a caribou/moose only hunt or whether the caribou hunting is part of a larger mixed game hunt for several species. Also, the general area to be hunted and how many hunters to the guide affects the price significantly.

A typical Alaskan caribou hunt would be combined with a moose hunt and would last about 10 days, costing the hunter around $2,000 in the process. Two hunters could share a guide and share a good bit of the chores and possibly trim this total cost a bit. When caribou are taken as part of a general, overall hunt that might include sheep and/or grizzly, the length of the hunt and the costs go up. If we're talking about 10 to 12 days for a

Caribou migrating on the Alaska Peninsula as photographed by Alaska Department of Fish and Game biologist Jim Faro.

This big bull caribou loping across the Alaskan tundra would provide a classic running big game shot for the hunter. Author only snapped his picture this time out.

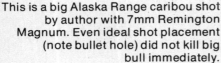

Caribou are often found, even during raw and stormy weather, on the high pastures that are actually the tops of "tabletop" mountains such as this one.

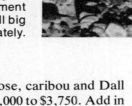

This is a big Alaska Range caribou shot by author with 7mm Remington Magnum. Even ideal shot placement (note bullet hole) did not kill big bull immediately.

"three animal" hunt (usually moose, caribou and Dall sheep), that would cost around $3,000 to $3,750. Add in grizzly or brown bear and possibly black bear to the first three for a "five animal" hunt and the length of the trip is now 15 to 18 days and the costs total a nosebleeding $4,500 to $6,000.

**The Yukon:** The Yukon boasts a very fine herd of about 140,000 caribou and the kill has historically been far lighter than Alaska's. There are perhaps 1,500 licensed sport hunting kills here each year as opposed to more than 20,000 in Alaska. Though the native kill is unlicensed and unrecorded in both areas, it also is undoubtedly far lighter than in the Yukon due to the very sparse population in this giant area. Though the Yukon herds have not yet been subjected to the wholesale slaughter by natives that Alaska's have, the upcoming completion of the Dempster Highway and other roads into the northern Yukon, cutting through some prime wintering grounds, does not bode well in this respect. Due to the historical evolution of the treaties and statutes governing native hunting rights, it does not appear that it will be possible to place any restrictions on this killing, and the results may be catastrophic.

By law the nonresident hunting in the Yukon is tightly regulated and well controlled. The number of outfitters are limited to 22, and these are examined regularly to insure that they and their equipment are up to standard. Most all hunting here is by the classic horseback, wilderness packstring usually trailing into already established camps but occasionally striking out through the country and setting up camp along the way. There are practically no caribou/moose only combo hunts. Both of these animals are usually taken as part of a larger mixed game hunt including sheep and bear as well as off chances at such "bonus" trophies as wolverine and wolf. The hunts average 15 days in length and about $3,500 to $4,000 in cost. Some shorter 10- and 12-day hunts are available, but if at all possible, it is usually a far better idea (from the hunter's point of view) to make the longer trip of 15 to 18 days and do it right. By and large, the Yukon offers hunting as good or better than Alaska's and at costs that would often run about 20 percent cheaper (sometimes more). The added thrill of making a classic wilderness horseback hunt, which to some of us is simply a more satisfying experience than a bush plane/backpack hunt, is another plus.

**British Columbia:** In many respects British Columbia, especially the northern third of the province, is the queen of all deep wilderness hunting areas on the continent. I'll never forget some magic hunts there with Johnny Holmes in the Cassiar Mountains when we worked some of the most beautiful country on earth and saw some of the largest caribou on earth.

British Columbia wilderness hunting has become ex-

Here a happy hunter and guide Gene Holmes (right) bring in an Osborn caribou taken in one of outfitter John Holmes' Cassiar Mountain camps.

ceedingly expensive even compared with similar hunting in other areas. However, due to their long history of outfitting and guiding American hunters, they do have more flexible arrangements and a greater variety of hunts than any other area. (See Chapter 19 for more information on special bargain priced late season hunts. There are also some specialized money saving opportunities for father/son and group hunts and most all of these opportunities are specifically tied into moose/caribou hunts.)

Some British Columbia caribou hunting is a horseback/packstring proposition from canvas back camps, but much of it involves hunting on horseback out of the outfitter's hard roofed base camp lodge. These hunts are usually 7 to 10 days in duration and will cost $1,500 to $2,500 depending upon the variables. These are good hunts to take the wife on, incidentally. If caribou are taken as part of a larger scale, mixed species hunt in British Columbia, the costs zoom. Figure $4,500 to $6,500 for mixed game hunts of 18 to 21 days duration. You may be able to trim these costs a bit on a cancellation by another hunter or some other very specialized situation but don't count on it if you want a quality hunt. British Columbia, in the Cassiars especially, offers a crack at the big bodied, heavy antlered mountain caribou which would make a nice counterpoint in the trophy room to a Barren Ground bull that you may already have taken elsewhere.

**Northwest Territories:** This is one of the most remote areas left on earth. Nonresident hunting was not even opened up until the mid-1960's, and there has been very little work done here in the area of population estimates

Nice Osborn caribou head taken by author in Northern British Columbia.

(Above) Guide Andy Dennis, the eternal hunter, glasses for game with big Osborn caribou shot by author loaded onto his horse for the trip back to camp.

(Left) A big Barren Ground double-shovel caribou such as this bull is enough to please most any hunter.

(Below) Author with a prime mountain caribou bull he took with John Holmes.

and general studies by trained biologists. There are perhaps half a million caribou roaming this vast area, though no one really knows. The nonresident hunting is limited to two (relatively) small areas in the extreme western end of this huge tract, right on the border with the Yukon. Hunting is good for moose, caribou, sheep and tundra grizzly. With only about 150 to 200 nonresidents hunting here each year, the place is not exactly being over harvested. The very sparse native population has not over shot this area, either.

Most of the hunting is by bush plane fly-in and then by walking, similar to much Alaskan hunting. However, dog team hunts (with dogs as pack animals rather than as sled pullers) and boat hunts have also been experimented with here and there. Horseback hunting is almost nonexistent. The costs are high, rivaling those of Alaska and a bit higher than the Yukon. I know of no moose/caribou only hunts such as are available in northern British Columbia and in some areas of Alaska. The general all-species mixed game hunt here runs about $4,000 and up for a hunt of 15 days and longer. Figure on $250 per day and up for a quality hunt. If you hanker to tread some of the wildest, most unspoiled country left on this or any other continent, this may be for you. However, be in top physical condition!

**Saskatchewan, Manitoba and Ontario:** Though there are fair populations in these three provinces (perhaps 80,000 caribou in Manitoba, for instance) there has been little or no nonresident sport hunting for them over the years. Seasons are frequently closed to nonresidents and, when open and unlimited, few hunters come.

The necessary outfitting and guiding services (for caribou) hardly exist in the first two areas, and Ontario usually reserves its caribou for residents.

It is almost impossible to accurately ascertain which "type" these animals in the middle of the continent fall into. The Boone & Crockett Club considers them to be Barren Grounds. The provincial governments often consider them to be woodlands or even to be of both groups, and some of the northern Manitoba and Saskatchewan animals have even been characterized as mountain caribou. I would not recommend that the man serious about getting a caribou try these places, though the casual hunter might luck into one as part of his fall fishing trip or other general outing there.

**Alberta:** Most caribou in Alberta are considered to be of the mountain variety. The herd is relatively small, probably no more than 4,000 or so on a year-around basis though they do get periodic infusions from the north as more animals wander south to winter. Costs here are a bit cheaper than British Columbia, but the hunting generally is not so good, and this is not a prime caribou area.

**Quebec/Labrador:** This herd of some 100,000 or more animals is very lightly hunted (no more than 1,800-2,000 taken per year under licensed hunting), and nonresident hunting was only approved as recently as the mid-60's with the discovery of how large the herd actually was. Good outfitting and guide services exist up on the Ungava Peninsula of northern Quebec but little or no services catering to visiting hunters are yet available in the remote territory of Labrador.

These hunts generally last for 7 to 10 days. The hunter is flown into camp and then hunts on foot. The cost of the hunt runs around $750 to $1,250, depending upon the proximity of the camp to the migration route and the desirability of the hunting area in general. This is not particularly spectacular country, and there is little other game available though some good fishing can often be had. However, this area does offer the advantage of being relatively close (about 900 air miles from New York City) to the crowded eastern seaboard of the U. S. Thus, the eastern hunter can get to and from the area with considerably less expense and faster than he can cross the continent to hunt the far northwest. There are some marvelous trophies available here. The highest scoring caribou head of all time, taken back in the early 1930's, was of this type and was shot in Labrador by an Eskimo. Many believe that if this record head is ever beaten, it will be by another sweeping, many spangled Quebec-Labrador head.

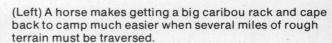

(Left) A horse makes getting a big caribou rack and cape back to camp much easier when several miles of rough terrain must be traversed.

(Below) Hunter returns to camp with caribou trophy tied aboard horse.

A big caribou bull such as this one may well be a trophy of a lifetime. Do you know how to properly skin out and care for the trophy as this Indian guide is doing?

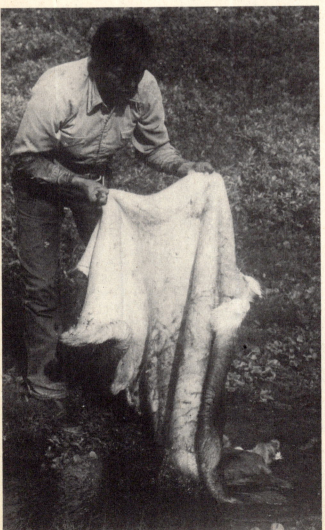

(Left) The white mane and neck of a caribou cape stains easily and the dried blood and grime is difficult and expensive to remove. It's a good idea to rinse the cape out in a clean stream before this happens.

(Below) On a busy deep wilderness hunt camp chores never end. Here outfitter guide John Holmes pauses a moment while sawing antlers off the head of a big caribou as guide Charlie Smith salts down a goat hide.

(Right) Fine fleshing a caribou head for trophy mounting takes patience and a bit of skill and practice. Watch others do two or three before you try it on one of your own precious heads!

(Below) A nice caribou head that is to be mounted demands the best of field care such as the careful skinning that Gene Holmes is doing on this relatively modest-sized but nicely symmetrical rack.

Successful caribou hunters load their roped together racks into a bush plane for the flight out at the end of a north Canadian hunt.

A young bull like this one that looks big to the deer hunter but is still small and indifferent as *caribou* racks go should never be taken.

## Guns for Caribou

Caribou are not hard to kill. They exhibit nothing like the vitality of a moose, elk or even a goat. It has been my experience that any cartridge that will kill mule deer well will work fine on caribou since they seem to have about the same amount of vitality, though a caribou bull may stay on his feet a moment or two longer after being hit than a mule deer buck might.

I have seen them killed promptly and with dispatch with such rounds as the .243, 6mm Remington (100-grain bullets or heavier) and the .257 and .25/06. If the hunter is out after nothing larger and shoots his gun well, these small .24 and .25 bores will perform well on caribou. For the average hunter the .270 is probably the

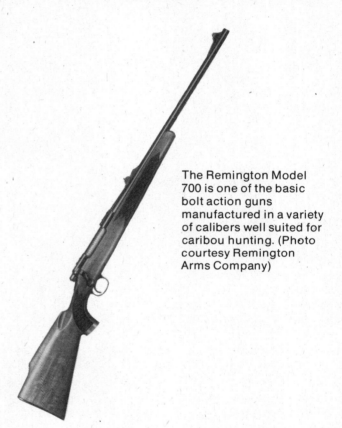

The Remington Model 700 is one of the basic bolt action guns manufactured in a variety of calibers well suited for caribou hunting. (Photo courtesy Remington Arms Company)

**Newfoundland:** This is now the only place where nonresidents can legally hunt the big bodied, short beamed true woodland type caribou. The herd on this large island runs around 15,000 to 18,000 animals, and the nonresident permits are becoming more severely limited in number and more astronomical in price each year. Most caribou hunting across the continent should offer a very high chance of success, upwards of 85 percent and higher, if one will spend the money to get back into a good caribou area and the time to hunt it properly once in there.

Newfoundland runs the lowest hunter success ratio on caribou (by far) and the costs, of both licenses and guides, are so high for what you are getting that this is not a recommended area to hunt. The caribou are generally far less impressive than comparable bulls of the other three types, and the country and many of the outfitting services are less than inspiring. The licenses for caribou have become so expensive as to be almost insulting, and unless you have already collected good, representative examples of the other three types of caribou and just have an undeniable itch for one of these woodland types, I would recommend you look elsewhere for your caribou hunting. Caribou hunts can often be combined with moose hunts but the moose, too, are among the smaller subspecies and not especially desirable as moose trophies go.

best bet as a caribou killer, offering a flat trajectory and a bit more punch than the smaller cartridges. Certainly nothing larger than the .270 with medium construction bullets weighing 130 grains, is needed.

Caribou are, except for pronghorn, the only game we have that might be called plains game. Sometimes they are shot at relatively long ranges and a vari-power scope of 2x to 7x is usually a good idea. The outsized caribou feet, huge in surface area to better negotiate the bogs and marshes encountered on his endless wanderings, can be taken for interesting secondary trophies. A good taxidermist can fashion them into highly attractive ashtrays, bookends or lamp bases. A nice caribou head adds grace and elegance to any trophy wall or trophy room.

# CHAPTER 6

# How To Get Your Moose

**THE MOOSE IS,** depending upon just how you define your terms, our largest big game animal. Though the bison is sometimes heavier, it is not as long nor nearly as tall as a large bull moose of the Alaska-Yukon race. More importantly, bison (or "buffalo" as they are frequently misnamed) are at best a fringe animal, not a widely available free-ranging game animal as is the moose. The largest Alaska brown bear may weigh over 1,000 pounds at the right time of year, and though they do qualify as more of a "basic" game animal than the bison, they are not as heavy, tall or long as the largest moose. Perhaps one might consider the walrus larger since a big bull walrus might weigh close to twice as much as a comparable bull moose but, again, a walrus is something of a limited, special situation game animal — not a "basic," widely available species like the moose.

In fact, for the hunter not used to seeing moose, the main problem is getting his whole scale of values adjusted to the sheer enormity of the beast. The largest bulls of the clan will exceed 10 feet in length with some perhaps reaching 12 feet. That's longer than some automobiles. The same bull would extend 8 feet in height

This bull, small by Canadian or Alaskan standards but fair for a Shiras or American type moose, was photographed crossing an open Wyoming meadow searching for a cow during the rut. Moose are often quite easy to approach during this period.

# MOOSE RANGE

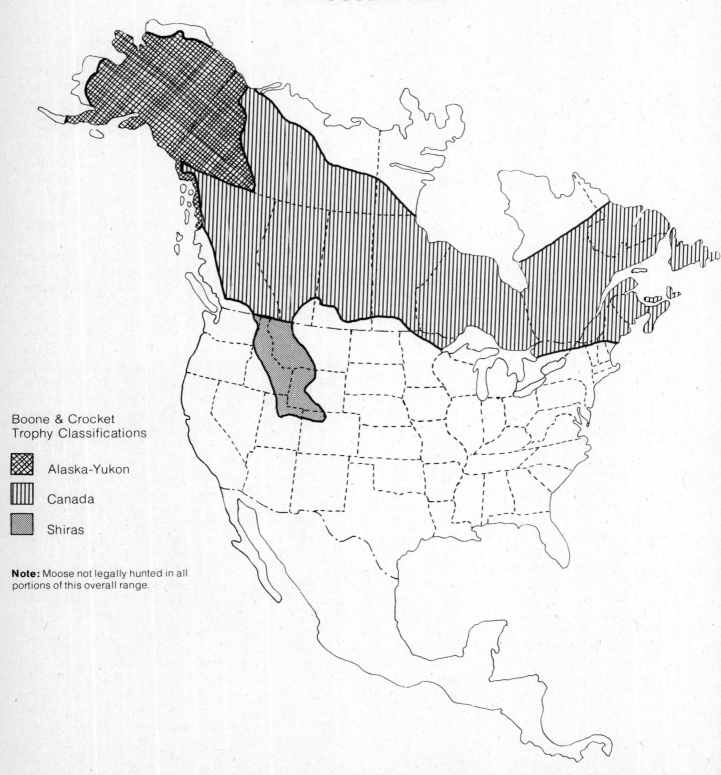

Boone & Crocket
Trophy Classifications

Alaska-Yukon

Canada

Shiras

**Note:** Moose not legally hunted in all
portions of this overall range.

72

Whenever you find moose, you'll find water not too far away. They love to feed on the tender aquatic vegetation and have been verified as diving as deeply as 20 feet to do so.

from the ground to the top of the front shoulder. That's as tall or taller than the ceiling of the average room — at *shoulder* height! With his head up, the antlers of this big bull would be over 12 feet off the ground or a bit taller than one 6-foot man standing on the shoulders of another 6-footer.

Moose simply dwarf most other North American game animals. The first time I ever saw moose tracks was on an elk hunt in western Canada. Though elk are rather large animals, they are somewhat dainty footed while moose have rather large, splayed out feet which serve somewhat as snowshoes to help him support his tremendous weight in many of the boggy muskegs and swamps that he likes to frequent. After several days of looking at elk tracks (which I then thought to be huge because I had never tracked anything larger than whitetail deer or pronghorn prior to that), I spotted some moose tracks one day. Splayed out even larger in the soft mud, they seemed like the track of some beast from another primeval world. Suddenly my elk seemed to shrink by comparison.

My first introduction to a live moose was unforgettable, and it taught me something I have never forgotten since: beware of amorous bull moose at the height of the rut. They can be crazier than the first three floors of any mental institution in the country put together. Here's what happened.

My Indian guide, Nick Dennis, was an artist of the *basso profundo* moose grunt. It was the latter part of September, and the moose were high in the rut here in the Rainy Pass section of the Alaska Range. We had been watching a big bull wandering around a boggy, small spruce dotted flat for some 10 minutes. We decided to get him in closer for a better look at those big antlers.

Nick started working on him at about 200 yards with what must have been a rather seductive set of grunts and *ooonnks*. Actually these noises sounded like nothing so much as a whole symphony of what we might delicately call anti-social sounds, but they were evidently coming through loud and clear to the big deer. He tossed his huge head this way and that with his small, red rimmed eyes pinwheeling around and then started lumbering our way with the awesome majesty of a Tiger tank. I'll never know whether the old boy thought Nick was another bull ready to fight or a lady fair moose winsomely calling him in for a tryst.

Either way, things were getting a bit tightly wound with him only 30 yards out and loping our way with romance in his heart. The shaggy hair was sticking out like a ruff on his neck, and as he moved purposefully toward us, one look at those pig-like little eyes showed that he meant business. He smelled like a paper mill facing the wrong way because, in typical moose-like fashion, he had been urinating in his scrapes and then rolling in the resulting odorous gumbo to announce to the world that YES! he was r-e-a-d-y! His lower parts

Moose have been called with birch bark horns for many years in Quebec, but modern day game call makers such as Johnny Stewart of Waco, Texas, are now pioneering with the electronic calling of moose (quite successfully as this photo of a Wyoming bull being called in graphically shows).

were plastered with this mud and he certainly did not resemble the beast portrayed on the typical barbershop calendar.

Nick and I stood up to show ourselves and, hopefully, end this little wilderness version of *The Dating Game*. We had already decided that his spread was only 55 inches or so, and thus he wasn't large enough to take. We waved our hands and yelled in a most unmooselike fashion. No dice. Our friend knew what he wanted, and if we were standing in the way of him getting to his girl friend — well, that was just too bad for us!

Finally when he was only 20 short paces out, I put a single 150-grain Nosler through his broad right antler palm where it wouldn't hurt him and quickly jacked in another shell in case that one didn't turn the trick. But it stopped him. In fact, he almost skidded to a halt on those big stilt-like legs. He stood there for a long moment, probably realizing dimly he'd been had, and eyeballed us in the most thoroughly jaundiced fashion imaginable. Then he shook himself, looking for all the world like a huge black dog in the process, and took off to find some proper lady moose to consort with.

Several days later I shot a moose. In fact, I shot two moose as that was still the limit in those days, and the outfitter had blandly assured me that, if I would help pack the meat out for later distribution to the local natives, he would be most happy for me to take two. Alas, being young and stout but not too brainy, I simply didn't know what I was getting into. However, this little experience also taught me something unforgettable. Namely that moose aren't large — they are ENORMOUS, and you should always shoot one with the idea of, "How am I going to get this thing out of here?" foremost in your mind.

As I put the two bulls down, the guide and I packed each of them out, making three trips apiece per bull. The first trip was the "easy" one with us carrying antlers, cape, heart and liver, two front feet to be fashioned into bookends (in one case) and various other smaller odd parts. I use the word "easy" only in a relative sense. The moose carries more weight on his head than any other horned or antlered animal in the world. Believe me, after thrashing around through several miles of damnably dense alders and willows with a rack over 5 feet wide and weighing about 75 pounds

(Above) Moose are enormous animals, dwarfing most all other North American big game. Here author Brakefield shows a nice though not particularly outstanding moose he took in British Columbia.

(Below) A good horse is a godsend in packing out a big moose. This load consisted of the antlers and cape on top and various smaller cuts of meat (tenderloins, heart, liver, tongue, etc.) filling the panniers or pack boxes. Two more trips were necessary for the horse to carry everything out, and he was very heavily loaded to accomplish it in even three trips!

Moose can be found almost anywhere in good mixed game country. Bulls were taken in the marshy valley below this hunter and also up on the peaks where he has just come from.

strapped onto my back, I will never ever, in my whole life, forget that little fact.

The second trip was tougher. On this one we each took a whole front quarter out. The third trip shouldn't happen to a professional Sherpa porter. On this one we each took a full hindquarter. Old *Alces alces gigas* has a right big fanny, and each of these things must have weighed a bit over 200 pounds. The only thing that kept me going was the fact that my guide was some 2 inches shorter and 20 pounds lighter, and *he* kept going.

Getting up with the third load took some doing. To arise like Lazarus with this kind of weight on your back required teamwork plus some fancy footwork. The man without a load had to literally stand on the feet of the poor loaded down pilgrim (who was crushed into the earth much as if he were laboring in the lead-like atmosphere of Jupiter), grasp his hands in a death grip and, on the count of three, help to heave-ho him upwards in a desperate attempt to get erect. Then the new standee, quivering and quaking in all his overloaded splendor, had to wait until the other man had squirmed into his own loaded packframe and then repeat the same drill to get *him* afloat.

Then we gingerly covered anywhere from a quarter-mile to a mile, depending upon the terrain and on where we found an appropriate steep bank. With both of us loaded down the way we were, that steep bank was our key to ever getting airborne again. When we found one, we would gratefully lower ourselves onto a steeper portion of the bank and rest the back breaking pack against it as we sat there in a more-or-less erect position due to the slope of the bank. When we were ready to lumber on again, we would sigh and launch ourselves forward out into the ether in order to regain our feet.

When we finally arrived at camp and that blessed meat rack that would support the awful load, the pack-straps had cut 1/2-inch deep trenches in my newly rounded shoulders. As I mercifully shucked the weight off my back, my head spun, my tummy turned flip-flops and I suddenly felt light enough to fly with the angels and the cherubs. Moose are that big.

## Moose as a Game Animal

Moose are relatively intelligent as animals go; they have an excellent sense of smell, and they hear well. This is in keeping with their background as being originally an animal of the boreal forests where these senses are particularly vital. Their eyesight, again in keeping with their background as a heavy cover rather than plains animal, is not particularly acute. Moose have thrived mightily in the modern era of the last hundred years or so, continually expanding both their range and numbers. From east to west, these animals have prospered. The island of Newfoundland off the eastern coast of Canada currently boasts a very large herd of some 35,000 to 40,000 moose, and yet these animals were not even introduced to that island until 1878, and it is believed that that introduction was a failure. The current herd stems from a 1904 introduction of two pair of New Brunswick animals (the first introduction was only a single pair of moose from the neighboring island of Nova Scotia). That's some population explosion!

Alaska is moose heaven with its gigantic herd of 150,000 or more moose, and these the largest members of the entire species. Moose seem to be adaptable, flexible and "well engineered" animals for the purpose of survival. For such an enormous animal to do so well in this modern era is almost unbelievable and no mean testimonial to the savvy of the beast. All of these survival characteristics also add up to making the big deer a fine game animal.

Moose vary considerably in how wary they are and how difficult they are to approach. Much of their range is so wild and deserted that the animals are not unduly chivied about, and in these cases, they are rather tame and easy to approach. Where the animals have been harried about a good bit, they become wary and difficult to spot during the day. (In some areas natives with snow machines, who with no limit on the amount of kill they can make because they are not bound by the white man's game regulations and have little of the white man's concept of game management, are rapidly becoming the number one conservation problem on the continent.)

These two Shiras moose were photographed during the rut in northwestern Wyoming by Johnny Stewart as they moved around constantly searching for cows.

Moose make quite good eating and are less affected by the rut than the meat of any of the five major North American deer. At its prime moose meat rivals the best game meat on this continent, that of elk and mountain sheep. I have never yet found a bull that, with proper field care and dressing, would not be good to eat — even a very large trophy bull who smells to high heaven at the height of the rut. However, the larger and older bulls, though tasty, can be quite tough to chew if one is strictly used to over-fattened, stall fed beef. This can be easily remedied though by a combination of knowing how to properly cook certain cuts, and judicious use of the chemical tenderizer or a bit of scoring and pounding with a cleaver or chef's knife. There is no excuse for a bad meal of moose meat!

A big 60-inch moose, such as this bull taken by John McCartt while hunting with Wes Brown in northern British Columbia, makes a dramatic focal point in any trophy room.

## Moose as Trophy Animals

Bull moose begin their antler growth in April, and it is completed in July when the racks begin to harden. By late August the bulls remove the last of the velvet by rubbing their antlers on small trees and bushes. The fact that an adult bull moose will, each year, grow some 50 to 90 pounds of solid bone material on his head in only 12 to 14 weeks is one of nature's miracles. These great antlers are, like all horns and antlers, a secondary sex characteristic (much similar to a man's beard) and, as such, they are used primarily by the bulls to establish breeding dominance among their own kind during the annual rut, rather than being used for defense against other animals or predators as some erroneously believe.

The big deer raise spikes their first year and funny little branched "shoe horns" or "boot jacks" that have little or no palmation (flattening), their second year. Their first set of cupped, palmated, moose-like antlers usually develops the third year and maximum sized trophy antlers come in the seventh through tenth years. After the tenth year, the antlers tend to regress in size and "freak" more in conformation. Few bulls will live this long, though they have been known to live for up to 17 years in the wild under ideal conditions.

Moose are browsers rather than grazers, and they consume some 50 to 75 pounds of food per day, depending upon the animal's size. One moose requires the same amount of forage as five or six deer. Moose dearly love water plants in the summer and have been known to dive to depths of over 18 feet to get to them! Moose are tremendously strong swimmers, and only the best paddlers can keep up with one in a canoe. They have been known to swim over 12 miles.

Moose thrive during the early stages of forest succession and regeneration, and they diminish as the forest climaxes. Lakes and marshes are very necessary for them, providing both favored summer feeding and protection from the heat and insect pests. Seeming to need an environment with a low average annual temperature, they are truly an animal of the northland.

They are hardy, prolific souls who are faring better than practically any other larger-than-deer game species in North America. Moose will increase their herd size rapidly under favorable conditions. An 18 percent to 25 percent net increase is not unusual in good years. Whereas 18 inches of snow will "yard up" deer and restrict their feeding area, it takes 30 inches or more to do the same to the much larger, longer-legged moose.

Moose are tough animals who are able to defend themselves well, even from the feared wolves. Observations have shown that when a moose resolutely stands its ground and defies the big gray canids, they generally will not continue to press a strong and vigorous animal in the 2- to 7-year-old range. Wolves do take a fearsome toll of the calves, yearlings and older animals, though.

Taxonomically there are four types of moose in North America with the animals generally becoming smaller in size the further south and east you look in their overall range. The Boone & Crockett Club recognizes three types of moose for scoring purposes in their trophy awarding system. The giant Alaska-Yukon

(Left) Here Elgin Gates and the Prince of Iran pose with a large Alaskan bull taken by the latter. Note the width and mass of the palms on this big fellow.

(Below) Andy Dennis is starting to cut up the back of the neck of this bull moose in order to cape out the head for a trophy mount.

moose lives just where the name indicates, and it is the largest deer that has ever trod the earth. The extinct Irish Elk, a gigantic freak of evolution that died off, was not quite as large in body size, but it did wear enormous antlers sometimes spreading to 12 feet! (Which is probably the reason why they became a casualty in the experimentation of evolution.)

The Canada moose classification in Boone & Crockett includes moose living anywhere in Canada except the Yukon. Generally the larger animals are in the more westerly and northerly parts of that giant country. This hunting oriented classification lumps together two separate races that the taxonomists (animal classifiers) make a distinction between. The smallest of all, the Shiras type, is limited to the western part of the U.S., primarily in the Rockies. The Shiras moose are smaller, much lighter antlered and often lighter in coloration than the larger northern moose. Actually, the moose must be regarded as being basically a Canadian animal (and Alaskan). Any fringe populations lapping over into the "southern 48" portion of the U.S. are marginal groups living on the very edge of the animal's acceptable range and thus do not achieve anywhere near the optimum size that is possible. The exact opposite may be said about the elk which is basically a U.S. animal that has penetrated into some areas of western Canada.

Moose are gigantic no matter what race of the beast we are considering. A big Shiras bull may weigh 900 pounds which is more than all but the largest elk recorded. The larger Canada bulls will scale 1,200 to 1,400 pounds, and the biggest Alaskan bulls may weigh as much as 1,600 to 1,800 pounds! A good Alaska bull will have antlers that spread in the neighborhood of 5 feet (though some have gone almost half again as much as that) while his equivalent Canada cousin will spread

50 to 60 inches. The Shiras are much less robustly antlered, and a bull over 40 inches is not bad while one over 45 inches is extremely good.

Moose heads are so large and so expensive to mount ($300 to $450 for a well-done, full head mount from leading taxidermy shops today) that the average sportsman probably should have only one mounted in that fashion. They simply take up too much wall space unless one lives in a very large house indeed. Otherwise, moose antlers can be nicely mounted on wood

Field dressing a moose takes an axe, a saw and lots of know-how and help.

(Above) A length of good rope can be tremendously helpful when field dressing large game like elk and moose. Here these fellows have trussed the bull moose into a better position so that they can completely skin him out and then quarter him. (The hide was made into a nice rug.)

(Left) Detaching the antlers from the skull of a big bull moose so that they can be mounted as a trophy really requires a heavy-duty hand saw or a chain saw. Impossible to do with a knife and rather difficult with a hatchet or even an axe.

plaques without the full head mount treatment and still make impressive but somewhat less bulky trophies. The sportsman can do this himself if he is "handy" and has the time, or he can have his taxidermist do it for him for about $75 to $125 plus any necessary crating and shipping. The bony link between the antlers can be covered by any number of materials ranging from the appropriate piece of headskin off the animal itself to buckskin to burlap or even upholsterer's flocking which can be applied to give a felt-like look and touch to the area.

There are any number of interesting secondary trophies a moose can yield to the shrewd sportsman. The feet (always the front ones) can be made into ashtrays, bookends, lampstands or other items in good

(Above) A nice bull moose butchers up about like a prime steer (though to many of us the moose tastes far better). These camp cooks are starting to rough butcher a hindquarter taken from a freshly killed bull in Canada.

(Left) Two packers carefully cinch a pair of moose antlers to a packhorse so that no points will inadvertently gouge him later and cause him to bolt. Note how much wider than the horse this rack, which isn't outsized, is.

(Below) A hunter and his guide happily bring in their moose trophy. The 55-inch antlers weighed about 50 to 60 pounds and the green, rough-skinned cape they are staggering under weighs over 100 pounds.

This little horse is very heavily loaded. Each of the two hindquarters off the not overly large bull moose that this hunter has just shot weigh a bit over 200 pounds so the horse is carrying upwards of 500 pounds as he stands. (This would only work on a short pack over relatively level and "easy" ground.)

taste. These often cost anywhere from $25 to $75 to have the taxidermist do them. The moose skin can either be tanned into an interesting hair-on rug (get the taxidermist to "shave" the leather to reduce its thickness and weight) or nice buckskin throw which can be hung on the wall or draped over the back of a couch or love seat.

Some people have even had the moose scrotum tanned into tobacco pouches for their pipe smoking friends! The moose is such a large beast that all possible use should be made of him for both trophy and meat purposes and nothing should be let go to waste.

Moose heads are, along with sheep, the one trophy that is almost always mounted in a straight eyes-front position. This is certainly understandable in the moose's case. The antler spread is so wide on big bulls that if the head were turned too much antlers would protrude into the wall. Besides, it is esthetically proper that the moose be staring straightforward rather than turned or canted in a more animated pose. Moose heads are so large that they are almost always hung in the center position on the trophy wall with other, smaller

heads grouped around them. The straightforward, eyes-ahead position accords well with this center location and with the general ponderous dignity of the huge and somewhat awkward looking head.

Moose are not "pretty" animals in the sense of the African kudu or sable or of our own elk or caribou. However, they are impressive, majestic and interesting, and one must place them high on any listing of top worldwide trophies available to the big game hunter.

## Ways to Hunt Moose

Moose inhabit such a vast geographic range that they are hunted in a wide variety of ways. In the dense lowland forests of Quebec and Ontario in the east they are often hunted by boat with the guide frequently trying to call the big deer in. It is usually not possible to spot them at long distances due to the thickness of the cover and the general lack of mountains and high hills to serve as vantage points.

In western Canada moose are most often taken as part of the general mixed game hunt, often conducted on horseback. The animals are usually spotted at long range on the mountainsides or out in the clearings on the flats as they move around to feed. Then they are stalked and shot much like any other classic mountain game, such as sheep or goats. There are also an increasing number of moose and caribou late season combo hunts and even some moose-only hunts in the more southwestern portions of western Canada.

In Alaska moose are often taken as part of a general three or five species hunt. The hunter is usually flown into camp with his guide, and then most of the hunting is via walking and glassing. Horses are used in some areas but overall much less so than in the Yukon, British Columbia or Alberta.

Horses can make a big difference on a moose hunt. Not only in covering more ground in order to look over more country but also, as mentioned earlier, in packing the animal out once he is down. *Never* shoot a moose — with or without horses at your disposal — where they will fall and die in the water. Try not to shoot them on the edge of the water as they may whirl around, mortally wounded and flounder out into the water to die. Dressing a bull moose out is quite a job under the best of conditions. Doing it in and partially under water is something that you'll never quite forget — even though you'll wish fervently you could!

Shiras moose are a permit-only affair, and the first thing the hunter must do is be fortunate enough to draw one of the limited permits. After that, getting the moose is rather easy as these animals are very tightly regulated and managed and many of them are about as wild as a barnyard heifer.

The charts on the following three pages will give you full detail on availability of current type moose hunts throughout North America and their approximate costs.

# Where and How to Get Your Moose

| HUNT AREA | ESTIMATED POPULATION | TYPE ANIMAL (TAXONOMICALLY) | TYPE OF HUNTS AVAILABLE | ESTIMATED COSTS (Not incl. transportation to and from, licenses, and incidentals). | REMARKS | FOR MORE INFO CONTACT: |
|---|---|---|---|---|---|---|
| **Alaska** | 130,000-150,000 | Alaska-Yukon (or *gigas*, the largest form of all) | Mostly fly-in by bush plane and then walk though some road hunting and some wilderness hunting by tracked vehicles available. Horseback hunting largely limited to a few outfitters in the Wrangell Mtns. in S.E. Alaska. | Available many ways. As part of a $3500 "5-animal" guided hunt, a $2500 "3-animal" hunt, a moose-caribou combo hunt ranging from about $1200 to $2000 depending on how long you hunt, where you hunt and whether horses or vehicles are also used or how extensive the flying is. Also, you can legally hunt moose in Alaska without employing a pro guide, thus saving a lot of money. However, this is only for *seasoned* woodsmen and hunters! | The best time to hunt is around mid-Sept. at the height of the rut when animals are moving and unwary. The bigger trophies are found the further south and east you go in Alaska with the Kenai and Alaska Peninsulas, the Talkeetnas and the southern Alaska Range heading the list for largest racks. | Alaska Dept. of Fish & Game Subport Building Juneau, Alaska 99801 Tel. 907/586-3392 |
| **Alberta** | 141,000 | Western Canadian (*Alces andersoni*) with some smaller Shiras moose in extreme S.W. | Mostly horseback hunting, either from ranch or permanent camp, or from wilderness camps. Best hunting in west-central and northwestern strip bordering the B. C. border. Standard hunt is 10 days though hunts are available from 7 days to 3 weeks in duration, depending on how many other species sought. | Hunts generally run from $750 to $2000 depending on how long (7 to 14 days), whether one or two hunters to the guide, and whether moose only sought or moose/caribou combo hunt or general mixed game hunt for several species. Figure $1000 for good moose-only hunt in good area. | Though much of the hunting in Alberta is not what it was, the west-country is still as spectacular as any on earth and the moose hunting is still quite good. | Gov. of Prov. of Alberta Dept. of Lands & Forests Natural Resources Bldg. 109th St. and 99th Ave. Edmonton, Alberta, Canada |
| **British Columbia** | 100,000 plus | Practically all West Canadian (*andersoni*) with a very few smaller *shirasi* in extreme S.E. tip of Prov. and a few larger *gigas* in ext. N.W. | Moose hunting varies tremendously in B. C. Most all hunting by horse in north half of province and rather expensive. In south half, horses may be used or hunting may be on foot from 4WD vehicles driven to logging or access roads. May also be afoot after flying into established tent camp well off road. Hunts in the north are usually either moose/caribou combo hunts (10 to 14 days) or as part of general mixed game hunt (14-21 days). In south they may be moose-only hunts (7 to 10 days) or part of smaller scale mixed game hunts (10-15 days). | Moose-caribou combo hunts on horseback in north half of prov. cost from $100 to $150 per day, depending on how many hunters to guide, etc. Thus, 10- to 14-day hunts run from about $1250 to $2000. Mixed game hunts in north much higher, from $2000 to $4000 depending on game, area and length of hunt. (Check on late season moose-caribou hunts for big savings. Cold, tough hunting but often actually see *more* trophy moose and can sometimes save 25% to 40%). Moose hunting in south half of B.C. much cheaper, ranging from about $500 to $1250. Figure an avg. of $650 without horses and $1000 with them for good hunt. Caribou often not available. | If you're a trophy hunter, the further north and east you go (with the limited exception of the small population of giant *gigas* in extreme N.W. tip), the larger the racks. However, moose hunting can be everybit as good for smaller trophies and meat in the central and southern areas at far less cost. Late season hunts come in late Oct. and Nov. (down clothing!) and also, check father-son specials and last minute hunt cancellations to save a buck. | Gov. of Prov. Of Brit. Col. Dept. of Recreation & Conservation Fish and Wildlife Branch Victoria, British Columbia, Can. |

| HUNT AREA | ESTIMATED POPULATION | TYPE ANIMAL (TAXONOMICALLY) | TYPE OF HUNTS AVAILABLE | ESTIMATED COSTS (Not incl. transportation to and from, licenses, and incidentals). | REMARKS | FOR MORE INFO CONTACT: |
|---|---|---|---|---|---|---|
| **Manitoba** | 45,000 | West-Canadian | Little or no horseback hunting. Drive or fly to cabins or lodge and hunt afoot or by boat from lodge. Also, some "spiking out" away from lodge by hunter and guide. Usually two or more moose hunters per guide here with meat hunting very substantial. Manitoba is not hunted very heavily by nonresidents, yet it is a good bet for the visiting moose hunter with some good trophies available at reasonable costs and, on the better hunts, a better than 50% chance of success. Most hunts run 5 to 7 days tho 10-day hunts are available and recommended if time and money allow. | Hunts range from about $200 (where you rent a "housekeeping" cabin and furnish your own food and cook it while sharing a guide with one or more other hunters) to $750-$1000 for longer hunts using boats and motors and having a guide to yourself. | When checked out carefully by a visiting sportsmen, some real bargains are available here with black bear a frequent "bonus" trophy tho caribou not available. | Dept. of Tourism, Recreational & Cultural Affairs Room 408, Norquay Bldg. Winnipeg, Manitoba Canada |
| **Newfoundland** | 50,000 | East-Canadian | Mostly afoot from cabins or lodge. Some hunting from roads or using vehicles indirectly. Most hunts run 7 days with the hunter sharing a guide with another hunter. | Though hunter success ratio is high (close to 50%) this is not the place for the trophy hunter trying for a large rack (though some are taken) and it is relatively expensive with 5- to 7-day hunts running $500 to $750 *plus* the most expensive moose license in North America at $350! | Though some of the underbrush is thick and the country a bit rough, this is (relatively) easy hunting. I know of no standard "bargain" opportunities here except for a possible last minute cancellation where another hunter forfeits his deposit. Photo opportunities are usually rather limited. | Gov. of Prov. Of Newfoundland Dept. of Tourism Confederation Bldg. St. John's, Newfoundland Canada |
| **Northwest Territories** | Unknown but large | West-Canadian | This is one of the remotest areas on earth, and the hunting is understandably expensive. Tho the moose are large and plentiful, there are no moose-only or moose-caribou only hunts offered to my knowledge. Rather, all moose come on the very expensive mixed game all-species hunts that last 15 to 21 days. Most of these hunts are by fly-in to camp and then walk (similar to Alaskan hunting). Very few horses used tho some outfitters have used jet boats to river hunt and pack dogs to move camp. Fantastic photo opportunities. | Mixed game hunts generally run $2700-$4000, depending on length of hunt, ground hunted and luxuriousness of accommodations. This is *not* the hunt for a fellow only interested in moose! | This savage, yet fragile area is little known and expensive. If you have the time and money, by all means try it. If not, moose can be had more cheaply and easily elsewhere. | TravelArctic Yellowknife, Northwest Territories XOE 1Ho Canada |

# Where and How to Get Your Moose

| HUNT AREA | ESTIMATED POPULATION | TYPE ANIMAL (TAXONOMICALLY) | TYPE OF HUNTS AVAILABLE | ESTIMATED COSTS (Not incl. transportation to and from, licenses, and incidentals). | REMARKS | FOR MORE INFO CONTACT: |
|---|---|---|---|---|---|---|
| **Ontario** | 125,000 | West-Canadian (western third of Prov.) and East-Canadian (eastern 2/3's of Prov.) | Mostly hunting afoot or by canoe from lodge or cabins. Many hunts from "housekeeping" cabins where hunter furnishes food and some or all gear, but uses guide, usually shared with one or more other hunters. Avg. hunt 7 days, though they range from 5 to 10 days. | From about $200-$250 for 5 days in housekeeping cottage and sharing a guide with one or more other hunters to $750-$1000 for longer hunt with more personalized service in deeper wilderness areas. Many good hunting opportunities for the sportsman who investigates carefully. | Ontario has, for many years, been the classic canoe hunting, calling 'em up with the birchbark horn grounds, and there is still much good hunting here 'at reasonable costs with whitetail deer and/or black bear often being taken as "bonus" trophies. Best Area: Sioux Lookout. | Dept. of Tourism & Information Prov. of Ontario Parliament Bldgs. Toronto, Ontario Canada |
| **Quebec** | 75,000 | East-Canadian | Very similar to Ontario hunting with possibly a slightly smaller hunter-success ratio, province wide. Many good hunting opportunities available at reasonable cost. Best area: Abitibi Region. | Similar in cost to Ontario hunting. | Similar to Ontario. Some whitetail deer and black bear also available in southern portions of province while the northerly areas offer the unique opportunity (for eastern Canada, that is) of also scoring on caribou or wolf in some camps. Caribou raise the hunt cost considerably, tho. Language can, though not often, be a problem here. | Gov. of Quebec Ministry of Tourism & Sport Hunting 2, place Ville-Marie Montreal, Quebec Canada |
| **Saskatchewan** | ? | West-Canadian | Similar to Manitoba. Boats used frequently, particularly in the deep wilderness area of the lake country in the northern portion of the province. | Similar to Manitoba. | Don't shoot your bull in the water! Black Bear a good possibility, plus some good ice fishing in north. | Gov. of Prov. of Saskatchewan Dept. of Natural Resources Regina, Saskatchewan Canada |
| **Yukon** | ? | Alaska-Yukon except for West-Canadian in small part of ext. s.e. prov. | Few or no moose or moose-caribou hunts offered. Moose available mostly as part of all-specie, mixed game hunts running 14-21 days and almost always on horseback. Good hunting for big moose here, especially in the southern and southwestern parts of territory but expensive if moose are your main quarry. | These mixed game hunts range from a low of $2000 to a high of $3800, depending on duration of hunt, luxury of accommodation and how many sheep and grizzly in general area. Figure about $2500 for a good average.14-day hunt. | One of the classic big game fields, the hunting, scenery and photo opportunities are generally superb, but moose can be hunted more cheaply elsewhere. Check for areas without many sheep for lower prices. | Gov. of Yukon Terr. Box 2703 Whitehorse, Yukon Canada |

## Guns for Moose

Moose, though very large animals, don't have a reputation as being particularly hard to kill. This squares with my own experiences as I have never had a moose run over 100 yards after being hit. Usually they don't move more than 20 feet.

As I have written in other places, there's a very apt saying that, ''Moose hurt a lot.'' That shorthands the whole situation on moose vitality about as well as any single statement that I have ever found. Moose *always* take some time to die. They are simply so huge that, I suppose, their great heart just will not stop as readily as smaller animals. I have never killed a moose as quickly as I have caribou, deer or even goat or elk. But, once hit well, moose just don't seem to want to stampede off into the next county as elk invariably do.

For this reason, whenever I shoot a moose, I never follow him up immediately as I would a similarly hit elk.

This hunter is confronting a young bull moose (almost hidden in the trees on the crest of the small knoll) which he decided to pass up as being too small.

Though moose are massive animals, they are surprisingly easy to bring down with any sort of decently placed shot from an appropriate caliber.

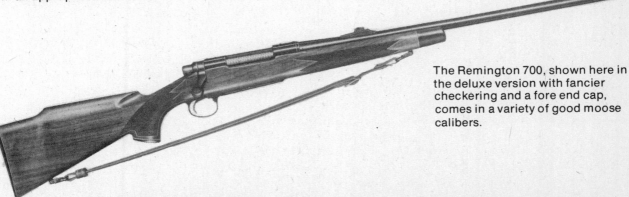

The Remington 700, shown here in the deluxe version with fancier checkering and a fore end cap, comes in a variety of good moose calibers.

(Above) Successful moose hunters, with antlers loaded aboard the packhorse, are "tailing" the horses together so they'll stay in train while trailing through the brush on the way back to base camp.

Guide Gene Holmes brings in a decent 50-plus-inch Canadian moose he had guided his hunter to.

Remembering the "hurt a lot" homily, it seems that moose really do, and if not pushed hard, they will usually lie down in a few moments and begin to stiffen up. In fact, usually a fairly hit moose will not move off at all unless pushed hard.

The ritual that the majority seem to follow is to walk around a bit in a few faltering circles, hump up and then gradually go down. Usually once down they will never get up, though I saw one exception to this one late fall hunt in British Columbia. Easy as they are to get down, they seem to sometimes take forever to die, though.

All in all, moose are not nearly as armor plated as a big bull elk, and often they appear easier to lay down than a big billy goat which might only weigh one-quarter as much as they do. While the .243, 6mm Remington, .257 Roberts class of cartridge is definitely too light for moose under average conditions, the .270 and .30/06

class of shell is perfectly suitable. The bullets should be reasonably heavily constructed since we are shooting at a large animal with heavy bones and an unbelievably thick hide. If you have ever skinned out a whole moose and then tried to pack out the over 200 pounds of wet, green hide, you would know exactly what I mean. The leather itself, during the rut when it thickens for combat with other bulls of his own kind, can run well over a inch thick up around the bull's neck and forequarters. That's a lot of leather to penetrate.

However, modern, well-constructed bullets such as the Remington Core-Lokt or Winchester Silvertip among factory types or the Nosler, Bitteroot or Barnes among the handloads are perfectly capable of penetrating this hide and reaching the vitals on a well placed shot. Actually, while I do regard the .270-.30/06 class of cartridge as a bit marginal for elk under some circumstances, I feel that they are more appropriate for moose even though the latter is much the larger animal.

Of course any of the newer .284 or .30 caliber magnums will do just dandy for moose hunting — providing you can handle the extra muzzle blast and recoil and still shoot these more powerful cartridges accurately, without flinching. In moose hunting as in all other big game hunting, it's far more important *where* you hit them than *what* you hit them with.

Some of the older "mid-30's" cartridges such as the venerable old .35 Whelen (.30/06 necked up to .35 caliber), the now discontinued .348 and the long discontinued .33 Winchester make fine short-range moose

A good weather tight camp where hunters can relax and keep clean is important during a grueling deep wilderness moose hunt.

stoppers out to about 150 yards. The .358 Winchester (.308 Winchester necked up to .35 caliber) and the .350 Remington will also work nicely on the big deer with the latter giving a bit more killing range due to its somewhat higher velocities. The real powerhouses such as the .338 Winchester or the .375 Magnum are certainly not necessary for clean kills on moose.

Many moose are still shot at relatively close ranges. Much of the hunting done in the dense woodlands of eastern Canada dictates short shots of necessity. Even out West where moose are now often found high on the mountains at or above timberline, often above the sheep, it is quite often possible to approach them rather closely. Moose as a rule do not appear to become as shy and wary as readily as do elk or deer. Although when

hunted hard, they certainly do become a bit more skittish and difficult to approach. It is often possible to approach within 100 yards of your quarry when moose hunting.

One unfortunate aspect of the moose's size is that the animal is so overwhelmingly large that there is often a tendency to just punch out a shot on the "hit him anywhere" basis and this often works, resulting in a wounded moose that may not be followed up and killed because the hunter felt he missed. Moose should be shot with the same care and precision that the much smaller mountain sheep or deer are taken with. They are a marvelous game animal and an impressive trophy, and they certainly deserve a good stalk, an accurate shot and a clean kill.

# CHAPTER 7

# How To Get Your Mountain Game: The Sheep And Goat

**FEW ANIMALS** and fewer people possess the thing called charisma. The mountain game, our goats and sheep, do project this aura, this special presence, in abundance. There is a unique drama to hunting high up on the rooftop of the world. The country itself — shimmering snow topped spires scalloped with lovely little alpine pastures and parks which are in turn laced with clear purling streams of coldest melt water — evokes a special feeling in even the most phlegmatic and stolid of hunters.

Mountain country often demands the best from a hunter. It takes extra stamina to hunt hard all day in the cold thin air, and the extra strain of constantly climbing to gain altitude in order to spot and locate game can place severe demands on the out-of-condition hunter used to the softer, easier lowlands.

Weather "makes up" rapidly and dramatically in the mountains. Everything up there is less predictable, more beautiful and more exciting. But the true ornament of these lovely North American highlands is the large game animals that inhabit them, and no species are more classically appropriate than the sheep and the goat. These robust animals, so different from each other in some ways and so similar in others, are magnificently adapted to the harsh and demanding lives that

A magnificent trophy. This big old "roman nosed" ram shows the ferocity of his recent fighting for ewes.

# NORTH AMERICAN MOUNTAIN SHEEP RANGES

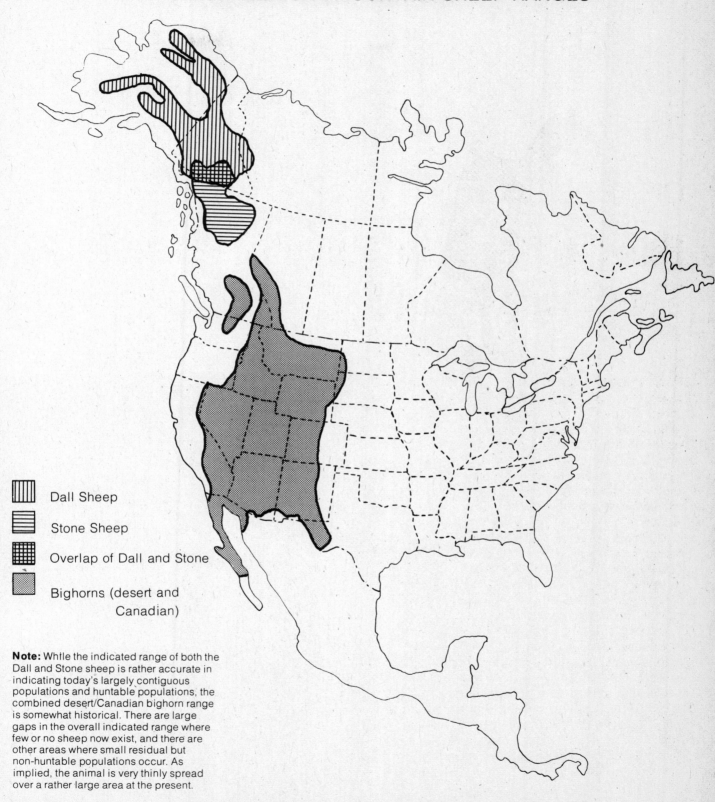

▥ Dall Sheep

▤ Stone Sheep

▦ Overlap of Dall and Stone

▨ Bighorns (desert and
      Canadian)

**Note:** While the indicated range of both the
Dall and Stone sheep is rather accurate in
indicating today's largely contiguous
populations and huntable populations, the
combined desert/Canadian bighorn range
is somewhat historical. There are large
gaps in the overall indicated range where
few or no sheep now exist, and there are
other areas where small residual but
non-huntable populations occur. As
implied, the animal is very thinly spread
over a rather large area at the present.

# MOUNTAIN GOAT RANGE

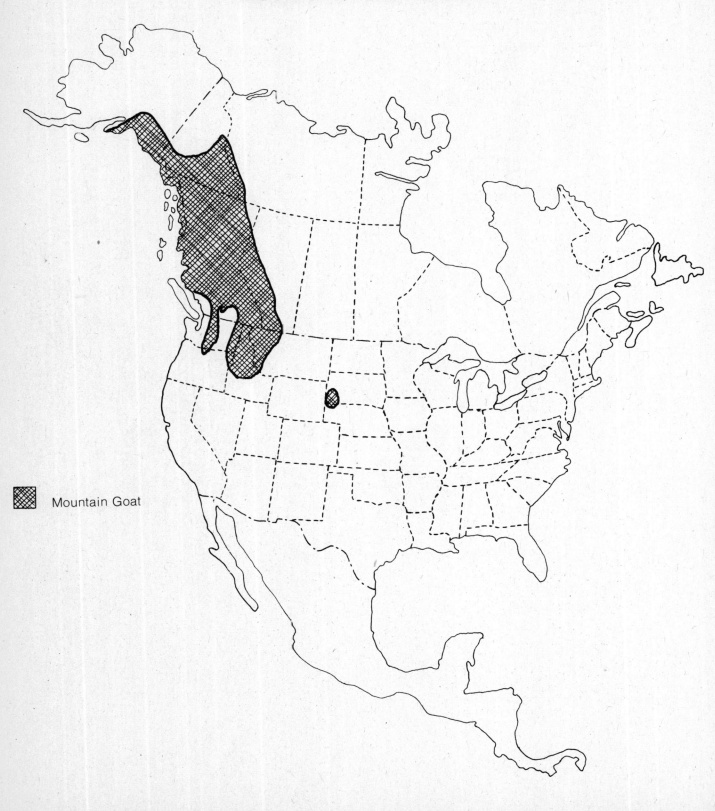

Mountain Goat

they must lead.

## General Mountain Hunting Conditions

Hunting both types of animals is somewhat different than most other North American big game stalking and shooting. The normally critical dawn and dusk hours are much less dominant when after sheep and goats. These species must usually be spotted at a very long range, before they have seen the hunter, and then stalked carefully, often over a period of several hours, in order for the hunter to maneuver himself in for a reasonable shot.

The animals feed up until mid- to late morning and then lie down for a couple of hours to chew their cuds and rest. Then they arise, feed some more, and in mid-

(Above) The sight every sheep hunter wants to see. Two large unsuspecting rams searching for danger from below while the hunter has slipped down on them from above.

(Right) A classic sheep basin being glassed by outfitter Johnny Holmes as he searches for Stone sheep in the Cassiars. There is abundant food and water for the sheep on the easy slopes to the left while safety lies in the steep cliffs to the right.

Today most mountain hunts for sheep and goat begin with a bush plane flight into base camp and then a packstring ride up into the higher altitudes.

to later afternoon they lie again for more cud chewing and rest. The quarries are usually spotted during these feeding periods when they are standing and moving around.

It is best to wait until they are bedded down and contentedly chewing away before investing several hours in the final stalk. Otherwise the feeding animals may move off during a lengthy stalk, much of which often has to be in the blind. You may lose the animals entirely or, due to their shifting positions, you may frighten them off by exposing yourself inadvertently.

Good, *properly fitting* boots are basic to all successful mountain hunts. Climbing and walking across the slopes ("side-hilling") is very punishing on city feet. Ankle and calf muscles that are seldom used under level, lowland conditions are stressed severely. Tender soles are easily bruised by the constant pounding of walking and climbing on hard rock or scree slopes. It's best to secure heavily reinforced boots made for mountain work and get them large enough to wear a set of the felt or leather-and-pile sole liners. These provide more cushioning for the soles and, in the case of the latter, more arch support. The boots should also be large enough to wear two pair of thick, heavy-duty hunting socks. These socks help cushion the entire foot and lower leg from wrenches and shocks, and the thickness

of the second pair helps to wick the inevitable (and dangerous) accumulated perspiration away from the feet.

These boots should have some sort of scree ring at the top to protect the feet from the smaller pebbles and pieces of talus that seem to exhibit a miraculous faculty for being able to work down into the boots where they become very painful to the feet and lower legs.

Sunglasses and chapstick are musts for high country work. So is some sort of suntan oil if one has a tendency to sunburn easily. The thin atmosphere of the heights is extremely deceptive. It is usually colder the higher one goes, and even a medium bright sun, without the protective screening of several thousand feet of lower, denser atmosphere, can quickly burn the skin and dry and crack the lips. This happens before you are even aware of it, and due to the cooler temperatures, it always comes as a bit of a surprise when it happens. My lips have become so cracked and chapped on more than one mountain hunt that it was painful to even drink water. I have used tallow from a fresh kill to coat them when I foolishly got caught without any sort of commercial lip balm. It's a bit messy, but it actually works out quite well and the relief is a blessing.

Dressing in layers, rather than bundling up in a few bulky garments, is vital to proper mountain comfort.

When climbing it is very easy to become overheated, and this results in too much perspiration (always dangerous) and, in turn, causes dehydration and thirst. Then when you stop to rest, the pendulum swings precipitously the other way, and it is quite easy to go from a huffing-puffing state of overheating to a shivering (partially caused by all that accumulated sweat), teeth chattering state of cold in a few moments. Being able to don and doff several layers of clothes at will gives one far more flexibility in combating these radical temperature swings, and the extra air trapped between the layers of clothing means more warmth with less bulk and weight to carry around.

Good optics, both binoculars and spotting scopes,

Though the first shot was a little far back, this proud youngster brought down his nice Dall ram with a second well placed shot. Sheep do not exhibit near the vitality that similar sized mountain goat do.

A quality high-power spotting scope, such as this Swift Telemaster 15x to 60x zoom, is an absolute necessity for serious goat and sheep hunting.

are critically important to the success of any mountain hunt. Time was when the 7x35 binocs were the most popular among knowledgeable hunters. This was in the era when quality binoculars automatically meant the classic Porro prism type of construction. The 8x, 9x models, not to mention the 10-power models, were generally too heavy and bulky to carry and rather difficult to hold steady for extended periods of glassing. The advent of the fine roof prism glasses in the early to mid-60's changed all of that, and now 8x and 10x glasses are probably the most popular types. I myself prefer the 10x type though I have and frequently use a pair of the magnificent 8x Leitz Trinovids. A spotting scope of approximately 20x can save the hunter many fruitless steps by helping him to accurately assess at long ranges

not only the desirability of a particular trophy (which means conformation as well as gross size) but also the feasibility of stalking it successfully in the difficult mountain terrain. For more on optics see Chapter 12.

## Hunting North American Sheep

Many widely held ideas about sheep hunting are false. Though sheep are among the best climbers in the world, they are most frequently not found at the very tops of mountains or on steep rocky slopes.

Sheep feed on the tender grasses found on the gently rolling slopes most often located on the intermediate and even lower shoulders of the mountain. These often easy-to-negotiate pastures are a far cry from the dizzying mountaintop cliffs often associated with "mountain sheep" in the minds of beginning sheep hunters.

It has often been said that sheep have vision equal to that of a man with 8-power binoculars, and I have found this to be, if anything, an understatement. Their visual resolving power is nothing short of astonishing. Their hearing isn't bad, but since there are often discordant noises in the mountains due to rock slides and the like, sheep frequently don't react to sounds quickly unless these are noises they associate with man, such as a regular or rhythmical tramping related to walking or climbing.

Unlike goats, sheep can often be found down at the edge of the timberline or even lying up in timber to find shelter from the wind or sun. They always like to have a steep, cliffy area nearby that they can repair to if hard pressed by wolves or other four legged predators, but

(Above) Classic sheep hunting scene. Hunter and his guide belly down on top of a ridge that they have climbed in order to slip in above the sheep.

(Right) Art Kolp, a hunting consultant of M & N Safaris in Torrance, California, proudly shows a nice Stone sheep that he recently bagged in northern British Columbia.

these little escape routes can be surprisingly small. Sheep will sometimes dash up and down or even around and around within a postage stamp sized ''rough'' until they wear the predator out, or to just demonstrate to him how fruitless it all is.

This may change a bit now that coyotes have worked their way as far north as Mount McKinley. The little wolves are extremely intelligent and co-operate with each other when hunting. I have seen them hold a cow elk in hock deep water for several days until she weakened, and then when she finally tried to break through, they brought her down rather easily. This example of how they work together to bring down prey far larger and more powerful than they could normally tackle alone, leads me to believe that they can and will learn to do the same with sheep, penning them in some of these small cliffy areas until they are literally starved out and can be run down rather easily.

The conventional wisdom has it that the best way to hunt sheep is to spot them at long range before they see you and then plan a stalk that brings you up over the mountain above and behind them or at least from another shoulder on their side of the mountain. According to the classic sheep hunting dictum, sheep aren't supposed to look up very often never having had to be much concerned with danger from above. While this is not necessarily a bad way to hunt sheep, it is less true now than it was 20 years ago. Sheep are much more hard pressed and wary nowadays, and most populations have learned to look in all directions and to be as concerned about the rear door as the front. It is still vitally important to spot the animals before they see you and to execute some sort of stalk, whether from below, above or beside, so that they are not alerted in the process.

## Guns for Sheep

Though sheep are powerfully built, medium sized animals, they are not particularly difficult to bring down. What is needed is a flat shooting rifle that is accurate and one that the hunter thoroughly knows and has confidence in, rather than a rifle/cartridge combination yielding a lot of raw power. In the past, sheep shots were either very close (less than a hundred yards) or very long (350 yards and father), depending upon whether the hunter was able to come up over the comb of the ridge and drop down on the unsuspecting quarry or whether the hunter had to work up toward the sheep and take a long-range shot, often at a moving target. Alas, today the long shot predominates far more than it did 20 years ago due to the spookier, more man-wise populations of sheep now encountered.

The .243 Winchester, 6mm Remington, .257 Weatherby, .25/06 and .257 Roberts all make fine sheep guns if bigger game, such as grizzly and moose, is not on the agenda. These cartridges can all be fashioned into lightweight rifles that are a joy to carry and that shoot accurately and flatly with very little recoil. The .270 Winchester is the classic sheep cartridge (along with all its near twins like the .284 Winchester, the .280 Remington and the equally classic and wonderfully balanced old .30/06). This class of cartridge does recoil a bit more; something to bear in mind when youngsters, some ladies or particularly recoil sensitive men are doing the shooting.

Certainly the big magnums such as the 7mm Remington and the .300 Winchester, to name but a couple, make fine sheep guns in the hands of those who can carry and climb with the necessarily heavier guns and then shoot them without flinching and jerking the trigger in spite of the significantly sharper muzzle blast and heavier recoil. These guns perform well not so much for the extra power they bring to bear, but because they offer flat trajectories that equal or exceed most of the lighter guns just mentioned, and they feature heavier bullets which are less wind sensitive. The mountains are filled with rising thermals, unpredictable eddies and localized wind currents here and there. Often these localized little booby traps are not even noticeable to the hunter 300 to 350 yards away but, downrange toward the animal, they can significantly float a bullet to one side or the other causing a miss or, worse yet, a bad hit which allows the animal to get away or to tumble down onto some inaccessible ledge or outcropping where he can't be recovered.

Fine optics are a must in order to utilize the flat shooting capabilities of these cartridges and most hunters today, including myself, opt for the 2x7 and 3x9 vari-power riflescopes feeling that a tad of extra scope weight and bulk are well worth the extra flexibility and long-legged view afforded by them. These modern vari-powers are now extremely rugged and offer optical quality as acute as the fixed power models.

### The Quarry

Though the mountain sheep is primarily an Asiatic animal, with the largest diversity of subspecies and races occurring there and with the animal achieving his maximum body and horn size there, North America is extremely fortunate in having some of the finest mem-

A band of Rocky Mountain bighorn rams. By today's realities all of these are fine trophies.

Here the author holds a magnificent set of massive, well-broomed bighorn horns which — sadly — he didn't take. These horns are so heavy they're difficult to lift for any period. It's remarkable that an animal hardly larger than a big man grows them and can carry them around on his head the year-around.

bers of this noble family of game animals. There are, depending upon whose classification(s) one accepts, perhaps 10 to 12 species of wild sheep in the world, and these further break down to perhaps 45 or so subspecies and races. It must be admitted though that some of these latter are pretty theoretical or describe variants that are practically extinct or of little or no interest to the hunter.

American sheep fall into two specie types: the bighorns *(Ovis canadensis)* and the thinhorns *(Ovis dalli)*. While these two separate species can be broken down into as many as a dozen separate races by the vigorous "splitters" among the taxonomists, the Boone & Crockett Club's system of further breaking the bighorns down into the bighorns and the desert bighorns and the thinhorns into the Dall (white) and the Stone (black) sheep is eminently practical and realistic for big game hunting purposes. Broadly speak-

ing on a worldwide basis all sheep can roughly be broken down into the running types and the climbing types. The huge sheep of Asia, heavier bodied and longer legged, are of the former type though they often live quite high (Elgin Gates tells of hunting the fabulous Marco Polo sheep at altitudes approaching 20,000 feet!). This is due to the fact that Asia is primarily a huge, very high plateau. These sheep feed on rounded rolling shoulders which are often well above 10,000 feet in altitude but look more like a high plain than anything else. They can climb quite well and, if pressed hard enough, will repair to the cliffs, but they prefer to run it out with many adversaries, reacting almost more like a pronghorn than an American sheep.

The American sheep are of the climbing type, shorter coupled and legged, chunkier bodies and preferring the precipices and cliffs to the rolling meadows when pressed.

## THE BIGHORNS

These sheep are both heavier bodied and heavier horned than the thinhorn or Dall type. Their horns are darker colored, more rounded in cross section and more likely to be broomed (worn) off at the tips. The horns tend to be curled in more closely to the head rather than flared out at the tips and these sheep live further to the south indicating that their distant ancestors came across the land bridge from Asia to Alaska several millenia earlier than the Dalls did.

**The Northern Bighorns:** These animals are heavier bodied and darker colored than their southern cousins, the desert bighorns. The heaviest of the North American sheep fall into this type with a very old and large Canadian bighorn ram weighing as much as 300-325 pounds and standing between 38 and 42 inches high at the shoulder. The horns on a really big old ram can weigh as much as 40 pounds, and they make a majestic trophy and an awesome weapon for fighting during the annual rut. Though once quite widespread throughout the continent and numbering perhaps 2 million or more at the coming of the white man, they have been reduced to a mere remnant species, numbering perhaps 15,000 to 20,000 animals on a continent-wide basis. The plight of all the American sheep is a sad one. For all their

Desert bighorn sheep are a thinly distributed, smaller race of the basic Rocky Mountain bighorns. This big ram, though carrying magnificent horns, probably weighs only about 165 pounds of which a full 20 percent to 22 percent is in horn weight.

An alerted bighorn ram, whose massive horns indicate that he's probably over 10 years old, scampers toward safety after being alerted to danger on his high vantage point. This calls for quick shooting!

This happy hunter is carefully tying down his prized sheep head for the long trek out of the mountains.

magnificence and glamor as a game animal, they are both highly susceptible to diseases carried by domestic sheep, and they are much less adaptable than the whitetail deer or even the elk or moose.

The best places to hunt for these animals are British Columbia, Alberta and Montana. Much of the hunting is by limited special permit, and the expensive permit must be applied for a year in advance and often for many years before one may be lucky enough to draw one. The best hunting on the continent for these animals, if you are lucky enough to secure one of the coveted 40 or so permits awarded each year for the area, is in the Sun River country of Montana. Any decent hunter who will work for his game is almost assured a crack at a good trophy from this herd of 800 to 1,000 sheep. Latching onto one of those elusive permits is the problem.

**The Desert Bighorns:** This is a smaller bodied (perhaps 160-170 pounds on a big ram), more specialized version of the basic bighorn. These animals, due to the low densities afforded by their sterile environments, were probably never anywhere near as common as were the more northerly bighorns once were.

The desert sheep's horns, interestingly enough, are often as massive and heavily based as the much larger

northern bighorns. This leads the old rams to have a singular appearance in which their rather thin faces and necks and spare, lean bodies simply appear too small to support the massive horns they may carry. Depending upon how one classifies some populations, there are probably somewhat less than 10,000 of these animals on the continent with the best populations located in California (no hunting due to a legislative fiat since 1854 but the population still declining due to competition with the feral burro and habitat loss), Arizona and Baja California.

Arizona offers some 70 or so permits per year on its rigidly controlled and well managed sheep hunting program with out-of-staters being limited to 10 percent of these. There is some extremely limited desert sheep hunting available in Nevada and New Mexico as this is written, but that is subject to closure at any time. In times gone by there was relatively good sheep hunting in Sonora (now largely closed) and Baja California. Though the former is supposed to be closed and the latter area limited to some 10 or so sheep per year, it's one of the world's worst kept secrets that an adequate amount of the coin of the realm brought into conjunction with the right palms in Mexican officialdom has often resulted in the granting of "extraordinary" permits. Some of the most shameful incidents in American hunting have occurred due to rich American sportsmen wanting to "get their tickets punched" so that they can qualify for a "grand slam" on the four North American sheep. This unfortunate slam concept, a cachet innocently originated by an outdoor writer and hunter in the late 40's when times were considerably different, has become — along with illicit brown and grizzly bear hunting from airplanes — one of the two most malodorous chapters in the American hunting tradition.

## THE THINHORNS

These sheep are more lightly built than the Canadian bighorns, and they feature lighter (often yellowish) horns that are more triangular in cross section, not as massive in circumference and weight, and often longer due to not being broken off at the tips as frequently. Due to their more isolated, northerly ranges these

(Right) Stone or "black sheep" are limited primarily to northern British Columbia, and with a total world-wide herd of less than 10,000, they are one of the world's most sought after trophies.

(Below) This beautiful Dall sheep ram, photographed in the central Alaska range, carries an unbroken right horn that is well over full curl.

Even an averaged sized Dall sheep head, such as this 33-inch ram taken in Alaska, makes an elegant addition to any trophy collection.

sheep have generally not suffered as much as the bighorns from the encroachments of civilization.

**The Dall:** This beautiful white sheep (often more off-white or cream-white in the older rams) is a magnificent addition to anyone's trophy room. A big ram stands 38 inches at the shoulder and will weigh up to 180-200 pounds.

Dalls are generally in good supply as sheep go with continental populations probably reaching 60,000 to 75,000 animals and good concentrations of them being found in Alaska, the western Northwest Territories and the Yukon. I would recommend the latter area as the best all-around spot for them at this time, but the other two grounds also offer hunting ranging from good to exceptional. The hunting pressure on Dalls has increased enormously in the past 15 years and though, with limited exceptions, this still has not resulted in a significantly decreased hunter success ratio, it has caused a substantial decrease in the average trophy size.

The average sheep being taken in Alaska now runs 32-33 inches in horn length, though nice ones up to and even beyond 40 inches are still taken occasionally. However, the 36-38-inch rams are much fewer and farther between than they were as late as the early 60's. Any relatively heavy Dall sheep with a 36-inch curl is a nice trophy nowadays, and the sportsman after his first sheep would do well to consider a smaller head, especially late in his hunt. The Dall's whitish pelt is so distinctive that it's a good idea to save the rear portion, after caping out the head and neck for a trophy mount, and have it tanned as an elegant little throw rug or wall hanging.

**The Stone:** In its own way this black sheep, with his contrasting white or buff rump and underparts, is as striking and beautiful as his whiter cousin to the north.

Stones are almost entirely limited to the northern third of British Columbia though a few do lap over into the southern Yukon. Within the past hundred years around the Yukon/British Columbia border the Stone and Dalls have apparently interbred. These salt-and-pepper sheep were at one time called a variety of names including Fannins and were thought to possibly be a distinctly different race of sheep rather than merely intergrades of the two basic subspecies of *Ovis dalli*.

*Ovis dalli stonei* is marginally larger than *Ovis dalli dalli* with a big ram reaching weights of perhaps 200-225 pounds and standing perhaps an inch taller (39 inches) at the shoulder than a comparable white sheep ram. The horns tend to be a bit larger at the bases and weigh a bit more, though in length the two sets of horns run about the same. The greatest American sheep ever killed, the fabled Chadwick ram shot in northeastern British Columbia in the late 30's was a Stone, and to this day it is the only American sheep with horns exceeding 50 inches (on both sides, to boot).

Stone sheep have been pressed harder than Dalls over the years, and since they are far more localized with smaller populations, it may well be that British Columbia will introduce some form of limited permit-only hunting in the near future. There are probably around 6,000-8,000 Stone sheep in British Columbia. Historically the Cassiar Mountains and, farther east, the Muskwa-Prophet River areas have been choice grounds for these sheep.

Good taxidermy preserves a great trophy forever if it is properly cared for, such as this 40-plus-inch Stone sheep from northern British Columbia.

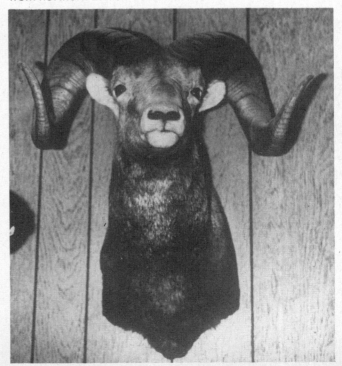

## Mountain Goat Hunting

Goat hunting is probably the most arduous general big game hunting on the continent as well as being among the most exciting (and dangerous) brand of the sport. Goats live higher than sheep and in much steeper and rougher terrain. In fact, goats live where many novices tend to look for sheep or, in other cases, they live in areas where novices would believe that no large game animal could survive. While sheep may be driven down quite low in the howling gales of mid-winter, nothing short of an earthquake will drive the goat down from his beloved heights. As long as there are steep, windy slopes to keep the snow from drifting too high over the rougher grasses and herbage that the goat prefers, he will stay up in the crags and patiently paw the snow away to expose his dinner.

Goats are entirely different in temperament and climbing method than the higher strung, faster running

Guide Gene Holmes pauses while fleshing out the head of a trophy goat for his hunter. This is exacting work.

Here the author shows a medium-sized goat he took in the Cassiar Mountains of northern British Columbia. This was a classic goat hunting situation with the animal being shot as it was about to disappear over the crest of the mountain (the notch directly behind him). It then tumbled several hundred feet down the brutally steep (and dangerous, due to loose rock) rock chute that he is sitting gingerly on with his snow white prize.

and climbing sheep. Over the years so much glamor has been attached to sheep hunting (and rightly so) that it has indirectly served to make some underrate the sport and drama inherent in goat stalking. Goats are phlegmatic, deliberate types who can absorb punishment all out of proportion to their size. A flat shooting rifle is a good idea just as it is in sheep hunting, but more power is often called for. I would not classify the milder .24 and .25 calibers as good goat guns, though in the hands of good stalkers and deliberate shots they can certainly take goats.

The .270/.30/06 class of cartridge makes a nice goat gun and the 7mm Remington Magnum/.300 Winchester Magnum is even better if the shooter can handle the

Guide Gene Holmes makes the basic
back-of-the-neck cut on a nice goat
as he begins the final fleshing out of
the head for a trophy mount.

additional punishment with no ill effects on accuracy. A big billy can absorb an enormous amount of punishment and carry on with vigor. This is partly because of their stolid temperament and partly because of their physical makeup. The goat carries one of the warmest coats in the wild, and a well furred, winter coated billy will offer an armor plated side protected by guard hairs reaching to 9 inches in length and finer, inner hair that is very thick and resilient. The goat is also relatively heavily boned for an animal his size.

The idea of climbing up the mountain behind a goat and dropping down on him from above has never particularly appealed to me. It is true that the goat seldom looks up. One glance at the short, downward look of his neck/shoulder conformation shows the most unpracticed of eyes that *this* fellow truly seldom needs to look above himself for danger. The problem is that goats live in such damnably steep country that walking all the way around a mountain to approach him from the other side may turn out to be fruitless, as the far face may be well nigh unclimbable by the average hunter! Even if climbed, the hunter can well approach to within 100 yards or even 50 yards above the animal and find that, due to the steepness of the terrain and the jutting outcroppings, he simply can't see the animal anymore nor maneuver into position to get off a shot. That can be

very frustrating to say the least!

Also, since trophy billies have a much noted and remarked about habit of flinging themselves off into the ether when mortally hit, it's a very good idea if at all possible to see if and where your goat will fall when you hit him. He may fall into an area where you can't recover him or he may do a swan dive straight down for 500 to 1,000 feet thus often breaking off his horns and doing grievous damage to that luxurious white trophy pelt. Even if you are immediately above him and can see the animal well enough for a good shot, seldom can you see well enough to tell what is below him and how he may fall.

Since goats are slower, more deliberate animals than sheep — less likely to spook and often slower about decamping after deciding to do so — I prefer to climb up to their level while hidden by a same-side-of-mountain shoulder and then side-hill around the mountain until I can get a shot. This allows you to chart your stalk on *this* side of the mountain without going all the way around it to see if you can readily negotiate the other side. It also serves to better insure that you will be able to spot and shoot the animal (from his own level), and also to see if he will fall far and where he will land when he does so.

Goats make a fine trophy, and I am just as impressed

Many sportsmen are missing a bet by not having their mountain goats mounted as a rug-with-full-headmount. This mount (similar to the classic bear skin rug) is unusual and dramatic.

than the largest Canadian bighorn rams, and they are built differently. A big billy runs a bit taller than a comparable ram, up to 40 inches and even 42 inches at the shoulder, and he is far more slab sided and deeper bodied. The ram is round like a stuffed sausage while the billy is deeper chested and flatter sided. Although the sheep is a faster, more dynamic aerialist, the goat's slab sided build, unique hooves and deliberate temperament enable him to level himself across or up sheer cliffs that would defeat a sheep.

Yes, sheep and goats do occasionally fall to their deaths. Nothing without wings can constantly live and climb in the country that they do without a periodic accident occurring. Goats have horns like sheep, meaning that they never shed their headgear. Their horns continue to grow larger as long as the animal lives (antlered game like the deer shed their racks every year and the very old males will raise smaller antlers than the bulls and bucks in their prime). A billy upwards of 9 inches is a decent goat; between 9 inches and 10 inches in horn length means a nice trophy; and over 10 inches

Guide Charlie Smith attends to the delicate task of properly skinning out this nice northern British Columbia goat.

when I see a big old mountain billy on a fellow's wall as I am when I see a fine ram. It is true that the goat's horns don't come anywhere close to matching the sheep's for sheer massive magnificence, and that — by and large — "if you see one goat, you've seen 'em all" because they are rather similar to each other in appearance except for the very largest and smallest or the occasional freak. But the knowledgeable hunter knows that there is far more to defining the value of a trophy than mere size and conformation. Though most goats may be relatively identical, goat *hunting* probably varies more from head to head, than any other. The fellow who shoots a big billy, one with horns of 10 inches or better, almost always earns his trophy twice over!

### Defining the Goat

Technically the North American mountain goat is not a "true" goat in the sense that it does not belong to the long-horned group of goats such as the ibex and markhor of Asia, and some have gone so far as to call it a "goat-antelope." For practical hunting purposes it looks like a goat, acts like a goat and lives like a goat, so that's what we'll consider it. A big old billy will always have a substantial amount of yellow or cream in his pelt (part of the aging process just as human hair tends to go gray) and can weigh over 300 pounds.

Though I have heard stories of mythical 500-pound goats, I've never been able to substantiate one anywhere close to that personally. However, it is obvious that the very largest goats probably weigh a bit more

Guide skins out trophy mountain goat in camp while being flanked
by caribou and moose racks that indicate a successful mixed game hunt.

means a potential record book head. Nannies also have horns, and they are as long or longer than a comparably-aged billy. However, they are much smaller at the bases and much thinner throughout their length.

Back when goat trophies were mistakenly evaluated solely on horn length, the world's record for some years was an old nanny. When horn circumference (thus mass) also was included, she dropped far down the list and the billies took over. It is rather difficult to tell nannies from billies at a distance. Some time and a practiced eye is necessary. The billy is more heavily built, more often solitary (a large and a smaller animal standing together most often means a nanny with a kid) and his horns are shaped differently. The nanny's horns are not only slimmer, they tend to jut more straight back and then hook down sharply within a inch or two of the end. The billy's horns arc back in a more even, gradual curve or parabola without the sharp hook near the end.

The best goat grounds are found adjacent to each other in southeastern (panhandle) Alaska and across to the east of the same coastal mountain range in northwestern British Columbia. Though goats are found throughout much of the giant province of British Columbia, they have been heavily hunted and much reduced in numbers throughout many of the southern and central portions of this area. There is little or no goat hunting in the Yukon or Northwest Territories, and Alberta has few remaining goats. There are fair populations of the animal in Montana, Idaho and Washington as well as a few scattered elsewhere in Oregon, South Dakota and Wyoming. However, the goat must be regarded as primarily a Canadian (and Alaskan) species.

104

# CHAPTER 8

# How To Get Your Black Bear

**MY FIRST SIGHT** of a wild North American black bear still ranks as one of my more pronounced big game hunting disappointments. Grazing along on the steep Alberta hillside, he looked like nothing so much as an oversized Labrador Retriever rather than a *bear*. An unlucky coin toss meant that my brother John put him away after a long climb and two shots with his .270. He weighed an honest 250 pounds and he later squared out just a hair shy of 6 feet — both being extremely respectable measurements for a truly wild, non-garbage fattened black bear. (The "square" of a bear hide is determined by the measurement across the front paws from one tip to the other added to the body length measurement from nose to tail and that total being divided by two.)

The next time Blackie and I got together was in Alaska. Even though I had a better idea what to expect by then and I also realized that all black or dark animals appear smaller at a distance than they actually are (just as white or buffy toned animals appear larger), I still wasn't too impressed with this average 200-pounder.

My first sight of a wild grizzly was something else again. The prime 500-pounder looked to be everything

A typical black bear is not a large animal. The boars average about 200 pounds unless they have been doing some panhandling at the local garbage dump.

# BLACK BEAR RANGE

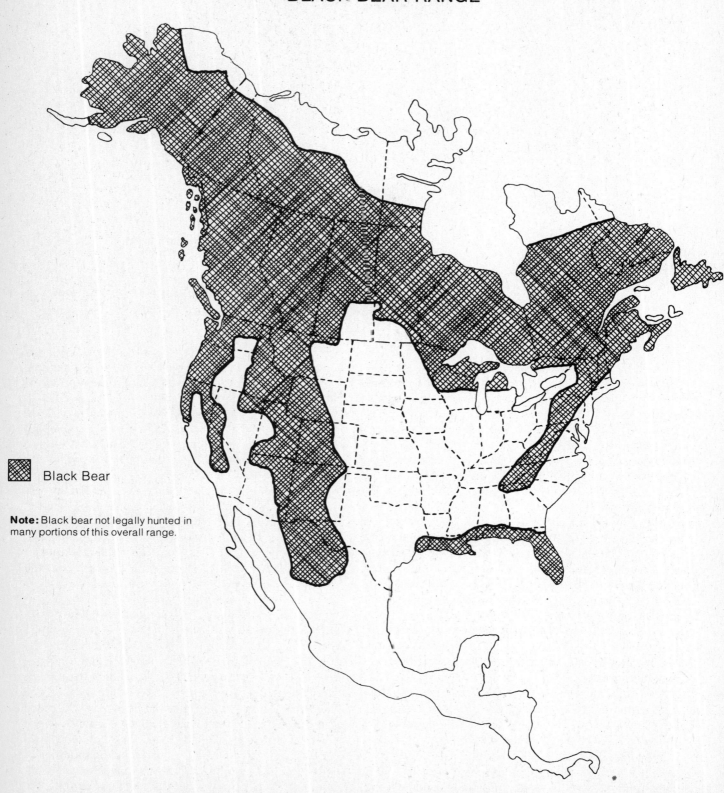

Black Bear

**Note:** Black bear not legally hunted in many portions of this overall range.

Hunter points to hole in shoulder where he shot black bear.

a *bear* should be as he peacefully carded blueberries through his ham-sized paws while perched halfway up the broad shoulder of a British Columbian mountain. He was a long way away, and there was no proper way to stalk him so I sat and watched him through the 30x scope. After he finished with his blueberry dessert, he apparently decided a little protein was in order. He ambled-shambled across the sidehill a couple of hundred yards and idly started digging for whistling marmots, or perhaps I should say he began *excavating* for the small, groundhog-sized rodents. The casual ease with which he tore away offending roots or dislodged bothersome boulders left no doubt as to his enormous strength. *This* was what a bear was supposed to be!

These incidents all occurred some years back, and since then my appreciation of wildlife has rounded and matured a bit. I still regard the grizzly as one of the most magnificent creatures on earth, but I now rate *americanus,* his smaller black cousin, much higher than I did then.

Fortunately, more and more other sportsmen are coming to recognize this and more fully appreciate the black bear which was in the past often either regarded with contempt ("vermin") especially by many Canadian hunters or fear ("ferocious") by the unversed. Both attitudes were equally misplaced.

Why shouldn't the black bear be rated highly? He's widely available and was, originally, the only large game animal found in all 48 contiguous states. As recently as 1944 he was still found in some 33 states, and today something over 200,000 black bear are alive and prospering in approximately 24 states. About a quarter of a million additional black bear reside in Canada. One can see that this is one animal in no imminent fear of extinction!

The black bear makes a fine trophy for several reasons. A well furred bearskin rug is impressive and comes in a variety of colors ranging from honey blonde and cinnamon brown (most commonly found in the Rocky Mountain West and some parts of western Canada; very rare in the eastern U.S. and relatively rare on the West Coast) through blue-gray (the "glacier bear" of southeastern Alaska) to the striking all white kermode bear found off the coast of British Columbia. Incidentally, this latter bear is truly a white bear and not an albino. It is a very localized white color phase of the basic black bear. True albinos do occur but only extremely rarely among this species.

Though generally over exaggerated by half in stories and conversations, the black bear does attain enough stature to make an impressive and attractive trophy. Actually, in a manner of speaking, there are two basic types of bear and one must generalize about them separately whenever discussing the size of the animal. The *wild* black bear is a furtive, nocturnal forest denizen who is among the most omnivorous of animals in the world. Though preferring meat, the average wild blackie (excluding some exceptions like the salmon eating coastal blacks of the Alaskan panhandle) probably averages about 5 percent animal matter in its diet, but even this paltry portion is largely comprised of insects! Winter kills and other scavenge provide practically all

(Left) Black bear are very wary and shy creatures in the wild, and it would be quite unusual to get this good of a shot at one before alarming him.

(Below) Skinning out a fat black bear is a time consuming chore that will dull the best knives repeatedly.

the additional meat that he will get under normal circumstances, as he is too slow to catch most healthy game animals except for the very young or the very old.

This bear will average around 175-225 pounds for an adult boar in good condition. Bears do naturally vary a great deal in weight, depending upon the time of the year. For example, a 200-pounder might gain 50 pounds immediately prior to denning up in the late fall. Instances of truly *wild* blacks weighing 400, 500 or even upwards of 600 pounds do occur. (Just about as frequently, I suspect, as instances of people weighing that much.) Sows will weigh about one-half to two-thirds as much as boars and, by and large, there are probably about as many 200-plus-pound male or female bears running around living off the wilds as there are 200-plus-pound men and women.

The "other" black bear is the feral animal that has found a free meal ticket and is living off handouts in parks or zoos or is scavenging regularly from the garbage dumps of small wilderness villages or hamlets or one that is picking up refuse from canneries or fishing camps. These animals are the ones that are generally so outsized and are reported in the press as "wild" bears when occasionally killed or trapped.

In 1957 New York state trapped 125 bears as part of a study project. Six males weighed over 400 pounds and the two largest of these beasts weighed 562 and 599 pounds, respectively. The heaviest female weighed 391 pounds. All of these outsized bruins were trapped at garbage dumps. These feral, civilization-haunting, man-wise bears are the most dangerous animals in North America. They have become accustomed to humans and human activity and, especially in the case of the "cute" panhandling park bears, they have lost all

fear of man. It's not so much that they are ferocious towards man, but more like they're just contemptuous.

Any wild animal is extremely powerful compared to man. Black bear are no exception, and when you skin one out, the ropy, sinewy muscles on the compact bowlegged frame amply attest to that. If you have ever seen a black bear, even a heavy adult, scoot up a vertical tree like a common gray squirrel with his pants on fire, you can tell immediately how powerful they are. Tree climbing is a vigorous sport! I have, through a long chain of weird circumstances, found myself in the un-

Packing in for a deep wilderness hunt usually means a bonus chance for black bear, whatever game the main attraction may be.

usual position of trying to wrestle to earth and subdue a "tame" black bear cub weighing less than 50 pounds. It was a chastening experience. Though I outweighed him three and half times, there was no doubt who was the stronger.

All bear skulls should be saved since they make interesting secondary trophies — a bonus from this type of hunting. Whenever making a rug mount or head mount from a bear trophy, most all taxidermists nowadays use the lightweight, last-forever head forms of synthetic material. These forms feature very realistic plastic teeth that, unlike the real thing, do not crack or split over the years.

The real skull should be boiled thoroughly for several hours in sal soda which can be purchased very inexpensively at most large supermarkets. A buck's worth will do all the bears you'll shoot in a lifetime. The skull can then be left outside to dry and sprinkled with borax (Boraxo will do fine) to kill any pesky varmints or mites remaining inside. After drying for several days the skull can then be bleached with peroxide if so desired to make it even whiter. All teeth should be wiggled and jiggled in order to pull out any loose ones. These are then glued back into their sockets so that they don't fall out later and get lost. Add a touch of glue as a safety measure around the base of all the teeth that you aren't able to pull out.

For an added touch you can neatly letter across the top of the skull the pertinent information about when and where the trophy was taken, the gun used, the range, names of your guide or hunting companions or whatever other data you want to include. Any of the finer pointed, felt-tipped marking pens work well in enabling you to do this neatly and permanently. But first you have to go shoot your bear, so let's find out where to go and how to hunt them.

Black bear hunting breaks down into several basic methods, often at wildly varying costs, when considered on a continent-wide basis. I'm leaving out all controlled situations such as "hunting preserves" featuring big game shooting and talking only about truly wild bear killed in ethical, fair, chase hunting situations.

### Eastern and Southern U. S. Black Bear Hunting

Most of the bear taken in this giant one-third-of-the-country patch of territory are taken by accident and incidental to whitetail deer hunting. In this area the best bear hunting is concentrated in the Smoky Mountains. Western North Carolina boasts a good population ranging from 6,000 to 10,000 bears, depending upon whose estimates you accept as most factual. A goodly number of these bruins are protected in the parks.

Professional guide services for outsiders are limited in this area, though. Tennessee, mostly in the nearby Tellico Plains area, offers limited hunting for about 300 to 500 free ranging bears (many of them trading back and forth between the two states) plus several "shooting preserves" that offer controlled black bear hunting as well as "wild boar" (often feral hogs).

West Virginia and Virginia offer about 2,000 bears between them which means the hunting, if considered basically as a bonus-to-deer-hunting or a secondary hunting situation, is decent. Though there are scattered bear populations in several other southern and mid-Atlantic states, none of them offers any viable bear hunting.

The northeastern region offers a bit more variety in its bear hunting. Pennsylvania supports a surprisingly large population of between 2,000 and 3,000 animals, but they are hotly pursued by the state's legions of big game hunters. The season is short, often only one day, so this is not a good opportunity for nonresidents, even though they can purchase a bear license.

Michigan and Minnesota both feature good bear hunting with some 10,000 and 6,000 animals, respectively, within their borders. Both have limited professional guiding services available for the out-of-state stranger. Maine offers about the same number of animals as either of the two preceding states (around 8,000), but the professional guiding services and facilities catering to out-of-staters are considerably

more developed here in this thinly populated state. This is the best area in the east for the nonresident visitor who is unfamiliar with the area.

### Eastern Canadian Black Bear Hunting

Some years ago the Canadians discovered that though most of their own countrymen might regard black bear more as vermin or a nuisance than as a fine big game animal, most Yanks further to the south didn't. And, more importantly, a goodly portion of these dollar-toting gringos were willing to part with some loot in order to find good hunting for the bruins. The giant provinces of Ontario and Quebec offer some 90,000 and 50,000 animals, respectively, and various services and facilities catering to the visiting hunter interested in finding himself a bearskin rug are well developed.

Much of this east Canadian bear hunting occurs in the spring and over bait. The bait can consist of many things from fish or offal (that usually has been allowed to sour or "cook" in a plastic bag for a while) to garbage dumps, old crowbait horses or other bear goodies guaranteed to give your Aunt Minnie a king-size case of the vapors.

Actually, where legal, there's nothing particularly wrong with hunting this way, though it has never appealed much to me personally. I am told by those who know, that after one sits motionless for several hours (or days) at the bait, often being eaten alive by noseeums and other insect pests, any bear that is taken is

Black bear skulls should always be saved as exciting secondary trophies from a successful bear hunt. Good taxidermy practices now include the use of a synthetic form (rather than the skull) because it is far longer lasting and more durable.

well earned. When you think about it, this type of bear hunting is rather similar to tiger hunting in India in the days of yore when the big cat was lured to a staked out bait (usually a bleating goat) while the hunter waited in ambush on his *machan* or platform built above the ground in the nearby trees. Tiger hunting used to be regarded by some as the height of glamorous adventure. Anyway, this type of baited bear hunting is generally rather effective *if* you do a good job on your pre-hunt desk work and thereby select a good outfitter in a good bear producing area.

Many of these hunts are quite inexpensive, ranging from $150 to $500 depending upon the length of the hunt, the accomodations and the level of the guide service provided. Many hunters make one or two guided hunts and learn about the area and the type of

denning period. (NOTE: Even on a spring hunt, check each trophy out carefully before shooting if at all possible. Sometimes a bear can rub its fur in the den, especially if it's a sow which has cubs [she shouldn't be shot anyway as you are killing two or three animals, not one].) The weather on spring hunts is salubrious, and the chances of finding a bear are, other things being equal, better than in the fall.

On the other hand, the fall hunt can often be teamed with a moose or whitetail hunt (or other game in different parts of the continent) and many hunters just naturally prefer to limit their big game hunting to the fall-winter months, feeling that the cold, nippy weather is more bracing and more appropriate. The costs of the spring and fall hunts are usually about the same since the outfitter or guide costs usually run pretty constant

Hunter and guide show black bear taken on Canadian hunt.

hunting and then return on their own for even cheaper hunting.

The length of the hunt may vary, but 5 to 7 days is a good allowance for a springtime, bear-only hunt in a good area. However, if I were seriously trying to take a moose or a deer along with my bear on a fall hunt, then I would definitely allow 2 weeks. Both types of hunts, spring and fall, have points to recommend them. The spring hunt gives the hunter a nice vacation at a time of the year when he normally can not hunt other game, and if he times it right and does his hunting immediately after they leave the den, he will be hunting them when their fur is in the best condition of the year. Even the best fall fur, in prime condition immediately before the bear dens up, can not match the best spring fur which has continued to grow longer and glossier during the

between the two seasons.

## The Rocky Mountain West

There is some hunting for bear only in this area, but most black bear are taken as added bonus trophies on mixed big game hunts of various types. Wyoming has something under 5,000 black bear, and Idaho and Montana both boast decent bear populations, probably better than 5,000 in each case though there are no official estimates to check. Black bear are taken "as they come" on fall mixed game hunts ranging from mule deer group hunts that can run as low as $50-$75 per day on up through trophy elk and deer hunts with a guide for each hunter and all the trimmings that may cost $150-$200 per diem. At least 10 days should be allowed on these mixed game hunts if the hunter wants to take a

Jack Atcheson and two of his young sons show a pair of well furred blacks taken on a spring hunt in Montana several years ago. A spring black bear hunt is a nice change of pace type of hunt and due to the generally agreeable weather, a good hunt for ladies or youngsters who aren't particularly interested in "roughing it."

good trophy of the main game sought *plus* have a decent chance for a "bonus blackie." Two weeks would be even better, if possible.

There is some spring bear-only hunting in Montana and Wyoming, but it is rather limited. These hunts usually last a week and cost $500 to $750 depending upon the area and the services and accomodations. Farther to the north in British Columbia (with a huge bear population estimated at 100,000!) there are far more bear-only spring hunts offered especially in the southern, southeastern and south central parts of that giant province.

Some of these springtime hunts, especially north of the border, offer added chances at wolverine and wolf, two of the most highly prized trophies in North America. Though it is illegal to do so in British Columbia, if the truth were known, many a spring killed black bear was taken over old crowbait horses that had sudden "coronaries" in propitious places. The cost of one of the 7- to 10-day excursions can vary wildly depending upon the usual variables, but $100 to $150 per day is a fair average with some hunts going for a bit more. Some outfitters charge an added "trophy fee" upon the taking of the trophy, and some of these "fees" are staggered in cost depending upon the size of the trophy.

Since British Columbia is such a game-rich province, the fall black bear hunting is almost always done in conjunction with the hunting of other species of big game. This can be mule deer or elk hunts further south or goat/caribou/moose hunts throughout most of the province. The cheapest hunts run about $100 per day and offer limited availability of other species and stripped down guide services (one guide per pair of hunters or more). The mid-range hunts run $150 or more per day and offer better game areas and accomodations and, sometimes, a more personalized guide service. The full scale packstring hunt for mixed game with one guide to the hunter now runs from $200 to $350 per day, depending upon the services and, primarily, whether there are sheep and grizzly in the area and, if so, how many of the latter of these two animals.

**The Pacific Coast**

California, Oregon and Washington are all good black bear states. Oregon fields some 20,000 ursines while Washington has at least 30,000 of the baggy pants fellows and California has about the same amount. However, considering it strictly on the basis of density of population, Washington state with much less geographic area than California is undoubtedly *the* black bear state nationwide.

Here much of the hunting is done with packs of bear hounds, and the success ratio is extremely high for nonresidents retaining the services of guides with good dogs. In certain areas of the state (mostly in the northwest), the bear are actually regarded as pests due to the extensive damage they do to the timber by girdling the trees. Bear hunts in Washington usually last from 5 to 7 days and cost around $750. This fee can be broken up several ways. Some guides want a down payment of $400 to $500 and then an additional payment of $250 to $300 upon the taking of the trophy while others want the full payment of $600 to $750 before the hunt ever commences.

Oregon's bear hunting is similar to Washington's, though there are fewer guides and outfitters available to

This proud youngster has just brought down this brown phase black bear or cinnamon bear. This secondary color phase of the basic black bear is far more common in the Rocky Mountain West than it is in the far West or in Alaska, and these brownies are almost never taken in the East.

serve the nonresident hunter. California has offered some dog hunting for nonresidents in the past, but this is declining.

### Alaskan Hunting

Black bear are frequently taken as bonus trophies on all-specie mixed game hunts. These fantastic and fantastically expensive "safari" hunts range from 10 to 17 days and cost from $200 to $350 per day depending upon game offered, services and accomodations.

Alaska fields a phenomenal population of some 45,000 to 50,000 black bear, and the hunting is superb in those areas of the giant state where the bear is present. A sleeper of a hunt is the "do-it-yourselfer" or "semi-do-it-yourselfer" in southeastern Alaska where you can often combine a fall bear expedition with a hunt for goat and the elfin Sitka blacktail deer. Alaska is a bonanza for goat hunters and many are just now beginning to discover the long neglected (by *nonresident* hunters) southeastern panhandle area where black bear, often oversized from feeding on salmon in similar fashion to the local brown bear, are very common.

Although some of the younger outfitters are now beginning to cater to this type of southeastern black bear/goat/blacktail hunt, it's still largely undeveloped compared to the far better known (and enormously more expensive) Alaskan general, mixed game hunts further to the north in the main body of the state. Most of these newer outfitters in the panhandle area are concentrating on the local brown bear and offering blacks mostly on a "take 'em as they come" bonus basis.

An enterprising fellow might well, with a bit of energetic and persuasive talking, work himself up an interesting, informally guided hunt with some like-minded citizen in Juneau if he went about it the right way. Perhaps by trading out "guided" hunts in their two home areas with the Alaskan visiting the "southern 48er" the following year.

The sportsman journeying to this panhandle area will find the hunting good, the weather unpredictable and often sour, the country dramatically exciting and the costs — relative to what you are getting — negligible. *WARNING:* be in extra good physical condition if goat are also on the menu. Otherwise the black bear can be hunted rather leisurely from boats in many of the coastal bays.

There are other scattered pockets of black bear hunting from Colorado to Utah in the West to New York state in the East. The diversity of both the range of this animal and the different ways in which he is hunted is unmatched by practically any other North American game animal except whitetail and, possibly, elk.

Though the truculent, inflexible grizzly has continually retreated before man and his advancing civilization, the wily and adaptable black has stayed and thrived mightily. And, if the ultimate test of an animal is how adaptable he is, his "survival quotient" if you

The Prince of Iran poses with an average black bear he took on an Alaskan hunt.

will, then the North American black bear has to rate very high on the worldwide scale of large game animals.

Many years ago black bear were valued highly for the bear grease, oil (used to make hair oil, among other things) and various other animal products which could be rendered from them. An interesting account of a Wisconsin black bear killed in 1867 itemizes the sale of products from a single bear:

$64 — for 8 gallons of pure, strained oil
        at $8 per gallon
$ 6 — for 2 gallons of crude oil at $3 per gallon
$10 — for the hide

$80 total — *exclusive of the meat*.

That was a pile of coin over 100 years ago, and it shows graphically how the animal was valued, even if only in a purely commercial sense. For some years after that, with the introduction of other oil products and various other substitutes, the black was less valued commercially and, at times, was regarded as a nuisance at best, and vermin at worst. In recent years more and more sportsmen have recognized the true worth, in recreational and sporting terms, of this fine game animal. In the whitetail woods of the East, especially, the black bear lends added spice to the annual deer hunt just by being in the same woods!

### Guns For Black Bear Hunting

Black bear are not, considering their size and strength, especially tenacious of their lives. Any gun

The Marlin lever action featuring the powerful 444 cartridge is another good bet for the black bear hunter favoring the lever gun but wanting a bit of extra close-in authority.

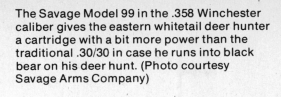

The Savage Model 99 in the .358 Winchester caliber gives the eastern whitetail deer hunter a cartridge with a bit more power than the traditional .30/30 in case he runs into black bear on his deer hunt. (Photo courtesy Savage Arms Company)

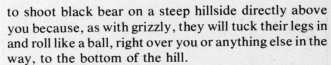

that will cleanly and regularly take whitetail or mule deer will do fine for blacks. The .30/30 and .35 Remington, both rather mild mannered, and after 200 yards, downright meek loads, will do fine for shorter range shots at *americanus*. And, over the years, hundreds have been killed by those two and similar powered rounds by eastern whitetail hunters who lucked out and happened to stumble onto a bear in the deer woods. However, I would keep my bear shooting to within 150 yards or less when using cartridges of this stripe.

The .243, 6mm Remington, .257 Roberts and .25/06 are fine rounds for blacks. They carry a bit more power at the muzzle than the older fashioned, snub nosed cartridges just covered, and they retain their muzzle energy out to 200 yards and farther in a much more efficient fashion due to the sharper pointed bullets they usually feature. One shot with any of these shells, providing it's anywhere in the heart/lung vitals, should dispatch blackie promptly.

The .270, .280, .30/06, 8mm Mauser and similar rounds have killed hundreds of black bears over the years. They make fine bear rounds though smaller cartridges will do equally well. Many hunters after other game such as moose, caribou, sheep, goat or even grizzly with these cartridges have used them to put away "bonus blacks" they happened to stumble upon.

Larger guns, speaking with more power at both ends, really aren't necessary for black bear unless you just happen to want to use your pet rifle. It's a good idea not to shoot black bear on a steep hillside directly above you because, as with grizzly, they will tuck their legs in and roll like a ball, right over you or anything else in the way, to the bottom of the hill.

Today's big game hunter is a confirmed scope sight user, and even though black bear, especially in the heavily wooded East, are an animal of the heavy coverts, I would still suggest the hunter use a low-powered scope rather than iron sights. The scope gives him a bit of magnification that he can handily use at times to tell whether what he sees is a flicking ear or merely a wind-nodding branch. Also, the scope with its greater light gathering powers, affords the hunter far better vision early and late during the low light periods.

For eastern hunters a 2½ fixed power scope will do fine but one of the lower range variables such as the 1.5x to 4.5x would do even better. For a reticle I would prefer the duplex type thick and thin cross hair (which I use for all big game hunting anyway) since it would enable me to aim in heavy cover and yet still draw a fine bead when necessary. The widened field type of feature now offered by leading scope makers (at an extra charge) would definitely come in handy here since these animals are occasionally jump shot at very close ranges like deer (or rabbit for that matter).

Hunters trying to put a black rug on their walls further to the north or west where there is much greater chance for the long shot could put a 4x or, better yet, one of the 2x to 7x variables to good use.

Black bear are fine game animals. They furnish several interesting types of trophies from the skull to the bearskin, and depending upon what they've been feeding on, they can be good to eat, also. They also are, along with grizzly bear, wolf and wolverine in some areas, the only major trophy that can still be hunted in spring as well as fall. They are cunning and adaptable animals who have learned to live with man and his axe and plow. With any sort of wise game management in years to come, black bear should be with us in good huntable numbers indefinitely.

# Chapter 9

# How To Get Your Alaska Brown Bear and Grizzly Bear

**THE PILOT SET** the wings and brought our little plane lazily spiraling down over the large draining tidal flats. Above the high water mark there were no trees on this bleak windswept Alaskan peninsula. Only tall lush grass and, here and there, clumps of twisted brush growing almost horizontal to the ground. We lost altitude a bit heavily as the Cessna struggled with the several hundred pounds of cameras, film and duffle that I would need to camp here and photograph the bears in the next few weeks.

We swept in over our first bear, a big sow with two roly-poly cubs of the year almost hidden in the tall grass. She didn't even deign to look up and acknowledge us, having gotten a bit used to man and his infernal machines here in this protected sanctuary. That didn't mean for a moment that she was a "tame" or "friendly" Walt Disney bear. Those words have no meaning when applied to *Ursus arctos*. She and others of her kind had learned, here in this one unique place, to more or less tolerate man. A fragile truce. Only that and nothing more.

A nice mountain grizzly striding along powerfully beside a small stream is an unforgettable sight for any sportsman and one that all too few will see in coming years.

# GRIZZLY AND ALASKA BROWN BEAR RANGE/S

(As defined by the Boone & Crockett Club)

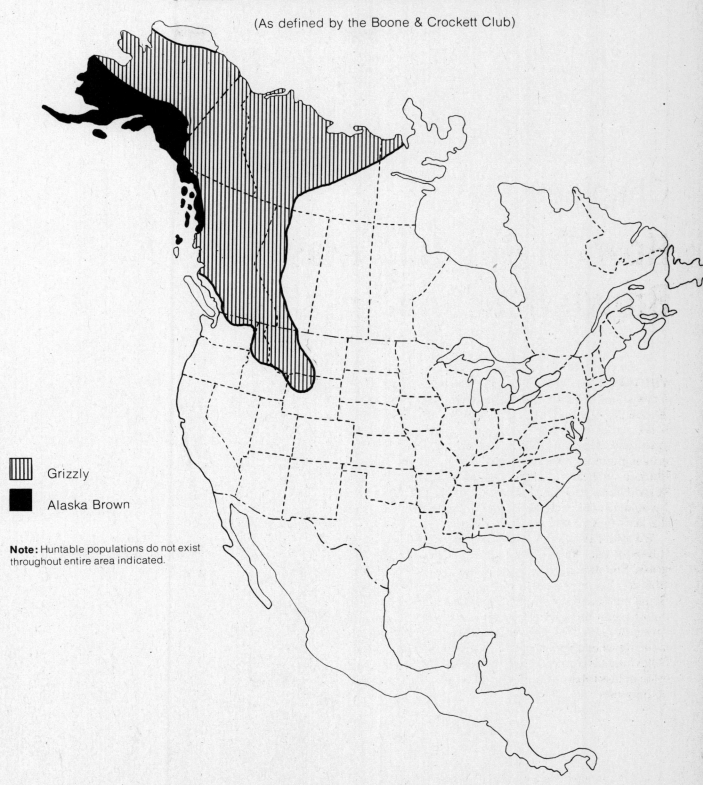

Grizzly

Alaska Brown

**Note:** Huntable populations do not exist throughout entire area indicated.

(Above) More good brown bear country. The bears come down out of the mountains of the interior of both Kodiak Island and the Alaska Peninsula to fish for salmon on the tidal flats when they are running.

(Right) Alaska brown bear congregate in great numbers at favored fishing holes during the height of the salmon runs.

(Below) A young Alaska brown bear leaping into the water to try to pin a salmon down. This is not good fishing technique, indicating that this bear has not yet learned how to fish properly by standing patiently until a salmon swims within striking range and then pinning it with a ham-sized paw. Brown bears, like people, vary greatly in their angling ability from individual to individual, and some never seem to get the knack of it.

118

Even now in late July, this arctic prairie was dotted with patches of year-round snow in the shady lees. It slid beneath us, a white-speckled, brown-green patchwork, as we glided in. Ahead of us the shimmering blue water of a small wilderness river sliced through the khaki checkerboard. Then I saw what I had crossed a continent for. To the right the river foamed its way over the McNeil River falls. Not very impressive as waterfalls go, this one would hardly qualify as big rapids on many larger and stronger rivers. But the falls were in exactly the right spot to bottleneck the salmon run as the tired fish paused momentarily to gather strength to breast the falls on their relentless march upstream.

The big bears know this, and they come down out of the mountains of the interior to this spot every year since before the coming of the first man to this land. Each year, at exactly the time the salmon come, the bear come — a not-so-minor miracle of nature. The living is good, and some bears gain hundreds of pounds in the short 4- to 6-week season. There were seven of them here today with the largest occupying the best fishing holes and the smaller 2-year-olds and sows without cubs constantly being bumped to less desirable fishing spots whenever bigger and stronger bears showed up. Nature is a beautiful but amoral lady. Might *does* make right in her infinite equation.

The weeks that followed were to be a very special experience. Though I had stalked, watched, hunted, photographed and killed the big bear before, as one idyllic summer day dissolved into another, I had more continuous and intimate exposure to this animal than would be possible in three lifetimes spent in most any other good bear country on earth. Bear are basically antisocial types, having very little tolerance for their own kind (except at mating time or during cubhood)

much less for man. In this one spot they have, over a period of years, developed a tentative and highly fragile acceptance of each other and man. However, too much intrusion by man or the wrong kind of behavior by him could easily upset this delicate balance.

Bears are, in common with blondes, fast horses and slow poker hands, creatures of myth and mystery. There is probably more disagreement and truth-stretching involved with them than with any animal in North America. However, I have spent a considerable amount of time observing and hunting them and even more time interviewing in depth others who know their bears. In the balance of this chapter we will attempt to clear up some popular misconceptions about these magnificent animals as well as advising where and how to best hunt and take them.

### The Game

Yes, Alaska brown bear and grizzly bear are considered by most authorities (and by myself) to be one and the same animal. At one time they were categorized separately but no more.

In fact, though the grizzly-brown bear is an entirely different animal than the much smaller and shyer American black bear, he is actually the same animal as the brown bear of Europe and Asia. One of the great behavorial mysteries of the wild is why the Eurasian brown (grizzly) bear is tractable enough to be taught intricate circus routines relatively easily while his American cousin is anything but a good subject for a trained animal act! Perhaps a longer exposure to man over on the other side of the water has something to do with this profound difference, but no one really knows.

Though grizzlies vary enormously in size, the average adult mountain grizzly boar will weigh about 400

Alaska brown bear grow to enormous size due to longer coastal growing seasons and all the free protein they are treated to during the salmon runs.

pounds, and with his hide off, will measure about 6½ feet over the back from nose to tail and about 7½ feet across his front arms from claw tip to claw tip. Females will average 30 percent to 40 percent less in weight and are proportionately smaller in length and width. Some wild bears are considerably larger than this, but it is hard to believe that many over 800 pounds now exist, though they have been recorded as large as 1,100 pounds. Incidentally, the now extinct "golden bears" of California, which were actually giant coastal dwelling grizzlies (or "brown bears") living on salmon but doing it in a more benign climate than that of present day Alaska's, appear to have equaled or even exceeded the very largest specimens of Alaskan brown bear ever recorded.

The giant plains grizzly, a true inland dwelling grizzly that also fattened and grew to enormous size due to the superabundance of buffalo, is also now extinct. Though these bear undoubtedly did kill calves and an occasional adult bison, probably most of their free protein came from bison that died of natural causes or from other, faster predators but were then preempted by the larger grizzly. General George A. Custer, who was to achieve a dubious kind of fame a few short years later, killed one huge old boar in the then Dakota Territory that weighed just a bare few pounds shy of half a ton. That's a lot of bear anywhere, and for any inland bear it's doubly remarkable.

Though bears, due to the amount of fat they store up for hibernation, regularly vary more in weight than most animals, the *average* adult inland mountain boar probably varies from about 375 to 450. Though much larger bear do exist in the mountains (I've seen some that weighed upwards of 700 to 750 pounds), the vast majority are far smaller. It's simply that most bears tend to grow rather than shrink as they are re-killed over the years in song and story. This is perfectly understandable, but it does lead to all sorts of exaggerated and erroneous ideas about their true size.

So-called Alaska brown bears, actually just coastal dwelling grizzlies, are a far different proposition due to two extended salmon meals per year and a generally warmer and longer growing season. So are the coastal dwelling grizzlies of British Columbia, for exactly the same reasons, though they aren't known as "brown bears" but rather simply as grizzlies.

These big coastal bears achieve an enormous size. A prime Alaska brown boar will probably average between 700 and 1,200 pounds, depending upon where he lives, what time of year it is and how old he is. A comparable female would run between 500 and 800 pounds (live weights in all cases) or, to put it another way, a coastal sow will weigh considerably more than a prime inland boar. However, in keeping with all bear stories everywhere, even these huge sizes are often exaggerated in the telling.

I have had more than one tale recounted to me, in all

The grizzly can be told from the smaller black bear by the pronounced shoulder hump of the former.

seriousness, about this brown bear or that one weighing 1,800, 1,900 or even "over a ton." Frankly I don't think any Alaska brown bear of the modern era has ever achieved anything like that size. Jim Faro, the Alaska Fish & Game Department's Biologist on the Alaska Peninsula where some of the very largest bears live, says that he has never seen or been able to authenticate any bear weighing over 1,600 pounds. Jim knows about as much about these big bruins as there is to know, and he has ten lifetimes of practical field experience with them and exposure to them.

### Are Grizzlies and Brown Bears Ferocious?

Both animals are supremely powerful beasts. Whenever a hunter skins out his first one, he is literally astounded at the size of those huge, ropy sinews and muscles. To see one of these animals casually moving large boulders aside to dig for marmots is a chastening experience.

Both types of grizzly certainly have the equipment to be "ferocious" if necessary. And, every year, there are a few unfortunate encounters between man and grizzly

Danger! An alert and aroused grizzly is scenting the air for trouble. This bear could, true to his unpredictable nature, do about anything though the danger of "charges" is often greatly over dramatized in the more purple type of bear story.

A mother grizzly with a young and curious cub. This is a potential trouble situation as the photographer (the author) was well aware when he snapped this photo!

wherein man definitely comes out the loser. But, these are few in number and usually special-circumstance situations. A bear with an abscessed tooth is a mean customer when surprised on a trail as is one recovering from an old gunshot or other natural wound. Of course inadvertently coming between a sow and her cubs is the classic problem situation with bears, but it is difficult to generalize about these situations. There have been a number of recorded instances where sows abandoned cubs in these cases. (Probably these were mostly large cubs 2 years old or older that, though still with their mother, were self-sufficient, and the bonds of cubhood had thus been considerably diluted.)

The bear that hunters encounter now, even in the remotest interior mountains of Canada and Alaska or the most deserted beaches of British Columbia or Alaska, is not the same bear that existed prior to the Lewis and Clark expedition in the early 1800's. When these redoubtable explorers crossed the continent, they encountered some truly ferocious "grisly" bears that, due to little or no exposure to man tended to approach fearlessly and often dispute the right of way. All that has changed in the ensuing 2 centuries. Man now rules the continent in undisputed power, and the big bears know this.

Perhaps in some of the remotest stretches of the tundra back in the Northwest Territories there are some bears still innocent enough to casually challenge man, though I doubt it. It appears that through genera-tions of exposure to man and consequent imprinting, the bears know full well that man's awesome weapons can reach out with a power to match or exceed their own and do it not just at arm's length but at 200 or 300 yards and even further. Bears are used to being, as adults anyway, the unchallenged rulers of their deep wilderness domains, but when man comes, they move off almost always giving way to him if given half a chance.

Some bears cause trouble when foolish campers, staying under canvas in good bear country, sleep with the bacon or other tantalizingly odored goodies almost under their pillows. Other problems surface when a hunter or hiker rounds the bend of a trail in tall grass or underbrush and suddenly surprises a bear. This can happen more easily than some imagine since most all of the trails that people use in good bear country are actually bear trails. The thick brush and a strong wind in the face of the hiker can easily mask his approach from a relaxed bear. Bear don't like to be suddenly confronted or "braced" in situations like this. They may, in the process of just looking for a way out, run the wrong way (*toward* you rather than away) and thus, rather innocently, leave a few bear tracks up and down your carcass in the process.

Actually most "charges" are rather innocent, though one would never know it when the tall tales start wafting around over cocktails and each hunter rekills his bear, making sure that it is more ferocious and larger than that of the guy sitting next to him. Bear are such potentially lethal animals that they have learned to set-

(Above) Mama grizzly with three large cubs. The author has found this to be the most dangerous type of situation as younger cubs are often more timid whereas these "teen-agers" can let their curiousity get themselves — and you — into trouble before you know it. Though grizzly sows have been known to abandon cubs under pressure — don't count on it!

(Right) A big Alaska brown bear is a magnificent trophy and the world's largest carnivore (with the possible exception of the polar bear).

A grizzly sow with three large cubs grazing out in a meadow like so many Hereford cows. Probably no more than 10 percent of the average mountain grizzly's year-around diet consists of meat and most of that is carrion.

tle most of their dominance disputes with threat gestures involving huffing and puffing, teeth clacking, eye contact and abortive "charges" rather than through outright no-quarter fighting. If they actually fought seriously each time there was a pecking order dispute, there soon wouldn't be any bears left. (Which puts them several steps ahead of us in development, in a manner of speaking.)

Thus, many "charges" are really more threat displays than outright, total commitment situations. I have been "charged" twice in this fashion, both times being sow-with-cubs situations. The first time I had a gun, and the old girl stopped at 20 feet. The second time all I had was two motor driven Nikon cameras and a cut bank at my back that boxed me in when that lady finally stopped at 6 feet. Both times I was certain that they didn't mean it, but I must admit that the second and closer instance took more than a little starch out of my shirttails. Interestingly enough both these cases, and most of the others I've heard about, involved long yearling cubs.

Apparently the very small cubs of the year are generally shy and timid for the first few months and don't often stray too far from mother — nor do they openly approach strange objects so readily. Two-year-olds and older are usually old enough to have some sense about strange objects and beings and, often, the sow does not seem as devoted to them as to the younger cubs. But yearlings and cubs a bit older can be very devilish. Old enough to have lost the timidity of very small, weak cubs and yet young enough not to have learned fear or discretion (with a devoted mother like that I guess I might not be afraid of anything much either), they tend to be very curious and outgoing and may often approach people or animals fairly openly depending upon what their past experiences have been. And, where they go, mama is soon to follow. She didn't really want to bother me on the closest "charge" because the cubs had approached me, rather than the other way around, and they were just trying to get a good look and a good whiff. However, I am glad neither cub took it in his head to let out a loud bawl at just the wrong time. That might have changed the complexion of matters a bit. Just because I don't subscribe to the idea that grizzlies go around dutifully charging at every other human they encounter doesn't mean that I'm not aware that it *can* happen and how fearful the consequences can be when it does.

This young grizzly was just shedding his winter coat when he was photographed in Alaska. (This is why his back looks so dried out and bleached out.) His fur would not be prime for a trophy mount in this condition.

## Where to Get Your Grizzly and Brown Bears

**Alaska:** This is big bear mecca. Only Russian Siberia could possibly rival it in numbers of bear and sizes of individual bears, and no one knows the exact status of that giant and mysterious game field. Alaska has some 15,000 to 20,000 of the big bear, including both inland mountain grizzlies and the coastal dwelling browns. Harvesting is running around 800 a year or about maximum or a bit over it. Bear hunting has become, necessarily, ever more tightly regulated and a nonresident hunter is only allowed to kill one of the big bruins (of either type) every 5 years.

Bear hunting is very expensive. On a specific bear-only hunt in the spring or fall on prime ground, figure on paying from $300 to $400+ per day for a 10- or 12-day hunt on the Alaska Peninsula or Kodiak Island. The hunts toward the upper end of this stratospheric cost scale include more luxurious camps and, often, a secondary chance at big moose and caribou. Farther to the south and east, the bear tend to run smaller and the hunting cheaper. Good comfortable boat hunts can be had along the coastal panhandle and the islands off of it in southeastern Alaska for $250 to $300 per day which, though still expensive, is considerably cheaper than comparable hunting on the Peninsula or on Kodiak.

For some reason that has never come to light, the bears of southeastern Alaska and its related islands are a bit different than those of Kodiak and the Alaska Peninsula. The very largest bears of Kodiak and the Peninsula have historically considerably exceeded in size the largest members of the southeastern tribe. Up until the early 1960's it was no trick at all to take a bear squaring out at 9 feet or a bit over (length of skinned hide from nose tip to tail plus length of skinned hide across front legs divided by two) and quite a few 10-footers were brought in. At this time a comparable southeastern Alaskan brown bear would square out about a foot shorter.

However, since that time the Peninsula and Kodiak have been hard hunted, and though there may still be a few solitary monarchs hiding in the interior of both areas, a sportsman will probably take as large a bear in the southeast. Nine-footers are few and far between now, and 10- and 11-footers are almost unheard of. The bear, still in relatively good shape as far as overall numbers, just aren't living long enough to raise many such Goliaths anymore. Another interesting distinction as Don McKnight (Chief of Research for the Game Division of Alaska Fish & Game Department) and a number of other experts can attest, is that the southeastern bear usually tend to be more truculent for some reason. Don tells me that when they have trapped large numbers of bear for various tagging and research projects, the bear on Kodiak and the Peninsula are usually at the other end of the chain when approached while

Elgin Gates, the well-known trophy hunter, poses here with an enormous brown bear he took on the Alaska Peninsula.

those from the southeast are at *this* end, lunging toward the person/s approaching them.

Admittedly this is atypical behavior and not to be compared with the more normal behavior of free roaming bear. But still, the difference seems to be rather widespread and predictable between the two populations, and the bear were under similar circumstances (partial restraint) at the time.

Mountain grizzlies are scattered throughout interior Alaska and usually run much smaller than their coastal cousins. They also have a long standing reputation as being a bit more pugnacious, probably due to the harsher life they lead. There is considerably more color variation among the inland animals ranging from "Toklat blondes" through the standard medium brown and dark chocolate shades to the gorgeously beautiful silvertips that, due to their long gray guard hairs, look almost like a blue-gray panda bear. Most all coastal bears are medium brown or dark brown. (For more on specifically where to hunt inland grizzlies in Alaska see

Chapter 18: Big Game Hunting in Alaska for details.)

Inland grizzlies are almost always taken in the fall as part of mixed game hunts running from $250 to $350 per day depending upon the type of hunt. Spring grizzly hunts (sometimes combined with black bear) cost about $250 to $300 but tend to run 7 to 10 days rather than 10 to 18 days as is the case with the more complicated "three-animal" or "five-animal" mixed game hunts in the fall.

**Yukon Territory:** With a total population less than that of a medium sized U. S. city this huge land is almost unpopulated. In fact, there are considerably less people in this giant larger-than-California area than there were at the turn of the century during the goldrush era. There are about 5,000 inland grizzlies here, running a bit smaller than their counterparts to the west in Alaska. The hunting is good since the recorded sporting (licensed) kill is barely over 100, though as is the case in Alaska, natives kill an additional unrecorded number of bear.

(Above) Mounting a proper grizzly hunt usually means quite an extensive (and expensive) expedition into deep wilderness.

(Left) Glassing for Alaska brown bear on the rugged Alaska Peninsula. This is typical brown bear country.

other game except bighorn sheep and, in some areas, desert sheep.)

**British Columbia:** This classic game field is about the same size as the Yukon with about the same number of bear or perhaps a few more with province-wide estimates running at about 5,000 to 8,000 animals. Between 350 and 400 of them are taken annually on sport hunting licenses so the kill is considerably heavier. However, there is still much good grizzly hunting left here for both the inland bears and, especially over around the Taku River on the northwestern coast, for the large coastal salmon-eating types. (Though they aren't called "brown bears" here, they are waxing fat and prosperous, living under the same conditions as their coastal cousins over in Alaska.)

In line with their long tradition of outfitted and guided hunting, British Columbia operators offer a wide variety of big bear hunts. Spring hunts for grizzly-only are available at $200 to $300 per day. On the fall hunts grizzly may be taken on various full scale mixed game hunts ($300 to $400 per day) as well as on "intermediate" hunts which offer a chance at grizzly and antlered game but not at sheep ($200 to $275) and on more limited mostly-bear-hunts with marginal chances at perhaps one other trophy (moose or caribou) for about $200 per day. Some very large inland bear have been taken in the Cassiar Mountains, and I have personally seen some quite large ones come into Johnny

There isn't much availability of spring grizzly-only hunting in the Yukon though some more southerly outfitters occasionally arrange hunts of this type. The fall bear hunts are almost always of the pack-string horseback type, and the bears are taken as part of the full-scale mixed game shoot. These hunts usually run 14 to 18 days, though some shorter and longer hunts are occasionally available. Costs range from $250 to $300 a day, and chances for a bear are relatively good in many areas. (You should be aware that, on truly ethical sport hunts, there is less chance by and large to take a mountain grizzly than almost any

Holme's and other outfitter's camps in that region.

**Northwest Territories:** This is one of the wildest territories left on earth which, with a population density considerably lower than that of Outer Mongolia, makes the pristine, deep wilderness Yukon Territories next door seem almost crowded. There are no estimates for grizzly bear in this area, but I would think the population must be around 10,000 or more. The tundra grizzly of this area is the only population of these animals in North America that may actually be increasing in numbers.

Around 100 bear are taken each year by licensed sport hunters, and the unlicensed native kill in this area should still be relatively negligible. There is little or no spring bear hunting here, and all of the fall bear hunting is part of generalized mixed game hunts for moose, caribou and Dall sheep. These hunts are expensive, running $250 to $350 per day and generally with no horses available.

**Other Areas:** Though there are a few grizzly still scattered around Montana and Wyoming and up in Alberta, the hunting for them in these three areas is inconsequential, and the visiting sportsman who is serious about getting a grizzly would do well to look elsewhere.

### Spring vs. Fall Grizzly Hunting

Bear hunting is one of the few types of hunting that still offers both a spring and fall season. There are advantages and disadvantages to both types of hunts.

Spring hunting usually means, other things being equal (which they often aren't), a better chance for a big bear. For one thing grizzly are usually the sole or at least the overwhelming priority on the hunt, even in those areas where wolf, black bear or wolverine may also be available. There are no sheep or antlered animals to distract the hunter. Thus he puts more time and

Proper salting of trophy capes and hides, such as this small bear, is all-important. You can't overdo it! Use plenty of salt, especially around the facial features, edges and feet and rub it in *hard* and *evenly*.

effort into his bear hunting.

Also, the bear have just come out of their dens. Or even if they didn't den up (all grizzlies don't den up all winter; some do for part of the time, some never go to den), they are still very hungry. They'll be out searching the bare slopes for food, and they're much easier to spot than they are later when much of the summer

Grizzlies are great grass eaters, putting away vast quantities of it during prime grass seasons.

vegatation is still cluttering up the fall landscape. The bear are moving around more searching for food, and they are more out in the open — all of which means they're easier to locate.

A grizzly trophy is primarily a rug type trophy, thus the condition and color of the pelage is all-important. A bear in prime spring coat, just out of the den and not yet starting to shed, will have a longer, glossier coat than he will when he's in prime fall coat. *CAUTION:* Contrary to some stories, bears can and sometimes *do* rub spots in their coats in the den. Just because your bear has just come out doesn't automatically mean he's in perfect fur. Always try to glass each bear carefully. *all over* before stalking and shooting him.

Another plus of spring hunting for many sportsmen is the fact that the weather is usually more benign. This offers two advantages. Less hunting time is lost due to snow, rain and fog. Also, the hunting itself is often more comfortable, and the days are longer, meaning more time afield. Hunting at this time of year offers an added insight into the country as opposed to always hunting only within a fairly restricted time frame in the fall and early winter weeks. Also, if the hunter is lucky enough to have the time and wherewithal to afford two vacations within a year or 15 months, a spring bear hunt offers a nice way to do it.

There are some potential disadvantages, also. Many hunters don't like the balmy breezes of spring and early summer, having an instinctive feeling that on a *hunt* the weather should be nippy and getting more so, not the other way around. Also, though the bear hunting may not be quite as good and the hunt may be a tad more expensive, for the hunter's first trip to this area or after these species, a fall mixed game hunt does offer a bit more for the money with three to five animals on the docket rather than one or two. Though it might seem that, since fewer trophies are being offered, a spring bear-only hunt should be considerably cheaper than a fall mixed game hunt, you must remember that the outfitter's basic costs (food, tentage, guide and cook wages, transportation, horses and saddlery, etc.) are about the same either way. It simply costs a certain amount to get back into wilderness country and stay there for 10 to 14 days, whether one happens to be after one animal or ten in the process. Probably the best approach is for the hunter to try both types of hunts, spring and fall, over a period of years in order to savor the two different experiences.

### Guns for Big Bear

*Ursus arctos* is a tough customer, whatever you call him, wherever he lives and however big he is. Especially if he is aroused and pumping adrenaline. Bears have a phlegmatic temperament, something like that of mountain goats or the world's wild swine and wild oxen, that seems to be particularly effective at sopping up the shocking power from rifle wounds and allowing

them to carry on. In addition to this they have a longer coat than that of black bear and most other big game animals. They are also, at many seasons of the year, armored with thick belts of fat to protect their vitals from all but the more powerful loads and strong, well constructed bullets.

Bears, even the biggest and most agitated ones, are, after all, flesh and blood and subject to the dreadful shocking power built into modern, high density, center-fire rifle loads. But they should be approached with caution and shot with accuracy. Though the basic maxim for taking most all other North American big game such as deer, elk, sheep and goats is to hit them behind the front leg and about a third of the way up in order to rip up the lung-heart complex in the thorax, this is not the best approach for big bear shooting.

Grizzlies and brown bears should be shot, if possible, in the front shoulders in order to break them down and anchor them to the spot. Breaking one or both of the front shoulders will immobilize the largest bear allowing the hunter to then finish him off safely. From a dead side view this means aiming right at the middle of the top of the front leg in order to break that shoulder. Breaking down the hindquarters will *not* immobilize an angry bruin. They can pull themselves along with surprising speed and agility using their front legs only, especially if they are coming downhill toward the hunter.

This brings up another all-important tip about taking big, potentially dangerous game like grizzlies. They should never be shot when directly uphill from the hunter. When any bear is hit on a hillside, the almost inevitable tendency, whether they've been hit seriously or not, is for them to tuck their legs in and roll down the hillside like an animated rubber ball. This gets them out of danger quickly and effectively. A bear rolling, bounding and slipping down a steep slope is extremely hard to hit. I can attest to that personally. Even if hit

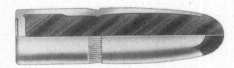

The Remington Core-Lokt bullet, shown here in both round nosed (above) and pointed conformations (below), is a good bear bullet due to its well designed controlled expansion characteristics. (Photos courtesy of Remington Arms Company)

(Left) Elgin Gates poses with what some believe to be the most regal trophy on earth, a large polar bear. Though not legally huntable as of this writing, there is a good chance that legal hunting will again be available on these magnificent creatures in the future.

(Below) The new 8mm Remington Magnum, offering factory loads in 185-grain and 220-grain bullets, both of which yield close to 2 tons of muzzle energy, is a fine choice for a powerful big bear rifle. (Photo courtesy Remington Arms Company)

properly in the front shoulders so that one or both are broken, a bear on a steep slope is not anchored since he has gravity working for him. More than one hunter has had the surprise of his life when his mortally wounded bear dribbled himself straight downhill and right over the hunter in the process. That can be dangerous, to put it mildly.

When selecting the specific cartridge and bullet combination to use for big bear (or any other potentially dangerous game), it becomes important to consider the situation on two levels. Cartridges that will do a good job of *killing* big bears will not necessarily do a first chop job of *stopping* them (or, to put it another way, of *right-now* killing them). A grizzly or brown bear, any grizzly or brown bear worth taking, is truly a trophy of a lifetime. Most sportsmen will never get one, and those that do usually will get only one. They should be killed cleanly and humanely.

Thus, though .270/.30-06 class cartridges have killed many big bear over the years, they would not be my first choice as either bear killers or bear stoppers in this era. Good bear killers, meaning that the hunter is working fairly open country and can usually count on shooting his bear from a distance, start with the .284 magnums and the .308 magnums. Cartridges, developing about 3,600 to 4,000 pounds of energy at the muzzle and doing it with heavily constructed bullets weighing from 175 grains to 250 grains, under good conditions when the hunter can pick his shots and be assured of follow-up shots, are fine and dandy.

Close-in hunting for big bear in thick cover is some-thing else again. That calls for bear stopping. Knocking the bear down and keeping him down, that is. Often the first shot must do it. Not so much because the bear will be "charging" but, because if the bear can struggle just a few feet away in the heavy cover, he is often completely hidden and set for an ambush.

Trailing up wounded grizzly bears, even mortally hit ones, in thick cover is not a good way to stay on friendly terms with your life insurance agent. For heavy-duty work of this type, you need rawboned power that speaks with the authority that even a hyped-up grizzly responds to. That means rounds like the .338 Winchester, the various .350 class wildcat Magnums and the .375 H. & H. Magnum. Cartridges developing 2 tons or more of muzzle energy and doing it with heavy-duty 200- to 300-grain bullets break up even the heaviest bones and create wide-mouthed wound channels that lay easy-to-follow blood trails and bleed the animal out quickly and effectively. There may be those that think I am overgunning them for big bear. They are the ones that have never heard the bawl of a wounded and enraged grizzly.

# CHAPTER 10

# What Is Killing Power?

**IN AN AGE** when doctors and clinicians can not even seem to come up with a universally legalistic definition of death, it is difficult to talk in biological absolutes. Yet it is important that we explore how animals are killed by modern high-powered rifles and that we examine the different elements that contribute to the efficiency of the act.

A modern, smokeless powder, high density rifle loading with a muzzle velocity of around 3,000 feet per second and a muzzle energy in the same neighborhood is fantastically destructive *when teamed with the right bullet* (more on that in a moment). Although few big game animals are killed outright — dropped as if they were a poleaxed steer, a well hit head of game will usually not run or flounder more than 20 feet to 20 yards from the point where it was shot.

This whole subject is filled paradoxes. Some animals don't die when they should, and others die much more promptly than their wound would appear to indicate. Some species of animals, other things being equal, seem much harder to kill than others twice their size.

Where you hit them is still more important than what you hit them with. Author's first shot at this running mountain caribou was too far back (note bullet hole to right of rifle), but it slowed the big (near 500-pound) bull up enough for a well placed second shot to finish him.

This interesting time lapse sequence of a bullet impacting in flesh simulating gelatin shows approaching **(A)**, entering and beginning to expand **(B)**, continuing to expand and creating a far larger wound channel as it does so **(C)**, fully penetrating the gelatin block with the wound channel continuing to grow **(D)**, and the secondary effect of the explosive wound channel (with small bits of gelatin also becoming lethal secondary particles) **(E)**. (Photos courtesy of Remington Arms Company)

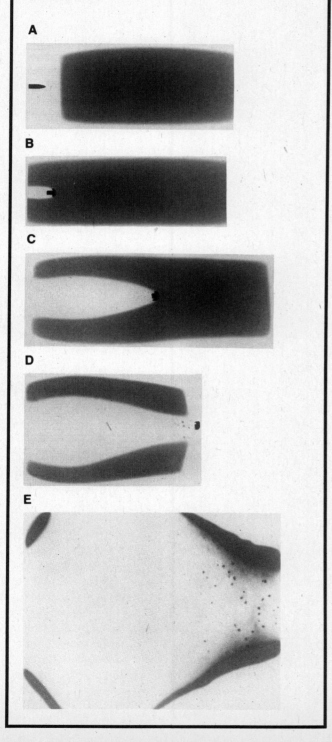

A

B

C

D

E

No one quite knows what constitutes vitality in either animals or humans, but it does appear, for reasons we don't fully understand, that some animals usually withstand the shocking effect of a high-powered rifle wound much better than others.

In North America, mountain goats and grizzly bears are celebrated in outdoor writing as being able to absorb punishment far out of proportion to their size. In Africa, cape buffalo and rhino are famed for being able to soak up lead in almost unbelievable quantities. Why? No one knows for sure. The most likely theory is that some animals' nervous systems seem less sensitive to shock than others, and thus this key aspect of a rifle's lethality simply does not work as well in their case.

But, we are getting ahead of ourselves.

### The Wound

The carnage caused by a well placed rifle shot is almost unimaginable to the uninitiated. When a beginning hunter opens up his first animal or two that has been well hit in the critical heart-lung area with the right type of bullet, he is astonished at the damage inside. (The right type of bullet is one that isn't too heavily constructed and therefore drills a hole neatly through the animal without adequate expansion or one that isn't too lightly constructed and thus blows up and fragments on the animal's outside without penetrating to the vitals.) The animal's vital organs are literally blown apart such is the extent of the devastation in many cases.

As the bullet penetrates the outer layer of hair and hide through the intermediate layer of muscle and flesh to reach the vital bone and organ area inside, several things begin to happen almost instantaneously. The bullet begins to both expand and also shed some of its own mass, starting with the outer jacket but sometimes including varying portions of the bullet core, also.

As this expansion starts, the bullet creates a funnel shaped wound channel, and the force of the high velocity, rapidly expanding projectile pushes ahead of it fragments of the animal's bones and also, displaced liquids such as blood and cellular material. These bone chips and this wave of fluid actually become lethal agents themselves, somewhat like shrapnel, and they multiply vastly the effect of the bullet.

The damage caused by this hydraulic displacement can hardly be exaggerated. It was discovered in World War II that much more damage could be caused by having a torpedo explode as it passed underneath a ship rather than trying to literally hit the ship itself with the torpedo. The shock wave of the displaced water almost always "broke the ship's back," and the torpedoes of both sides were quickly fitted with proximity fuses of various types rather than contact fuses.

Immediately upon bullet impact, the animal begins to suffer from the two major effects of the wound — hemorrhage and shock. Hemorrhage is the chief killer in a wound caused by a large, slow moving projectile

This young whitetail buck was killed quickly and effectively with one shot
from the 308 Winchester leaning on the tree.

such as an arrow, but in a wound caused by a high velocity bullet, shock also plays a critical role. I have discussed and analyzed in detail with several doctors exactly what role each of these two deadly forces plays in the "typical" high velocity rifle wound. I found more disagreement than agreement. Some felt simple hemorrhaging was the more critical factor while others placed more emphasis on shock. When we began discussing shock, there was even some disagreement as to exactly how it functioned and affected the animal. As I said before, there are few absolutes in this area so I might as well give you a few of my own layman's medical theories about this. I didn't go to medical school, but I have killed a lot of game and have been present when others have killed many animals. Although both wound-effects are important, I believe that shock plays a larger role in most kills made by high velocity ammunition. Especially those outright or semi-outright kills where a large animal dies before hemorrhage effect could have killed it.

I have had shock-effect and how it works explained to me a number of times by differing medicos. Some of their definitions not only didn't agree but actually differed on one particular or another. My own feeling is that shock is transmitted along the nerves to the brain, and when an animal is greatly enough over-shocked, the amount of shock waves the brain is receiving is literally enough to "short out" the brain and thus kill the animal.

Actually, there are probably two types of shock involved in these wounds. The massive hemorrhaging would and does induce shock itself. But, there also appears to be a more instant shock effect than can be accounted for solely on that level. This immediate shock is why an animal usually can absorb a second or third wound which have a far less *immediate* effect than the initial wound. Anyone who has killed much game knows that the first wound is always the one that most drastically affects the animal. Some animals' propensity to soak up other *killing* wounds, after an initial badly placed shot, and appear to carry on for an unduly long time has been well remarked for many years.

This is a good thing. It is almost certain that the animal, after the initial impact, feels little if any of the pain that might be associated with this sort of massive damage. Thus, the "blinding" effect of this initial shock is to the good, as no sportsman wants his quarry to suffer unduly.

## The Killing Effect of Velocity

Ever since physicists gave us the complex formulas to calculate kinetic energy, we have had a marvelous tool at our disposal. However, in some ways it has raised as many arguments as it has quashed. For now the principal debate hinges not on how much energy a given bullet traveling at a known velocity can impart (we know that), but how *directly* this energy relates to that elusive thing called killing power. No one has yet been able to provide us with a yardstick to measure that. Thus, the interminable hassle rages between the big bore/big bullet/slow velocity partisans on the one hand and the small bore/small bullet/high velocity boys on the other.

Here is what is known. A gun with 3,000 pounds of kinetic energy is, theoretically, generating enough

bullet, even though the two left the firing chamber at exactly the same initial velocity. This means that out at extended hunting ranges, of perhaps 250 to 300 yards, the very shape of the bullet plays a substantial role in its retained velocity and energy, thus its "killing power." For instance, let's compare three different 180-grain .30/06 factory loads, all leaving the barrel at a calculated 2,700 feet per second but shaped differently. Bullet #1 is a round nosed Remington Core-Lokt while #2 is the same construction but a *pointed* Core-Lokt and #3 is a boat tail type of target bullet (the most streamlined of all, pointed at rear as well as nose):

| Bullet | Muzzle Vel. ft./sec. | Muzzle Energy ft./lbs. | Vel. at 300 yds. ft./sec. | Energy at 300 yds. ft./lbs. |
|---|---|---|---|---|
| #1 | 2700 | 2910 | 1740 | 1210 |
| #2 | 2700 | 2910 | 2040 | 1660 |
| #3 | 2700 | 2910 | 2190 | 2200 |

One of the first prices we begin paying for increased velocity is increased recoil. Another old and hallowed rule of physics is that for every action there is an equal and opposite reaction. Thus, in theory, if the cartridge were fired in a completely weightless rifle (obviously

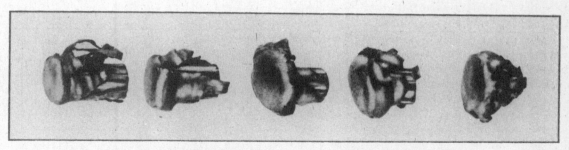

This is proper bullet performance. The three bullets on the left were fired into gelatin blocks closer to the muzzle, thus expanding more than the two on the right due to the higher impact velocity. A good bullet must be able to expand, in a *controlled* manner, under a very wide variety of conditions.

power to lift 1 pound 3,000 feet into the air (or, if you will, 3,000 pounds 1 foot off the ground). *Whenever the velocity of a bullet doubles, its calculated kinetic energy quadruples. Whenever a bullet's weight doubles, its calculated kinetic energy only doubles.*

Still another factor to keep in mind, whether considering a small, fast moving bullet or a large, slow velocity projectile is a thing called sectional density. This essentially refers to the fact that a longer thinner bullet will penetrate things better (including the air) than a shorter, fatter bullet. Or, to complicate it a bit, two bullets of the same caliber and weight, but shaped differently, will have differing trajectories and retained energies.

A blunt, round nosed 180-grain .30 caliber bullet will shed velocity (thus energy) much more rapidly than a sharply pointed, spitzer shaped 180-grain .30 caliber

impossible), the recoil at the butt end of the gun would be as powerful as the energy coming out the front end. The heavier we make the rifle, the more we damp down this "opposite reaction" that we call recoil, but this also means a heavier and more cumbersome firearm that we must muscle around often at high altitudes and over rough country.

So, every time we double the velocity, we quadruple the muzzle energy coming out the front end. But, at the same time we also quadruple the recoil coming out the butt end and into our sensitive shoulders. This is alright up to a point. But, if we set for ourselves the goal of keeping the total weight of our firearm to somewhere between 7½ and 9 pounds (in most cases), then it is obvious that, based solely on this immutable law of physics, there is a fairly precise and constant limit to the

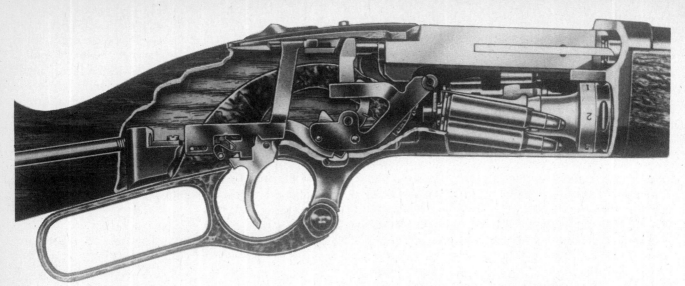

amount of additional velocity we can purchase via added recoil.

Another rather disagreeable aspect of added velocity is partly psychological but nevertheless very real to most hunters. Muzzle blast of any sort increases *apparent* recoil and probably has as much to do with aggravating that bane of accurate shooting — flinching —as the recoil itself. Whenever added energy is purchased by greatly increasing velocity, the resulting high pitched *c-r-a-c-k* of this type of muzzle blast is much more upsetting than the deeper toned *b-o-o-m* resulting from increasing energy by using a heavier bullet.

Also, added velocity has finite limits due to the efficiency of existing gunpowders. Beyond a certain point, more velocity is achievable only by adding amounts of gunpowder all out of proportion to the amount of velocity obtained. Powder burning efficiency is not a linear situation whereby simply adding "X" amount of extra powder one realizes "X" amount of added velocity. Beyond each powder's peak efficiency, it takes two-X, then three-X then four-X and so on of added powder in order to get another "X" increment of increase in the velocity. As more efficient and slower burning smokeless powders become available these peak points of powder efficiency may be raised, thus enabling us to achieve higher velocities with reasonable increases in the amount of powder used, but it is doubtful if we will see any quantum jumps in this efficiency as we did in the conversion from black to smokeless powder cartridges back in the late 19th century.

Existing smokeless powder cartridge ballistics appear to be a rather "mature" technology (similar, say, to the gasoline fired, internal combustion automotive engine) and the existing "state of the art" does not imply any great breakthroughs. Added refinements and marginal improvements here and there yes, but nothing truly spectacular. We stand at about the same point in firearm's ballistics today that aeronautical technology stood at the end of World War II when the internal

The rotary magazine of this Savage Model 99 allows the use of sharper pointed bullets than is safe in lever guns featuring tubular feed magazines where a sharp enough jar might cause a spitzer pointed bullet to detonate the primer of the shell in front of it. Sharper pointed bullets translate into flatter trajectories and more killing power at long ranges.

A hunter may come thousands of miles to collect on a trophy caribou like this one. Having the right gun and knowing how to handle it are all-important.

combustion, gasoline fired engine peaked out in airplanes traveling at about 450 to 500mph and for any substantial improvement in efficiency a whole new technology, that of the jet engine, was necessary.

Added velocity also has the disadvantage of far more rapidly wearing out the rifle barrel. Though newer and harder steels that have become available to the barrel maker in the last 10 or 15 years have partially obviated this, greatly increased velocity increases barrel wear all out of proportion to increased bullet weight (or worse, creeping partial wear in the throat which affects velocity marginally before it becomes obvious that the barrel is just completely "shot out").

A final disadvantage of truly phenomenal velocities is the added strain they place on the bullet designer. As we shall see later in this chapter, bullet design is a science unto itself, and the wider the spread of potential impact velocities that the bullet designer must engineer for, the more difficult becomes his task. To build a bullet that must expand adequately and yet hold together at velocities ranging from 1,000 feet per second to 3,500 feet per second is obviously considerably more difficult than handling velocities of 1,000 to 2,000 feet

Within the span of time that men still alive have witnessed, we have seen this kill zone extended from the range of 75 to 150 yards (evident during the later blackpowder era) to the current 275 to 375 yard ranges now obtained in the most modern magnums. Within the last 20 years this range has roughly increased about 50 yards.

In addition to flatter shooting guns, added velocity has also given us more destructive guns with higher killing power. As we have seen, greatly increased shock-effect makes cartridges far more formidable. And finally, added killing power derived almost solely from increasing bullet weights has its limits, also. As the hole in the gun barrel increases from .40 to .50 to even (in some instances in the past) .60 caliber and more, the gun becomes enormously heavy and unwieldy, and the cartridges, with their paperweight sized bullets, become terribly expensive and heavy to lug around.

When the incomparable Frederick Courteney Selous, the legendary African elephant hunter, was roving around Rhodesia in the 1870's market hunting for ivory, he used some fearful four-bore muzzleloaders, each

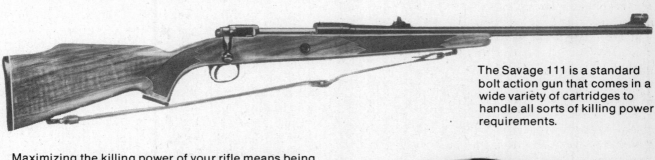

The Savage 111 is a standard bolt action gun that comes in a wide variety of cartridges to handle all sorts of killing power requirements.

Maximizing the killing power of your rifle means being able to shoot it accurately and that, in turn, means consistent range practice. Good quality shooting glasses are an important safety factor for sustained shooting especially when using the more powerful cartridges.

per second. Far more variables are introduced into the wider span situation. Though it appears at times that bullet designers are miracle men, there are limits to even their powers of ingenuity, and increasing velocity tests these powers to the utmost.

Before we leave the subject of velocity, it's best not to close while stressing these negative considerations alone. Velocity is critically important and precisely *because* it has been instrumental in affording us the increased killing range and effectiveness is it necessary to occasionally stress the limits of its efficiency.

Velocity enables us to shoot with flatter trajectory thus increase the range at which we may reasonably shoot at game. If we define the killing range as that area in which the bullet rises or falls no more than 4 inches above or below the line of sight, then greater velocity extends this "kill zone" mightily.

firing a ball weighing 4 ounces! That's a quarter of a pound! When hunting afoot in the Tsetse fly infested interior (horses that had survived an attack of the "sleeping sickness" and thus were immune were too expensive for him to use and other horses were worthless), Selous had to dig out the soft lead projectiles from each dead elephant and re-cast them for re-use. At a quarter-pound apiece, one doesn't carry too much ammo around on one's back! These guns were frightful things, incidentally. Selous started off using a pair of 12½-pound smooth bores in 1871. His standard "load" was a *handful* of powder ("I find that an ordinary

The Winchester Model 70 Magnum bolt action rifle is available in the most powerful centerfire calibers, offering a maximum of killing power. (Photo courtesy of Winchester Western)

44 REMINGTON MAG.

375 H.&H. MAG.    38-40 WIN.    44-40 WIN.    444 MARLIN    45-70 GOV.    458 WIN. MAG.

Cartridges come in all shapes and sizes, and appearances can be highly deceiving.

handful of powder is over 20 drachms''). The thought of shooting a gun that light that fired such a monstrous charge is awe inspiring. Selous himself many years later said, "They kicked most frightfully, and in my case the punishment I received from these guns has affected my nerves to such an extent as to have materially influenced my shooting ever since, and I am heartily sorry that I ever had anything to do with them." Thus, the greatest modern hunter who ever lived was himself a consistent victim of flinching.

Incidentally, consider the weight of that quarter-pound "bullet" for a moment. The standard .270 loadings feature bullets running from 130 to 150 grains while the .30/30 and .30/06 feature their most common hunting bullets in the weights of 150 to 220 grains in various loadings. The heaviest factory load available for the .375 Magnum is 300 grains, and the .458 Winchester,

one of the most powerful factory rounds now loaded in this country, features a 510-grain bullet as its heaviest. The legendary .600 Nitro Express, largest factory smokeless powder cartridge made (in bore diameter anyway) smote elephants with a 900-grain softball sized bullet. This blunderbuss of Selous' that fired a quarter-pound ball was in reality firing a 1750-grain projectile. Awesome!

Thus, gaining added killing power by heavying up the bullet also has its obvious limits.

### The Killing Effect of Bullets

Most beginning hunters far underestimate the importance of proper bullet selection. Remember — the only part of the whole enormously complex and delicately balanced shooter-gun-cartridge continuum that actually comes in contact with the living game is — the bullet. The shooter can make a highly accurate shot, the rifle can be capable of pinhole accuracy, the cartridge can be of the right power and yet, if the bullet doesn't function properly, you can very easily lose your trophy.

Bullets can go wrong in one of two basic ways. One, they can blow up on the outside of the animal and expend both their energy and their mass in inflicting what are basically surface wounds that will not kill. This can occur either because the bullet malfunctions through bad design or manufacture, or much more likely, because the incorrect bullet is chosen for the job by the sportsman.

The second thing bullets can do wrong is to penetrate straight through the animal with little or no expansion and then proceed to expend about 98 percent of their precious energy on the landscape behind the beast rather than inside of him. All the energy in the world is no good if it's used only to break up rocks and displace clods of earth behind the game animal.

The meek, mild-mannered, standard high velocity loading of the .22 Long Rifle rimfire round pushes a diminutive 40-grain bullet along at some 1,285 feet per second for a rather uninspiring muzzle energy of 147-foot pounds. The .50 machine gun round used so effectively on the wings of many World War II fighter planes to shoot down other planes featured various loadings usually pushing a bullet of about 1.71 ounces or 750 grains (still less than half the weight of Selous' fantastic bullets!) along at right respectable velocities of around 3,000 feet per second. The muzzle energies of

Checking out your rifle when arriving in camp is vital. Strange gremlins due to changes in altitude, moisture content or just rough handling by the baggage people can sometimes drastically alter the point of impact. This could cause the loss of an expensive and irreplaceable trophy if not caught by a checkout off the benchrest before the hunt begins.

these loadings ran in the neighborhood of 15,000-foot pounds of energy or about five times as much energy as the typical .270 or .30/06 big game load!

And yet, if you hit a whitetail deer in the stomach at 40 yards with the metal-cased, non-expanding .50 caliber machine gun bullet and the pip-squeak .22 Long Rifle bullet, chances are the little rimfire round would do more damage than the huge machine gun cartridge. The .22 would probably penetrate the relatively soft and thin deer hide and expand a bit to cause damage inside. This is certainly not the right kind of cartridge to use for deer, but it would probably *eventually* kill the animal. On the other hand, depending upon exactly where it struck, the much heavier, non-expanding machine gun bullet would probably drill straight on through and expend both itself and 99.9 percent of its energy rather harmlessly on the landscape behind the deer. That's just fine for moving dirt around, cutting down trees and making little rocks out of big rocks, but it doesn't serve so well to kill deer.

Admittedly this is a bit of a far-fetched example, and the results would vary a bit depending upon the specific circumstances involved, but it does, I believe, serve to make the point. There is no inherently "good" bullet

nor "bad" bullet. Every bullet, like every rifle, knife or other tool is basically a set of compromises, and a bullet is only "good" in relation to its performance on the particular job at hand. A "good" woodchuck bullet is, almost by definition, a "bad" moose bullet — and vice versa.

The key to good bullet performance is simple — expansion without undue fragmentation. And, to carry matters a step further, the ability to perform these functions well over a wide range of impact velocities against widely varying types and amounts of resistances.

Bullet expansion varies all over the lot and can range from almost nil to total fragmentation. The key is to have the bullet greatly expand without flying apart. Any bullet will usually shed a bit of its outer, gilding metal jacket and some of this is to be expected, especially on close-in, high velocity impacts against very solid (the shoulder of a moose or grizzly) resistance. The problem becomes more acute when the bullet also starts shedding or unraveling its solid core and thus substantially shedding its mass.

Good bullet expansion at reasonable hunting ranges, say from about 50 yards to 300 yards, will run from around 30 percent to 60 percent depending upon the

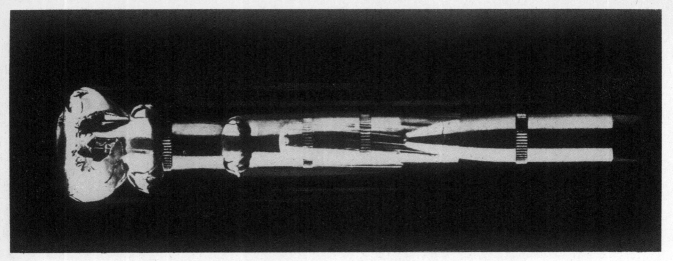

Special photo shows the varying impact and expansion stages of a
Winchester Silvertip bullet. (Photo courtesy Winchester Western)

bullet construction, impact velocity, type of resistance met and other variables down to and even including a minute variance based on the ambient temperature. Retained weight can also vary all over the lot from perhaps 95 percent to as little as 50 percent. In most cases if a big game bullet sheds more than 40 percent of its original weight, it is demonstrably poor performance or else the bullet was badly chosen for the job at hand.

Most heart-lung shots taken at the basic 150- to 250-yard hunting range will see a bullet shedding around 10 percent to 25 percent of its weight due to fragmentation. There are extreme examples of varying types though. A 150-grain Remington Core-Lokt bullet, one of the best of the factory types, fragmented considerably more than that when I drilled a British Columbia grizzly literally between the eyes. I was using a 7mm Remington Magnum rifle and straight factory loads, and the bear immediately dropped as if poleaxed when I fired the 140-yard shot (one of the very few animals that I have ever had to do that to.) The bullet took him head on and penetrated the brain pan then exited out the left side of his head, blowing off most of the lower jaw and zygomatic arch in the process and then reburied itself into his left front shoulder, after penetrating his thick hide and some 2 inches of sinewy muscle tissue.

Though the old myth that a big grizzly or Alaska brown bear's skull will "turn" a bullet is just that (assuming anything like an appropriate bullet was used to begin with), I must say that that long suffering projectile did encounter considerable resistance. The fact that the remnant of the bullet had shed a bit of its core and that its original 150-grain weight was reduced a bit over two-thirds to 48 grains did not indicate a complete failure in this case. I know bullets that would have done better (Nosler and Bitterroot for two), but the faithful Core-Lokt performed well and dispatched the big bruin

so readily that he was literally dead before he hit the ground after toppling off the big 4-foot diameter log that he had been standing on.

Whenever game is struck by a rapidly traveling bullet, you can generally hear the impact. Especially if the shot is a bit out beyond 200 yards, and the initial muzzle blast has partially died down and therefore doesn't mask the impact sound. The experienced hunter can usually pretty well tell about where his bullet hit by the sound. A rump shot into the meaty hindquarter, especially from the side rather than the rear hits with a resounding *SPLAT*. Something like a flat hand slapping hard onto still water except magnified considerably.

A bullet entering the stomach or paunch of an animal often hits with a *PLOP*, but the timbre of this general sound varies considerably depending upon how much food the animal has in both its stomach and intestines and on exactly where in the paunch the bullet impacts. A proper shot into the heart-lung area lands with a medium-timbred sound or a *WHUNK*. A shot into the shoulder of a massive animal like a moose, grizzly or big bull elk lands with a *THUD*.

### Measuring Bullet Effectiveness

Even though bullets are a key link, quite possibly *the* key link in the whole rifle-cartridge-primer-powder-bullet chain, for some mystifying reason no company, group or organization has even taken it upon themselves to try to propound any sort of informal "efficiency index" that might apply to bullets. Admittedly no one system could be all encompassing, but there are things that could be done to greatly clear away the fog for the average sportsman/hunter about which bullet is best for what.

One possibility might be to try to measure the three factors that I believe to be the key elements in bullet effectiveness: penetration, expansion and weight reten-

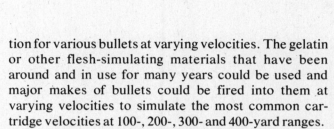

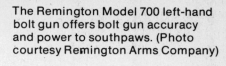
The Remington Model 700 left-hand bolt gun offers bolt gun accuracy and power to southpaws. (Photo courtesy Remington Arms Company)

tion for various bullets at varying velocities. The gelatin or other flesh-simulating materials that have been around and in use for many years could be used and major makes of bullets could be fired into them at varying velocities to simulate the most common cartridge velocities at 100-, 200-, 300- and 400-yard ranges.

Depending upon how far one wanted to take matters, the density of the gelatin material could be varied to simulate the differing game one might pursue from woodchucks and whitetails on the one hand to moose and grizzly on the other. Considering the vastly thicker, tougher hides of the latter two along with their somewhat different musculature and heavier bone structures, a "light," "medium" and "heavy" game animal categorization for bullet testing would be rather interesting.

However, the main thing would be to recover the bullets and measure both their expansion and their retained weights, for the various "ranges" mentioned. The "wound channel" in the gelatin blocks should also be measured for both length and volume displaced. These two "wound factors" should be then combined in some fashion to form an index.

The way to make all these figures more interesting and usable by the general sporting public would be to combine them all — bullet expansion, retained bullet weight and wound index — into a *master* index in some

fashion by either adding all together or multiplying one by another. This would take a more statistically minded type than myself to figure out exactly how to insure maximum rationality. (e.g.: That no one of the factors involved tended to unduly distort or dominate the final overall index.) Food for thought! And a considerable benefit to the hunter who wants to know which bullet is "best" for his purposes.

No investigation of this subject should close without emphasizing that the most important factor of all is a coolheaded hunter. Make sure you are shooting a game animal and not another hunter, an automobile or livestock. Make sure you are shooting the animal you *want* to and not an illegal doe, cow, fawn or calf or a small buck or bull that you later wish you hadn't taken.

Take the extra split second and the extra breath to try to place your bullet where you want to. A clean shot usually means a clean kill — and a bad shot usually means a long, tiring chase that at best results in an exhausted hunter and some thoroughly tainted (by adrenaline) meat and, at worst, means a lost trophy and/or possibly even a lost hunter.

As important as bullets are, ultimately it's hunters even more than bullets, that kill game!

# CHAPTER 11

# How To Spot Game

**ANDY DENNIS,** the Indian guide who has held my hand more than once on extended deep wilderness big game hunts in northern British Columbia, once told me, "Huntin' is all-ee time looking for game . . . looking, looking, looking." We had been sitting on a frigid mountaintop in the Cassiars for over 3 hours, or just about long enough to turn my freezing nether parts to stone, searching vainly for sheep. Andy must have noticed I was beginning to get a bit restive so he delivered himself up of this pearl.

I've thought about that casual remark hundreds of times over the years since then. He was right. So right. Basically, big game hunting *is* "looking for game." Sure, there are various types of hunts such as driving for whitetail in the East or for elk in certain parts of the West which don't fit this category. But, most hunting basically involves *looking* for game. And most game is taken by hunters who spotted their quarry before they themselves were spotted and who then successfully stalked and shot the animal.

And yet, even though spotting and locating game is a prime element of most any hunt (some would say that, along with accurate shooting, it is *the* prime element), it's amazing how many misconceptions there are about

It is important to use a rest when seriously glassing an area. The sitting position is the most common one, but it should be alternated with others.

140

Bear such as this large grizzly are among the most difficult of all game to spot at long distances. They lack antlers or horns that might call attention to them, and they are usually more or less dark or neutral colored without contrasting rumps or underparts that stand out. (The only exception being some black bears that have large enough white chest patches to be noticeable at long distances.)

it. Do "good eyes" or keen eyesight automatically mean that one is better at spotting game? (No!) Are some people just inherently better at it than others? (Yes.) Can you teach yourself to be better at it? (Yes.) Is it hard to master this important skill? (No.) Ask most any group of hunters, even some fairly seasoned veterans, the above questions, and you'll be amazed at how many wrong answers you'll get.

To clear away a bit of the fog we need to talk a bit about vision in general. Then we'll get around to finding out how to best put that vision to work and to train it to be better at spotting game animals. Actually, as eyesight goes, we human beings are gifted with extraordinarily good vision. In fact, we have about as good all-around vision as exists in the bird or animal kingdom. While it is true that many of the large herbivores, who make up most of our big game animal population, can see a bit more acutely than we can, they do not see color. Birds see color, but among the mammals, only man and the great apes possess this marvelous ability. Thus, though a pronghorn antelope or a mountain sheep (probably our two sharpest-eyed North American big game animals) can see more keenly than we and can discern movement or motion at truly phenomenal distances, their resolving power on stationary objects may, in the right situation, not match our own.

Imagine how different it would be if you saw the world only in varying shades of gray. It's true that these animals can see far more than simple black and white and that, much like modern black and white camera film, they can differentiate much about texture and depth by being able to see these varying tones of gray. But, this is a far cry from being able to see the world in full color. Thus, it is often possible to actually walk right up to a wild animal if you are dressed in either a camouflage outfit or a neutral toned outfit that more or less corresponds with your background and if you only move when the animal is looking away from you or has its head down feeding. As long as the animal sees no motion and you do not alter the angle at which you are approaching him, you can pull off some pretty amazing stunts with patience and care. I have walked to within 50 feet of wild animals, varying from elk and moose down to black bear and mule deer, in order to photograph them.

These large herbivores are prey species, and thus they generally have their eyes set rather far apart on the sides of their heads in order to extend their peripheral or panoramic vision. Again, the pronghorn antelope with his enormous, bulging eyes set high up on his head is the undoubted champ at peripheral vision. He has an almost insect-like ability to see partly behind him, and that's a good thing to bear in mind when trying to stalk him. Make sure his head is down completely or facing *directly* away from you. Otherwise, you will be seen approaching as you quarter in from the rear.

(Above) A hunter hastily glassing the area might well miss this caribou bull, almost completely hidden except for his towering antlers.

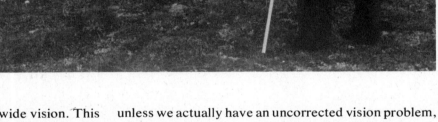

A spotting scope can be invaluable in sizing up game that has been spotted with binoculars as Cassiar Mountain outfitter Johnny Holmes is doing here while looking over some caribou bulls at the far end of the valley.

However, they pay a price for this wide vision. This means that there is usually a smaller arc at which their vision overlaps adequately in order to afford them true binocular vision which, in turn, yields maximum depth perception. Man, on the other hand, is an eyes-front predator with somewhat less peripheral vision but with a very wide arc of overlapping binocular vision meaning that he has maximum depth perception throughout a relatively wide angle.

It is true that the birds see color and that the sharpest-eyed of all — certain of the major hawks, eagles and vultures — can see four to eight times as well as we can, but when compared with other large mammals, man doesn't come off half badly in the eyesight department.

Okay, so we all see pretty well, but why is it some, like our faithful wilderness guide, seem to see so much better than we do? Well, the fact is — they don't. Not

unless we actually have an uncorrected vision problem, that is. The two factors that make our wilderness stalwart *appear* to see better than his city dude hunter are:
1. An aggressive, self-confidence that he *can* see whatever he needs to while the dude, often in strange and even intimidating surroundings, begins to wonder if he — and his eyes — will "measure up."
2. The wilderness native knows what he is looking for. Our eyes are actually an input device constantly feeding data into the computer known as the brain. The brain must then correlate or match up this incoming data with data already stored in its memory banks. The city man simply does not have the rich store of

This would be a good vantage point to do some extended glassing for several reasons. First, a lot of general country is visible so a lot of territory can be covered. Perhaps even more importantly, there is a lot of "edge" area (dividing line between treed and open areas) also visible where game often likes to feed or can just be spotted momentarily as it moves through the area.

Successful glassing for game takes patience and persistence. Here British Columbia outfitter Johnny Holmes shows how it's done by "worming in and settling down" so that he can get comfortable and glass the far slope in a leisurely and effective way. It worked too! About 2 minutes after this picture was snapped a nice band of caribou were spotted near the top right of the picture.

memories that his wilderness counterpart does. The dude may actually be seeing as well or better than his guide but may be unable to match up this input so that his brain knows what he is seeing. The city man is used to looking at entirely different things in differing surroundings and at differing (usually far shorter) distances. His memory bank reflects these differences. The city man might well be better able to read the legend on the speeding subway car or the quickly glimpsed interstate exit sign as he goes whizzing by.

### How to Improve Your Game Spotting Vision

Can the average city man see almost as well as his wilderness counterpart? Yes, most definitely, if he follows this step-by-step program.

### 1. Have Your Vision Checked Annually.

Sounds elementary, eh? Maybe so, but it's amazing how many good hunters take to the field each year with less than adequate vision. Your vision may have unknowingly slipped to 20/30 or even worse. You may have been able to get along fine in the city, in familiar surroundings and with less demand placed on your eyes (20/40 is borderline but usually adequate to drive a car, but these deficiencies will become painfully apparent when you begin placing far heavier demands on your

eyes during the long awaited hunt). Differentiating a small piece of horn or antler from a similarly colored mass of brush or tree limb is one of the tougher things you can ask your eyes to do for you.

Have your vision checked each year before taking to the field. Especially if you're edging up toward 40. Do it in ample time to have your glasses or contact lenses corrected, fitted and then adequately wear tested.

### 2. Buy Quality Hunting Optics.

This is another elementary point that simply can't be overemphasized. Imported cheapies (binoculars or spotting scopes) that are filled with all sorts of optical aberrations even though they "magnify" an image, are just going to give you a headache and insure that the game you're after dies of old age. Optical science is an enormously complex discipline. The production of truly first rate optical instruments, *those that will hold up* under the often difficult field use we hunters must put them to, is one of the more difficult and expensive of industries. Good optics don't come cheap. Spend some time and money selecting and purchasing your hunting optics. (See Chapter 12 for more on this.)

### 3. Be Patient.

The greenhorn thrusts his glasses up to his eyes, swings them back and forth rather rapidly over the

Glassing for game is not only a key element in hunting, but with the right frame of mind, it is challenging and interesting.

Classic sheep hunting scene. The hunter and his guide have climbed up the back of a high ridge and are now glassing sheep on the far slope. One thing's wrong — the guide is obviously using the hunter's binoculars since the hunter is having to use his riflescope, and this is never an effective (or safe) way to spot or size up game.

landscape, sighs and announces that "there's no game here." There may or may not be. But he didn't spend enough time and attention to really find out. Even if there isn't, there may well be something in sight in the next moment or two.

All too often the beginner equates "hunting" with "movement" and does not realize that, as Andy succinctly put it, "Hunting is all-ee time lookin' for game . . . looking, looking, looking." The experienced hand enjoys glassing for game, and he is in no hurry. He takes just pride in his ability to puzzle out pieces of game animals and identify them and then evaluate whether they are worth a stalk. In other words, he *enjoys* glassing. He also realizes that, whether he has been glassing from that same spot for a few minutes or for several hours, the situation can change drastically in the next 10 seconds when a trophy-sized head of game happens to amble out of the tree line where it had been hidden up until then.

### 4. Know What You're Looking For.

Most people who haven't looked over a lot of game invariably expect deer-sized animals to be a good bit larger than they are and moose-sized animals to be considerably smaller. Deer are actually belt buckle height, and looking for them is more like looking for a long legged German shepherd dog or a rather large goat than it is looking for the chest high, pony-sized beast that some imagine them to be. Moose, and elk to a

A game animal that is stationary, even if fairly well exposed, is extremely easy to overlook without the aid of quality optics.

144

(Left) To get the most out of a spotting scope of 20x or higher power, it is almost mandatory to use a tripod or at least a sturdily constructed rest of stones so that the scope may be held vice-steady.

(Below) Many eastern whitetail hunters don't adequately rely on binoculars when hunting. This big Pennsylvania whitetail would be easy to miss in this thicket if the hunter was relying solely on his naked eye.

lesser degree, are enormous animals, and a hunter whose eyes are used to seeing deer-sized game and smaller varmints is simply going to be boggled the first few times he sees a moose in the flesh.

Go to your local zoo and take a look at the animal/s you plan to hunt (or similar sized animals if your particular species aren't in the collection). An even simpler method is to measure off hash marks on a wall or tree showing the shoulder heights of the various animals you are interested in (see Chapters 1 thru 9 for this information).

Realize that 99 times out of 100 you will see a piece of an animal rather than the whole beast. And usually a rather small and misleading piece at that. The hint of a rounded rump protruding from behind some rocks. The tips of a few antler points or a flicking ear tip sticking out from among a tangle of brush.

Check the *pattern* of the background as you glass. Are the hills or folds in the landscape sharp or rounded? Are the trees tall and straight or is the area dotted with brush and short, spreading trees? Is the predominant color green, brown, gray or what? This is the ''stage'' upon which you must spot your quarry.

*About your quarry.* In addition to the general height and size of the animal, what are the other factors you are looking for? If the weather is still rather warmish and insects are out, do you expect to see flicking tails and twitching ears? Do you expect to see white underbellies? What general coloration do you expect to see? If the elk you are looking for is a big bull, then he will generally be a bit blonder (often called "buckskin bulls" by some) than the cows or younger bulls. In some areas the whitetail deer are much more rufous than gray, especially if the weather is still a bit warmish. Old caribou bulls usually (though not always) sport a magnificent white mane that is not only easy to see but also distinguishes them from the cows and younger bulls. If the bucks or bulls are just coming out of velvet, look for those bleached out antlers that they haven't stained yet by horning up the brush. These whitish antlers are very easy to spot but beware — they always make the rack look larger, especially if the animal is in direct sunlight, and the light is coming from behind you.

### 5. Practice *Seeing*.

There's "looking" and there's "seeing" and a world of difference between the two. When in unfamiliar

teresting. You'll be surprised how much it helps, and how quickly you get better at it.

Have a friend plant objects that don't "belong" in an area that you aren't familiar with. And then in one quick scan, try to spot the object (or part object). These non-belongers can be any kind of pick-ups: old tires, cans, bottles, paper, cardboard boxes, etc.

You can invent all sorts of exercises to help train yourself to see better. And you *can* train yourself to see better, make no mistake about that! In the days before World War II, elite Japanese navy fighter pilots used to resort to all sorts of tricks to develop better vision. One of their favorites was to develop better peripheral vision by trying to identify distant objects with a side-wise, snap glance.

Another was to try to discover the brighter stars during daylight hours. This is no mean feat, and without

Successful pronghorn hunting places great emphasis on good game spotting. The trick isn't to find these animals that tend to stay in the open anyway, it's to find them *before* they find you — which means very long-distance game spotting indeed since this is the sharpest-eyed of all North American big game in the author's opinion.

areas, scan the general landscape thoroughly but quickly and then look away. Try to remember what you've seen and describe it to yourself or an observer-friend. What was the "character" of the landscape? How much cover was there, and where and what was it? Where might be the most likely places for game to be bedded down or feeding? Learn to *see*, not just look. It'll help you spot more game, and it'll help you keep from getting lost. Incidentally, though this is a bit laborious at first, with constant practice it becomes second nature and requires no more "work" than the other, lazier approach did.

Practice estimating distances and then pace them off to see how close you were. Do it with a friend and make a mild sort of competition out of it to keep things in-

above-average eyes to begin with, it is virtually impossible to accomplish. However, all of these students were gifted with extraordinary eyesight as a base requirement. With much practice the students would become more adept at their star hunting, and then they would add an additional wrinkle. When they had sighted and fixed the position of a particular star, they would jerk their eyes away 90 degrees and then snap them back to see if they could locate the same star immediately. Of such things are fighter pilots, and superior vision, made.

### 6. Be Aggressive . . . Be Confident.

Though this point overlaps the preceding one a bit, it simply cannot be overemphasized. Scan an area *aggressively,* not passively. Know that you will spot any game that is there (though maybe not on the first few passes).

*Work* at *seeing.* Don't overdo it so that you become fatigued and your eyes begin to water early on. But try to keep a mental "edge" on so that you are positively not passively viewing the landscape and trying to locate game. The man who doesn't expect to see anything usually doesn't.

Be confident. If you think you will locate whatever game there is out there, you usually will. Try to enjoy yourself and don't regard glassing for game as drudgery. Unfortunately, all too many hunters do just that. Glassing for and locating game is one of the basic hunting skills, and any chance to practice it afield is a plus. Besides, you will find yourself spotting all sorts of interesting natural history phenomena, involving other species or non-trophy animals as a part of looking for your game.

## 7. Use Good General Technique.

Keep your eyes moving as you scan an area. It has been proven that small objects tend to disappear or fog up when you strain to see them with a fixed eye. The visual system is a dynamic system, and if you are investigating a particular object, do it by moving the eyes slightly past it and then snapping them back onto it. (There is one exception to this — if you are checking movement then hold your eyes still.) Be aware that the

(Above) One optical quirk in *sizing up* a trophy after you have spotted him is that white animals, such as this Dall sheep, tend to look larger and closer than they are while dark animals such as black bear tend to appear smaller and further away than they actually are.

(Below) Standing up on your hind legs and supporting your glasses unassisted is *not* good technique. These hunters would have been better off to sit or lie prone, or, if that was not advisable because the ground was too marshy or it made for too low a visual angle, to have one hunter hold and steady the most docile mount while the other leaned (lightly) across the saddle to rest his glasses.

Some sort of rest, however informal, is always necessary to properly use a high-powered spotting scope. Here author uses crown of his hat for a quick, informal rest.

If a high-power spotting scope is to be used for extended game spotting rather than used momentarily to size up game that has already been spotted with lower powered binoculars, some sort of secure rest such as this small tripod is absolutely necessary. (Photo courtesy Swift Instruments, Inc.)

tendency is toward eye movement (which is good) when you are stalking and moving, but it is toward keeping the eyes still (bad) when you are on a stand.

Before you ever start glassing an area, scan it thoroughly with the naked eyes. That's right. Sometimes you can locate something much more readily with the naked eye and then "home in" on it with glasses. Also, when you begin looking for game from a particular vantage point, always work from the foreground out rather than the other way around. I know it sounds elementary, but most hunters don't do it that way. I must confess that I have spotted more than one head of game rather close up with the naked eye only after I had intently scanned the far vistas with glasses for sometime and then set my glasses down to rest my eyes momentarily and idly looked around at the nearby landscape.

Use binoculars to look for game. Spotting scopes certainly have their place, but *locating* game isn't one of them, except under highly unusual circumstances. Binoculars afford three dimensional vision while spotting scopes don't. Spotting scopes have a narrow field of view and are tiring to use. Their main purpose is to

size up game after you have located it through the binoculars.

I do not recommend using a riflescope to look for game or to try to make out what a strange object is. For one thing that "strange object" may be another hunter and many, myself included, get downright testy when we find a gun pointed anywhere in our general direction. I don't care if the safety is on, if there is no cartridge in the chamber or even in the gun, or if the bolt is removed, I don't want any guns pointed at me. You probably feel the same way. Besides, riflescopes were not intended to be used to locate game, and they do a rather poor job with their narrow fields of view, low powers (relatively) and lack of three-dimensional viewing.

Try to keep yourself tuned to the right mental pitch which is not nervousness nor complete relaxation but rather a middle area of relaxed alertness. When it becomes fatiguing to maintain this mental "set," put the glasses down for a bit and relax. Better to be "right" when you're glassing and take a few breaks to do it than to keep the glasses up but be using the wrong approach.

Use a rest, or better yet, several rests when glassing an area for an extended period. Standing up to glass is okay but soon becomes tiring as your arms get the wibble-wobbles.

The most common rest is to sit and rest your elbows on your knees. That's fine but vary it a bit. Lie prone if possible and rest your glasses on your hat or a pile of stones or brush. Stand and lean against a tree or rock

Binoculars should always be kept handy, even around camp or where you don't "expect" to see game. This hunter has made it more convenient to keep his glasses with him at all times by informally rigging a strap of elastic to keep them from flopping against his chest when walking or riding horseback.

and rest your arms and glasses. Change your vantage point a bit. Often it helps to move on a couple hundred yards even though you are still glassing the same basic area. Slightly different vistas are presented which may, at best, allow you to see something you could almost but not quite spot before. At a minimum, the change in position provides a tad of variety and eye relief and helps to keep you "fresh."

Vary what you are looking for. If you can't locate any animal parts, then look for anything that doesn't "belong." Often this is the first step toward locating game. That wrong-colored rock may be an animal rump. That funny shaped stick or piece of brush may be an antler. Anything at all that doesn't seem to jibe with the overall color and character of the background may be something that you can eventually resolve into an animal.

Be aware that when seeing conditions are poor — at twilight during a light rain or fog, when there is a haze in the air —*that* is the time to redouble your visual aggressiveness.

When you feel yourself working too hard at trying to make a deer or a sheep out of what's probably a rock, set your glasses down momentarily and look elsewhere. Relax a bit to get the edge back on your vision. Don't completely neglect the object in question as you may miss a momentary flicker of motion which would instantly confirm that it's an animal but move your eyes around a bit and relax mentally before trying again.

Spotting game is a key element in effective hunting and anyone can, with a modest amount of effort, vastly improve their ability to locate and identify game. Besides, it's fun!

# CHAPTER 12

# How To Choose Your Hunting Optics

**ON AN ALASKAN HUNT** some years back it seemed that the luck of the draw had me hunting with a particularly surly native guide. When this fellow found that I had plenty of aspirin in the small medicine kit that I always carry with me into the bush, he started gobbling them up like a kid after his favorite gumdrops.

One sunny afternoon while we were lying beside a sparkling alpine stream and glassing the high meadows for game, I inadvertently picked up his binoculars to check out what later turned out to be only an attractive dun colored rock. They were strictly trading post cheapies; a pair of shoddily made imports that our Nipponese friends would never brag about at trade fairs. I continued to use them for over an hour as the guide took himself a little siesta. A little later I was smitten with a skull cracker of a headache myself, and since I had left the aspirin back in the tent, it'll be a long time before I forget that 8-mile hike back into camp.

That evening it took three pills to chase away the infernal pain in my head. As I sat writing in my journal, sure enough, my friend showed up again for a few pills

If the high-power spotting scope isn't going to be used for extended periods of time without a break, a highly effective "mount" can be improvised such as the author did with his broad brimmed western hat so guide Andy Dennis could take another look at a — highly attractive rock about a mile out!

to tide him through the night. Inspiration struck. I pulled out the spare pair of Zeiss binoculars I happened to have along and suggested that Nick use them tomorrow to "see how he liked them." He did and —*voila!* — no anvil chorus in the head that day or the following night. To make a predictable story short, he used my quality glasses for the rest of the trip and suffered nary another head hurt. In fact, when I left he offered me about everything up to and including the southern half of Alaska for those glasses.

This is a story with several morals. One is that poor quality optics not only degrade your effectiveness in the field, but if used over prolonged periods and under demanding conditions, they can actually cause you pain and discomfort. (The two barrels of these shoddy binoculars were probably out of alignment and thus caused the eyes undue strain as they constantly attempted to force the two images to merge properly into a single, well focused, and perfect circle.) Another is that this kind of severe eyestrain caused by poor quality optics is an insidious thing. It may not strike instantly when one is first using the offending glass, and there may not be anything visually noticeable to the viewer that calls his attention directly to the nature of the problem. He can pick up a comparable pair of high quality glasses and, using them side by side, instantly note that the better pair gives him a far brighter and sharper image. However, this does not necessarily flag him that the bad pair are actually causing him pain.

For the big game hunter it is hard to overemphasize the importance of optics. Binoculars help him to spot and locate game at intermediate to long ranges. They also enable him to keep up with a buddy who is circling around behind the game to drive them his way, or to tell what a friend over on the other ridge is trying to signal. They help him to evaluate, before he wastes a lot of steps and time, whether a particular swamp is negotiable or whether the face of a hill is safely climbable. Good binoculars aid the hunter in plotting the strategy of an extended stalk after game is located. What is the

Even a white animal like this mountain goat can sometimes be very difficult to spot against light colored talus slopes under certain lighting conditions. It took us some time to spot this fellow even though he was out in the open. Quality optics make the difference!

The immensity of good deep wilderness game country is sometimes downright intimidating. Here outfitter Johnny Holmes relaxes on a high cliff that overlooks many miles of the Cassiar Mountains. To properly hunt huge areas like this requires good binoculars and a high quality zoom spotting scope or spotting scope with several different eyepieces ranging in power from perhaps 15 or 20 to 45x or even higher.

best vantage point to try to shoot from? What is the fastest and safest route to get to that point? Good glasses help him to decide from far away before the animal can spot him.

Once in position to shoot, a good riflescope insures more accurate shooting at far longer ranges than was possible years ago even with the finest of peep sights or, worse yet, the often crude open sights that most center-fire factory rifles came "equipped" with. Better yet, a riflescope with its efficient, light gathering powers enables the hunter to confidently and accurately make those early dawn and late dusk shots that would be the sheerest folly without the assistance of *quality* optics. A good riflescope not only makes more accurate shooting technically possible, but it also gives the shooter the *confidence* that often makes the difference on the longer shots. It enables him not to just hit the animal but to hit him in the vitals where clean kills are assured.

The spotting scope, the third leg in the hunter's vital arsenal of optics, is the one that is most neglected, though more and more hunters are coming to recognize its importance. Spotting scopes are helpful in locating game at extremely long ranges, beyond the reach of even the best hand held binoculars. They are also extremely valuable in enabling the hunter to accurately size up the quality of a trophy at intermediate to long ranges. The hunter who tramps several miles, most of it uphill or through other rough terrain, only to discover that there aren't any bucks or bulls in the group of game animals he was stalking (or that they were only yearlings and therefore not what he was looking for while trophy hunting) soon becomes a convert to the fraternity of spotting scope users. Closer to home, the spotting scope can be put to good use at the rifle range, enabling the hunter to score his shooting at 100 yards and further without the awkwardness of always having to leave the benchrest and walk the target. This makes trips to the range more convenient and more enjoyable. Anything that encourages more consistent, year-around rifle practice is going to be a great aid in getting trophies on the wall and meat on the table.

In a moment we'll cover each of these three major categories of hunting optics in more detail, but first it would be of value to explain some general optical terms that apply to all three classes of hunting optics in varying degrees. This will avoid confusion as we go along.

### Optical Terms

*Power:* The magnification of the object is the "power." Thus, an 8x glass magnifies the object eight times larger than the naked eye, making it appear eight times closer. The majority of hunting binoculars range from 7x to 10x in power, while most spotting scopes used for hunting purposes range from 15x to 45x with the occasional model going all the way to 60x. Hunting riflescopes range in power from 1x to 9x for big game use, but specialized scopes on up to 20x and more are sometimes used for long-range, precision shooting of woodchucks, crows, marmots and other pests.

Far too many beginners base their selection of optics primarily on the power, believing that the more power, the more they are getting for their money. Not so! The power of the glass must be selected to best fulfill your needs. Too much power can be as bad or worse than not enough.

The optical design for any particular set of binoculars or scope is, like the design of any other type of tool, a set of compromises. Other things being equal (which they sometimes aren't), the higher the power, the smaller the field of view and the less brilliant the image. Clarity and definition greatly decrease as power increases. In a sense, it is about three times harder to make a 10x binocular that resolves brilliantly and cleanly than it is to make a 7x glass that does the same, even though the former glass is only about half again more powerful, and do it at a salable price in the marketplace.

Another aspect of added power is that the greater magnification also emphasizes any shake involved with hand holding the glasses or any vibration involved with trying to use the optics from a moving car, horse or boat. Many big game hunters can and should use the higher powered optics of various types, but they should select these instruments with great care, realizing that it is far harder to design and build the higher powered glasses than those with the lower magnification. Good glass doesn't come cheap and nowhere more so than at the higher powers.

*Ocular Lens:* This is the lens closest to the eye when the optics are in use, and it is usually the smaller of the two external lenses.

*Objective Lens:* This is the larger lens farthest from the eye when the optics are in use. Binoculars are usually referred to as 7x-35, 7x-50, 8x-32, etc. The first number in the series refers to the power or magnification, and the latter number refers to the diameter of the objective lens in millimeters. The larger the diameter of the objective lens, the greater the light gathering ability.

*Exit Pupil:* The exit pupil of a set of binoculars is the small circle of light that one sees when holding the binoculars at arm's length and pointing toward a bright light. This factor is determined mathematically by dividing the objective lens (in millimeters) by the power of the optic. Thus the exit pupil of a pair of 7x-35mm binoculars is 5 (or 35 divided by 7). If the exit pupil is as large as or larger than the diameter of the eye pupil, then the image received is of normal brightness. If, however, the exit pupil is smaller than the diameter of the eye pupil then the image brightness is diminished.

It is good to bear in mind that the average diameter of an individual's eye pupil during the day is 4 to 4½mm. Thus, a binocular with an exit pupil greater than 5mm would be wasted during average daytime viewing. However, at night an indivdual's pupil expands to 7 to

These Tasco 8 x 20 binoculars are very lightweight at only 7 ounces.

In recent years the 2-7x variable power riflescope has probably become the single most popular type among various categories of big game hunters.

Many hunters, including the author, still prefer the fixed power model spotting scopes with several interchangeable eyepieces of different powers to the zoom models.

(Left) The peerless Leitz Trinovids were the first quality roof prism compact binoculars on the market though there are now many makes. These Leitz glasses are ferociously expensive, but the 10x Trinovid is unrivaled for mountain hunting and the glass that I reach for and use more than any other.

(Below) A recent development in binocular design among several makes has been the lever or "instant focus" type of focusing arrangement rather than the twisting of one or two calibrated dials in order to focus.

7½mm, thus many people whose viewing is largely nocturnal opt for the bulky and heavy 7x-50 binoculars with their very large 7-plus (50mm divided by 7) exit pupil. These large glasses are not recommended for the big game hunter, however.

*Relative Brightness:* This is another optical factor that is derived mathematically. The relative brightness is derived by squaring the exit pupil. Thus, the relative brightness of a pair of 7x-35 binoculars is 25 or the square of the exit pupil of 5 (35 divided by 7). The relative brightness of a pair of 8x-32 binoculars is 16 or the square of the exit pupil of 4 (32 divided by 8).

*Relative Light Efficiency:* This relatively new term reflects the added light transmission efficiency of today's newer, multi-coated optics. This is derived by increasing the basic *Relative Brightness* factor by 50 percent. Thus the *R.L.E.* of the 7x-35mm binoculars cited above is 37.5 or 50 percent more than their brightness factor of 25. Similarly, the *R.L.E.* (for appropriately high quality, well coated optics that is) of the 8x-32mm's is 24 or 50 percent more than their brightness factor of 16.

Some very sophisticated and efficient coating methods can increase the *R.L.E.* an additional 10 percent to 15 percent beyond the standard 50 percent increment over brightness. Proper coating of lenses, both internal and external, greatly decreases internal glare and reflection and significantly increases light transmission. *R.L.E.* is the concept that properly reflects these added efficiencies.

*Field of View:* This is the diameter of the area seen through the optical instrument. Today's modern roof prism binoculars generally offer a substantially wider field of view than did even the best of the Porro prism binoculars of an earlier era. Field of view is particularly important when trying to track with running animals or flying birds. It is also helpful when trying to keep your eye simultaneously on a number of animals fairly widely separated when bedded down or feeding.

*Central Focusing and Individual Focusing:* These two terms apply to binoculars only. Central focusing binoculars are focused by a single knurled wheel (or, in some cases nowadays, a single lever). An adjustable right eyepiece is provided to take into account any differences between the two eyes. These are the most convenient to use and thus the most in-demand type on today's market. Individual focusing binoculars are adjusted for each eye at the eyepiece. Though a bit more awkward to use, they are more moisture proof and sturdy in construction, especially in the Porro prism type binocular.

Here are four high quality compact binoculars actually in use on a British Columbian hunt. (Left to Right) The Leitz, Bushnell, Nikon and Zeiss. The completely waterproof, rubber covered Zeiss binoculars, patterned after the N.A.T.O. tanker's glasses, are particularly durable and interesting.

### Binoculars

Binoculars should be basic equipment with every big game hunter. I am amazed at how many Easterners still take to the deer woods each fall without binoculars. I would feel absolutely undressed doing so. No matter how thick the cover, there are always power line right-of-ways, open ridge tops and farm fields that need to be glassed or glassed across. Even in the thick cover itself, good binoculars help you to decide whether that telltale motion 75 yards out through the thick cover is a squirrel twitching his tail, a small bird hopping around on the branches or a deer flicking its ear impatiently. Especially at dusk or dawn. More binoculars in the field might help to decrease the number of hunting accidents involving both livestock and other hunters.

Up until the early 1960's the basic type of binocular construction for quality glasses was of the Porro prism type. This is the relatively bulky type of binocular with the right angle "knees" jutting out from the ocular lenses. Leitz pioneered the development of the lighter, more compact roof prism binoculars in the 1960's, but now most quality makers offer their own roof prism types. Many quality models of both types of construction are now available on the market, but I generally prefer the roof prism types due to their added compactness and generally wider field of view. (They are also usually a bit more expensive, other things being equal.)

Actually, the main thing is to buy quality glasses in the power that you need. Construction type is secondary to this. For general big game hunting use in the Porro prism type of glass, I prefer the 7x-35mm models,

though I have used 8x glasses and been perfectly happy. For the longer legged needs of mountain hunting I have used 9x-35mm glasses (especially the peerless Bausch & Lomb models of yesteryear), but these are getting rather cumbersome, and they are not the most holdable glasses for extended glassing sessions.

In the roof prism types I prefer the 8x and 10x mod-

This diagram clearly shows why the newer roof prism design is lighter weight (left) and more compact than the older Porro prism design (right). (Photo courtesy Ernst Leitz)

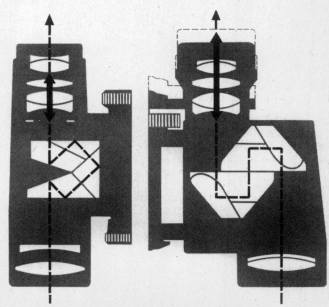

Some Porro prism type binoculars are surprisingly compact and lightweight (in the lower powers) almost rivaling the larger roof prism models in compactness. These 6x Bushnell compacts wouldn't be a good bet for mountain hunting but would do fine for the eastern whitetail deer hunter and double nicely as a stadium type binocular.

els. I started off using the fabulous (and fabulously expensive) Leitz Trinovids in 8x simply because, due to "Porro prism thinking," I simply could not conceive of using 10x glasses effectively in the field. I used the 8x binoculars happily on many successful trips but have since found that the 10x roof prisms are perfectly usable and carryable in the field. And the extra power, *in expensive and high-power glasses*, often comes in handy. Binoculars, in common with most sealed optics, require little or no maintenance. Just keep them out of water and sand.

Though I have both hard and semi-hard cases to carry my binoculars in when traveling or to pack them away in, I always just hang them around my neck without the case — usually tucked inside my shirt or jacket — when actually using them afield. Good binoculars not only make the hunt more productive, they make it far more enjoyable. Is that speck way over there on the dead snag merely a wood formation or is it a majestic golden eagle perched there? Those animals that aren't worth stalking and shooting certainly are worth observing "close up" through good binoculars as they disport themselves in a natural and unalarmed fashion. This makes interesting viewing and teaches one far more about animal behavior, thus ultimately making you a better hunter. It's not a bad idea to carry along a spare pair of binocs on an extended deep wil-

derness trip. Even the best binoculars can get broken, misplaced or stolen, and a backup pair can make all the difference. Besides, binoculars are good for everything from stadium sports to bird watching, and after all, the wife should have a pair, shouldn't she?

### Riflescopes

There is a supposedly authentic anecdote that I haven't personally verified, but I certainly don't doubt that it could happen. Whether it did so or not, I pass it on to you. It speaks volumes about the evolution of today's modern riflescopes from the bulky, fragile and generally cantankerous creations of the 30's and 40's to the sturdy, precision instruments of today.

Supposedly a hapless hunter (out in Oregon, I believe) dropped his scope sighted .30/06 into a fast flowing river, and try as he might, he couldn't fish it out. Over a year later during a lower water stage, the same rifle was found several miles down the river after being washed down along the rocky bottom by the current. The rifle itself was a rusty wreck after over a year of total immersion and all kinds of jostling around on the bottom. The bolt was completely frozen shut. The hunter found that all he needed to do was throughly clean off his scope and it was as good as new! No water leakage, no broken lenses, not even any lenses out of position which would cause vision distortion.

Extra high, "see through" mounts, like trading stamps and short hemlines, seem to be in and out of fashion periodically. The theory is that you can use either iron sights or scope interchangeably. Maybe so but the whole thing has always been rather awkward for me though some seem to swear by this approach. This type of mounting is seen far more frequently in Europe than here by the way. (Photo courtesy W. R. Weaver Company)

Now I'm not guaranteeing that if you toss your favorite scoped up hogleg into the river that your scope will be as lucky — but then again it just might be. I can well remember growing up on a diet of sage gun writing that told us all about selecting and using riflescopes and then conscientiously insured that equal time (more or less) was given to discussion of the best types of iron sights, including various types of bead and ramp front sights and various open and peep rear sights. No more, my friends. If iron sights turn you on, by all means use them. But, for practically any general big game hunting purpose, use of optical sights has become almost universal. Even with the rainbow trajectoried .30-30's and similar shells. Even with guns that inconveniently eject at the top (like the Winchester 94) and thus cause some awkward scope mounting considerations. Even for

longer young, they are a godsend.

In times gone by steel tubed scope sights ruled the field but no more. Now Weaver is one of the few major makers that continues offering quality scopes in these sturdy but somewhat heavier constructions. Most makers have switched to the lighter weight aluminum alloy and duraluminum type tubes, having found them to be adequately rugged for average field use if reasonable care and protection is afforded them by the hunter. (All Oregon hunter stories notwithstanding, any precision optical instrument is breakable and somewhat less indestructible than a pickax and should be cared for accordingly.)

After the iron sight vs. optical sight discussions were largely laid to rest, there was a mini-era of fixed power scope sights vs. variable power sights argumentation.

(Left) Since a riflescope also magnifies the shooter's wobbles as well as the size of the target, the kneeling or sitting position, which is steadier, is preferred to "offhand" or standing up without any support.

(Below) Good, properly fitting and waterproof lense caps are a good idea to protect your expensive riflescope. A fogged or broken scope, at the wrong moment, could cost you a whole expensive hunt, not just the cost of repairing or replacing the scope itself!

guns used in the heaviest of cover for the closest in type of shooting.

The benefits accrued from the use of good riflescopes can hardly be oversold. A prime example is the fact that they enable many older hunters to continue hunting effectively whereas the opposite would be true if those same hunters were using iron sights. One of the basic facts of life about aging is the tricks that begin to be played on our vision beyond the age of 40. Since iron sights must be focused in two planes, and these must then be superimposed on a third plane (the target itself), shooting with iron is at any age and under any condition a less than exact science. Scope sights, since they show cross hairs and target in a single plane, are far easier for all of us to work with, and for those of us with eyes no

The vari-powers were generally cited as being heavier and more expensive (they still are but not overly so) and were called into doubt as being too frangible in general and too subject to leakage by water or moisture. That one's now largely been laid to rest, also. In fact, if memory serves me correctly, our Oregon friend's scope was a quality make 2x-7x vari-power.

I suppose in theory the quality fixed power scopes are still a bit more rugged than their equivalent vari-power brethren, but the latter have never yet let me down, and I've put them to some pretty rugged tests. Moreover, the vari-power tubes do offer the considerable advantage of added flexibility as compared to the fixed power models.

If you are shopping for fixed power scopes, the mod-

# HANDWORK IN MAKING RIFLESCOPE LENSES

Quality riflescopes are one of the biggest bargains, among any type of product, on today's market. Whatever your choice of make or model, it is far lighter, brighter, and stronger and yet costs the same or less than it did 10 or 20 years ago.

Few hunters realize the amount of handwork necessary to produce quality optics. Here riflescope lenses are measured in thousandths of an inch after **(A)** edge grinding and **(B)** polishing and **(C)** in *millionths of an inch* to measure the radius of the curvature of the final lenses (to check its conformity). Photos courtesy of W. R. Weaver Company.

**A.** The lens is measured after edge grinding.

**B.** Surface inspection of the lens element is conducted by Jose Giron immediately after polishing.

**C.** The refracted light method of measuring the radius of curvature uses wavelengths of light from a monochromatic light source. When the test plate is placed over the lens the conformity to radius of curvature can be measured in millionths of an inch.

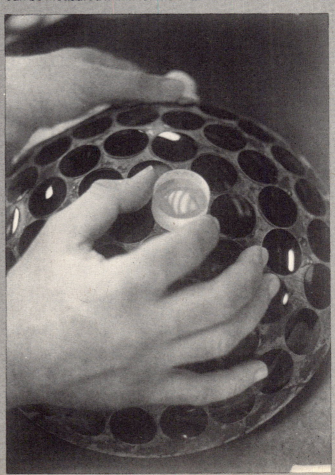

Strange glitches can suddenly appear after an extended trip in even a properly scoped rifle that is as familiar as an old shoe to the hunter. Here author checks his gun upon arrival at base camp for British Columbian hunt even though he had just checked it 3 days earlier — 3,000 miles away and 3,000 feet lower in altitude. It was "on," but it might not have been!

A rigid bridge type top mount is one of the most durable and functional of all riflescope mounts for general hunting usage.

els around 2x to 2½x are generally cited as those best for use in close-in eastern deer hunting situations and other heavy brush hunts. The 4x is usually offered as the "best all-around" model, and the 6x is recommended as best for many mountain hunts, pronghorn hunts or other hunting situations involving long shots in open country. Some do go for the 8x and even 10x fixed models in certain limited and usually non-typical big game hunting circumstances, but these scopes are most often used for long-range varmint hunting.

The vari-power scopes generally fall into four approximate ranges. There are those models offering a "zoom" of from approximately 1x through 3½x to 4x. These are best used in the closer, thicker situations, and they double well for turkey hunting and small game shooting. The most widely used models run roughly 2x to 7x or 2½x to 8x. This scope is almost an ideal compromise between expense and bulk on the one hand and flexibility and usability on the other. If in doubt, it's hard to go wrong with one of these numbers.

The 3x to 9x scope offers a bit more magnification, and since its objective lens is practically always larger than the comparable 2x to 7x model, it offers more brightness and resolving power in the higher magnifications (6x through 9x). However, these larger objective lenses also mean more weight and bulk as well as more expense. Many hunters favoring the newer and hotter shooting magnums opt for this scope over the 2x to 7x. I've used a good 3x to 9x for years on my old standby 7mm Remington Magnum, and it's been an ideal marriage. There is a newer class of 4x to 12x vari-power that is rather large and bulky and very expensive. It has found some favor in very long-range big game hunting situations, but it is more useful for the hunter that feels he must use the same scope for big game hunting and long-range varmint shooting and/or long-range target shooting. There are now some even higher powered vari-power scopes, but these are of no interest to the general big game hunter.

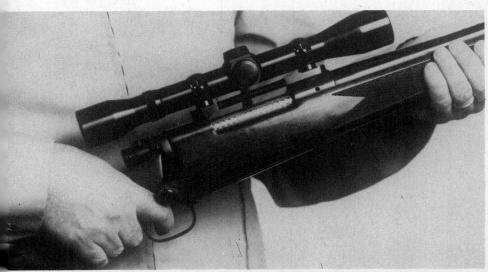

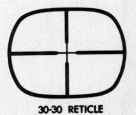

**30-30 RETICLE**

This diagram indicates two developments that have dominated the riflescope reticle picture in recent years — the overwhelming popularity of the "duplex" or tapered cross hair reticle to all other types and the recent emergence of the wider-field or "TV Tube" scope.

159

## Spotting Scopes

These marvelous tools can be a leg saver for the hunter who must decide from a long distance whether a particular head of game is worth going after. They come in both vari-powers and fixed powers with the latter usually offering interchangeable eyepieces in different powers so that the hunter using them has more flexibility than his counterpart with the fixed power riflescope. I have used both and tend to personally prefer the fixed power models with interchangeable eyepieces, but there are many fine vari-powers on the market.

Actually, most spotting scope usage will be at 15x to 20x. The higher powers, especially 40x and above, are very difficult to use under all but ideal conditions, and even then they leave a bit to be desired. The least bit of mirage caused by heat waves, too much wind which makes steadying the scope difficult, or less than the brightest light which makes the higher powers awfully dark cause the higher magnifications to be unacceptable. The vari-powers usually come in 15x-45x ranges on through 20x - 60x ranges. I personally prefer a fixed model with a 15x or 20x ''workhorse eyepiece'' and an additional 25x or 30x eyepiece for those occasions when it's needed and usable. With the lower powers in use, I often just lay the spotting scope across the crown of my wide brimmed western hat, and I find that this makes a perfectly adequate rest on all but the windiest of days.

Two final words on optics — one on safety and the other on quality. First, the safety. Some hunters mistakenly think they can save a buck and try to use their riflescope as a pair of binoculars also. This just doesn't work for several reasons. Their ''binocular'' is just too heavy and awkward for any extended use for one thing. For another the single tube vision doesn't offer the all-important depth perception or ''3-D'' vision of a pair of binoculars, and thus the hunter is much less efficient in being able to properly distinguish game when he sees it. Finally, any hunter who is looking at me over the end of his centerfire rifle has just lost a friend (and maybe a few other things). I don't care if he has his bolt out and lying on the ground, his gun unloaded and the nearest ammo for his cannon is nestling

Zoom spotting scopes have improved so much in quality in recent years that the better makes, such as this Bausch & Lomb 20 to 60x model, are almost the equal of the fixed power models in quality, and the choice between the two has become largely a matter of personal preference.

Spotting scopes, though absolute necessities for mountain hunting, can be awkward to carry and get at easily when needed. Outfitter Johnny Holmes solved the problem neatly with his custom made padded case made of lightweight aluminum that carries his spotting scope, extra eyepieces and small tripod behind his saddle.

160

in a sporting goods emporium in Boise, Idaho. Think about it. I'm sure you feel the same way.

Now, for the quality. It's an oft passed truism that cheapie Brand X optics are "made in the same plant by the same people" as expensive Brand Y optics. One hears this all the time about camera lenses, microscopes and various other glass instruments as well as spotting scopes, binoculars and riflescopes. And, many times, it's true. But, like most truisms, it's only true as far as it goes. It just doesn't go far enough.

Lens design and optical manufacture is still an arcane and recondite science that at times mystifies even the experts. Even under the most controlled of circumstances in lens grinding and instrument assembly, there will be a considerable variation in quality from instrument to instrument. If you are lucky, you may get one of the best of the lot in the "cheapie" model, and it may be almost as good as or even as good as the average of the lot in the expensive line. That may happen.

Chances are it won't.

The extra price tag tacked onto the expensive line means that these instruments are inspected more often, more intensively and that they must cleave to a higher standard to be accepted as salable. If not, they are junked or sold to some other cheapie line for distribution under another name. When you pay more money, that is usually your assurance of more uniform and higher quality, from scope to scope or binocular to binocular. If the manufacturer is to reject more pieces in order to maintain higher standards, then that must inevitably be reflected in higher prices at the sales counter. But, it's well worth it to you, the hunter, to spend the few extra bucks. An optical instrument that is used for 10, 20 or more years is cheap indeed on a per year basis even if it is the highest priced there is. And it won't let you down just when you need it so desperately on that lonely mountaintop with the trophy of a lifetime in your sights.

The design and manufacture of precision riflescope lenses is a demanding business with absolute emphasis on quality control. (Photo courtesy W. R. Weaver Company)

# CHAPTER 13

# The Big Game Hunter's Knife

**THE FIRST GRIZZLY** I ever killed was instructive in several ways. The particular lesson that will probably remain with me the longest of all is that it demonstrated to me, in a fashion that no amount of writing or reading about it could, the difference in having at hand a good knife and a bad knife. Bear are rather rotund citizens, especially when the living is good and they are fattening up for the winter as was this late September British Columbian grizzly.

As we began peeling the hide off, we found him literally swathed in layers of milky white fat, ranging from 1/2-inch to over 2 inches deep. We could have rendered more lard out of that guy than from a prize winning 4-H bacon hog! I quickly noted that the soft bladed, indifferent quality folder that I had with me that day was requiring about 15 swipes against the whetstone for every five swipes against *arctos'* hide to keep me halfway in business.

The bear had fallen in an overgrown spot that made working on him difficult, and as the morning dragged on, Larry and I found it brutally tough work to get that hide off. If the old pearl about the *work* of a deer hunt

Here custom knife maker Tommy Lee of Gaffney, South Carolina, uses one of his creations to skin out his own deer. A fine custom knife offers certain owner satisfactions that even the very best off-the-shelf models can't quite match.

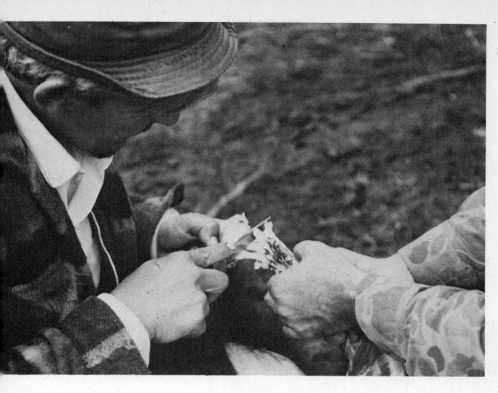

A sharply honed folding hunter excels in "close work" such as skinning out the foot of this wolverine for a full rug mount.

The classic older design of the two-blade folder, though still popular, seems to be giving ground to the one blade, locking-blade folder. (Photo courtesy of W.R. Case Company)

beginning after the buck is down is true, it's doubly true about bear hunts! Bear fat will dull the edge of the best of knives in remarkably short order. With poorer grade cutlery, such as the knife I happened to have along, the way the edge degrades has to be seen to be believed.

Finally we got that green hide off. With the head and feet still in and rough fleshed as badly as we did it, the thing weighed a bit over 200 pounds. Done properly it should have weighed hardly half that. I'll never forget the memorable tramp back. We had about 7 miles to go. For a while we'd try making our way through the almost impenetrable willows and alder and then find us a creek to follow. After trying to leap from wet stone to wet stone like an overloaded chamois and falling dangerously several times in the process, we'd then seek the safer but more tiring underbrush route again. Back and forth we alternated, switching the wet, balled up hide from one of us to the other. The other would "take it easy" carrying both rifles and all our other gear on his pack frame. On that trip I made a fervent vow that never would I be caught in the bush again with an inferior knife and that never would I be a party to such a bad skinning job again, even if I had to work all night getting the hide off right the first time.

Even after we got back to camp (well after dark that night), the fun still wasn't over. I spent a long day the following day, "manicuring" and fine fleshing that

blasted hide. Nothing will make a hide go hair-slipped* like leaving little pieces of suet adhering here and there, especially on bear hides. And, once any cape or hide does start to slip, there is no way to save it. So, I fumed and cursed and painstakingly sliced off little slivers (and big ones too) of fat all day long. No matter how awkwardly placed the animal is when it falls, it is at least five times easier to skin the hide off right to begin with — while the hide is still fresh, the animal still supple and

---

*Rotting of an animal hide caused by improper skinning and resulting in the eventual loss of hide hair.

Though every knife book, manual and article since the invention of the printing press and paper solemnly tells the reader that knives should never-ever be used to pry, poke or prod but only to cut, I'm here to tell you that, if you do much hunting and serious field work, you're inevitably going to find it necessary to occasionally break these sacred rules one and all. Here, Andy Dennis is poking out the remaining cranial matter and meat after sawing the author's big caribou antlers off skull of animal. The trick, when breaking these rules, is to *know* you're doing it and to be careful. Having a fine knife that's up to heavy-duty use doesn't hurt either!

On a custom folder, such as this one by Tommy Lee, the customer can specify the type and degree of engraving or other ornamentation that he may prefer — depending on how much money he has to spend and how distinctively different and "one-of-a-kind" he wants his knife to be.

warm and the hide still attached to the animal so that there is resistance to skin against — than it is to re-skin it later with the hide already off and starting to dry.

I have always been a bit of a knife nut and usually keep a couple of dozen around for this purpose or that. My temporary aberration in having that bad blade with me that day was due to an oddball set of circumstances that doesn't bear going into here. Suffice to say that Larry's oldest boy inherited a pocketknife as a "gift" that very day.

Nor do I think I'm at all unusual in having, using and experimenting with (some dastardly folks have used the term "playing with") a goodly number of edged instruments. That's actually pretty common among big game hunters for any number of reasons.

First is that, simply and bluntly, few if any of man's tools have the raw *sex appeal* that emanates from fine knives. To see a gleaming, artfully curved blade crowned by a beautiful yet sturdy handle is to gaze at an art object that changing fashion will never dim. Ultimate functionality is never out of fashion. To test the keenness of a well honed and stropped edge is to commune, however briefly, with some of man's most primeval instincts. Fine knives were being crafted many centuries before guns and gunpowder were a gleam in the Oriental eye. Quite simply — a fine knife is the *essence* of hunting, distilled and compressed into a bare few inches and ounces.

Secondly, is the fact that a hunter needs a good knife (or, if you agree with me, several good knives) for so many purposes. Sure, skinning and dressing game or fish is the first task that pops to mind, but truth be told, the hunter will put his knife to other uses far more often than he will use it on game even on the most successful of hunts. Slicing bread, pies and other kitchen goodies, whittling fuzz sticks to start fires, or just whittling to while away an idle rainy day hour in camp, cutting canvas or leather to mend tentage, clothing, saddlery or tack and myriads of other utility uses that demand the attention of the hunter's blade seem to constantly pop up. A good knife is often instrumental in keeping the hunter safe and effective in the field so he can get his game as well as in being crucial to the care of that game once he does get it.

Any good hunting blade, of whatever size or type, should be kept *sharp* and that means sessions with the whetstone every day you're in the field if you're using it every day (as you most likely are).

A third reason is that, amazingly enough for such a basic (I didn't say simple) tool, there has been a product revolution since the mid-60's, rivaling anything that has happened in the firearms and ammunition fields. Time was that, with a few limited exceptions, most off-the-shelf hunting knives were depressingly similar in both design and manufacture. Practically all were fixed blade models with few medium large to large folders available, and none of the latter ever seemed to have the highly desirable feature of a locking blade. There was a rather short range of quality level knives with most of these off-the-shelfers being of relatively indifferent quality. Though this was partly because certain advances in metallurgy and tooling were still to come, the primary reason for it was a massive amount of incorrect thinking in the cutlery industry about how much sportsmen would pay for good knives.

Up until the late 1950's there weren't many custom knife men around. Old timer R. H. Ruana out in Bonner, Montana, was making a very inexpensive line of knives that weren't as finely detailed and finished as many custom blades but were (and still are) magnificent values for the money. A small skinner that I had him make up for me some years ago remains as one of my prized possessions. As I remember, I got a goodly

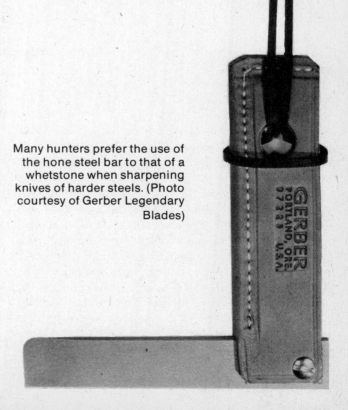

Many hunters prefer the use of the hone steel bar to that of a whetstone when sharpening knives of harder steels. (Photo courtesy of Gerber Legendary Blades)

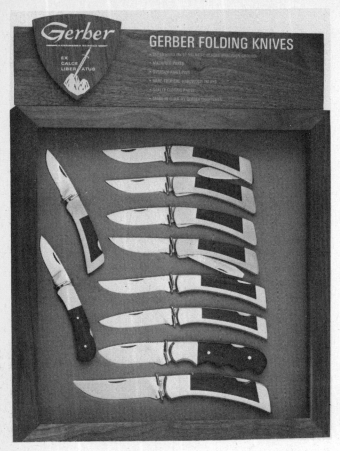

The better off-the-shelf makers have discovered the popularity of the expensive, relatively heavy-duty folding hunting knife among today's big game hunters. Here's a look at the rather complete line of Gerber folding hunters, with a knife to fit most any conceivable hunting need.

A fine custom knife with the handle fashioned from a piece of Dall sheep horn that the customer himself picked up in Alaska while on a hunt. (Knife and photo by Tommy Lee)

amount of change back from a $10 bill when I paid for it at the time.

"Bo" Randall started making elegantly beautiful knives down in Orlando, Florida, in the 30's, and he gained quite a bit of renown with his combat models during World War II and the Korean fracas. Many were the stories circulating around about servicemen cutting escape doors through the sides of helicopters while angry little men were shooting at them. These and similar incidents were often true, and there are many men alive today who owe that state of existence to their expensively crafted custom combat knives. In the 50's and especially in the 60's a new generation of custom knifesmiths, led by such men as Bob Loveless, broke new ground in the use of certain steels and in the offering of a wider variety of designs.

There are a couple hundred custom knife makers around who are full-time professionals nowadays. This is a far cry from the handful of craftsmen operating in the field a generation ago. These men and their advanced design thinking and extreme emphasis on quality have, in turn, spurred many off-the-shelf houses to come out with their own premier grade lines of hunting knives that are excellent in quality and far higher in price than these makers would have thought the market would absorb as recently as 10 years ago. Now, in the field of cutlery as well as those of firearms, ammunition, clothing and other gear the hunter has an abundant range of choice, and the ill-bladed hunter of today has only himself to blame. There is ample choice in both quality and design among both stock models and custom knives to satisfy any field need.

### Knife Design

The first argument about the "good big knife vs. the good little knife" undoubtedly occurred in some dim cave thousands of years before the iron age even began. Few subjects can cause as many heated arguments among equally well informed sportsmen as can knife design. A knife is such a *personal* thing. Rather than making grand pronouncements on this booby-trapped subject, perhaps I can just tell you what works best for me and why.

I currently have between 20 and 30 knives lying around with about half of them being custom blades and the other half quality factory models. Both fixed blades and folders are represented, and blade lengths range from 2 inches to a bit over 6 inches. Various sorts of steels are involved from straight carbon steel through "semi-stainless" on to the straight stain resistant types like 440-C. Blade shapes range from straight bladed/raised point "small game" models through deep bellied/raised point skinners to dropped point/semi-curve bladed "all-arounders." Over the years I have used most all of these to one degree or another.

Most of the time I will use a folding knife with a blade running around 3 to 4 inches in length, a medium dropped point and a mild curve in the cutting edge of the blade. That doesn't mean I don't use the other models as my needs and moods vary. But this is the type of knife that gets the nod more than any other.

Here's why. I like the compactness of the folder. Though still bulky enough so that, in most cases, I still must wear them on a belt sheath rather than in my pocket, they don't tend to poke and prod when sitting in the saddle or on the ground as a longer, fixed bladed model often does. I've found that the awkwardness of the longer knives can be reduced by wearing them "cross draw" on the belt (right-hand scabbard worn on left side at angle with blade edge forward). However, they are still longer and heavier than the folders.

Except for specialized skinning work (and that should be handled with a special second knife), the basic hunter's knife should always have a dropped point. A dropped point design gets that point down where the work is and therefore does half the work for the sportsman. The hunter using a fully raised point knife must labor mightily and practically break his wrists in the process. Sure, there are times when fully raised point designs and longer blades come in handy, but they are strictly secondary. As Tommy Lee, of Gaffney, South Carolina, and one of the finest of the younger custom knife makers now at work says: "The difference between using a dropped point blade and a raised point blade in the field is the difference between farming with a tractor and farming with a mule." Although many of his designs are picked up by collectors, Tommy still caters primarily to the discriminating field user, and hundreds of his blades are in use throughout the world today. He knows what he's talking about.

If "animated discussions" about knife design have been the mode of the day for hundreds of years, no aspect of that issue is as burning as knife size — or more

I takes a good sharp knife to skin out small, thin-hide trophies like this wolverine. It is much easier to slip and "ding" or put holes in this hide than in the far thicker heavier cape of an elk or moose or even a deer.

Some off-the-shelf makers offer magnificent quality at astonishingly cheap prices. This Schrade-Walden "sharp finger" knife isn't cheap but considering that it is almost entirely handmade, the price is modest indeed.

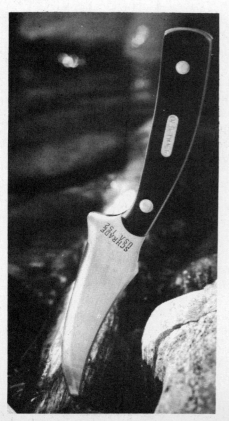

"Do as I say, not as I do." Here author gets caught short and finds it necessary to hack off a chunk of frozen moose meat for cooking. A heinous task to put a sharply honed blade to, but if you're hungry after a 20-mile horse ride in a driving snowstorm and this is all that's in sight to eat, it doesn't seem such a sin!

specifically, blade size. Different sizes come in handy for different uses. Very small 2-inch to 2½-inch round bellied blades are handy for the man that must do a lot of demanding, fine fleshing on heads to skin them out for trophy mounts. Blades of around 6 inches can come in handy in heavyweight knives that must, of necessity, occasionally be used for those basic Knife-No-No's: chopping, hacking and prying. And you can bet that if you spend a lot of time afield and particularly if some portion of it is heavy-duty deep wilderness work, you are going to find yourself occasionally in those situations where you must do things with your knife that the book says not to.

Day in and day out the ideal blade size probably runs 3½ inches to 4 inches. That's big enough to slice and butcher any game on this side of the water and small enough to be easily portable and to serve well in the kitchen or the tent for those equally important but finer toned cutting chores. The big folders usually feature blades in this size range and with the desired medium-dropped point. The folders are available in both stainless steel and non-stainless with Buck offering models using a steel that seems about halfway between the two. The trend seems to be toward the stainless variety. However, on factory models anyway, I prefer the non-stainless types. They take an edge much easier and

seem to hold it at least as well.

The only time I opt for stainless type factory blades is for sustained use around salt water. Actually, there is no such thing as the perfect all-around knife just as there is no perfect all-round rifle, vehicle, bird dog or anything else of note. The best thing to do is to try several types and see what works best for you. That way you'll be equipped to meet varying situations, and besides, you'll have the fun of owning, experimenting with and using several different fine knives!

## Custom vs. Quality Factory Knives

This is an interesting question to put it mildly. The answer is no longer as clear cut as it might have been a few years back. Factory lines from such quality makes as Buck, Gerber, Schrade-Walden and others offer a wide variety of sizes, designs, types and price ranges. Some very good knives indeed are being made and sold off the shelf in this country. Figure on paying around $20 to $50 for good factory folders and that much or more for good fixed blades, depending upon how much extra "chrome" ("presentation cases," "commemorative" interest, limited engraving, etc.) that you may be picking up the freight for on the latter.

Custom knives cost more, there's no doubt about it. But they offer added advantages. They can be designed, or at least altered a bit here and there in such features as handle material, hilt design and material, finger grooves in the handle and a variety of other "customized" fine points.

The maker's name is usually engraved on the knife blade, and it is standard procedure to get your own name engraved on the other side of the blade. This helps identify the knife and protect it from loss or theft. These nice little touches add to the pride of ownership. And the quality of the better custom jobs is superlative. If, like most, you delight in owning beautiful and useful items, items that are handmade and created with an artist's eye, then an expensive custom hunting knife is one of the biggest bargains around.

Folders, which actually cost more to make (other things being equal), are usually priced at $100 and up. With special adornment, this can double and triple easily. Fixed blades start around $75 and go on up to about $200. With a few exceptions if you are paying much over $200, then you are generally buying a collector's item rather than a field-use item. With some careful shopping around you should be able to find just the knife to fit your needs and one that will delight the eye and the hand for the rest of your lifetime — and then for the lifetime of your son and his son — for around $100 or so. Divided on a per year basis, that's a cheap investment indeed. And, if one wants to approach this strictly on a crass commercial basis, any really first rate knife made by a quality custom man is going to appreciate far faster than the general inflation, so that a few years after the purchase you can usually sell one of these items for far more than you paid for it. A good investment in the strictest sense of the term.

## Maintaining Your Knives

Good knives need little care. The primary thing is not to store your knife inside its leather sheath for months at a time. Leather contains certain oils and acids that can, over a long period of time, discolor your blade. When you have finished using your knife, wipe it clean and dry. Avoid using water unless you have had it in salt water or unless it is absolutely necessary to clean the knife. Water can help to corrode non-stainless blades if only wiped off casually. When using a folder, use another knife blade or other sharply pointed object to pick out any scale, or grit that inevitably becomes lodged inside the knife or at the head of the blade.

Keep your knives sharp. The dull knife *is* the dangerous knife — the one that you cut yourself with. Set up the initial edge when you get the knife and then keep it sharp. When using the knife, hit it a few licks with the stone every now and then even if it really doesn't drastically "need" it. It's far easier to keep a knife sharp than it is to start with a dull blade and sharpen it from scratch — especially with some of the super-hard steels now in use on the more expensive knives.

# CHAPTER 14

# Choosing And Using The Right Clothing And Duffle

**A SKILLED CRAFTSMAN** is known by his tool box and the assortment of items inside. A knowing eye can quickly survey the contents of that box and tell much about its owner. The tools that are (and aren't) inside, their condition, age and brand names and even how effectively and neatly they are stored within the tool chest all team up to tell a story about how experienced the craftsman is, what his specialities are and how much pride he takes in his work — in short, *how effective* he is at his job.

And so it is when a seasoned hand scans another hunter, quickly noting and appraising his clothes and duffle. What the hunter is wearing and what he pulls out of his kit bag, how old these items are and of what quality they are as well as how well maintained the lot is, all add together to tell much about the owner. How much of this clothing and duffle there is, how well it has been selected for the particular hunt and how well it's packed round out the story.

A well made, heavy-duty down coat is expensive but well worth the money. When covered by a rain suit to meet wet conditions, it is the big game hunter's most basic line of defense'' in maintaining comfort and efficiency in the field under difficult conditions. A wide brimmed western type hat is also good for windy, open country. (Photo courtesy Browning Company)

Clothes have become largely ornamental for most of us in today's urban society. Near total climate control in the buildings where we spend most of our waking hours has ushered out the era of markedly differing summer and winter wardrobes. Now it is generally warmer in the winter in these halls of commerce and industry than it is in the summer months, and the 10-month-a-year business suit has come into its own for men. The difference between summer and winter clothes is now more often one of color and cut (fashion) than of weight or warmth (function).

Not so with the big game hunter. Your clothes play a vital role in how effective you will be. They are utilitarian in the most basic sense, and whatever "fashion" there is in serious outdoor clothing (and I contend that there is, in a sense) is derived from how well designed and made they are to perform certain *functional* roles and how well chosen they are for a particular situation. Fashion in outdoor clothing is determined solely by these down-to-earth criteria and not by any abstract "creativity," based almost completely on the "look" of the clothing, of a far removed designer.

It's a fact of life that most of us weren't born rich. Sad but true. Thus, we're usually not able to buy all or even most of a quality outdoor wardrobe at once. Rather, we must painstakingly accumulate our treasured gear over a period of time, often several years. Knowing what to buy first and when to concentrate on only the very highest quality and when temporary substitutes of middle-level quality are allowable can save you both discomfort in the field and money in the pocket.

So, we'll approach our coverage of outdoor clothing and duffle in just that fashion. However, before outlining the basic outfit for a general big game hunter, we need to discuss the various types of materials used and their insulating properties since these considerations will touch, in a general way, upon most every item on our general checklist. Then we'll return to talk about the specific items on the checklist itself.

## Insulating Properties of Varying Materials

Insulation is there to keep you warm, dry and well cushioned. Though these three important characteristics are listed in rough order of importance, the relative weighting of each of the three varies a bit depending upon what item we are considering (underwear vs. shirts vs. jackets vs. sleeping bags, etc.) and what type of hunting we are doing (desert big game hunting is obviously less concerned with keeping the hunter dry).

In turn, the efficiency of any insulation is roughly determined by its ability to create and sustain a thick layer of non-conducting still air. Some of the newer synthetics are approaching even in some respects surpassing down, but to date the right kind of top grade northern goose down still ranks as the best all-around insulation material for the outdoorsman in most (not all)

Camouflage suits, where allowed by law, are often very effective. Since big game animals are literally color blind, more manufacturers should offer camo items in such colors as Day-Glo orange. This would break up the hunter's outline in the eyes of the game and yet provide the safety factor of bright colors visible to human eyes. (Photo courtesy Eddie Bauer, Inc.)

situations. This kind of down is the warmest, lightest insulating material known to man — and the most expensive.

Down is a natural miracle in its ability to create this thick layer of dead air and still "breathe." This means that though it traps the dead air for warmth it still allows your worst enemy, your own body moisture, to efficiently pass or "wick" through to the outside. This also means that the all-important comfort *range* of down is far wider than most other materials.

The same down sleeping bag that can carry you to 20 degrees below zero (Fahrenheit) should, with a bit of judicious venting by unzipping the closure to one degree or another, be comfortable when it's 50 degrees warmer. This gives you tremendous flexibility since radical swings in temperature, or more importantly, *apparent* temperature (where added wind and moisture team to make it much "colder" than the thermometer may indicate) are the norm in the outdoors. Especially if you are "living close to the ground" as you will do on most all backpacking and do-it-yourself hunts that don't offer any expensive frills.

Also, the best grade of down has a fantastic ability to be compressed to almost nothing and then spring back to its full loft (or full effectiveness). This means that you can compress your down gear, especially that bulky

Since feathers and down do have some disadvantages, I would usually choose the best synthetics to these pig-in-a-poke situations. Feathers and down do absorb water readily, and once thoroughly wetted, they lose almost 100 percent of their effectiveness. Wet down is not only useless, it will make you cold. Good synthetics are far more efficient when wet, though they too lose much of their effectiveness. Also, down and feathers require special and expensive types of construction if their full effectiveness is to be properly utilized in sleeping bags or clothing. Down can easily mat together if not compartmentalized internally within the item in some fashion. This matting results in "cold spots" and uneven cushioning. The tiny little down

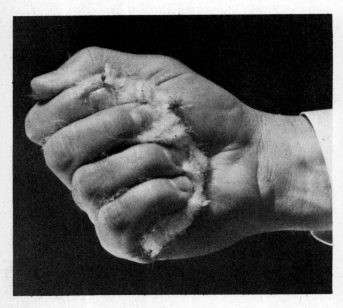

Down is still the most efficient of all insulators. The enormous compressibility or "loft" of down is responsible for this. (Handful of down (above) expands to amount shown in photo on right when not compressed.) (Photos courtesy of Eddie Bauer, Inc.)

sleeping bag, down to much more "carryable" proportions by the use of "stuff sacks" into which you cram the item. Best of all, down has practically no "memory" and thus never seems to lose its ability to spring back to its full loft. (After many years of use however, it may take a bit longer to reassume its full loft when unpacked after extended periods of compression.)

There are several grades of down and other feather-type insulating materials. Lowest in the pecking order and, in my judgment, not as effective as today's best synthetics are items variously labeled as "waterfowl feathers" and "duck feathers." This labeling does not identify the type of fowl, the type of feathers (except you can bet that they aren't down!) nor when the bird was plucked or whether it was a northern or southern bird.

plumes show an absolute genius at being able to pierce through outer coverings and then work their way through the smallest of pinholes. Feathers are also harder to contain than the more uniform and controllable man-made insulating materials.

Next up the line in both effectiveness and expense is a mixture of feathers and down. Here again, the exact and specific nature of the feathers is seldom volunteered nor is that of the down. The ratio of the mix is important. An item made of 60 percent down/40 percent feathers is, other things being equal, better than one with the proportions reversed. The choice between this bag or garment and the one made of best quality synthetics is less clear. Costs of the two must be considered as well as the exact nature of the ratio (feathers to down) and the general workmanship that is evident in

Down items can be compressed, through the use of a "stuff sack" into very small areas. The bag this man is carrying on his belt actually contains a fairly substantial light down jacket. (Photo courtesy Browning Company)

the two items. More and more, though, I tend to lean toward the better grade synthetics.

The best type, and the kind I use and recommend strongly to you, is a bag or garment made of "prime northern goose down." Why? Well, *down* is best because these ultra-light, soft feathers are the most efficient on the bird. They come from his breast, the part that comes into direct contact with that icy winter water so they have to be the most efficient.

This down should be *goose* down because their down is simply more efficient than comparable quality duck down (more individual feather filaments, something over two million of them to the ounce of down, in fact!). The down should be *prime* because that indicates the best grade of *winter plucked* down. This is far and away better than would be plucked from the same birds in the spring or summer. It should be *northern* down because these cold country birds grow much better down than do their cousins living in warmer climes. Thus, the best quality of all is *100 percent prime northern goose down.*

All of these desirable features combine to make this the most expensive insulating material now available. I do look for the better grades of synthetic materials to continually improve, so that under the impetus of "space age" technology, they will eventually equal and then surpass the best down in all-around effectiveness. Undoubtedly these synthetics will be a bit less expensive, too, as there is a limited quantity of the best grade down available to the world markets. (This down comes from domestic geese, by the way, and not wild geese which have been shot.) Right now the nod goes to down, and since I'm a bit of a romantic, I'm sort of glad.

Down is used most often in sleeping bags or the

One of the great advantages of down clothing is that not only is it very warm for its weight but it has the widest comfort range of any insulating material by far. The fact that very heavy-duty down parkas such as this one, capable of taking the wearer down well below zero, are relatively comfortable in weather 25 to 35 degrees Fahrenheit is remarkable and extremely useful. (Photo courtesy Woolrich)

rather bulky, heavy-duty outer jacket. There is also increasing use of down in an item that I highly recommend — the lightweight down "sweater" which is more of an inner or mid-layer clothing item, though it can be impressed into duty as the outer jacket in mild weather or for short exposures.

Other materials are more commonly used for such things as shirts, sweaters, trousers and socks. Wool has its advantages and disadvantages. Chief among the former is the fact that of all the insulators it is by far the most efficient when wet. It is possible to remain warm in good quality wool even when quite wet if the conditions are not too extreme. This is very difficult to almost impossible with any other material if the exposure is extended — even in weather that is almost balmy if the least amount of wind is blowing.

Wool's chief disadvantage is that it is very heavy and

not usually recommended. However, some of the wool and synthetic blends do work quite well for specific uses. Note any small print quite carefully on the tags, ads or promotional material accompanying wool garments. Some of the copy explaining that this is actually a wool *blend* is set quite small and very easy to miss. A final potential disadvantage to wool for some is the fact that it is "itchy-scrathcy" to them, and they have a skin reaction that is unpleasant. This occurs far less frequently with the best quality new wool than with wool that it is "itchy-scratchy" to them, and they have a skin of predominantly wool and best grade synthetics are completely free of this bothersome side effect for those prone to it.

Cotton is used in a multitude of ways for hunting garments, and it serves quite well in some cases and less so in others. In a general way cotton is light, cool,

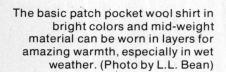

The basic patch pocket wool shirt in bright colors and mid-weight material can be worn in layers for amazing warmth, especially in wet weather. (Photo by L.L. Bean)

bulky. It takes up far more space to pack in the duffle bag than the highly compressible down, and it is considerably heavier to wear around than down. Its comfort range, though respectable, is nothing like down's and under dry conditions, it is not as warm. One major advantage to wool outer garments that the big game hunter particularly appreciates is that it is "quiet." When stalking through heavy cover, cotton is quite noisy and the various types of nylon outer facings usually used on down garments are positive screamers. Wool is very quiet and very briar resistant.

There are several grades of wool, also. The best grades of all new wool are also quite expensive, and the proper type of quality sewing and construction to hold this heavy material in place throughout years of heavy-duty use afield also adds to the cost of the garments. The various wool/reprocessed wool blends are

relatively inexpensive and, in the case of denim type materials, wears quite well. It does not add much warmth; it is not efficient when wet; and it is "noisy" in thick cover. It is not briar or stick resistant, giving the wearer little or no cushioning effect depending upon the exact nature of the garment being considered.

Cotton does not do a good job of "sopping up" such field filth as mud and blood. This type of grime can be much more readily absorbed by wool with less loss of insulating effectiveness. Wool is also easier to clean by brushing off after dry, whereas cotton, if really begrimmed, must usually be washed thoroughly.

The various synthetics like Dacron and Fiberfill and others can be rated in efficiency generally by reading the manufacturer's material accompanying the garments and also by that ultimate yardstick of price. Quality costs money.

## Basic Clothing and Duffle Outfit

Now back to that basic list of clothing and duffle for the big game hunter. This is a skeleton list that would need to be fleshed out for any special purpose trip, but by and large, if the hunter is properly outfitted with all the items included on this list, he will be able to handle about 95 percent of the hunting situations that he will run into in North America from a weekend in an eastern whitetail deer camp to a 2- or 3-week deep wilderness mixed game hunt. I have listed the following items in rough order of importance here. Obviously this is somewhat arbitrary in spots as a hunter must have trousers as well as shirts or socks, so listing one as "more important" than another is only a relative undertaking and not an absolute. However, this approach will let me emphasize certain aspects that do help to establish a rough priority to which things you buy first or buy in only best quality.

Here's the basic outfit for the generalized big game hunter:

1. Heavy-duty sleeping bag and mattress
2. Heavy-duty leather boots for climbing and rough country work
3. Insulated rubber boots for cold country work and wet weather going (in some cases the combination leather/rubber "pacs" can be substituted here)
4. Rainwear
5. Sturdy walking shoes for camp wear and less arduous tramping
6. Jacket
7. Shirts and sweaters
8. Trousers
9. Headgear
10. Underwear
11. Socks
12. Gloves and mittens
13. Belt and suspenders
14. Duffle bag (to carry everything else around in)

That's the basic stripped-down assortment of items you will need. Selected well, this outfit will see you through the worst conditions that North America has to offer with the exception of the most extreme Arctic and desert situations. All these items are indispensable at one time or another. But, like the old Philadelphia dowager who was all for democracy said, "I just want to be a bit *more* democratic than the others," some of these items can be even more critical than others at times.

First, a parenthetical general comment that I have made elsewhere in this book but one that simply can not be overemphasized. It's always a good idea to buy the best quality outdoor items of any type that you can afford. You'll be more comfortable and effective afield, and the difference between good and bad quality could

(Above and Below) Quality insulated clothing, whether fashioned of down or the better synthetics, demands clean and well organized work rooms and skilled labor. All of which adds to the costs. But, if taken care of, these items last for many years and — most importantly — they don't let you down under tough field conditions when you most need them! (Photos courtesy Eddie Bauer, Inc.)

even, in some cases, mean the difference between life and death. Also, most outdoor types are pretty practical and down-to-earth people. It's simply cheaper, in the long run, to buy first rate gear that lasts a lifetime rather than cheap shoddy gear which may look good on the store shelf but falls apart the first time or two that you put it to a severe test. And, invariably, this is when you need it most.

### 1. Sleeping Bag and Mattress:

I put these two items at the top of the list, because if you can't sleep, you can't hunt. It's just that simple. Big game hunting, even at its most relaxed, is a strenuous undertaking, and a good night's rest is critical. You might even say that there is a "misery scale" that hunters should be fully aware of. You can hunt for surprisingly long periods when you are hungry, thirsty or wet and generally uncomfortable (if you're in good general physical condition). Take away that good night's rest though, which is so necessary to rebuild the tissue destroyed in a hard day afield, and in 1 or 2 days you'll fold up like a cheap accordion.

Expect to pay from $75 to $200 for a really good lifetime sleeping bag depending upon what insulation you buy, what construction and cut the bag is, and where you buy it. The better synthetics run in the lower half of that price range (for a bag that can take you down almost to zero) while the better down bags run in the upper half. But, when you pay $150 for a bag and use it for 25 years and then pass it on to your children for use, it doesn't seem quite so expensive. And, many of these bags can be pressed into double duty to serve as lap robes in the winter stadium while attending football games or other events, or to serve as extra coverlets thrown over the bed at home or at the weekend cabin during cold snaps.

The shape of the bag is a matter of individual prefer-

A down mummy bag is lighter, more compact and warmer than its equivalent square ended, rectangular shaped bag and is the author's personal favorite among types of sleeping bags.

ence. Many claim that they must have the freedom and leg room of the larger, square cornered rectangular bags in order to sleep well. This means the bag will be bulkier, heavier and more expensive than some other, more compact cuts and constructions. At the other end of the spectrum is the "mummy" bag which is a cocoon shaped, tubular bag which allows less room to turn around in but is warmer and cheaper for the same weight and bulk. In between these two extremes some leading manufacturers have been offering in recent years a compromise "trim line" shape where the bag tapers a bit at both ends but does offer squared off corners and a bit more room (and weight and expense) than the mummy bag.

Fortunately, after a tough day's hunting and climbing, I usually sleep a bit sounder than a poleaxed steer. Therefore, I use the mummy type bag. This is handy since I also do a good bit of backpacking and do-it-yourself hunting as well as the more opulent type of hunting where you have a horse or vehicle to carry your heavy and bulky gear.

My own bag, still giving good service after almost a decade of ridiculously hard use, features a bit over 4 pounds of prime northern goose down, and I can per-

sonally vouch that, with the right mattress and liner, it's snug and toasty warm at 30 below zero. The outer shell of these bags is most frequently fabricated from either rip-retarding nylon or a durable blend of nylon/cotton. The all-nylon is lighter than the blend, but I chose the latter since I felt it would take the extra abrasion of the heavy-duty wear I put on a bag better and also because it would be a bit more resistant to damage from possible flying cinders or strong direct heat of the campfire. This bag has never let me down from Alaska to Florida. The whole bag, crammed into its amazingly compact "stuff sack" weighs in at a tad under 8 pounds.

There are a few commonsense tips that will greatly extend the life of your expensive sleeping bag and the range of service it can give you when you are afield. Hang your sleeping bag up on a tree or convenient bush outside, turned inside out, in order for it to dry out and air out fully on dry days. When it's damp and may rain, at least turn your bag inside out when leaving it in the tent. This gives your bag a chance to "breathe" a bit and dry out the moisture that collected from your body in the bag overnight. If you do not air out your bag for several nights, you will notice a significant decrease in its ability to keep you warm and comfortable, even the top quality down bags.

If anything heavy has been sitting on your sleeping bag during the day in the tent (including the duffs of your good hunting buddies who may have been sitting around kibitzing), fluff and plump the bag up before you crawl in for the night. This helps it to regain full loft (and thus efficiency) immediately.

Do not store your bag tightly compressed for long periods of time, especially if it is one of the less expensive synthetics that may have more "memory" than down or the better man-mades. Do not store your bag in a damp area nor anywhere close to direct heat. Keep your bag clean. A dirty bag is an inefficient bag. Inspect the bag closely before beginning to use it for the cold weather fall-winter season. If it's getting a bit dirty and wilted looking, by all means spend the money to have it dry cleaned properly. (NOTE: Be sure to check that your cleaners can properly handle this specialty cleaning job before releasing the bag to them. Then pay the rather hefty $10 to $15 cleaning cost happily. Cleaning your bag periodically [how often depends upon how frequently you use the bag, how you use it, and how careful you are when using it] will extend its useful life many years.)

By all means buy yourself (or have your wife make for you) several sleeping bag liners. These liners serve several purposes. They can help you to keep your bag cleaner because you can dry out each liner (or even wash it) in the field easier than you can dry out your bag itself. Also, you can lend your bag to someone else or borrow someone else's bag if necessary and do it much more pleasantly if there is always a clean liner to slip into the bag. The liners also add a bit of warmth to the bag. My favorite type of liner is one made of light colored inexpensive cotton flannel with tabs sewn in to tie the liner into the bag. (In using cotton, I can spot dirt more easily and keep it well washed.) The cotton flannel is lightweight and costs little. This type of liner breathes well and probably adds about 5 to 7 degrees more to the bottom end of the ''comfort range'' of your bag. Depending upon how many members of your family use the bag, it's a good idea to have two or three of these liners handy.

A second, more specialized liner can be made of a heavier weight (and much more expensive) pile or ''furry'' material. This liner is considerably heavier and more difficult to wash, but it will usually add about 15 degrees to the bottom end of your comfort range and may be necessary if you should have to press your bag into duty for extreme cold weather use that it was not originally designed for.

Keeping your bag clean and well aired simply can't be overemphasized. When I first came into camp on an Alaska Range hunt one day, another hunter was complaining about how he was ''swindled'' when he purchased his expensive down sleeping bag. It simply wasn't keeping him warm. I asked how long he'd been in camp, and he told me about 2 weeks. Then I asked how often he had aired out the bag, and all I got was a blank look in response. When he showed me the bag, it was damp enough to grow mushrooms in! (Though I'm not sure those hardy plants could have survived the odor.) A good sunny day's airing had the bag functioning as it was originally intended to. The very finest custom built car runs rough if you don't keep the engine tuned, and the best sleeping bag is cold and damp if you don't keep it aired out and relatively clean.

The most important thing you can do to extend the use and the life of your bag is to make sure you have the right thing between that bag and the ground. And, unless you're some sort of teeth-gritting masochist, you'll need something more under you than a tarpaulin if you are to sleep comfortably on the ground for several nights running. Especially if it's a mite cold or damp which it often is. Or at least *I* need more than a thickness or two of cloth between the bag and the ground, and I'm the fellow that collapses into a coma each night — not a finicky sleeper.

No matter how expensive and efficient your bag, it is difficult for it to keep you warm at the bearing points where your shoulders, buttocks and lower legs mash

Down is a difficult material to work with, requiring much hand work. This, plus the high cost of the down itself, accounts for the very high costs of top quality down sleeping bags and garments.

down the insulation and come into contact with the ground. *Any* insulation, however effective (and expensive) does not work well when heavily compressed. True, you can scoop out hollows in the ground for your shoulders and buttocks and lay in spruce or pine boughs to make your sleeping more comfortable. But this routine is troublesome to go through if you are moving camp often and the right kind of boughs may not be handily available. In many camping and hunting areas the ordinances now forbid the cutting of any wood.

A good mattress is always with you, always smooth, soft and non-prickly, and it helps you to keep as warm on the bottom side as on the top side when sleeping on the ground.

There are two basic types of mattresses now in widespread use for hunting and camping — the old faithful air mattresses and the newer synthetic foam mattresses. I personally prefer the latter for most jobs, but both have their advantages and disadvantages.

An air mattress should *not* be fully inflated for use afield. Once another hunter who was in the same elk camp with me kept complaining about not being able to get a good night's sleep. After several days of complaints, with the pilgrim becoming increasingly haggard, I wandered over to his tent one day and noted that he had pumped up his air mattress to epic proportions. When I asked him if he always kept it that way, he proudly assured me that he did, even going to the trouble of pumping it up to the last seam-stretching inch every night before turning in. Then the poor chap must have rolled around all night like a pea perched on a watermelon. No wonder he didn't sleep well!

The air mattress should be inflated, depending upon

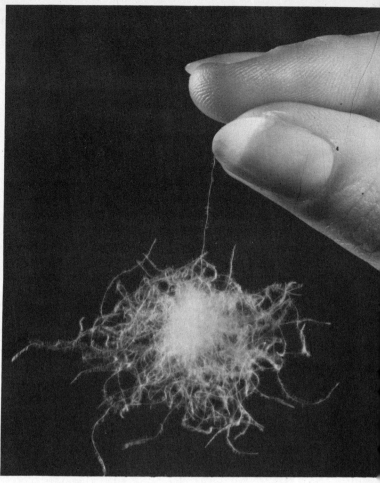

Down is a magnificently efficient insulator as long as it's dry but almost useless when it becomes wet and matted.

The turtle neck dickey, whether fashioned of wool, synthetics or a blend, is an inexpensive, lightweight "secret weapon" to combat the cold. Everyone should have one in his jacket pocket for any sort of cold weather hunting.

personal preference, to somewhere between one half and two thirds of its capacity. The idea is for the air mattress to cradle you *in* it, not for you to lay up *on* it.

There's no sense in buying less than the best in air mattresses. Second rate ones simply won't hold up under tough field use. A mattress that you must always be patching, worse yet, one that is always leaking air through one of those almost impossible to find and infuriating slow leaks so that you wake up flat on the cold, hard ground about 2 AM every morning is about as useful as last week's newspaper.

Top quality air mattresses weigh as much and cost as much as the best synthetic foam mattresses. They do offer the advantage of being somewhat less bulky when deflated. Get the kind that either comes with its own built-in foot pump or a small hand pump. Blowing them up by mouth isn't the best way to do it. It can give you apoplexy and the warm, moist breath from your lungs doesn't do the inside of the mattress any good.

I prefer the foam mattresses because they are (to me, anyway) warmer and softer, and I sleep better on them. I have two that I use frequently. One is a shortie sized mat that is only long enough to reach from my head to my hips (which are the two main ground-bearing points). Due to this shortness and its thinner, 1-inch thickness, it weighs only a svelte 2 pounds. Ideal for backpacking or any situation where weight is at a premium.

My main, workhorse mattress — the one that gets the most use — is 3 inches thick, 77½ inches long and weighs in at 9 pounds. It rolls into a substantial package that measures about 30 inches by 10 inches. However, it makes the wilderness sleeping more comfortable than most over-soft, overaged mattresses in use in homes. I have slept on this mattress for periods of up to 2 months at a time and returned to civilization as refreshed as a teenager after a cold shower.

Foam mattresses will, if used in a damp tent over a period of time, accumulate dampness themselves much as a sleeping bag will. Thus it is also a good idea to air them out and turn them over from time to time to reverse the "top" and the "bottom." Placing your mattress on completely non-porous, non-breathing ground covers such as heavy-duty plastic means that eventually enough moisture (from you) will wick through the mattress until the bottom becomes damp and then actually wet if it is not properly aired. Thus I prefer a heavy-duty duck tarp that protects the mattress from abrasion due to ground contact and yet helps protect you from dampness because it "breathes" and thus will pass a major part (not all) of your moisture through.

Of course your problems with moisture will vary a good bit depending upon how damp the general prevailing weather is, how large your tent is and how many hunters are sleeping in it, and probably most important, how much moisture you yourself tend to throw off. People vary significantly as to how much they perspire. The thing to remember is that you must sleep dry, and your biggest and most implacable enemy is not the driving rain or the chilling snow — it's your own porous body which is constantly exuding and exhaling moisture to one degree or another.

## 2. Boots and shoes:

After your sleeping bag and its related accessories, boots and shoes are probably the most critical items in your outdoor and big game hunting wardrobe. If it's true that when you don't sleep you can't hunt, it's equally true that when you can't walk you can't hunt. If you do any sort of halfway serious big game hunting,

The well equipped big game hunter should have a pair of both high quality all leather boots (above) and all rubber boots (below) to meet varying field conditions.

you will encounter all sorts of terrain and weather in surprisingly short order. You must walk to hunt, and this truism holds true no matter how you hunt. Even on a fully outfitted horseback hunt, sooner or later you'll end up putting your own legs and feet to hard use. You can't shoot game from atop the horse, and you'll have to climb and walk hard because there are places where it isn't safe nor even possible to go while mounted.

If your boots don't adequately protect your tender feet in rough country or if they don't fit well, you soon find that you have all the mobility of a Galapagos Island tortoise. You can't hunt. Twisted ankles, aching insteps, bruised or blistered foot balls knock you (no pun intended) right off your feet. I have seen men travel over 5,000 miles to take a trophy and then not be able to walk or climb the last half mile for the shot. What a tragedy!

To properly handle the wide array of country and conditions you will run into, you need several types of footwear. First, you must have top quality, heavy-duty boots for general dry to moderately wet climbing and hard tramping in rough country. These boots must, of necessity, be rather heavy, and they should have strongly reinforced heels, insteps and box toes to protect your rather sensitive feet from the pounding they will take.

I recommend 8-inch high, best quality leather boots. Any higher and they tend to cramp and bind the calf, and they really don't afford much additional protection (except possibly in snake country and that can better be handled by lightweight, breathable leggings especially designed for that purpose). Less than 8 inches doesn't give your ankles and lower legs the added support they need for the roughest punishment.

Your basic dry weather boot should be of leather, not rubber or rubber/leather combinations. Leather breathes better than any other material used to make quality footwear, and by and large, it is the most comfortable to wear. The newer types of silicone impregnated leathers and better boot constructions are amazingly waterproof. Though standing submersed in water will eventually result in wet feet, well maintained leather boots can take an amazing amount of damp walking and even quick scurrying through standing water without allowing your feet to get wet.

These boots should have a sewn-in tongue and scree ring around the top to minimize the possibility of small pebbles working their pesky way into your boots. These are more than convenience factors. When doing a lot of hard walking and climbing on shale slides or even churning through the pea gravel found on many sandbars or riverbeds, these small bits of rock show an almost malevolent ability to penetrate into your boots and wedge themselves in the most painful positions inside. Oftentimes when this happens, you must stop wherever you are in order to remove the irritation before you can move on. I almost fell off a peak in Montana's glorious Sun River country one afternoon because I had to take a boot off in a place that would have given a mountain goat pause. I was tired, it was late in the day and very cold, and the combination of stiff joints and tiredness-caused carelessness almost resulted in my taking wing into a 500-foot gorge.

Although in the past many experienced hunters and climbers swore by the use of hobnailed soles for hunting involving a lot of serious rock work, that is no longer necessary, thank goodness. The rubber lugged Vibram and similar soles are far more flexible and don't require that you have an extra pair of boots, one hobnailed and one not. They will do about everything the awkward hobs will (more on dry rock surfaces in my opinion) and only lose out to the nailed constructions on extended ice work which few hunters ever face in their climbing and trekking.

Check the fit of any outdoor footwear most carefully. Your foot is truly an amazingly engineered construction having 26 different bones in it and offering not a single flat plane anywhere on it. To properly fit such a variable item, which will always swell (often a half-size or more) during a day's hard work afield, takes some doing. For myself, I always get my heavy-duty boots a full size wider and longer than I do my street shoes.

For extreme cold weather usage the two layer boot with an inner liner of thick, absorbent felt and an outer layer of leather and rubber is hard to beat. (Photo courtesy of the Browning Company)

This is because I often wear two pair of *heavy* socks, rather than one. Also, I use a pair of hard, felt-topped arch supports placed inside the boots. If any of you are "semi-flat-footed" as I am, you will find these arch supports make a world of difference in allowing you to stay afield and remain as mobile in the afternoon as the morning during a tough day's hiking.

Since your feet do swell a bit during a day's use (even sidewalk walking in the city), it's important that your boots be a bit loose rather than too tight. Loose boots can usually be worked and jimmied to fit (unless just ridiculously oversized) with extra socks, pads or arch supports. Since these boots are very expensive ($50 and up nowadays) and will last you for years, be especially careful about buying them through the mail. They must fit properly. Also, even though you "usually" wear a certain size of hunting boot, if you change brands or even style numbers within the same brand, approach the fit of the boots with due care. All shoes and boots are constructed over lasts (wooden carvings of the foot), and last making is a bit of a variable art. Depending upon exactly how an individual boot last is made (and how the boot itself is "lasted" during the manufacturing) and depending upon the exact proportions of your own feet, you may find that a different boot requires a different size for best fit (either width or length or both). Also, make sure *both* feet are fitted well by the pair of boots. A pair of boots are identical in size but your feet aren't. If you are right-handed, and thus right-footed, your starboard foot will be a bit larger than your left one. In some people this difference can be extreme, even requiring shoes (or boots) from two different sized pairs for proper fit. Chances are you won't have this kind of problem but always try on *both* boots to be sure.

All hunting boots and shoes should be *completely* broken in before the hunt. Do not decide to buy a new pair of boots and then immediately wear them on a hard hunt. One trick to greatly accelerate breaking in leather boots is to fill them with water and let them stand awhile (away from all heat or direct sunlight) and soak up the water. Then put them on and "walk them dry" on a hike or just mowing the lawn. This will mold them to your feet in much the same fashion as fine saddlemakers mold holsters and scabbards to shape by working the dampened leather over forms during their construction.

Your boot laces should be as heavy as possible. It's extremely inconvenient to always be repairing broken laces afield, and once this starts, it never seems to end. These laces should be much longer than comparable city shoelaces would be. Though they do not lend themselves to the standard bow tie used on street shoes, it's surprising how many hunters still cleave to this approach. They do so out of habit I suppose, though the boots never stay tied. Some use the "double bow" (two bow ties, one on top of the other), but there

is a much better way.

I far prefer to make the one single tie in my boot lace (just like the first step in the standard bow tie) and then wrap the laces all the way around the upper boot once or twice, finally wrapping or whipping the loose ends around and around the loop around the boot. There is no tie to come loose (the multiple wraps secure the laces), and they'll stay that way, all day, giving your upper boot a tad of added support. They can easily be loosened or tightened, as the occasion may demand, without undoing them all the way.

Leather-type synthetics like Corfam may eventually overtake leather in the use of these "No. 1" hunting boots but not yet. Corfam was rather expensive, did not breathe nearly as well as leather and was a bit heavier. It was fully waterproof and with additional devel-

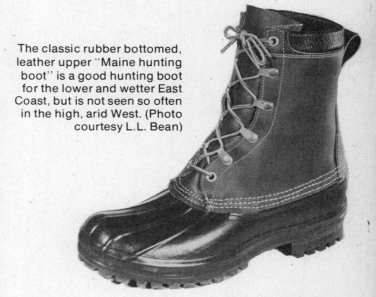

The classic rubber bottomed, leather upper "Maine hunting boot" is a good hunting boot for the lower and wetter East Coast, but is not seen so often in the high, arid West. (Photo courtesy L.L. Bean)

opment, it will probably someday surpass leather for field use. Corfam usually outlasted leather as it was less subject to drying out due to dissipation of the natural oils in leather (however, this can be largely remedied by following the simple leather care instructions found in Chapter 21.)

### 3. Rubber boots:

These boots are secondary to the all-leather editions just covered only in the sense that they are usually not worn as often. When they *are* needed, they are as fully important as the leather boots, and the latter make a poor substitute at best. The well equipped big game hunter definitely needs both types of boots in his closet.

These rubber boots can be of either the insulated or uninsulated type, depending upon the types of uses they will be put to. Generally if the hunter lives in the northern part of the country or if he will be doing any hunting in the high West or the far northern parts of the

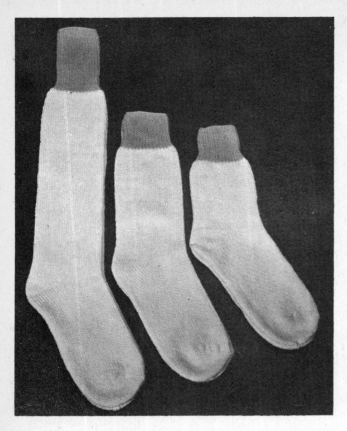

The well equipped hunter should have good quality wool stockings in several lengths to fit his 6-inch high walking shoes, 8-inch high basic leather boot and 10-inch high rubber boot as recommended by author.

which tend to be a bit ''sticky'' due to electrostatic binding). Some canny hunters always carry an extra pair of clean, dry socks afield with them as well as a smidgen of foot or talcum powder in case their feet get too wet afield. They can then pause a moment, dry their feet off and apply a quick dusting of powder and don a dry pair of socks.

All boots should be taken off when you return to camp and set out to dry as soon as possible. This is especially so with rubber footwear of any type. Stuffing them with newspapers and sprinkling a bit of powder in them will help dry them as will sitting them adjacent to (not right next to) the mild warmth from a stove. Hanging boots upside down will help enhance the drying process as well. Good rubber boots, sturdily made and with the right type of soles don't come cheap either. Expect to pay around $40 to $60 for them.

### 4. Rainwear:

This is one of the most underrated yet important items of all. Rainwear serves three basic functions: to shed water and keep the hunter dry; to help ward off the

continent, he would probably be better off with the insulated type.

In these type boots either the 8-inch or 10-inch height is allowable. The rubber of the uppers has more give to it than does the heavy-duty leather of the dry country boots and thus will not unduly bind your calves if you select the 10-inch boots. The latter are, of course, a bit heavier and bulkier, but they will protect you better in deeper snow or water. I prefer the Vibram type sole on this sort of boot, also. These boots should also feature a fully sewn-in tongue both to keep loose gravel and dry matter out as well as extra insurance that moisture doesn't leak through the boots at the tongue area.

When wearing these rubber boots, foot dampness is far more of a problem than with all-leather boots since rubber doesn't breathe at all and the natural perspiration from your feet has nowhere to go but to accumulate in your boots. Thus, two pairs of socks are especially recommended with any rubber boot but most especially with the warmer, heavier insulated type. Much of the accumulated moisture will ''wick through'' the inner pair of spongy, heavy socks and accumulate in the outer pair, thus helping, to a degree, to keep your feet a bit drier and more well cushioned.

When wearing rubber boots (or any boots for that matter), there are a few extra precautions one can take to greatly extend your comfort. Sprinkle some foot powder, both on your bare feet (to help keep them dry) and on the outer pair of heavy socks (to make it easier to pull on the heavy boots, especially the rubber ones

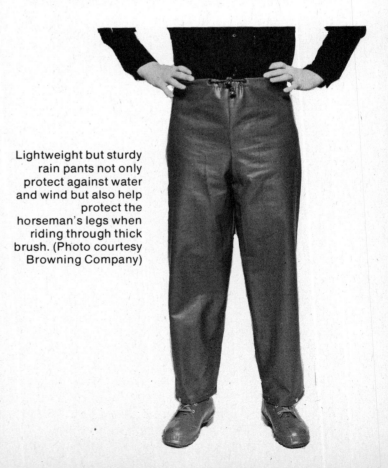

Lightweight but sturdy rain pants not only protect against water and wind but also help protect the horseman's legs when riding through thick brush. (Photo courtesy Browning Company)

A lightweight, "breathing" (or well-ventilated) rain suit should be carried everywhere in deep wilderness hunting and is a good idea for general hunting. The outdoor weather is highly changeable during the hunting season, and even if precipitation isn't encountered, the suit helps cut the wind and keep the hunter dry when he often must sit or lay on the damp ground as outfitter Johnny Holmes is doing here while glassing for game. Note patches of melting snow on seemingly dry ground. This is practically a sump, and without the rain suit he'd quickly be soaked even though it isn't raining or snowing a drop!

chilling wind; and to give an added (lightweight) layer of clothing for warmth. Weather is unpredictable during the fall-winter hunting seasons and especially in many of the wilderness or high altitude areas where much of the best big game hunting remains. A wet hunter is cold and uncomfortable, even in mild temperatures, and his efficiency quickly plummets to near zero as his teeth chatter and he shivers, quickly losing interest in the hunting while he looks for a place to build a fire and try to get warm. In really cold weather, the wet hunter is in danger of suffering from exposure and hypothermia which are far more serious than merely being a bit uncomfortable.

There are two basic options here: the two-piece rain suit and the one-piece, knee-length poncho. Either should be made of lightweight nylon and should feature a non-corroding nylon zipper and a tuck-in or foldaway hood. As might be expected, each has its pluses and minuses. Whichever you choose initially, I would suggest that when you eventually get around to your secondary or fill-in items, that you also pick up a rainsuit of the other type. Though I use the two-piece suit a bit more than the poncho, I have and use both types quite frequently.

The two-piece suit offers complete protection all the way down to your boots, and it is far better to walk in (the type of rain trousers that unzip at the bottom are very easy to get on and off over bulky boots and hunting trousers). The suit should be loose fitting and have ample vents under the arms so that it breathes rather well. Camouflage is a good color. (Blaze-orange camouflage would be even better since mammals, at least among the big game species, do not see color. But I can't seem to con any manufacturers into making this preeminently sensible item!) Prices run from $35 to $45 for the rainsuit, and it's well worth it since it takes top quality to offer the necessary durability *and* lightness.

The one-piece poncho is somewhat lighter and less bulky to carry if backpacking. I prefer it for much horseback riding since it allows me to hold an expensive camera or two underneath it and yet have them instantly available if needed. These ponchos are a mixed blessing for horseback use. Their spread allows you to somewhat drape them over the horse's saddle, keeping it dry and perhaps even the saddle bags which may have items in them you don't want to get wet. However, if you are riding through heavy cover, the limbs and branches are constantly snagging this "blousey" garment and ripping or tearing it. When backpacking some ponchos can be extended over the full pack on the back, thus protecting both the hiker and all his gear. This usually makes walking a bit easier since the poncho is not hanging as low around the legs and flapping and binding. Some of these poncho type garments are cunningly contrived so that they can be unfolded or unzipped to form a small rectangular all-purpose tarp.

They can even be used to rig a very small lean-to shelter that works better to shelter gear rather than a person.

### 5. Hunting shoes:

This is probably the most overlooked category of hunting footwear and yet, especially on extended or particularly arduous hunting trips, they can be equally as important as the other two types of boots. I prefer a medium weight, 6-inch high walking shoe. It should also have a sewn-in tongue and scree ring as well as a Vibram® type sole.

When you return to camp after a hard day afield, doffing the heavier boots immediately not only gives them more time to dry out before morning but donning the lighter, ''fresher'' footwear will also give you a surprising lift. I used to know some leading executives from one of the largest shoe companies in the world who made it a point of changing one pair of lightweight street shoes for another each day at the office in the midafternoon. This change both decreased their personal fatigue and also extended the life of their shoes.

On all three types of boots and shoes I have just discussed, I prefer the design that features eyelets rather than bent-prong type ''buttons'' around which you wrap the laces. Eyelets usually don't wear out your laces as quickly, and you can untie and loosen the laces momentarily without them coming all apart. Also, these bent-prongs are forever catching on rocks and sticks and getting bent out of shape or even, at times, torn from the shoes themselves.

There is somewhat more price spread on hunting shoes depending upon how light or heavy you want them. At one extreme they are almost like a shortie version of your heavy hunting boots, and at the other end, they are only fit for lounging around the center of camp. You will end up paying about $25 to $65 for them depending upon your preferences and pocketbook. I

An extra pair of camp shoes to relax in and rest your feet while your boots are drying out at night is a good idea. However, even these relatively lightweight shoes should be rather sturdy by city-pavement-walking standards in order to protect your feet even around camp.

A lightweight, waterproof slip-over shirt of the mountaineer ''Anorak'' variety is a very useful all-purpose garment, easy for the big game hunter to carry anywhere.

would strongly recommend that you purchase at least medium weight, relatively heavy and sturdy shoes, even though they are primarily for lounging around camp. The temptation there is to get shoes that are too soft and lightweight, forgetting that even in camp it will get muddy and sloppy and that there is always the chance that you may be called out of camp unexpectedly to help a buddy cut some wood or drag his deer in. Unless you want to be constantly changing from shoes to boots, you will find yourself ruining those unreinforced, ''butter soft'' buckskin shoes and similar type loungers which are better used at home in the family room than outdoors anywhere.

I have found it a good idea to stay away from the very lightweight and soft ''quail shooter'' type boots, used by upland bird hunters. These boots are very attractive and comfortable — on the showroom floor of the store — but they simply will not stand up to any sort of extended big game hunting use. Upland bird hunting and big game hunting are, even if done in the same country, entirely different sports requiring differing kinds of footwear.

No slip-on type cowboy or Wellington boots should be used afield by the big game hunter. They slip too much and will quickly chafe and blister the foot, and that open top has a miraculous ability to collect dirt and debris. I do not even recommend them for use around camp. When you're back in the bush, good boots are a treasure, and second rate ones or poorly fitting ones are an abomination. I have had very little stolen from me in the wilderness over the years, but interestingly enough, I have had more boots taken than anything. When you consider all the expensive and enticing gear that a well equipped big game hunter carries afield, that makes for something to ponder, doesn't it?

## 6. Jackets:

This key item is your first line of defense against the unfriendly elements for your critical upper body/torso area. Here again, my vote goes for down. Wool is far heavier, doesn't breathe as well and doesn't compress

A good down vest is one of the most flexible items of clothing in the hunter's closet and one of the best investments.

for packing as well. For these reasons I prefer wool for my medium weight shirts and trousers and leave the heavy-duty outer wear task to down (properly protected when necessary by good rainwear since down is useless when wet!).

Prime northern goose down is the ticket here as we've already discussed, and nylon is the best outer shell due to its lightness, durability and ability to keep the down plumules from escaping. Unfortunately, nylon is very loud when walking or riding through heavy cover.

I prefer to use the light and medium weight down shirts and jackets rather than the very heavy and bulky down "parkas." Two outer items, say a lightweight down shirt and a medium weight down jacket, are no more expensive than a single very heavy-duty down parka and, due to the extra warmth of the layering principle, they are usually as warm as or warmer than

the parka (except that they may not extend as far below the waist as the larger single garment). The two garments give you considerably more flexibility in being able to dress for different kinds of weather and to properly "vent" yourself (adding and shucking garments) as needed when suffering extreme temperature swings such as when mountain climbing.

My two current favorites are a lightweight down "sweater" or "shirt" and a medium weight, reversible jacket that zips to the top of its turtleneck cut, padded collar and is fluorescent orange on one side and brown/green camouflage on the other. The "shirt" tips the scale at a wispy 16 ounces and it compresses, with the help of a stuff sack, into a tiny cylinder hardly larger than a carton of cigarettes.

This garment is fantastically warm for its weight and bulk and well worth the $25 to $35 price tag. Two of these shirts can be teamed together, as I often have, for astonishing warmth due both to the down plus the layer of dead air trapped between the two garments. I always carry one of these shirts with me, suitably compressed to minimum size, in my day pack or jacket pocket on all but the mildest days.

The medium weight down jacket weighs a bit more, but it is warmer. The snug fitting, padded collar helps to keep out the cold that insidiously seeps into the neck hole of most garments, and the two color combination allows me to hunt most anywhere in the U. S. and Canada and comply with the local regulations. This type of jacket costs around $50 to $65 and, teamed with the lighter weight down "shirt," it will see you through all but the worst weather.

It is impossible for me to choose between these two items so, rationalizing that they do in a sense replace a single very heavy down coat, I must consider them *both* to be basic and actually to be the two compatible parts of a single garment. When you begin securing those secondary items, I strongly suggest that you put a down vest at the very top of the list. This item is even lighter, more compact and less expensive (around $18 - $30), and it allows you to dress with *three* layers of down and still not unduly restrict your arm movements due to binding. Incidentally, though my normal size is "medium," I purchased the outer jacket in "large" so it would be rather loose fitting. All down garments (and other types, too) in order to work well, should be rather loose fitting. It's a good idea to get the size that allows extra roominess so that you have a maximum sized "envelope" of insulating air built up around you by the garment. Also, looser garments allow you to wear other garments and gear underneath as necessary. And finally, the loose garment does not bind or restrict the big game hunter during his heavy exertions and some of the occasionally outlandish contortions that necessarily crop up from time to time. Sleekly cut, tight fitting "continental" style clothing is for the city or for the ads of many outdoor manufacturers who want to flatter the

(Right) The wool shirt is, with the down jacket, among the big game hunter's most important items of wearing apparel. The author prefers light and medium weight (10- to 14-ounce material) wool shirts to the heavy 20-ounce type "jacket shirts" that are bulky, heavy and often uncomfortable.

(Below) The bright red plaid "deer hunting suit" of wool has been popular for years in the East because the bright colors are a safety factor in the crowded woods, and the wool is both silent in the heavy undergrowth and remains warm in the often wet conditions. This type of clothing is not used very frequently outside the eastern U.S. for general big game hunting, though.

eye of the viewer used to the fit of urban clothing. Hunting clothes should be loose, baggy and, in a word, a bit "frumpy" looking in this respect in order to function at their most flexible best.

All of these garments — the jacket, the shirt and the vest — should be a tad long (another reason for going to a larger size so that they cover the vital lower back, lumbar region over the kidneys where it's so easy to get cold). Although I have a very expensive (over a hundred bucks at today's prices) and heavy down outer coat that I bought by mistake years ago, I seldom ever wear it. The fact is, it's almost like new since I quickly learned that aside from some specialized situations, it didn't do well the jobs I needed doing.

### 7. Shirts and sweaters:

My clear preference on hunting shirts is for best quality, new 100 percent wool, made of fabric of the 10- to 12-ounce weight. I don't like the far heavier "jac-shirt" types made of the bulky, boiler plate stiff 18- to

22-ounce weight material so often depicted on outdoor calenders or magazine covers. This is not a lightly held bias, by the way; I simply will not own or use one of the very heavy shirts. The lighter shirts are much less bulky, less expensive, less "itchy-scratchy" and — again using the layering principle — much warmer when teamed together with another light shirt. The heavyweights are difficult to keep tucked in, and they usually tend, due to their stiffness, to periodically unbutton themselves automatically as you move around strenuously.

As far as color, any kind will do, but the woodsman's plaids (usually red-and-black or black-and-white) are undoubtedly the two most popular and two of the most attractive. I prefer the shirts with the bottom in the shirt tail cut rather than in the squared off, non-vented jacket cut, since the latter is too bulky to keep tucked in properly while the former works perfectly well if one wants to wear the shirt untucked during warm weather. For warm weather hunting cotton flannel or cotton/synthetic blends do fine. Expect to pay $8 to $18 for the cotton or cotton blend shirts and $15 to $25 for the wool shirts.

Shirts should, like all other gear, be kept clean. Dirty ones aren't as attractive or efficient. If dirty, have your wool shirts cleaned before you take to the field. Buttons should be large sized for secure closure and for handling with bulky gloves or mittens, and they should be as non-breakable as possible. It's a good idea to have them double sewn with some additional heavy-duty thread after you purchase the shirt (your dry cleaners can do this for you). This saves lost buttons later.

## 8. Trousers:

Candor forces me to admit that, in this category at least, I do not always practice what I preach as the trite old bromide has it. Probably the best all-around trousers for most serious big game hunting are medium weight wool trousers (10- to 12-ounce fabric). As with shirts, I'd stay away from the 18- to 22- and even 30-ounce weight fabric. These boiler plates can almost stand without you, and they are very heavy, binding and bulky. If you need them for specialized work such as sitting motionless in a blind or over bait for long hours in very cold and/or damp weather, so be it, but I would not say they belong in the big game hunters basic wardrobe list but more appropriately near the middle or bottom of the list of secondary, fill-in items.

These medium weight trousers should be cut loosely around the seat and crotch so that they don't bind and so that the extra layer of air in that area is both warmer and handles the heavy perspiration generated in the crotch area (the most dangerous type to the hunter) more effectively. The pants should be several inches larger around the waist than your city pants. This allows you to tuck in bulky and perhaps multiple shirt

Though denims and jeans are probably the most common big game hunting pants encountered in the field, loose fitting light to mid-weight wool trousers offer many advantages over denim.

tails and not get chafed when you're constantly twisting and turning during a heavy day's work afield.

The trousers should also be a bit more wide legged than some of the stovepipe legged street pants or jeans commonly seen today, and they should be uncuffed so as not to collect dirt and debris. They should be a bit shorter than street trousers so that they aren't constantly getting dirty and wet due to dragging in mud or water. Yep, I know trousers with the "look" that I'm advocating may not exactly make you a candidate for the Marlboro man in the next TV ad but, this is the cut that works. Forget the svelte look of the models in the magazines and catalogs. Those trimline cuts are portrayed to sell garments and magazines or other products; what I am recommending is what works and, to the knowing eye, is what actually looks best. As I said before, attractiveness in the field is strictly a reflection of functionality, not "fashion."

Wool offers many advantages over cotton in trousers. It's warmer, more silent, sheds dirt and damp-gunk better, is warmer when wet and not that much more expensive than today's high priced denims. Having said all these things, I must now admit that I probably take to the field as often in denim levis as in any other type trouser. They are generally cut a bit too snug and thus bind. (However, if you're as thin as you need to be for the more active types of hunts, this is only moderately restraining.) They are cold when wet and, if new, very loud in heavy cover. (My ancient, thousand-wash favorites are almost as silent as wool.)

I like them for several reasons. They wear like iron, and considering that they can be patched much cheaper than wool can be rewoven, they often last longer for a lower long-run cost. They are lighter and more compact, and I can carry several more pairs on a long trip. With the proper underwear, they can almost match wool in many respects. Best of all, when I'm to be afield for a long time and weight is at a premium (backpacking or a stripped down spike camp outing), two pairs of jeans enable me to wash one pair and have it drying while I wear the other pair. Thus, I'm always in (relatively) clean trousers. Two pair of wool pants take up more room, and though they sop up dirt and gummy grime far better than denims, when they *do* need cleaning, it's difficult to find a dry cleaner out in the wilderness!

Suffice it to say that both denims and medium weight woolen trousers have their uses, and I try never to be afield for longer than several days without at least one pair of each. I always use only well-worn levis to keep the binding to a minimum. If you have new denims, wash them continually and wear them around the house until they are well "broken in." In this era of rising prices and shoddy copies, top quality denims are no longer inexpensive by any means, but they are a must. The cheapie lower quality denims are much lighter weight and very stiff when new. They seem to dissolve just about the time you have them well broken in. The better grade jeans wear almost forever, no matter how well-worn they appear. I treasure mine so much that when the sad day inevitably comes when holes start appearing, usually in the knees, I patch them and go right on using them rather than throwing away these cherished companions of many a long hunt.

### 9. Headgear:

The wide brimmed hat is the king of outdoor hats for the big game hunter in most situations. Not just because it's picturesque either. It's lightweight, comfortable, shades your face from wind, rain and sun and keeps you relatively cool or warm, whichever is needed. That wide 2½-inch to 3½-inch brim does an unexcelled job of protecting your sensitive face and eyes from sun, wind, dust, sleet, snow, rain and snow-glare. A well styled, wide brimmed hat — whether the straight "westerner" type, the "white hunter" style or the cocked brim Aussie "digger" type — in top quality felt will cost you anywhere from $25 to $50.

I have just bought a new one after bidding a sad farewell to my old friend that accompanied me on countless hunts and outdoor excursions for a decade. As in the case of leather, when drying out these wet felt hats, do not expose them to direct heat. They may shrink, and even if they don't, this forced drying will age the felt before its time.

The big game hunter also needs other cold weather

The basic stocking cap comes in an almost unlimited variety of materials and slightly modified designs (including ski masks and watch caps), and it's one of the best buys available to the big game hunter. This one has a crown of down insulation. (Photo courtesy Eddie Bauer, Inc.)

Wide brimmed hats, whether of straw for desert country (top) or felt for mountains or general use (below), are extremely valuable in protecting the hunter's face from sunburn and wind.

Most hunters don't realize that, depending upon the exact kind of weather conditions and how they are dressed, upwards of 50 percent of their body heat loss can be from a bare head. The down-insulated type cap with ear flaps is a good option to combat this.

headgear in addition to his basic, wide brimmed fedora. For simplicity and convenience sake, I usually stick to the ski mask or Navy watch cap design type of stocking cap. These come in all-wool, dacron/wool blends and straight dacron. I prefer the blends, but all are good. Although these may not be quite as warm as some of the fancier types, you can wear two of them if necessary and they are quite warm.

I usually stick to them for several reasons: they are generally inexpensive ($4 to $10); they can be folded up and stuffed into your jacket pocket so that they are always there and ready for use; and they give your head and upper neck total protection with no "cold spots." The Navy watch cap with single large opening rather than three or four openings for your eyes, nose and mouth (such as featured on ski masks) is particularly flexible. It can be worn perched up on top of the head, at several differing attitudes of "half mast" partially down over the face or completely down with the single opening at minimal size just to barely expose your eyes and nose.

## 10. Underwear:

I have probably seen more hunters ill equipped in this clothing area than any other. A surprisingly large number of sportsmen take to the field clad in all sorts of painstakingly selected expensive outerwear and, as an afterthought, merely don the same T-shirts and shorts or briefs that they wear in the city. Underwear performs several functions for the hunter. It is your final line of defense and against cold, wind and moisture, and it is the one layer of clothing that comes fully into contact with that shivering, palpitating *Homo sapien* carcass that is not too well engineered by nature to perform some of the tasks that we hunters put it to on a long, tough hunt.

I do usually take several changes of city underwear with me on long hunts. I wear them coming and going (always save a fresh set for the trip home!) and, sometimes, under my hunting underwear. Although I have both hanging in my closet, I almost never use the quilted, heavily insulated underwear suits of dacron or down. Most (not all though) big game hunting is very active, and these suits will get too hot and sweaty for the strenuous hunter. Since perspiration is absolutely your worst enemy afield, I don't use these suits unless the situation is very specialized, calling for very cold and stationary circumstances. I have used these suits to sleep in at night and put them to good use when huddling for hours in a chilly duck blind.

I prefer two other somewhat similar types of underwear: the waffle weave, cotton thermal two-piece suit and the two-ply cotton (inside layer) and wool (outside) type. The first type is inexpensive, lightweight, breathes well and relatively warm. The second type is more expensive, warmer and under some circumstances a bit sweatier. Both suits offer the added plus of all long underwear suits, namely cushioning protection of the arms and legs against brush, abrasions and bruises as well as protection against the cold. I usually carry several of the cotton suits with me and one of the two-ply suits on any long hunt into cold weather country.

I do not like the extremely open weave fish-net type of underwear suits. The tops work okay allowing your

Long underwear, made of various materials and of differing designs, serves the valuable function not only of keeping the hunter warmer but of helping protect his body (especially legs and shins) from the inevitable abrasions and knocks and jolts picked up in strenuous outdoor hunting.

body to breathe very efficiently, but the bottoms usually end up branding your bottom indelibly (and uncomfortably) with that dratted fish-net pattern if you must sit much while afield or in the saddle.

### 11. Socks:

Good socks are surprisingly expensive ($3 to $10 per pair) but well worth it. I prefer the long bulky type

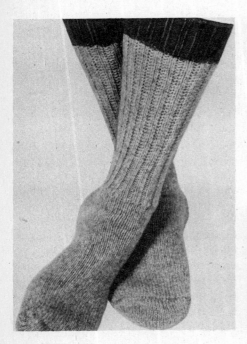

Good, high quality wool hunting socks are expensive but well worth the cost. Two layers are more than twice as efficient for really cold conditions, and clean socks are far warmer than dirty ones. Canny big game hunters carry an extra pair afield in case the pair they're wearing becomes too wet due to wet weather or perspiration.

Some mittens, even of the two layer persuasion, have a flapped slit so that the trigger finger or all fingers of the right hand can be extended for limited use without removing the mittens. The elasticized cuffs make for added warmth by closing out the cold air more effectively.

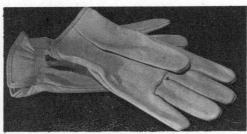

Gloves of leather or light buckskin are good for dry weather work where the temperature doesn't get below about 15 degrees Fahrenheit. Wool is necessary for damp weather work and mittens for colder work.

for most use and generally choose a wool/nylon or wool/dacron blend. Occasionally there are good allover-stretchable wool/spandex blends that aren't quite as warm and spongy as the former two blends but do keep their shape and fit better under hard use. They also serve to give the foot and calf a bit more support due to the allover elasticity. These will never ride down into your boots under hard tramping.

Dirty, damp socks are an abomination afield. Carry enough socks with you to always have clean ones in reserve and do a bit of washing afield (which is another reason for steering away from the all-wools).

### 12. Gloves and mittens:

There seem to be about as many types of gloves and mittens around as there are people to wear them; the choice is almost endless and a bit mind-boggling at times. Stay away from all the gimmicks like the battery powered, "heated" gloves or socks. Gloves and mittens are made of leather, cotton, down, various blends and synthetics. There are gloves that are gloves, semi-mittens, mittens, mittens with a hole in them for the trigger finger to protrude, etc., etc.

I've owned and used most of these over the years at one time or another but for simplicity sake have finally settled on the newer thermal type of synthetic material

with a cuffed top. These are lightweight, relatively inexpensive ($3 to $5), warm when wet, and they offer a surprising amount of protection in cool to moderately cold situations. Leather gloves can be an abomination in cold, wet weather. They constantly get wet and then freeze up into grotesque, rock hard claws. The thermal gloves are much easier to keep manageable when wet. Also, I am always losing gloves so I buy these cheapies several pair at a time which costs me about the same as one really expensive pair of fur lined, leather gloves.

I take several along with me on long trips, stuffing a pair into each jacket pocket (if it's cold country) just to be sure. When they get too dirty or worn, I just discard them and start using another pair.

Everyone's individual thermostat varies, but most people find that gloves aren't quite warm enough whenever the exposure gets down around 20 degrees (above zero) Fahrenheit for extended periods. I can take it lower because for some reason my hands don't seem to get cold easily, but when it's about 10 degrees above zero, I start getting uncomfortable. Then I haul out the double layer mittens that I prefer for really cold weather work. These mittens feature leather outers (to knock off the wind more effectively) and warm wool liners. The extra layer of air between the inners and outers helps these mittens to keep your hands toasty

Mittens offer, other things being equal, more warmth than gloves but less dexterity and flexibility. Two layer wool and leather mittens such as these are good for heavy-duty cold weather work.

has accompanied me on jaunts all over much of the world, becoming a bit of a treasured keepsake by now. It's just shy of 2 inches wide, of heavyweight, top quality leather. It's actually an old Navy belt, and though I don't remember where I got it by now, it carries a solid brass buckle that is stamped 1946. The wide leather strap makes an excellent strop to put an edge on my knife in a pinch when performing fine-detail work skinning out a head. I have also used it, in a pinch, to help strap everything from game heads to small outboard motors to my packframe.

Your hunting belt should be several inches longer than your normal dress belt for city wear. You will often be wearing it with bulky, outsized woolen trousers that have bulky woolen shirts tucked into them, and you can use the extra flexibility that this added length gives to you. Also, the longer belt serves better to perform any of the emergency tasks that you may have to put it to. (I have even seen belts used to bind splints temporarily to broken bones in the field until the

warm in all but the most severe weather. For really extreme cold, I use a pair of oversized sheepskin gauntlets, cut to the Eskimo pattern, that I had especially made for me. These gauntlets fit right over the mittens and come almost all the way up to my elbows. That three-layer mitten/gauntlet combo can (and has) taken me down to −40 degrees. However, I would not classify these expensive ($50) custom-made gauntlets as part of your *basic* rig. If your two-layer mittens (assuming they're warm and clean) won't take you through the cold, then chances are you shouldn't be out hunting in those conditions, anyway. As implied here, the well equipped big game hunter needs both the gloves and the mittens unless he lives and hunts exclusively in the southern part of the country.

### 13. Belts & Suspenders:

These seemingly unimportant minor items can be of more value to you if properly chosen. Hunters have a tendency to dangle all sorts of impedimenta (hunting knives, ammunition holders full of heavy cartridges, hatchets, sunglasses in cases, belt-sheathed whetstones or compasses, etc.) from their belts at one time or another. Some hunters overdo this, and I often think they could take a note from the military or the police and use a good Sam Browne belt. In any event, a wide and sturdy belt — one of full grain cowhide and running 1½ inches to 2½ inches in width — is less liable to break or wear out under these strains, and it will chafe or cut your waist less. Also, they can be put to other uses better than narrower belts.

I have used the same one for over 20 years now, and it

The importance of a good, heavyweight leather belt is underrated by most beginning big game hunters. A 1½- to 2-inch width is about right.

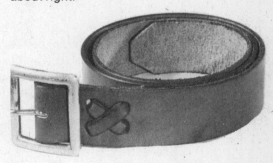

The big game hunter's pockets and belt always seem to be overloaded with heavy items; whatever his quarry and wherever he is hunting. Good heavy suspenders, in addition to his belt, are always a good idea. (Photo courtesy of L.L. Bean)

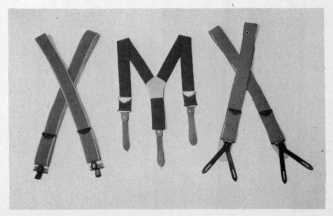

hunter could be taken to a doctor for proper care.)

Suspenders of the wide, heavy-duty woodsman type are invaluable in helping you to shoulder these heavy loads (literally!). Used in conjunction with your wide belt, they will help you to support those heavy belt loads and still keep your trousers belted loosely enough to be comfortable. Helping distribute some of the pressure onto your shoulders as well as around that long suffering waist means you will be fresher and stronger in the latter half of the day, too.

### 14. Duffle bag:

Duffle bags provide far more carrying capacity for

Well made duffle bags are the best way for the big game hunter to transport his clothing and gear on long trips. (Note the carry handles stitched to webbing completely encircle bags.) (Photo courtesy L.L. Bean)

heavy-duty use these cylindrical bags should be completely encircled with two or three sturdy straps of either leather or heavy webbing which then (hopefully) loop up to form self-handles. The bag thus will not have handles that can rip off at just the wrong time under extremely heavy loads since they actually cradle the bag due to encircling it and the leather or webbing itself would have to break which is highly unlikely. The bags should be well sewn and so much the better if they are bar tacked and reinforced with pieces of leather at bearing points or points particularly susceptible to wear.

A nice convenience feature is to have "D" rings

less weight and expense than any rigid or hard type of bag. Furthermore, if they are designed and made properly, they will outlast the hard bags, especially under rough airline handling. If you pack your gear right with all the more delicate and/or breakable items well padded by wrapping them in your assorted insulated jackets and sleeping bags and then placing this in the center of your duffle, the soft-type duffle bag will provide adequate protection for all but the most delicate items.

Your bag or bags should be large and roomy, something on the order of 23 inches to 27 inches long and 14 inches to 16 inches in diameter when fully packed. They should be made of a heavy duck or cotton twill that is water resistant (but not water*proof* because it is important that they breathe) and mildew resistant. For

sewn onto one or both of the top sides of the bag so that you can secure fishing rod cases or other items too long to fit into the bag to its outside. Figure on paying about $25-$50 for the duck bag/webbing strap model and $35-$85 perhaps even more for the cotton twill/leather strap model. The cheaper model, aside from being a bit heavier, is not quite as snazzy looking, but it is every bit as serviceable as the more expensive type.

There are some secondary items of duffle and equipment that you will need to handle special situations but this basic war bag list will see you through the basic circumstances you will run into during your big game hunting. Shop carefully, buy quality and take good care of these items and most of them will see you through for many years of hard use.

CHAPTER 15

# Getting The Most Out Of Your Trophies And Meat

**TIMES CHANGE** and this can affect hunting attitudes as much as any other set of traditions and habits. For instance, through the 1800's when many people were subsistence hunting for their very survival and beef cattle and poultry were often hard to come by, "meat hunting" was elevated to become one of the eternal verities while "trophy hunting" was often considered to be a somewhat trivial if not downright un-American activity.

That set of relative values no longer applies. Though game meat remains as tasty and nourishing as ever, and it still remains one of the sportsman's basic responsibilities to be competent and conscientious in the care of meat, the trophy value of large game animals now at least equals if not exceeds their value as raw protein.

Livestock is readily available nowadays while herds of large game animals have, in many cases, become further and further removed from the large population centers. To tastefully preserve and present a big game animal through the art of modern taxidermy is to give many people a chance to see and enjoy a marvelous creature that they might otherwise not have had the chance to observe. And today's taxidermist, with the

A life-sized mount such as this big Alaskan brown bear is very expensive and difficult to do. Spend the money to get the very best work, and you'll never be sorry!

If you have a local taxidermist nearby, get to know him and try to spend a bit of time in his shop. You'll be amazed at how interesting and instructive it will be.

Fine detail work, such as these finishing touches being checked by taxidermist Jack Atcheson on the mouth of this life-sized Alaskan brown bear mount, take many years of skillful experience.

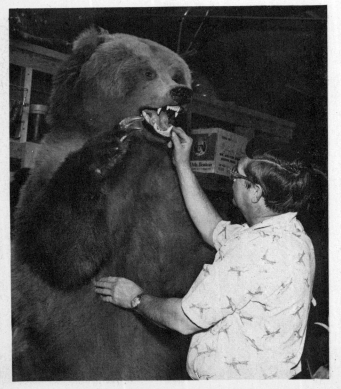

right sort of cooperation from the hunter, is able to present an animal that is almost *alive* and one that will, with proper care and attention, be there for your grand-children to enjoy. All of this takes some knowledge and cooperation on the part of the hunter, however.

## How Does the Taxidermist Do It?

Taxidermy has undergone a radical transformation since the turn of the century. Better methods and materials are now used. Trophies look far more lifelike and last much longer (with proper care). As recently as 50 years ago most taxidermy was of the "stuffed animal" variety. Hides were mostly pickled rather than being tanned by one of a number of more modern methods. This meant that they would inevitably, sometimes sooner sometimes later, begin to contract and crack. The pickled hides were then mounted over wooden forms, often nothing more than a crudely nailed together "neck" and "head" with a several spars sticking out for width and dimension.

Then some soft material, usually straw or excelsior, was packed and tied around the frame for the "body" before the final mounting of the pickled hide. When the hide inevitably began contracting around the soft, malleable "body," the resulting contractions and contortions were often a bit grotesque to put it mildly. Though the life of these trophies varied a bit depending upon how well they had been put up to begin with, and where and how they were displayed, seldom did one retain its attractiveness for more than 5 to 10 years, and many were never attractive to begin with!

Today's taxidermist has ready access to last-forever forms of various paper and synthetic materials that are molded to extremely lifelike contours and proportions. These forms come in a wide variety of sizes so that your particular trophy can be mounted over a "body" of exactly the right size. Better yet, many of these forms (especially for the more popular species such as whitetail deer, mule deer and elk) come in an almost endless variety of poses. You can have the head turned to whichever side you prefer or looking straight ahead, and the head can be up and "alert" or stretched out fully in a "sneak" pose. You can, at your choice, literally custom "engineer" your own trophy so that it will fit well into the particular spot that it will later occupy, and it will feature the "attitude" that you prefer.

Individual skill and craftsmanship are still important even in this era of mass produced forms. The conscientious taxidermist will stock a wide range of form sizes so that he can properly mount your trophy whatever its size, and the knowledgeable student of anatomy will know which among these forms is the best one for your mount. The bad taxidermist won't go to the bother of carrying such a large form inventory or, even if he does, won't have the eye to unerringly select the best one in each case.

Many mounts must have some "buildup" on the basic smooth synthetic form in order to best fit your cape and head skin. These hand molded contours, using plaster or plastic wood or a variety of materials to add planes and muscles and pieces of string or small rope to simulate veins, give the mount added character. They are especially important in the case of the older and larger animals that make the most outstanding trophies. Younger animals (in much the same fashion as people) often have more rounded, regular faces and body con-

Good taxidermy is so expensive due to the high degree of skilled and artistic handwork necessary. It can be argued that fine taxidermy is an art, and it is most certainly a craft! (Shown here — a sable antelope from Africa)

A good taxidermist should have a large and varied selection of forms for mounting so that he has the proper size for your mount. Animals vary considerably more in size than is readily apparent to the inexperienced eye.

and thick-skinned citizens such as elk, moose and the big bear. However, it's usually necessary to shave around the inside of the eyes and facial features even on smaller animals such as deer. This insures that the hide is supple enough to properly "taxi" it onto the form.

3. He must also inspect the hide very carefully to find and mend any bullet holes or any rips that occurred from field skinning or later processing at the tannery.

4. Then he must select the proper form, one that is the right size and that properly jibes with customer instructions as to what sort of pose he wants and which way he wants the animal to face.

5. The taxidermist must then do any necessary build-up on the basic form in order to make the hide fit well and properly simulate the more angular, craggy facial contours of older and larger trophies.

6. Then the taxidermist must sew the hide up around the form, letting it "set up" and thoroughly dry for about 4 to 6 days.

7. After the cape has dried and set up fully, the taxidermist must then carefully inspect the entire mount for any places requiring a touch-up. It is usually necessary to use lacquer or paint in order to add the proper "moist look" around the mouth and nostrils and to properly color the mouth or eyes. Paint may also be necessary to hide very small staple holes or blemishes.

8. The final step, and a critical one, is the proper packing, crating and shipping of the finished mount/s.

## How and When to Choose Your Taxidermist

The "when" is the easier part of this equation. The taxidermist should always be chosen *before* the hunt. Then it is possible to ship the trophies directly to him from the field rather than via the hunter's home. This is usually cheaper, faster and safer. Also, after the hunt there is a bit of a letdown, and sweeping up loose ends like looking for a taxidermist becomes anticlimactic. All too often this means the proper time and attention aren't spent on the process. Still another reason is that about half the fun of any major hunt is the pre-hunt planning and "work up." This kind of desk work is far from drudgery. It acquaints the hunter with interesting new areas and types of hunts, and it often shows him how to save money and increase his enjoyment of the hunt. Contacting and selecting the right taxidermist is (or should be) a part of this pre-hunt strategy. It gives the winter bound hunter something enjoyable and interesting to do, and it stretches out the total hunt experience into a many-month situation.

The "*how*" of selecting a taxidermist can vary a bit depending upon how far away from your home the the taxidermist in question is, how extensive a mounting job you anticipate (how many trophies and how large they are) and a number of other variables. However, some basics do apply throughout. First, the best way to judge a man is by his work not by words. If at all possible, review actual heads that he has mounted. Use

Coleman Jonas, one of the foremost originators and innovators in modern taxidermy, is shown here with a leopard mount.

tours while the older animals have developed craggier, more individual countenances. They literally have more "character." Only the better craftsmen, starting from the base of outstanding forms and glass eyes, can hand model in these individual touches to bring your trophy most fully to life.

Though some taxidermists tan their own hides, many don't and prefer to rely on one of the major tanneries for this service. Tanning often requires 6 months or more until the hide is returned to the taxidermist ready for mounting.

When the hide is returned from tanning, the taxidermist then follows these basic steps:

1. First he must soak the stiff, unyielding hide in order to make it pliable for mounting.

2. Then the taxidermist must generally shave the hide to reduce its thickness, especially on very large

pictures to supplement if necessary but the actual mounts are far better. Check to see if the heads are holding up well if mounted some years back, if the poses and proportions are lifelike, if the hide is soft and realistic, and if the eyes are lively and alive looking.

If at all possible, try to review at least one or two heads of the same species you are interested in. Just because a man does outstanding work on mule deer and pronghorn doesn't mean that his bear and mountain sheep will be equally good. Every animal is different, each takes a bit of a "knack" to do a really outstanding job. (Incidentally, a good general idea is to always — in the company of other experienced hunters if possible — view as many different trophies of all kinds as possible. Head mounts, wall rugs, life-sized mounts, North American game, African game, birds and fish. All of it is grist for the mill. The more taxidermy you see and analyze, the more discriminating an eye you cultivate, and the better you are able to separate flashy from artistic work.)

When contacting out-of-town taxidermists ask for the following items:

1. A copy of their basic brochure and price list.

2. A list of any other prices not included on the basic price list such as crating and shipping and repair work. Ask how the man usually packs and ships the trophies. This is vitally important. Fine taxidermy has been ruined more than once due to sloppy crating

and shipping. Ask how much it costs to pack and crate trophies — giving the taxidermist a specific example such as, one average sized whitetail deer shoulder mount. A good idea to control the rather elastic and, at times, unreasonable costs of repair work is to set up arrangements with the taxidermist to the effect that he can perform repair work up to the extent of $25 (with itemized explanation to accompany final bill when rendered), but for more expensive work, he is to call you collect and explain what he feels is necessary and how much it will cost before proceeding with the work.

3. A list of references. You are particularly interested in:

a. People who have had the same animal/s mounted that you anticipate taking

b. People who live near to you so that you can possibly review the work personally.

4. His basic terms. It is standard to deposit approximately one-third to one-half down upon initially shipping the trophies in and receiving the taxidermist's estimated bill.

Usually, if a very large job is anticipated, the percentage deposit can be less. A job involving three to five trophies from a major Alaskan expedition or one covering possibly 12 to 15 trophies from Africa might well call for a deposit more on the order of 20-25 percent. Also, the amount of the deposit should be roughly related to

A major taxidermist's workshop is a fascinating place! Here Jack Atcheson, a Butte, Montana, taxidermist and hunting consultant, supervises an outgoing shipment of finished trophies.

the delivery time. Most good taxidermy takes 6 to 9 months to complete and often this can run upwards of a year. This is partially because taxidermy is highly seasonal with most of the work piling up in the fall and winter and partly because (with the exception of the one or two operators in the country practicing the new freeze-dried mode of work) good taxidermy is basically a very time-consuming process involving a lot of handwork. However, some operators are now stretching this out to ridiculous lengths whereby trophies are taking up to 2 and 3 years to complete. Frankly, I would not accept this kind of delivery on my personal work. It's my feeling that the taxidermist in this position ought to either hire more staff or turn away the work until he can get a bit more current. However, if this is acceptable to you, at the very least it should call for a decreased deposit of only 5 percent to 10 percent which is now serving more as a simple binder than as a basic deposit.

When choosing a taxidermist, do not let price be the overriding consideration. Good taxidermy is an expensive proposition and undue scrimping will result in bad work that does not last. One artistically modeled trophy that is a joy to the eye and calls up pleasant memories over the years is worth more than several indifferent "heads" that one almost feels constrained to apologize for.

### Trophy Care in the Field

The most common mistake made in field trophy care is in not having salt available to adequately salt the hide. This is very easy to do because on most hunts no one "plans" to take that buck of a lifetime. The smart thing is to keep a supply of salt always at hand in car or camp. Use fine grained table salt not coarse industrial grade

(Above) It's a good idea to wash any blood, grit and other residue off a hide or cape before it "sets" as guide Gene Holmes is doing here on a caribou cape.

(Below) It is impossible to over salt a valued trophy like this bear hide, but you sure can under salt — and lose it!

rock salt. The finer stuff has more surface area by weight thus does a far better job of leeching the moisture out of wet capes and hides. Also, being smaller it works into those minute nooks and crannies far better.

The next dictum is to begin the necessary skinning operation as soon as possible. Sure, go ahead and take your trophy pictures and pause for a minute for a smoke and a moment of contemplation. But don't tarry too long. There can be an astonishing amount of heat build-up, even on very cold days, when very large game like elk and moose is involved. Also, the fresher the trophy is, the easier that it is to move around and handle as well as being much, much easier to skin. You'll appreciate this as you get into the work at hand!

When salting, the hide should be as wet (fresh) as possible, and the salt should be as dry as can be. Wet or damp salt doesn't spread well and — obviously — doesn't soak up additional moisture very efficiently. If your salt has become damp, heat it and dry it out and then pound out all lumps. When salting a hide or cape (neck and headskin), spread the hide out as evenly as possible on the ground and salt thoroughly. Be particularly careful of getting enough salt around the edges of the hide and around any bullet holes and facial features as these are the areas that begin to spoil first. Ironically, the natural inclination of most hunters is to dump the salt out into the middle of the hide and work it outward in increasing concentric circles toward the edges. This almost insures that the edges and facial features will get short changed. The center of the hide is usually the last area to go bad. Start with the trouble areas, doing them first when you are fresh and probably doing a more conscientious job.

Rub the salt in *hard* and evenly. If the hide has already begun drying out a bit and thus forming a natural seal (though it will still be wet underneath this dried out film), it may be necessary to lightly crosshatch the area with your knife to give the salt a head start in working through the "seal" and down to the hair follicles. When the salting is finished, fold the edges up first to make a sort of leak proof pan and keep the salty brine from draining out unduly as it begins to "draw" the hide and pull the moisture out.

Then fold the hide up carefully and store it out of the way in the shade. DO NOT STORE IT NEAR HEAT OR IN DIRECT SUNLIGHT. This will often cause the hide to "burn" and ruin. The hide should be folded so that the skin side is in and only hair is exposed to the outside. If there are scavengers about, then the hide should be stored out of their reach, possibly up in a tree. The hide should then be left to "cure" for several days. After curing (leeching out moisture from the green hide), the hide should then be hung up to drain and dry. It can be hung over a fence rail, tree limb or hitching rack — whatever is handy. Again, it should be hung where direct sunlight won't be on it, and a tarp can be placed over it to protect it from rain and the elements.

Below are some estimates for how much salt to use on different types of trophies. The amount actually required can vary greatly depending upon how good a job of skinning was done in the first instance and how briskly and evenly the salt was applied in the second instance. However, these figures should see most any job through successfully unless the initial skinning was just impossible to begin with (too much meat left adhering to the hide):

| | Whole hide (life-sized mount) | Cape and head-skin only (shoulder mount) |
|---|---|---|
| 1. **Moose** | 20-25 lbs. | 12-15 lbs. |
| 2. **Elk** | 15-20 lbs. | 7-10 lbs. |
| 3. **Caribou** | 12-15 lbs. | 5-7 lbs. |
| 4. **Deer, pronghorn, sheep or goat weighing 175-250 lbs.** | 8 lbs. | 5 lbs. |

5. **Bear.** For the whole hide of a medium fat bear weighing about 250 pounds and squaring out at 5-5½ feet, use about 15 pounds of salt. For a larger bear scale the amount of salt upward proportionately. Bear are fat animals and tough to skin and salt well and easy to go hair-slipped and ruin. When in doubt, pour the salt on! You can't use too much, but you sure can use too little.

Good trophy care means a lot of work in camp. Here outfitter Johnny Holmes saws the antlers off a big caribou skull while guide Charlie Smith salts down two goat hides. Also visible is a big grizzly hide in the foreground.

Caping out a big bull moose is a lot of work taking either help from one or two other hunters or lots of experience or — preferably — both!

## How to Skin Out Your Trophies in the Field

Actually, this step comes before the salting of the hide in real life. I have covered the latter operation first and out of order, so to speak, in order to emphasize it. Though skinning is of great importance, and if done badly enough, it alone can almost guarantee a ruined trophy, far more hides are lost due to uneven and inadequate salting than due to bad skinning.

There are two main things to remember about skinning — all the rest is background music. These two points are the utmost in simplicity and common sense,

but not paying heed to them causes most of the skinning-related problems. They are — start early and take your time. Start before the animal begins to stiffen up. Move the animal around to where it is in a handy position for skinning. Deer are easy to skin, but very large animals like moose, caribou and elk can be considerably harder (or easier) to skin depending upon how one positions them.

Always skin as cleanly as possible the first time. It is much, much easier to avoid small pieces of meat and fat (which can cause the ruination of your trophy) adhering to the hide by skinning out the hide right the first time rather than by trying to "manicure" them off the hide

Trophies like these bighorn sheep are tremendously expensive to hunt and often a once in a lifetime proposition when a hunter takes one. They should receive the most careful field attention possible in order to insure a beautiful and life-like mount.

after the initial skinning. Take your time and work at a steady pace. Most novices start off skinning too slow and then, after a while, get impatient and start working too fast. The problem is not so much with cutting holes or "dings" in the hide, the taxidermist can mend them later (at extra charge, of course) as it is in not doing a clean job of sliding away most of the meat and fat from the hide. Hurried work means sloppy skinning with layers of fat left on the hide that can impede the working of the salt and thus cause hide spoilage. Incidentally, though taxidermists can work many minor miracles in mending and restoring, once a hide starts rotting and going hair-slipped, there is no way known to man at any price to save it. All the hair will eventually fall out, and the trophy will be ruined. So, avoid leaving on that rot-causing fat when you first skin out the hide!

## Skinning for a Shoulder Mount

The old-fashioned neck mount is to be avoided at all costs. The shoulder mount, showing the animal's brisket and indicating the beginning of the body contour is far more attractive. The former mount merely looks "amputated" while the latter has presence and dimension.

When skinning for a shoulder mount, start behind the foreleg and cut up over the back, slightly behind the withers and back down the other side, scalloping your cut over each foreleg several inches down from the body to complete the cut behind the brisket. This type of cut gives the taxidermist a bit of extra hide to work with to cover shrinkage or to use if needed for repairs on other areas. Now make another cut up the back of the neck, directly over the backbone and then branch in a "T" to the back of each antler or horn at its base.

The next step is to skin out the neck, below the cut you have made up the backbone, and then to disjoint the head from the body at the first neck joint. If you are close enough to a taxidermist, it's a good bet to salt the

1. **Skin heads** as shown in diagram. Make initial cut along back of neck and a second cut forming a "T" running to the base of the horns. Cut carefully around the horns or antlers, and cut the skin away from the base. On antlered game a heavy screwdriver is useful in prying skin loose around the antlers. (Courtesy Jonas Brothers, Inc.)

Here guide Andy Dennis capes out a big Osborn caribou shot by author for trophy mount. Basic cut is made around body behind front legs then scalloped over front legs (about 6 or 8 inches down allowing taxidermist extra hide to work with). Then cut is made up back of neck along spine and "T"ed at end to two antlers.

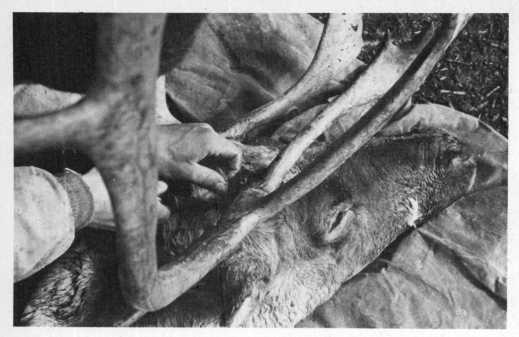

Skinning out around antlers is rather difficult on any deer mount. Although a knife is being used here, actually a blunt edged screwdriver is better and safer — enabling you to literally scrape the tightly binding skin away rather than cutting it and dulling your knife in the process.

Skinning out the head for a trophy mount is exacting work that takes time and patience to do well. Though an experienced hand like guide Gene Holmes (shown here) can make it look easy. It isn't unless you've had a lot of experience.

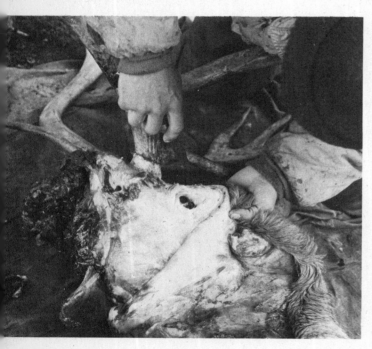

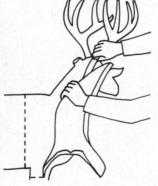

2. **Cut ear cartilage** from skull on the inside and clean meat away from the base of ear. (Skin out the back sides of the ears to approximately within one quarter inch of the edges.) Skin down the skull, being careful not to cut through the skin, especially around the eyes. Preserve the eyelids. Use the fingers of the free hand as a guide on the outside to be certain you are not cutting into the lids.

neckskin liberally, fold it back so that meat doesn't touch meat and take your trophy on into the taxidermist with the head still in. But, if this isn't feasible to do, due to distance or time, then here's how to go about skinning out the head yourself.

The first step is to skin out around the bases of the antlers or horns. This can sometimes be surprisingly difficult, and I have found that a blunt edged instrument like a screwdriver is actually better (and safer) to use for this than is your knife. Skin on down to the ears, turning them out as you skin them. The ears must first be cut loose from the skull at their bases in order to allow the skinning and turning, of course.

Skin out the rest of the head, being particularly careful not to cut through the hide where the skin is thinner such as around the eyes. Also, take care not to cut off the eyelids. They will make the finished mount much more lifelike and realistic. Use your fingers on the outside of the hide as a guide to keep you from severing them with your knife from the inside. Cut the lips loose from the skull leaving them attached to the skin and then split them and salt them liberally. They are fleshy and can spoil easily if not well split and salted. Be particularly careful with large animals having thick, meaty lips such as moose or elk. These lips should be split in many places with parallel slits and as much meat

(Above) Splitting and skinning out the lips is one of the more delicate aspects of fine fleshing a head for trophy mounting. You should never attempt this on a valuable trophy without watching someone else do it properly several times beforehand.

(Below) Antlers or horns must be sawed off the skull for a trophy mount on a line approximately through the eye sockets.

3. **The lips** should be cut close to the skull, leaving the lips attached to the skin. The inside of the lips should then be slit.

as possible cleaned out and then salted extremely liberally.

The final operation is to saw off those prized horns or antlers by cutting off the top of the skull on a line running through the center of the eyes. The top of the skull with the antlers or horns still attached is all the taxidermist needs to attach them to the artificial form. Then quickly clean out the matter adhering to the inside of the skull and eyesockets with your knife, salt the area (just for general hygiene, the skull or antlers won't "go bad" of course) and set them out, skull area up, for the magpies, jays and other camp robbers to finish helping you clean it up. (NOTE: If you think there may be some possibility of your rack of horns or antlers qualifying for Boone & Crockett Record Book consideration, *never* saw the skullpiece in two, thus separating the horns or antlers into two pieces for easier packing and shipping. Doing this, automatically and irrevocably, disqualifies any head from B & C trophy consideration.)

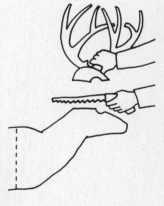

4. **Make sure scalps** are cut long enough for the type of mount desired. Shoulder mounts show more of the true form and character of the animal. Scalps for these mounts should be cut at the forelegs in order to include enough of the brisket for a full shoulder mount. It is not necessary to clean the skull. The top of the skull with horns or antlers attached is all that is needed. Merely saw off the top of the skull through center of eyes after skinning is completed.

## Skinning for Life-Sized Mounts

This is an extremely expensive proposition, but on a trophy of a lifetime, it just may be worth it to you. Cut from the brisket to the tail with one cut down the belly as shown below.

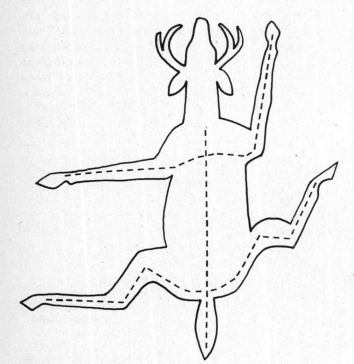

Then cut along each leg, at the rear of the leg, from the hoofs to the center line. The head should be skinned out just as it is in the case of a shoulder mount except do not detach the cape from the rest of the body skin. The skin and head should be all in one piece.

It would pay you to spend a fairly lengthy visit with a local taxidermist and watch him or one of his assistants actually skin out a head or two. This is the most exacting and difficult aspect of skinning out a trophy and watching a skilled technician do one or two heads, with you being able to ask questions along the way, is better than reading whole volumes on this particular aspect of the subject. Besides, it's a fascinating and interesting way to spend an hour or two.

## Skinning for Rugs

Bear, cougar, bobcats, coyotes and similar trophies are skinned for rugs in the same way as they are for life-sized mounts — with one exception: Do *not* cut off the foot pads if you want a life-sized mount. Make the central cut along the belly, running from the end of the tail up to the throat within 3 inches or so of the back of the jaw. Do *not* cut through the lips. Skin out the head from this bottom cut. On non-hoofed, soft footed animals, leg cuts are made from the center of the foot pads up the back of the legs to the central or belly cut. Skin out the feet to the last joints leaving the claws (or hooves) attached. Use the same care in skinning out the lips, ears and eyes as you would with any other type of trophy mount.

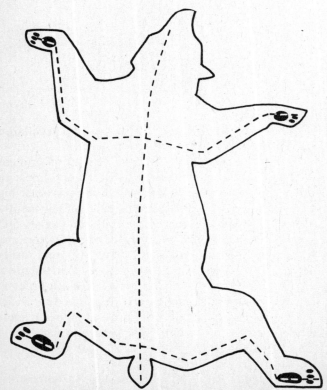

Here a nice array of African trophies is shown with the continental type bleached skull mounting. This is less expensive and very striking when compared with a full head mount and more American sportsmen should probably consider having the occasional trophy put up in this fashion.

## Field Care of Your Meat

Again, as soon as possible before the animal begins to stiffen up, you should start your field dressing procedure. Roll the animal over more or less on its back with the head end pointed slightly uphill. If necessary you can pile a few stones or boughs under the back of the front half of the animal to secure this elevation of the head and shoulders. This presents the abdominal cavity for easier access and promotes drainage of blood and other fluids. Very large animals such as moose and elk often must be cinched into position with a rope and I usually carry a 30- to 50-foot length of parachute cord or light rope when after these animals. This rope, when cut into shorter pieces tailored for the situation at hand, can make life much, much easier when having to field

I prefer to open the animal up a bit differently, making my first incision up forward immediately behind the brisket and then work backwards *toward* the anus rather than away from it. I do it this way because if the carcass is lying properly on its back, there is actually a small cavity of some 2 to 4 inches (depending upon the size of the animal) between the outer hide and muscle and the inner viscera. This is because of the elevated bridge of ribs which is literally holding the hide and muscle away from the inner organs at this spot. Thus, you have an extra margin of safety when inserting your knife and trying to avoid slicing into the inner organs.

Again, when doing it this way, I also use the "flying V" of fingers moving ahead of the knife edge and serving as a guide/safety factor. Especially when getting toward the rear end of the belly cavity where the softer

If your big game hunting has been limited to deer-sized animals, you'd better have an experienced hand along to help you butcher game such as this big bull moose!

dress very large animals such as these.

The first step is to open up the belly cavity. Most hunters do this by inserting the knife carefully through the skin and muscle enclosing the belly, starting immediately in front of the genitals and working the knife forward toward the brisket, thereby opening up the entire belly cavity in the process. When doing it this way, you should slice forward, with the edge of the knife up or forward, using the index and ring fingers of your other hand to act as a moving "V" in front of the knife blade. With this moving "V" you hold the stomach skin up away from the intestines inside so that the knife can slide forward without inadvertently cutting through any of the inner organs. Great care should be taken to avoid puncturing any of this inner viscera because that would cause leakage of various fluids that would degrade the flavor of the meat.

belly has allowed the outer skin and muscles to collapse into closer proximity to the inner organs.

Next it is time to skin the testicles right off and cut them loose. Then it is easier to slice by them almost all the way to the anus when opening a deer or other big game animal up. Next you should pull (actually gently ROLL) the lower intestines out of the body cavity and gently pile them beside the animal. Take your time and be gentle. They will come out very easily and rather cleanly if you avoid tearing or cutting them in the process. Now it's time to split the pelvis open in order to free the lower bladder and ureter. Deer-sized game can be split at the pelvis with a big hunting knife and some strong energy, but for larger game an axe, hatchet or small saw is absolutely necessary. These items make life easier for the deer hunter, also.

Now reach forward into the chest cavity and cut the

diaphragm membrane free in order to get to the forward portion of the chest. The diaphragm is that thin wall of muscle that divides the heart and lung cavity from the intestinal cavity. Cut the diaphragm free all the way around the rib walls and then pull out the heart and lungs, cutting them free by severing the windpipe, esophagus and blood vessels as far forward as possible.

These forward organs can be rolled back gently and removed out of the opening made in the belly. I don't like to wash out the belly cavity with water even if it is handy. Water contains bacteria, and if it's rather warm, you can actually accelerate spoilage by using water. Handle the hide with great care, especially on rutting animals. In fact, try to avoid touching it as much as possible. Make sure your hands and clothes are hair-free before handling the meat as you continue dressing the animal. If some hair has gotten into the body cavity during your work thus far, be sure to pick or brush it out. Again, washing with water usually won't remove it.

Incidentally, though it is one of the most persistent of myths, it is *not* necessary to cut the prominent tarsal

A wolverine is a marvelous bonus trophy to any big game hunt. Many hunters spend the money for a full life-sized mount when they take one of these rare and unique little trophies.

Guide saws antlers off skull of caribou so that they can later be fashioned into a trophy mount.

gland off of whitetail deer (located on the inside of the hock of the hindleg). Oil will not travel through the dead animal from this prominent gland and, in fact, it probably does more harm than good to try to remove it as that's how accidents occur. If the gland is accidentally sliced open during its removal, the oil that exudes most definitely *will* sour any meat that it touches. If you must remove the gland (though I don't) then be sure to cut well around it and very deeply beneath it in order to guard against accidentally rupturing it.

After the carcass has been emptied, you should try to drain it as thoroughly as possible. On smaller, deer-sized animals, try to hang it, head up. If that isn't possible, at least try to turn it over belly down to continue the draining. Avoid getting dirt and refuse into the body cavity during this process. It's not a good idea to leave deer or other big game carcasses on the ground. Ground contact over a large surface area, even in cold weather, means that the animal's body heat doesn't dissipate fast enough. Prop the animal open with a stick or two and then either get deer-sized animals off the ground by hanging them from a tree or something similar. Larger animals should be quartered up just as soon as possible.

Caribou, elk and moose all carry enormous internal body heat and merely opening them up is not enough even in the coldest weather. Even though the meat is quite cold to the touch on the outside, it is souring from the inside out due to that high locked-in body heat. A deer-sized animal can be quartered rather easily. The front quarters from even the larger animals can be disjointed at the shoulder with only a knife as these quarters are joined to the body with only muscle and cartilage. The hindquarters take some bone cutting but the small hunter's saws will do nicely for deer, and a small hacksaw will handle any game. You can cut the ribs into smaller sections with the same saw after disjointing the front quarters from the thorax. Good field care of big game meat is not difficult. All it takes is a modicum of neatness and care. And the eating is worth it many times over!

For more information on trophy care it's a good idea to order the *Field Guide For The Trophy Hunter* from: Denver Jonas Brothers, Taxidermists and Hunting Consultants, 1037 Broadway, Denver, Colorado 80203. This handy little 24-page booklet only costs 50¢ and it covers the area in detail and clearly. It is pocket-sized and thus can be carried along in the field for handy reference.

(Above) The end of a successful hunt with those precious trophies being carefully packed for the trip out. Note how much wider than the horse these Canadian moose antlers are.

Though there's no undue problem with these rather small moose antlers, sometimes it's difficult to get outsized moose and caribou racks into smaller bush planes for the trip out.

# CHAPTER 16

# How To Book A Hunt With A Professional Outfitter

**THE BIG GAME** hunter who is hunting for a new animal or in an unfamiliar area for the first time, no matter how experienced and skilled he may be, is well advised to hunt with someone who *does* know the country and the game. This can be a personal friend of his who happens to be familiar with these goings-on, but more times than not, it means that he must engage the services of a professional hunting outfitter. An outfitter who can then provide all necessary transportation into hunting country, gear and equipment necessary for comfortable living while there and, most importantly, a professional hunting guide familiar with the game and the terrain. Even professional guides or outfitters in one area practically always retain the services of another professional when they are making a long and expensive hunt far away from home in a new area (usually by swapping hunts with each other).

My friend Sam Sands, a longtime outfitter and guide hunting out of Rocky Mountain House, Alberta, has been a professional hunter all his adult life as was his father before him. He has taken record book trophies in several species of game, including bighorn sheep, and he has spent about as much time hunting, watching and

When booking a packstring hunt, tell your outfitter or guide your experience with horses. Be honest. It'll help him to better plan the hunt to match your objectives and capabilities.

learning about bighorns as most. Yet, when Sam went on his first hunt for Dall sheep up in the Yukon Territory, he did the sensible thing. He started corresponding with a well-known outfitter in that area and engaged him for a full scale 21-day hunt. The fact that Sam himself was a professional outfitter and guide made little difference. He was hunting a new trophy for the first time and in an area that he had never seen before, and being a sensible fellow, he decided he needed some help to even up the odds. About the only difference in Sam's situation in this case and that of a neophyte hunter making his first trip was that, rather than paying for the hunt outright, Sam swapped his outfitter for an

(Top) Even a large youngster such as this one, though he may have the physical capabilities of an adult, often should be hunted a bit differently. His attention span and patience are usually lower than an adult's, and his expectations on size per head are often lower since he's done less shooting.

(Middle) When booking the hunt, if your outfitter suggests you do some practice riding before the hunt — do it!

(Bottom) A successful mixed game hunt takes careful planning and booking.

equivalent hunt the following year in the Alberta Rockies for bighorn. (They both took fine rams, incidentally.)

When I tell this story occasionally, some hunters are quite surprised. After all, Sam is a *professional* isn't he? Then why does he need "help" to hunt? Also, since Sam owns all the necessary hunting gear, including a full packstring of horses, why should he pay to use someone else's (and he certainly did as his time spent guiding the Yukon outfitter was certainly worth money)?

First, some U. S. states and Canadian Provinces or Territories require by law that any nonresident retain the services of a professional guide or at least be accompanied by an adult resident of the area. This kind of legislation arises due to several reasons. In some cases, as one might imagine, the intent is to be sure that every visiting hunter more or less must pay someone to help him hunt that area. Many of the best game fields are, not surprisingly, the deep wilderness areas which are chronically cash-poor due to the lack of industry and jobs. This kind of law insures that most visitors will leave a bit of change around when they pass through.

But, that isn't the only reason for this sort of legislation, by any means. With the enormous growth of both real incomes and ready credit in the last generation, many hunters are able to take deep wilderness hunting trips at a rather early and, at times, inexperienced age. No longer is it always necessary for the sportsman to

build up to the "big" trips over a period of many years. Thus, more and more states and provinces got more and more tired of mounting arduous, expensive and — at times — dangerous search and rescue missions to locate and save legions of well meaning greenhorns who suddenly found themselves lost and/or stuck on the top of some strange mountain. Laws requiring strangers to be accompanied by knowledgeable locals are one way of at least partially avoiding that kind of imbroglio.

But, that wasn't the reason why Sam opted for the full treatment from his outfitter. After many years of experience in wilderness country, Sam wasn't about to get lost, and he could easily have worked out a more informal arrangement with the outfitter whereby the legal conventions would have been observed and yet he would not have been fully engaging the outfitter in such expensive fashion.

First, Sam, like most of the rest of us, had a limited amount of time. He simply couldn't dawdle long enough to get into vast and unknown game country and then "start from scratch." Secondly, he needed good horseflesh and lots of good tack, gear and food to get him back into pristine wilderness (which is where the trophy rams are found) and keep him there in comfort and security. Sure, he owned all of this gear himself, but it simple wasn't feasible for him to transport it all over 1,000 miles and then pay to get it all back into the wilderness. Like the rest of us, he found it more expeditious to "rent" the outfitter's outfit which was already established back in prime country.

And, finally, it was a new game to Sam. There is a saying that "a whitetail deer is a whitetail deer," whether hunted in the Missouri breaks of eastern Montana, the pine swamps of southern Alabama or the rolling ridges of Vermont. Well, yes and no. The saying

is true, as far as it goes. It just doesn't go far enough.

A sheep may be a sheep but Sam had never hunted *Dall* sheep before, only the larger and more southerly bighorn. Even if he had had extensive experience with the snow white thinhorn sheep, animals do vary by locale and by local conditions. They learn varying patterns of behavior and make varying adjustments in order to live. Darwin had something to say about all that many years ago. Point is — a completely strange animal is not as predictable (as if *any* truly wild animal was really predictable!) for the hunter unfamiliar with them and their ways. Starting off with an experienced guide who knows both game and country puts any hunter, no matter how seasoned, way, way ahead.

Selecting the right outfitter is a critical and relatively complex task. However, it is also an interesting and — to most hunters — highly enjoyable one. It should not be approached as a "chore" by the hunter but rather as a chance to learn more about the game and the country in question and as a way of stretching out the enjoyment

If you're after a trophy caribou, *be specific* as to both your wants and your minimum expectations. Adjectives such as "long" or "nice" or "big" are too open to differing interpretations. All caribou look "nice" to the deer hunter used to seeing only whitetail and mule deer.

210

of the hunt many extra months.

The process of selecting the right outfitter can vary a bit since there are so many different types of hunts, different outfitters and different objectives that the hunter may have. Obviously, the hunter's physical condition is considerably more important on a high altitude mountain hunt for 3 weeks when after sheep in northern British Columbia or the Yukon than it is on a much less expensive and less arduous hunt for moose by boat in the lowlands of Quebec or Ontario.

However, good physical condition is a prime ingredient of any wilderness hunt, and it will be so treated in the following analysis. Even "easy" wilderness hunts are considerably more of a physical experience than a day on the links or an afternoon of tennis. Also, obviously, the amount of time and money involved on a given hunt roughly determines the amount of time and energy that the outfitter can devote to answering your questions and requests for information. Bear this in mind. Don't negotiate a $500 meat hunt the way you would a $5,000 mixed game trophy hunt in Alaska. It's not necessary, and it won't work. In the following analysis, I'll give a number of general guidelines which should, in a commonsense fashion, be interpreted "up" or "down" depending upon the specific nature of the trip you have in mind, its complexity and expense.

### Recognize Where the Primary Responsibility Lies

It lies with *you* the hunter making the trip. Every year I hear a number of hunters blame their outfitter and/or guide for a bad hunt. In exploring these situations further and sorting out fact from fancy, I find that many times it is really the hunter himself who is at fault. Yes, there are certainly bad outfitters around who can unethically and even, at times, fraudulently dupe the sportsman.

But in many cases the sportsman is at fault for not checking out, in even the most cursory fashion, some of the inflated claims that the outfitter has made about his area or his services. In still other cases, the hunter may have booked with a perfectly good outfitter who, for the money he was charging and the types of hunts he was providing, was doing an outstanding job. Unfortunately, these services may not have properly fitted the sportsman's requirements and goals. Booking with a good outfitter who does not meet your requirements can be as bad as booking with a bad operator to begin with.

When most intelligent people buy a house, a car or make any other major purchase, they realize directly or indirectly that the main responsibility for making the right decision lies with themselves. They realize that others are trying to sell them something and thus, naturally, present their "product" in the best light possible. This can be a bit misleading at times, even when there is no conscious attempt to do so. There are always semantical problems when people communicate on complex matters. Words, like "good," "bad," "easy," "hard," and others that always seem to crop up when negotiating, all have highly variable and imprecise meanings.

So, start out with the right outlook. Take the responsibility on your own shoulders for coming up with a good hunt. After all, it's *your* hunt, *your* vacation, and *your* hard earned cash.

### Where to Locate Good Outfitters

Talk to friends and acquaintances. If they have had a good hunt within the last year or two with an outfitter, that is certainly a good lead. One prime advantage of this kind of source is that you have fewer communications problems with a friend whom you know and know well.

Other good sources are the ads in the national and regional outdoor magazines. These listings, usually arranged by geographic area, tell you the names of many leading outfitters and the game they offer on their hunts. Also, check with good, reputable taxidermists. These can be either local or national level taxidermy houses. Often they can suggest the names of outfitters who seem to be outstandingly successful in the trophies that they are sending in to the taxidermists. One of the more obvious sources is to check with full-fledged professional booking agents or hunting consultants. This is covered in complete detail in Chapter 20.

Also be sure to consider the various Fish and Game Departments in the states or provinces which you are interested in hunting. Also, you can contact the various professional guides and outfitter's associations for a listing of their members and any information on the particular types of hunts you want to check out. Still another potential source is the hunting or outdoor columnist in your local newspaper or favorite outdoor magazine.

### How to Make the Initial Contact With Outfitters

Start off with a basic list of between three and five outfitters whom you have selected to contact first. Don't just write to one or two. They may be away for several weeks, or there may be other delays that will have you sitting around waiting for answers too long. When you do contact these first outfitters (and this goes for the later contacts beyond the initial phase, also), try to keep your letters to them relatively similar so you can compare their responses more legitimately. If one outfitter gives you a much more courteous and complete response than another only because your original letter to the first man was much clearer and more organized than your letter to the second man, then you are left wondering if that outfitter is really a better operator or if he just started off ahead of the game due to a better approach by you.

If you're booking a packstring hunt, find out how many hunters will be operating on each packstring (preferably no more than four) and how many extra saddle mounts will be available if needed.

*Keep this initial contact brief and to the point!* The outfitter is all too used to "window shoppers" who want a lot of information but will never end up booking a hunt. Since the outfitter is a businessman, he must ration his time where he thinks it will bring him more business. Don't try to go into too much detail on the first contact.

Before you write the first word to an outfitter, you must make your own mind up about several things. You must decide how much money you can reasonably spend and what is the maximum amount of total money you can spend under any circumstances. Then, from these two totals (I always end up spending the latter, larger figure it seems) you must deduct such basics as what you must spend for hunting licenses, for transportation to and from the outfitter, for souvenirs or other incidental purchases and for any additional clothing, equipment or other gear that you must purchase in order to make the hunt. Then, save back an additional amount for "just in case" money. This little hoard can cover your tip to your guide and give you a small safety margin in case you are stranded somewhere for an extra day or two.

After subtracting all these items you are left with the net amount that you should and that you can (at furtherest stretch) spend on the hunt itself. You should know these figures before you ever begin the first step in negotiating or setting up a hunt.

Next, you should decide which animal you are primarily after. If you are planning a mixed game hunt in which you are after two or more animals, sit down and list the animals in order of importance to you. At times this takes some difficult soul searching, especially if you have never shot any of them before.

However, more hunts are ruined at this stage than at any other. Foggy, incomplete and unclear objectives hamstring any hunt from the beginning. If *you* don't know specifically what you want, how can you communicate your objectives to anyone else?

Even after listing your trophies in order of importance, you still are not through if you are trophy hunting. Beside each trophy you should list two columns: "Trophy I *want;*" and "Minimum trophy I will settle for." These two sets of figures, which can be in Boone & Crockett points, inches of spread or main beam length or number of antler points or some combination of all, are your yardstick to use in determining how long you need to plan on hunting and how much money you will need to spend. Obviously, the more animals you want to take, and the better the trophies you want under each species, the more time and money you had better plan on investing.

A sample list of this type for a hypothetical 21-day mixed game hunt in the Yukon might read as follows:

| Species | Desired trophy | Minimum trophy |
|---|---|---|
| Dall sheep | 38" around curl | 33" around curl |
| Moose | 60" spread or 200 points B & C score | 53" spread or 180 points B & C score |
| Caribou | 400 B & C score or 50" main beams | 350 B & C score or 42" main beam length (possibly will consider smaller bull if well developed double-shovels) |

### Bonus trophies

(These are too rare to be ''counted on'' as are the ''basics'' above, but they should be included in this process where you logic-out your hunt beforehand.)

| Grizzly | Any *adult* that is unrubbed and well furred. |
|---|---|
| Wolf | Any color or size that is well furred. |
| Wolverine | Any color or size that is well furred. |

Even though you probably won't find it necessary to get this specific to the outfitter about either your finances or trophy objectives in your very first contact, you should still do this ''desk work'' before you start so that you will have these factors in mind throughout the entire process.

Here are the things you should specifically cover in your first contact:

1. Ask him for a copy of his current brochure and any other literature that he may have put together on his hunting services.

2. Ask him for a list of references. These should be

If you're after expensive and highly prized trophies such as mountain sheep (above) or grizzly bear (below), plan on concentrating on them to the exclusion of all other potential trophies when setting up your hunt.

the names and addresses of hunters who have hunted with him in that area within the last year or two. *Beware of a list of references that includes mostly hunts from many years back.*

3. Tell him, quite simply, the trophies you are most interested in in order of importance. Tell him a bit about yourself (age, do you smoke or not, general physical condition especially if you are overweight, and your previous hunting experience). All this should be done crisply and in few words. More details can come later from both parties, if things progress that far. Ask him for the names of any hunters who took particularly good trophies of your "most wanted" species.

4. Thank him for any information he can give you and tell him that you are serious about the hunt, and if the information you receive from him warrants it, you will be back in touch with him shortly.

Remember: Outfitters generally don't tend to be good writers nor people who like to spend the time spinning out long, cumbersome letters (though there are some interesting exceptions to this general rule). Even though technically it's the outfitter's job to convey this information to you, keeping things brief and to the point at this stage tends to elicit more complete info at later stages in the process.

### How to Check References Properly

Call as many references as possible rather than writing to them. Even though it may be the outfitter's business to furnish you with hunting information, the references are just other hunters like yourself, and they are strictly doing you a favor by communicating information. It's much more convenient for them to do so over the telephone rather than by letter. You can keep your costs surprisingly low by:

1. Calling during cheap rate periods in the late evening or on weekends.

2. Direct dialing station-to-station rather than person-to-person operator assisted call.

3. Setting a watch in front of you to time the call or using a cooking timer that will "ding" after 5 or 6 minutes or whatever allowance you give yourself.

4. Outlining the questions you want to ask and jotting down the references' answers so that you can keep track of who said what after several calls to differing people. Be prepared to tactfully but briskly keep the conversation on the track. Those friendly anecdotes you can trade with each other are fun but expensive and not really the reason why you called.

When contacting references by mail, you can still make it convenient to them to reply to you by following several simple procedures. Introduce yourself in a brief personal letter. Type the letter if possible so that they can read it easily. If your handwriting is no more legible than mine, they'll have to struggle to read it. *Don't* send them a xerox copy of a single master typed letter. I

Be honest about your shooting ability when booking a hunt. Nowhere does it say you must be an expert marksman. Lying to the guide or outfitter may result in a shot that shouldn't have been taken. Check the sighting on your rifle as soon as you reach camp if possible.

When booking an extended and expensive hunt, try to check out the prospective guides as well as the outfitter. You'll be spending more time with the guides — a good outfitter and a bum guide usually will add up to a bum hunt.

personally feel this is rather rude and impolite even though some may regard it as being "efficient." If I am asking the sportsman for a personal favor, namely that he take the time to reply to my questions, then I can show him the courtesy of a personal letter. When I get one of these letter-copies, I do answer the questions and provide the requested information, but I must admit that it doesn't "inspire" me to go into as much detail as I otherwise might. I have a feeling that the effect is the same on other sportsmen.

I always include a fill-in-the-blank and/or multiple choice note for the reference to fill out that answers my basic questions. This makes it most convenient for him to respond to you, and since in effect it is a forced-format letter, it insures that you at least get all the basic answers you are after. Naturally I don't limit the reference to this form note. I also suggest that if he has anything else to cover that he please feel free to add to the note or, if he deems it important enough, that he call me collect some evening.

Most sportsmen will feel that you are sincerely interested in possibly making a hunt with the outfitter when you approach them on this basis. They will usually bend over forwards and backwards to furnish you with very complete information. A final nicety is to include a stamped, self-addressed envelope for their convenience in mailing their response.

What are some of the questions you should ask these references? Well, here again these can vary a bit depending upon what type of hunt you are investigating and other variables. However, a "shopping list" of possibilities is as follows:

- When did the reference hunt there and what species (and sizes) did he shoot? How long did he hunt and was this his first hunt with that outfitter or in that general area?
- How many other hunters were in camp and what species did they take?
- Did he see much game? How would he rate the country in general and what species was it best for? (It's often a good idea to ask the reference "based on what you saw and heard, please list — from best to worst — which species I have the best chance for in this area?")
- How would you rate the outfitter's gear and tentage (good/satisfactory/unsatisfactory); staff including cooks, guides and wranglers; horses and saddlery?
- How many hunters hunted out of each camp? How many camps did you hunt from? How many hunters to the guide?
- Please send names and addresses or telephone numbers of other hunters you met while in camp. (Note: This is especially important because it gives you other references to check besides those that the outfitter gave you.)
- How was the food, camp organization and "feeling"

Check out the camp accommodations carefully when booking a hunt. There are tents and then — there are more tents. This semi-permanent hard frame, built up foundation framing is the basis for a snug canvas camp as opposed to too small, haphazardly pitched tents that aren't weathertight.

of the hunt in general — enjoyable or disorganized? Would you go on another hunt with this outfitter? Would you recommend him as being a good outfitter? What would you do differently on another hunt with him? What other comments or suggestions would you make? Do I need any special equipment? Is this hunt more or less physically demanding than other comparable hunts or is it about average?

Checking out references can be very enjoyable and interesting. It's a chance to meet and learn from other hunters with similar interests, and occasionally you will make new friends to hunt with and correspond with over a period of years. So, don't begrudge the time spent reference-checking. Not only can it save you from making a very costly mistake — it can (and should) be fun!

### Additional Follow-up Contact With Outfitter

Okay, so far you have written to and received the basic "boiler plate" info and literature from the outfitter with perhaps a limited amount of specific information relating to your planned hunt. Then you have followed up by contacting some references, both those volunteered by the outfitter himself and some that you unearthed while checking the first group. What next?

Now it's time to get back in touch with the outfitter to follow up with further questions. When writing this time, you should tell him (briefly) when you wrote to him the first time and what he sent to you at that time.

Then you should mention the names of some or all of the references that you have contacted do date. This lets him know that you are obviously rather serious about the whole thing.

Then you should tell him more specifically what animals you want and in which order and how large you would like your trophies, especially your main target. You can also state any questions that may have come up during your reference checking. Then you should go into a basic list of questions that you want the outfitter to cover. Here again it's often a good idea to use the form letter fill-in-the-blank and/or multiple choice question approach that you used in some of your reference checking for the very same reasons — the ease and convenience of the outfitter.

What are some of these basic questions? Well, for purposes of this example, let's assume you are writing to the outfitter about that mixed game hunt in the Yukon that we mentioned a while back (where you wanted a Dall sheep, moose and caribou, in that order, as your basic objectives on a 21-day-hunt, and you hoped for a possibility at one of the bonus trophies of grizzly, wolf or wolverine). You might ask the outfitter the following (preferably using the fill-in-the-blank format):

1. *Sheep oriented questions:* How many of the hunters wanting sheep this past year got one and how many didn't? The year before? What was the *average* length

If you're booking a moose hunt, try to be specific about what size bull you're after. All moose are "big" and "nice." Such words have an infinite number of meanings depending on the hunter.

of curl on your sheep taken during each of the last 2 years? What were some of the larger sheep taken last year? Assuming I start out concentrating on sheep and am in reasonably good physical condition (by city standards) and can shoot well enough to consistently hit sheep-sized animals out to 250 yards, what would you say my chances of taking a 33-inch sheep are (____%). Of taking a 38-inch sheep under the same circumstances? Please give me additional references of the hunters taking some of your larger rams last year. On average, how long does it take most hunters to bag an average (33 - 35-inch) ram, assuming they hunt hard every day and lose no time due to bad weather?

2. *Moose oriented questions:* What were the two largest moose taken by your hunters last year? The year before? What is the *average* size moose your hunters have taken in the last 2 years? What are my chances of getting a 60-inch moose, assuming that I am willing to pass up some smaller bulls and work hard in order to be able to look over a number of moose? How many hunters wanting moose during the past season took one? The season before? What are my chances of taking a 53-inch moose which I have informally set as my (hopeful) minimum size moose. (Note: Please be assured that I know there are no "guarantees" in sport hunting and by asking you what my "chances" are, I am not asking for committments but, rather, for your honest opinion in each case, assuming it is an average year with average winter kill the preceding winter, average amount of hunting time lost due to bad weather during our trip, etc.)

3. *Caribou oriented questions:* (similar to moose and sheep questions).

4. *General questions:* Relative to the species I want, which is your area best and worst for? (Please rank in order from best to worst.) How many grizzly were

(Facing page) When booking a hunt be sure to be completely honest with your potential guide or outfitter about your physical condition. Country like this is tough to get around in, even on horseback, if you're out of shape.

(Left) If you have any special dietary needs, the time to let your outfitter know it is when booking the hunt, not after you're already out in the field!

taken last *fall?* How many wolves and wolverine? For how many total hunters? When, considering my objectives, would you suggest as the best time for me to come? How long do you think I need to hunt as a minimum in order to be pretty sure of taking my three "basics" and having them all at least meet my desired minimums?

Though these questions may well have to be adapted a bit here or there to serve your specific needs, they should give you a good idea of how to "audit" the outfitter at this stage. However, I should make several comments concerning this type approach.

*Thank him for furnishing the information.* In your covering letter accompanying the fill-in-the-blank or multiple choice question sheet, it's a good idea to let the outfitter know that you realize he is busy and you are sorry to bother him with so many questions but, at this final stage when you are making the decision whether to sign up for the hunt or not, you do feel you need this kind of information. You are not exactly apologizing to the outfitter — after all you're the customer. You are just letting him know you realize it will take some time for him to scrape up all these answers, and you are reemphasizing that you are just on the verge of signing up therefore, by implication, it's worth his while to answer all your questions fully and promptly.

*Make sure he knows you aren't trying to over-commit him.* The small cautionary note I included in the example — wherein you indicate that in all those instances where you are asking about "what are my chances ___% of doing one thing or another, you realize that

these are not guarantees or iron-clad commitments, just honest estimates — is always a good idea. All too many beginning hunters seem to think when they buy a hunt they are buying *animals*. They aren't, they're buying an experience.

The outfitter is supposed to provide the services he said he would in the kind of game country that he represented his area to be. He is not necessarily guaranteeing you animals. Most outfitters (and guides) are a bit on the individualistic and independent side or they wouldn't be in such a chancey, mostly thankless occupation to begin with. They realize that a major hunt is expensive and a big decision for most of us, and they don't mind furnishing information to *serious* possible clients. However, if they do get the idea that you are approaching their hunt strictly with an accountant's eye, more or less like you are buying so many pounds of potatoes and beans at the store, it may just "turn them off" to the point that they aren't that interested in taking you.

There's a bit of a fine line between wanting good and complete information (which inevitably gets into some numbers in the estimates about next season as well in the history of last season) on the one hand and appearing to be trying to get the outfitter to commit himself to all sorts of things on the other hand. This "fine line" can be walked very well, as long as you know it's there and take care to deal with it properly.

*Phone call:* It's often a good idea to tell the outfitter that after he returns the answers to these questions you would like to call him for one final conversation and to

ask where you can reach him by phone in the next month or so.

*Special personal considerations of yours:* If you have any special dietary needs or other health considerations, now is the time to explain them fully and honestly to your outfitter and then to ask him if they will affect your hunt and if so, how. Do *not* arrive in camp and suddenly spring this on the outfitter. It isn't fair to him, and it may hurt your hunt in double portion as he may have been able to make certain adjustments in advance to work around these things if he had known about them in time but can not now do so.

*Be honest:* I simply can not emphasize this one enough. If you knew how many times the average outfitter finds that his client lied (yes that's what I said) outright to him about his physical condition, marksmanship or any number of other things — most of you would be amazed. Don't tell the outfitter you are in good physical condition and want to work hard for a trophy sheep and then let him find out later that you are so flat-footed you can't climb a step ladder without problems. Don't tell him you are in excellent physical condition and then arrive in camp 20 pounds overweight, chuckling and claiming that you "gained it all in the last couple of weeks or so." Some clients have even been known to send the outfitter pictures of themselves made 20 or 30 years earlier! (No, I'm not kidding. I personally know of more than one instance where this has happened.)

Sure, if it's optional the outfitter would rather have his hunters all be young, in the peak of physical condition and brimming over with physical and emotional fortitude so that they will hunt and hunt hard for their trophies and be able to stoically accept any of the inevitable setbacks that crop up periodically on all ethical fair chase sport hunts. But, the outfitter is a realist. He knows that only a certain (small) percentage of his clients are going to be so gifted and that most of the rest of us will be molded of humbler clay.

If he's a good outfitter, he will be able to (almost) pull wonders in working around the various limitations of his differing clients. If he knows, frankly and fully and well in advance, all about your limitations and outlook on the hunt he can make adjustments. (Don't tell him you want to hunt hard and then grouse about getting up before 9 AM each morning after you get there!) By hunting you in some areas rather than others, in some camps rather than others, matching you with the right type of guide and horses, scheduling your hunt at the best time of the season, putting you in camp with the right kinds of other hunters and making various other adjustments, the really good outfitter can go a long, long way toward insuring that you will have a hunt that is both productive and enjoyable. One that is, in a word, well matched to you.

*Special equipment:* If it is a horseback hunt and you do not have your own saddlebags and rifle scabbard, try to borrow some to take with you. It's always a good idea to be as self-contained as is reasonably possible. If you can't borrow them, ask your outfitter specifically if he can furnish you with them. Let him know well in advance.

Most outfitters furnish a list of suggested duffle and personal equipment you will need. If yours did not do so, ask him if there is anything special you should bring along. (If it's a mountain hunt *always* take your own binoculars and spotting scope.) If he did not include a map of his area, showing where it is in relation to the overall state or province, you may want to ask him for one.

## Handling the Formal Agreement and the Financial Transactions

Some outfitters request that their clients sign a formal contract with them while others do not. Either way is alright, providing you go about things right. If he wants you to sign his contract, read it and review it over a period of time so that you have ample time to digest it. If anything about it bothers you, have a buddy or two review and/or contact some of the references again to see what they did about it or if it caused them any problems.

If there is no formal contract, when you mail your deposit in to the outfitter or his agent, it's a good practice to briefly review the terms under which you are contracting for the hunt (e. g.: no more than one hunter per guide nor four hunters per camp except under unusual and temporary conditions; a separate cook and wrangler with each camp or packstring; no more than two or four hunters, depending, per packstring; etc.).

Don't overdo this write-up. It is not a contract. It is merely an informal capsule of your agreement and what you are paying for. To overdo things by getting too detailed and too legalistic is not only probably going to make the outfitter a bit miffed, it isn't necessary. Keep it to no more than eight or ten lines of simple wording at most.

Plan to pay a deposit of approximately 25 percent to

33 1/3 percent down to bind the hunt with the outfitter. Some have recently been asking for as much as 40 percent or 50 percent down but, unless you are asking the outfitter to undertake some sort of special expense in order to provide a hunt that meets your requirements, I do not feel these higher deposits are warranted and would not pay them. Most all outfitters will accept a personal check for this phase of the payment since it will have plenty of time to clear before the hunt and that is usually the way I pay deposits since the checks make good receipts.

However, it is a good idea to check with the outfitter to see how he wants the balance of the hunt paid (usually due at the beginning of the hunt). Many outfitters require, and all prefer, that these balances be paid in some sort of guaranteed fashion such as with travelers checks or certified checks (or cash, of course).

When you go on your hunt, it's a good idea to take facsimile copies of all your correspondence with the outfitter as your hunt evolved. Leave the originals of these papers at home. If any disagreements do come up, having these papers with you can sometimes clarify things with a minimum of fuss and friction. On the more positive side, some questions may come up that aren't even to the stage of being disagreements and having this documentation along may keep them from becoming such.

## Recourse for Fraudulent or Misrepresented Hunts

Notice in the above title it does not say "recourse for *unsuccessful* hunts." All sport hunting runs the danger of occasionally being unsuccessful if it is truly ethical and open to the vagaries of weather, chance and fate. Nobody likes to bomb out on a hunt but it happens, and it happens to the best of both hunters and outfitters. After all, trite as it is to say it, "it's the misses (or unsuccessful hunts) that make the hits (or successful hunts) so much fun."

So, if your hunt was unsuccessful, don't immediately start blaming the outfitter or guide. Chances are it was more due to circumstance, bad luck or even — perish the thought — you might even have contributed, however innocently, to the lack of success yourself.

A hunt can go bad because of almost countless reasons or some patchwork quilt combination of these many reasons. Perhaps there was an abnormally high winter kill the winter before your hunt. Maybe the season is early or late getting started, and this sudden change in the weather has affected the general migrations or local movements of the game. Possibly some new industrial development — a dam or highway or seismic exploration many miles from your hunting area — may have adversely affected the availability of game. Or, you may just run into more bad weather than your share which may reduce your hunting time afield and, particularly on the shorter hunts of 5, 7 or 10 days, this can drastically affect the overall success of your hunt.

If you are unhappy with a hunt, I strongly suggest that you come home and put the whole thing on the back burner for a few days or weeks. A major hunt is a substantial emotional as well as physical happening and often a hunter may feel one way about events while he is out in the field in strange surroundings and far away from home and then, weeks later back at home, he may feel entirely different about the same thing. It happens frequently.

So, come home and let the whole thing sit for awhile to insure that you are approaching it with the right perspective. Think back carefully over the hunt to be sure of your ground. Did the outfitter furnish good tentage, food and horseflesh as he promised in his brochure or letter? Was the staff generally helpful and professional in their duties whether they be cook, wrangler, assistant guide or guide? The fact that you may have had a disagreeement with one of them doesn't necessarily mean that the staff was incompetent. Perhaps they may not have been as diplomatic as your next door neighbor, but that's not the same thing as incompetency.

If you didn't see much game, step back mentally and review the situation. Perhaps your own expectations were overblown to begin with. Although the western U. S. or northern Canada or Alaska may feature game in almost superabundance compared to the heavily populated East, Southeast or Midwest, you should not expect to see whole herds of game running free as if on an African savannah.

If your own expectations weren't at fault, think back to the general circumstances of the hunt. From speaking to the guides, outfitter, other hunters in camp who may have hunted there before or perhaps re-contacting the references, it is obvious that up until this season there was more game there than you saw and that, based on all experience to date, the outfitter did *not* misrepresent the quality of the game field.

All these cautionary comments are not designed to discourage any hunter from lodging legitimate complaints against misrepresentation and inferior service. Far from it! Most hunters don't do enough of that. Therefore, the bad eggs in the outfitting business aren't weeded out soon enough. If you had a bad hunt and someone else had been energetic enough to complain, perhaps you might have avoided that costly mistake.

Just be sure of your ground. I have heard hundreds of complaints against outfitters and guides and have, over the years, taken the time to delve into any number of them in some detail. Honesty constrains me to say that the outfitter was innocent in at least as many times as he was guilty. The culprits were often bad communications, a misunderstanding of what he was actually contracting for by the sportsman and, at times, just a plain unreasonable hunter or client who wanted to blame the outfitter for his own shortcomings.

However, let's assume that after carefully reviewing

the facts in your mind and after allowing ample time for the memories of the hunt to percolate and season so that you are approaching the whole thing objectively you still feel that you have an open-and-shut case of bad service and misrepresentation, then here are your options:

1. You can write to the Fish and Game Department of the state or province in which your hunt occurred and complain to them. List the commitments the outfitter made and the things he actually delivered, pointing out the difference between the two clearly and succinctly. Stay away from personalities ("he wasn't a very nice person") and loose value judgments ("he didn't seem to care much about how the hunt was going or the camps were running") and stick to the demonstrable facts.

Send along any documentation to support your case such as facsimile copies of the original correspondence between you and the outfitter (the commitments) and copies of letters from other hunters supporting your contentions (the actual delivery). Even though you may have been bilked by one of the biggest charlatans around and thus, quite naturally, are doing a slow burn about it, try to make your letter and the case it presents as objective and balanced as possible.

Ask the Department what, if anything, they can do to prevent this sort of sad occurrence from happening again and if there is any possible way you may be able to recover some of your fee. Chances are low on the latter prospect but it doesn't hurt to ask. Complaining to the Fish and Game people can have varying results, but if this is a state or province where the outfitter must be licensed by the state, the potential for recourse is certainly there.

2. You can write to the Guides and Outfitters Association (if your man belongs to one) and complain. Here again, work doubly hard so that your presentation of the facts is crisp, clear and unemotional. Remember: you are talking to a group of other outfitters who have all had ample experience dealing with overexpectant and overemotional clients of their own. If you have a strong case, and you certainly should if you are pressing matters to this extent, let it speak largely for itself.

Admittedly, if this is only the first or second written complaint against the man, chances are nothing much of note will happen by pursuing this approach. However, you are putting the complaint "on the record" and that can be considerably more important than it may sound. If numerous other similar complaints are received about the same man, chances are the ruling body of the Association may see fit to mention it and

censure the man if, for nothing else, reasons of simple self-interest. And, in many respects, peer pressure of this sort can be one of the strongest of all agents for reform. It may not get your money back (though it may get you a significant reduction in the cost of a repeat hunt with the man if you're interested in pursuing that approach), but it can sure help the next pilgrim to avoid the same unfortunate situation. Think how much that would have meant to you if positions were reversed.

3. A third, more general approach, is to try to contact a "Bureau of Consumer Protection" or similar office in the state or provincial government. More and more states and Canadian provinces are setting up departments of this type within their governments. Try to locate one in the governmental apparatus that you are dealing with and then contact them just as you might have if you had an unsatisfactory business dealing of a more generalized nature within their political boundaries.

4. If your outfitter is listed in the annual *N. R. A. Hunting Annual,* you can complain to their "Denali Complaint Advisory Board." This Board is made up of leading outfitters in Canada and the U. S. and to date they have established a rather good track record on resolving disputes of this nature. If the dispute is not resolved and the outfitter is deemed to be guilty of misdeeds, then his listing in the influential N. R. A. sponsored *Annual* is dropped in the future. Admittedly this is a more limited option (applying only to those outfitters listed in the *Annual* to begin with) but, in the right circumstances, it can be a highly effective one.

I don't want to close this chapter on such a purely negative note. Remember that the vast majority of outfitters are decent, honest operators struggling to give good service in one of the toughest vocations there is. Set out on your hunt with an open minded attitude of cooperation and patience and give your man the benefit of the doubt repeatedly. You'll find that, with the right fair-minded approach, things will work out well in the vast majority of cases, and you can avoid the regrettable and time consuming "final resort" options mentioned here.

One final thought. Before instituting these final recourse actions yourself, contact the outfitter to see if you can't work out some sort of mutually satisfactory resolution yourselves. Perhaps partial recovery against another hunt the following year would work well. Try this option as your next-to-last resort before instituting the other contacts which will, inevitably, heat the situation up and make a calm settlement more difficult.

# CHAPTER 17

# Tips On How To Save Money

**A FEW YEARS** back during an idle moment on a rainy Sunday, I mentally started counting up how much money I had invested in hunting clothing, gear and equipment of various descriptions. After a few moments I had to get pencil and paper to help me keep things straight, the totals were mounting up so high. As I kept at it, constantly thinking of whole new categories of items that were used more for hunting than for anything else (though many of them can be pressed into double duty for general cold weather use around house and yard), my reaction gradually escalated from surprise to astonishment to near shock. Why, without realizing it, over a period of years I had invested literally thousands of dollars in my favorite sport of big game hunting!

That did not include all of the out-of-pocket expenses that I had spent on various "big" faraway hunts over the years. Adding in such things as transportation costs, license fees, taxidermy costs, hunting and guide

Different men derive their satisfactions differently. To some the companionship and help of an experienced guide make the hunt far more *enjoyable* (which is really what the sport is all about, whatever the cost), while to others the idea of "doing it all on your own" makes the trip much more enjoyable even if it is more arduous and less productive. These are all factors in the personal equation that you must weigh for yourself.

Don't go off on a do-it-yourself trip in true wilderness such as this unless you have plenty of bush experience and feel *comfortable* in such country on your own. The ability to read a compass and start a fire and a few other talents are not enough here — experience and bush savvy count.

fees, tips and various other miscellaneous "nondurable" purchases raised the total cost to truly stratospheric heights! And I'm sure that if I added up these same costs today, they would have at least tripled, counting in the additional moneys I have spent since then as well as the higher replacement costs of the older equipment, constantly increasing due to "dat ole debbil" inflation.

Yet I am not wealthy by any stretch of the imagination so how did I spend so much money? Of course the secret is that this was spent on my primary hobby and over a long period of years, thus adding up to surprisingly high totals. Over these years I have learned a number of ways to reduce, even at times eliminate, some of these costs. Some of these "cost cutters" are straightforward and orthodox in treatment, and most anyone can avail himself of the savings easily and relatively conveniently.

Others are unorthodox and take a bit of doing. These options often require time, a certain amount of work, and possibly a few special talents of one sort or another. Some of these are not so easily performed, but as one might imagine, these are the ones that often yield the largest potential savings.

Or, to put it another way, the second more unorthodox group of "savers" are really options that require the sportsman to invest relatively substantial amounts of his time and energy and (occasionally) require him to put up with a bit of bother and aggravation in lieu of investing money. Nothing on this earth is "free" in the total sense, and the hunter must often pay

Caribou are the deep wilderness animal most easily hunted without a guide or expensive outfitted hunt.

for his hunts in one coin or another. However, for the man who loves his sport and is interested in making it a year-around adventure, many of these projects can actually be interesting, and they allow him to make hunts that he might not otherwise ever get to experience if he had to pay for everything in cold cash.

## Basic Ways to Save Money

1. *Buy high quality equipment and gear:* My binoculars are over 10 years old, and several of my pet hunting rifles are twice that old. My down outer garments for cold weather wear range from 3 to 8 years in age, and the down sleeping bag I have used numerous times each year for periods of up to 10 weeks at a time on extended wilderness trips is 9 years old. My light overnighter tent is 6 seasons old, and the lighter weight cotton or cotton/synthetic blend shirts and outer wear I have are mostly over 3 years old. All of these items are still giving me good service.

All of these items were painstakingly selected, of best quality and quite expensive. However, over the long run they have been very modest in cost. When you start dividing the cost of expensive items like top grade binoculars by 10, 20 or even more years of usage, the cost per year is quite low. Much lower than having to continually buy and replace or repair cheap, inferior grades of the same items. Best yet, all of these expensive items make you far more comfortable and productive afield than do the cheaper goods.

Cheap binoculars constantly seem to be out of collimation and therefore cause the wearer eyestrain. Inferior optics of all sorts from hunting scopes and spotting scopes on through binoculars just don't have the brightness and resolving ability of the higher grade optics (even though they may be of the same "power").

The guide costs you money, but he saves you time with his extra pair of hands, and he usually means more insurance for a successful hunt due to his expertise and familiarity with the area.

A major deep wilderness out-camp such as this one means an expensive hunt. But it also means more efficient hunting. If you cut corners to save money, you must accept that you will probably take less game, other things being equal.

224

Mountain sheep are, along with grizzly and Alaska brown bear, "expensive" animals to hunt with fewer cost cutting possibilities than exist with some other species such as deer, elk, and caribou.

The cheapies are also invariably larger and heavier to carry around, and they tend to "leak" thus losing their gas filling and/or absorb moisture which makes them "fog" and become practically worthless. And a hunting item is doubly worthless if it goes out in the field right when you need it most.

Cheap clothing and sleeping bags do not keep you as warm, they are not as flexible in allowing your body to "breathe" during the frequent and sometimes drastic pendulum swings of temperature encountered outdoors, and they are usually heavy and bulky. They rip and tear, and their insulation mats up and becomes inefficient.

Cheap boots and footgear do not give your feet the heavy-duty protection they need outdoors, and they tend to blister and chafe due to bad fit and bad construction. They wear out — usually at just the wrong time — and when made of leather, usually leak like sieves whereas the higher priced leather outdoor boots will often be almost waterproof as long as they aren't totally immersed in water and held there.

Low grade tents, tarps and dining flys are heavy, usually start leaking and smelling early in life and do not stand up to heavy use. It is not a humorous situation to be caught outdoors during a sustained 2- to 3-day downpour or snowstorm in a tent that constantly leaks and smells.

It's alright to shop for bargains. That's what we're exploring in this chapter. But, if you think you will use your outdoor gear over a period of several years, always buy the best you can. Try to get bargain prices on top quality goods; don't falsely "economize" by buying cheapies. It may take you longer to build up your complete array of outdoor gear and equipment this way, but when you do have it, it will be such that you can point to it with pride and count on it (with proper maintenance) never to let you down when you need it. Having critical equipment go out on you when afield in deep wilderness can be more than inconvenient, it can be downright dangerous at times.

2. *Shop at the best places:* Shop around a lot, learn the prices of the gear you are interested in and locate all the different types of outlets where it is available. Sporting goods stores usually are a bit more expensive than other outlets because usually they offer better sales service in advising and waiting on customers. Frequently some of the larger discount stores carry surprisingly high grade outdoor items and usually offer them at prices ranging from 15 percent to 20 percent less than many small sporting goods stores.

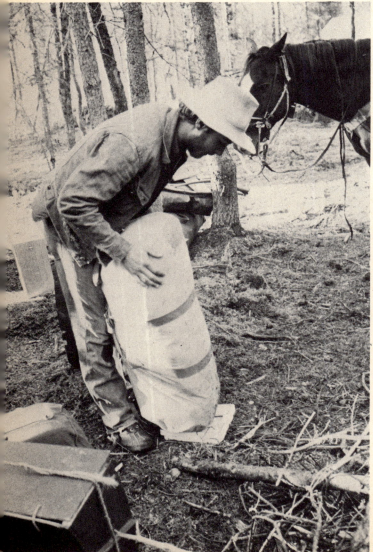

(Above) The ability to walk in and start hunting out of permanent, weather-tight camps costs money. Camping in your own tents is far cheaper.

(Left) Horses greatly expand a hunter's effective range, but they also make expenses zoom. Here a packer weighs some duffle to be sure he is properly balancing the loads on both sides of the packhorse.

In this era any grizzly hunt that has a reasonable chance of success must be fully outfitted and guided and expensive. There are not cheap and effective grizzly hunts anymore.

You should also have all the major catalogs of the outdoor oriented mail-order houses. These "wish books" offer a tremendous selection of goods. Perusing them on long winter nights is not only fun, it's one of the best ways I know to learn more about quality gear and equipment: how it's made; what special features it offers; and what new developments are on the scene. The prices from these mail-order houses are usually quite reasonable, considering the quality of the items involved. In some cases the prices are rather high, but they are related to unique items, made as well as sold by the mail-order house, that are among the best in their field and are not available elsewhere.

In recent years some new type outlets have originated. Some offer partially completed "do-it-yourself" kits whereby the handy sportsman (or his wife) can complete the construction of quality down outer wear or sleeping bags or other cut-and-sew type items. These kits are usually very well thought out and well designed. The directions are clear and uncluttered, and the various kits are often helpfully tagged (in the mail-order catalog) as being for "beginners" or requiring "advanced work." Some of these projects take a good bit of time, energy and patience, but the savings of 40 percent to 50 percent can make that investment well worthwhile if you have the time to devote to the project and are inclined along those lines.

Another newer type outdoor equipment outlet is the co-op type organization whereby you "join" and thus share in the savings which may come in the form of somewhat reduced prices on gear (10 percent-15 percent) or in the form of outright "dividends" at the end of the year based on what sort of business year the organization had in general and what amount of purchases you made in particular. These outlets have had varying degrees of success, but they are worth investigating.

3. *Shop at the right times.* There is a seasonal rhythm in the world of merchandising and commerce just as surely as there is one in the outdoor world. Most stores, be they discounters, retail sporting goods establishments, or even at times, the mail-order houses, like to clear their shelves at the end of each season. To carry over goods from year to year costs them money tied up in capital invested in dead inventory until next year, in the extra costs of required storage space and handling, in spoilage over the year and in decreased sales potential for the following year due to new developments in the field.

Usually it is cheaper and makes better business sense for the store to offer clearance sales at the end of the season whereby the goods may be marked down anywhere from 10 percent to 50 percent. Look for these sales to usually start after the first of the calendar year when the various hunting seasons are largely closed and the Christmas selling season is over. As the store prepares to begin featuring its spring camping and fishing lines, out comes the red pencil, reducing the prices on the fall-winter hunting and cold weather sports equipment. Stay alert and shop these sales. Sometimes outstanding bargains are available that, depending upon that store's exact stock position, may not be repeated there or elsewhere.

4. *Take care of your equipment:* Even though best quality outdoor gear is hardy and serviceable, it is far from indestructible. The kind of handling and maintenance you give your duffle can double or halve the useful life of it. Do not fold up or put away tents or down outer garments when wet or extremely dirty. Spread them out and hang them up to dry and wash or have them cleaned if necessary. Store your "soft," cloth-type items in the right places — namely cool and dry spots not hot, damp or dirty areas. Basements are frequently the *worst* places for prolonged storage as they are often damp, humid or subject to pests like mice.

Pack your breakables like cameras and optics carefully for travel to and from the hunt and handle them carefully when afield. Do not loop the straps of binoculars or cameras over saddlehorns where obliging branches seem to seek them out with religious fervor as you ride by and then toss them off or break them when snagged. Keep all your optics dry, out of the broiling direct sun or ultra-humid tents. Keep your leather goods clean by saddle soaping them when they need it and by oiling with neat's-foot oil or better yet, Lexol when they begin drying out.

In a word, lavish all the care and attention on your prized outdoor gear that you would on any other expensive possession. Whether you call this "saving money" or "deferring costs," either way the result is the same — more money in your pocket.

5. *Consider buying used equipment:* When exercising proper care, this option can make sense. As a general rule it is far better to purchase well maintained, top quality used equipment than it is to buy new shoddy equipment that costs as much or more, does not have the quality or the features and will not last as long. If necessary, get an independent expert opinion on the item. If an expensive gun is involved, many reputable gun shops or gunsmiths will let you, upon your furnishing proper identification and possibly leaving a security deposit, take the gun to the range for a trial shooting session. At the same time you can have another gunsmith appraise the condition and worth of the gun for you to insure that it is not overpriced.

Even soft equipment such as tents or sleeping bags can be safely purchased after being used under some conditions. Check your stores for "display" or "demonstrator" items that may have been handled a bit, might even have faded just a tad from prolonged show window exposure or may have been erected on the showroom floor. Often these items may be had for 25 percent to 40 percent reductions.

If you have a friend who has used a tent for some years and you know that it has been properly cared for and well maintained, you may be able to pick up the old one for a song when he goes to get a larger or more expensive model. Used optics such as binoculars, scopes, even cameras can sometimes be had at bargain prices when purchased from individuals. When doing so, have these items professionally checked and appraised. This is complicated, technical equipment that might have defects not immediately visible to the layman. Usually the prices charged by camera stores for used optics are not highly attractive, often ranging no more than 20 percent - 25 percent off. At these rates, unless it is a "demonstrator" that has received practically no meaningful use, it is hardly worthwhile to

from the mail-order houses) by buying them all in one, large quantity order. Frequently a mail-order house will pay the freight on large orders where otherwise you would have to pay it. (You are already saving the cost of all local and state sales taxes on purchases from out-of-state mail-order companies.)

Also, large orders can often mean an additional 1 percent or 2 percent rebate on the value of the order or perhaps a modest "free gift" for large purchases. When dealing with local sporting goods stores, it is sometimes possible, especially if a very large order for several hundred dollars is involved (perhaps covering guns and equipment for you and several of your friends) to negotiate special prices and terms.

In addition to strict quantity buying, it is also possible

Doing all your own cooking means you can't sleep that extra hour and still be away before dawn with a hot breakfast in you or stay out hunting until dark and return utterly spent to have a hot meal waiting for you.

purchase used goods.

I am not recommending that the sportsman get into the purchase of used gear in a wholesale fashion. Far better to buy new items in unopened manufacturer's pack with full warranty in effect. What I am saying is that, if used occasionally and judiciously monitored, this approach can make sense.

6. *Coordinate your purchases – buy in quantity:* Work with several buddies to coordinate your outdoor purchases to a degree reasonably possible. This can work to your advantage in several ways. Simple bulk buying often can help. If you all want to buy some wool shirts, outdoor socks and other miscellaneous items, you can often pick up some nice savings (especially

to a degree to defer some purchases if you coordinate *what* you buy as well as *when* you buy with several of your hunting buddies.

This is a bit inconvenient at times, but it can help to tide you over during the early years when you are accumulating your battery of outdoor gear a piece or two at a time. Here's how it works. Perhaps you and a friend can decide between you that he will buy the tent if you purchase the sleeping bag and several interchangeable bag liners. Thus, on certain weekends or periods, one of you can "borrow" the tent or the other can "borrow" the sleeping bag (using your own personal liners).

Another good "coordinated" purchase approach in-

(Right) Even an Easterner can still, if he does his homework to select a good area and spends the time and energy to hunt it properly, often take a nice mule deer like this with transportation and license costs being his main expenses.

(Below) Whitetail deer hunting, with careful study of the most productive areas, can be done rather inexpensively and yet still be effective.

volves handloading. Perhaps if two or three of you chip in together, you may be able to buy a far larger stock of components (possibly at lower unit prices due to quantity purchasing). Also, you may find that by pooling your money you can buy a larger, more automated handloading rig that will enable you to load ammunition for the several hunters more flexibly and inexpensively (considering that your time is worth something). In fact, I have even known of particularly enterprising types who have, after the purchase of larger and faster loading rigs, loaded rounds for their friends for a price. It is quite possible to load your buddy's ammunition, using his cartridge cases and components and merely investing your time and the use of your loading equipment, and even after saving him 25 percent or so over the retail cost of centerfire ammo, still make a tidy pile of coin for yourself. You can often earn back the entire cost of your loading rig within 6 months or so, given enough buddies wanting cheap ammunition.

Actually, handloading in a general sense is a real dollar stretcher. Depending upon what you are loading, how you bought your components, how many times you re-use your cartridge cases and a number of other variables, it is quite feasible to save anywhere from 40 percent to 75 percent or more on the cost of your ammunition. An added bonus is that handloading, besides being just plain enjoyable, enables you to add far more flexibility to your shooting by cooking up special purpose rounds with unusual bullet weights or types not offered by the factories. Also, the handloader can invariably, by trial and error, work up certain loads that are more accurate in his rifle than standard factory fodder.

7. *Save on transportation costs:* Some of the cross-country or Canadian hunts mean that you are investing significant money in transportation for both yourself, your duffle and (hopefully) your trophies on the return

Transportation is a big part of big game hunting expenses, especially getting back into deep wilderness country. Chartered bush planes such as this DeHaviland Otter are the quickest, easiest — and most expensive way to do it. Try to avoid chartering a small plane by yourself if you must fly. Sharing a larger plane with several hunters is almost always cheaper.

trip home. There are a number of ways to cut down on these costs if you are willing to devote a little time and energy to the task.

If you are going by plane, often it may be cheaper to ship some of your duffle on ahead by air freight (which is priced by the hundredweight) rather than by excess baggage (which is by the individual excess pound on international flights to Canada). It can even be cheaper to *mail* your duffle on ahead by Parcel Post or Air Parcel Post. (One not-so-secret secret relating to Parcel Post is that parcels shipped that way from the "southern 48" to Alaska actually go via Air Parcel due to the geographical separation of the two areas. Thus, the cheaper overall Parcel Post rate actually nets you fast Air Parcel Post service in this case.)

Another canny device some of us resort to on those long-range domestic flights that charge excess baggage by the number of bags in excess of the standard allowance (usually one carry-on bag and two baggage compartment bags) is to *rope together* various duffle bags into "*one*" bag. I have roped together up to three bags into one king-sized parcel and thus reduced nine excess bags to three at a tidy savings when multiplied by two (for going and coming legs of the trip).

All of these possibilities are highly variable depending upon how much weight you are carrying, how many bags it takes to pack all this in and where you are going. The point of all this is that it definitely is worth your time to check out which option is best rather than

casually packing everything up at the last moment and then carrying it with you, letting whatever is excess be charged that way.

Weigh your gear and duffle. Check out all the various shipping options (air freight, Air Parcel Post, Parcel Post, excess baggage, Passenger Accompanied Freight, etc.) as to both length of time in transit and cost (including insurance). You should do all of this well in advance of your trip so that you have ample time to work it all out and then to perhaps use one of the slower moving options. Major trips involve surprising weights if you are carrying a couple of scope sighted rifles, ammunition, cameras and film, gear to live outdoors for 3 weeks or so, optics and other "heavies." It's well worth your while to spend some time checking and manipulating here in order to get the lowest costs.

As for yourself, if you are flying, spend the time to check out (or have a travel agent check out) the various alternatives open to you. Sometimes there are enough options among the different routes that you could take, the special "plans" you can fly under and the different departure times, that they would confuse a Solomon. Don't just sign up for the first flight that will get you there and don't automatically accept the travel agent's word that he or she has checked out all the options on a long and complicated trip. I have even called the same airline several times, and each time I talked with a different ticket agent, I got differing recommended routings and at significantly differing costs. Spend some time here!

8. *Stay alert:* This general axiom can't be overemphasized. Spend the time to become familiar with the gear and equipment that you want and also to familiarize yourself with the outlets that sell these items. Then stay alert and "shop" constantly, even if in a passive sense.

"Bargains" come along all the time and at unpredictable times. Sometimes the businessman may be low on cash and need to raise some money by running a special sale. Or, he may be opening up a new branch store, relocating to a new sales location or going out of business. Any of these events can result in some unusually attractive prices. Keep your eyes open and remember that the general rule is that the *worst* time to buy hunting clothing and equipment (worst in a price sense, that is) is during the hunting season. Buy early or late for the savings.

### Intermediate Level Ways to Save

1. *Transportation:* There are still other, more complex potential ways to save money. Some trips might actually be cheaper in transportation costs if several of you charter a small airplane rather than fly via scheduled air carrier and then have to pay the high rates to charter a bush plane for the final leg. This is a very specialized option that takes a lot of careful shopping around. Often it makes the most sense on intermediate trips (500 to 800 miles), and for it to be worthwhile, you must almost always be able to fly directly from your hometown to the final destination via the small plane you charter. This can result in substantial savings when compared to the *combined* costs of the scheduled airline carrier and the nonscheduled bush plane you would have had to hire for the last leg.

This option can make for an interesting and unique experience if the pieces happen to fit. Also, this approach can offer you a more flexible and, at times, convenient way of doing things since you can literally go when you want to and where you want to with

(Above) Doing all your own chores and setting up your own camps means savings in money but loss in time. The latter can sometimes be more important.

(Right) A packstring hunt is the queen of all North American hunting trips, and some feel their life just won't be complete until they take at least one such trip — whatever the expense.

"your" airplane.

2. *Taxidermy:* Good taxidermy is frightfully expensive these days, and there's no sense in buying any other kind than quality work. Sometimes you can get your per unit prices lowered a bit by negotiating a quantity deal whereby you give the taxidermist a very large order. You can do this by saving up your own trophies for several years and giving them to him all at once. (Do *not* have them tanned initially if you're going to do this.) Or, you can get your buddies to use the same taxidermist so that, among you, you place quite a substantial order with him.

You can often save some money by shipping your trophies directly from the hunt to the taxidermist rather than shipping or carrying them home with you and then shipping them back to the taxidermist.

Whether this proves to be worthwhile depends in large measure on the relative locations of your home, your hunt and your taxidermist. One thing some eastern sportsmen do when they go west for a pronghorn, mule deer or elk hunt is to leave their trophies out there with a nearby taxidermist and then pick them up the following year on a return hunt. This saves them expensive packing and crating (of the finished trophies) as well as the high cross-country freight costs.

You can also save some money by having some of your trophies mounted as antler-only mounts or "skull" mounts rather than the more expensive complete head mount. There are other possibilities here. also. For more detail, check Chapter 15.

3. *Buying and Selling:* There are more and more gun shows, flea markets and similar informal trading fairs springing up every year. If you have done your "homework" well and know what you want and what the values are, often you can pick up some good values on the specific items you want or you can make some money on general buying and selling of some hunting related items. (Check your local ordinances to see if you need any sort of licensing when dealing in certain volumes.) If nothing else, these trading fairs can be an enjoyable way to spend a Saturday or Sunday afternoon. "Barn sales" or estate auctions offer other interesting possibilities. Watch the listings in your local newspaper or check with local auction agents.

4. *Use Discipline:* This may sound like an odd one, but I assure you, it can amount to substantial dollar savings. Hunting license costs, especially for the more exotic and faraway species are increasing phenomenally. If you are going on a moose hunt with only the barest outside chance at caribou or mountain goat, resist the "temptation" to get licenses (at $200 to $350 each) for the two lesser animals "just in case." That's pretty expensive "just in case" coverage. Make up your mind what you are specifically hunting and then go after it. Avoid the ultra-expensive "sidelines" that you probably won't even see, much less collect.

Another way of using discipline is to save an extra year or so if necessary in order to go to the best area and stay long enough on a "big" hunt. I assure you, two separate 5-day hunts are much more expensive than one 10-day hunt! The two hunts require duplicate transportation expenses and hunting licenses and, being so short, both are far more vulnerable to being ruined by bad weather. Losing 3 days of a 10-day hunt is bad. Losing 3 days of a 5-day hunt is catastrophic. No hunt, whatever the cost, is "cheap" if it is unsatisfactory.

## More Sophisticated (and Complex) Ways to Save

(Note: Most of these options relate to the longer, more expensive wilderness hunts that naturally tend to lend themselves to these possibilities. These are usually not easy "savers" to pull off. They take time, energy, patience, skill and discretion. However, they can be — for many of us — the only way we'll ever take some of those expensive "dream trips." And, for those advanced students of hunting, they can be rather interesting and fun to pursue.)

1. *Father/son, father/daughter, husband/wife special deals:* Some of the larger outfitters allow, especially on their longer and more expensive hunts, special prices for these types of hunts. Sometimes the "child" (who usually must be 18 years of age or younger) or wife may come along as a hunter for as little as 50 percent of the normal rate or as a nonhunting member of the party for as little as one-third to one-half the normal rate.

This deal is not as farfetched as it sounds. Usually two close relatives of this sort are not nearly as expensive for the outfitter to hunt as two independent hunters. They usually want to hunt together (often with only one guide between them), and they tend not to squabble between themselves about who shoots what as much as two independent hunters in the same situation might. Though this option was pioneered by the northern British Columbia mixed game outfitters, check out this possibility with Albertan, Yukon or Alaskan operators.

Depending upon how the outfitter organizes and conducts his hunts, this may be a very viable possibility. Especially so if this option is what really enables the basic, full-paying hunter to make the trip to begin with. Often it's far easier for a hunter to justify spending this kind of money on an expensive hunt if he is able to take his son, daughter, wife or some combination of them along with him and amortize part of the trip on the basis of it being a unique all-family adventure. Usually the second (or third) hunters — the children and/or wife — are not nearly as demanding about the number and size of the trophies they shoot as is the average hunter.

2. *Late season special bargain hunts:* This is a marvelous option, readily available with many major outfitters. Check Chapter 19 for full details.

3. *Last minute hunt cancellations:* Sometimes, especially if you are working through a professional

If you are on an expense cutting "do-it-yourselfer" type hunt, make sure that you or one of your hunting buddies in camp knows how to properly care for any trophies. These men have just skinned and salted a bear hide, and they are inserting the rolled up bearskin into a burlap bag to "cure" (give the salt time to work out the moisture).

hunting consultant or booking agent, it is possible to pick up canceled hunts and fill in for the aborting hunter. Usually these are last minute deals, but often you can save most or all of the other hunter's deposit and payments to date. That can amount to anywhere from 25 percent to 50 percent of the hunt! Check Chapter 20 for more details on this one.

4. *Booking in other hunters:* This is the most complex, delicate and potentially rewarding money-saver of all. Most major outfitters work through hunting consultants or booking agents to one degree or another already. These booking agents usually pocket a fee of 10 percent to 15 percent of each hunter's total fee that they book with an outfitter. If you can book in some other hunters, chances are you can do the same.

However, be advised that most outfitters have been approached by con artists of various stripes and ilks, and they tend to not want to "pay" any amateur booking agents until they have the other promised hunters in camp and their money in pocket. Then they usually grant the "booking agent" a rebate on his hunt to the extent that they collected on the other hunters. For instance, if you book a $2,000 hunt for yourself and bring along three more paying hunters on $2,000 trips, you might well pick up 15 percent each or a total of $900 reduction on your hunt cost. If the outfitter is con-

vinced that you can bring him other hunters, he may even grant you the booking agent fee on *your own* hunt, thus bringing your savings up to $1,200. It's a heck of a lot easier to afford a $800 hunt than a $2,000 hunt, my friends!

There are some potential pitfalls you should know about. Chances are these hunters you book in will be personal friends, and they will be hunting at the same time you are. If your hunt should go much better than theirs, one or two of them may get a little sour and claim that you are "getting all the game" because of your "inside connections." There can be some very real resentment on the part of one or the other of them if they don't do well themselves.

You can partially allay this by explaining very clearly to them all the ramifications of your "deal" in advance so that they know just what is happening. (Otherwise they tend to think you're making far more money off the operation than you are. And it always gets out around camp, one way or another, that you have some sort of mysterious "deal" with the outfitter. Better not to make a big secret of the whole arrangement.)

You can go a step further and share some of your savings with the other hunters. Perhaps you give them one-third (5 percent) of the savings on their hunt and keep the other 10 percent yourself for the arranging and coordinating you will inevitably have to perform. This makes them "fellow savers" and really not in a position to gripe too much about "special deals." It is perfectly fair for you to pocket the larger, 10 percent share since you are responsible for handling the bothersome details like shipping and clearing trophies through customs and any other minor "housekeeping" items that come up.

You can even pick up some attractive "booking agent" savings by referring all their taxidermy (again, in an aboveboard fashion) to a reputable, top quality taxidermist who gives you a rebate on your own taxidermy for all the business you bring him.

This kind of work takes tact, skill and — at times — a rather high "aggravation-quotient." (Ask any full-time professional hunting consultant.) But, if you persevere, some astonishing results are possible. My stepbrother, John, has made one African safari at half price and another completely free and is currently planning a hunt in Iran completely gratis. All this due to the number of hunters he has been able to book with the various outfitters across the water. Also, all his taxidermy work is now performed free of charge by a first rate taxidermy house due to the business he has brought to them.

All of this took a lot of work and energy. It didn't come easy. John personally advised, accompanied and hunted with all the hunters he has booked, and all his trips have been highly successful. Work, patience and a bit of luck played a part in all this, but the results have enabled him to make several enormously expensive "dream trips" that he might otherwise never have been able to afford.

# CHAPTER 18

# Big Game Hunting In Alaska

**ALASKA IS AN** enormous land. Just as Europeans visiting America for the first time must completely readjust their values in order to properly comprehend the scale of our continent-sized nation, so it is with folks from the "southern 48" who are visiting Alaska for the first time.

Alaska's 586,000 square miles make it more than twice the size of Texas. Or, to put it another way, large enough to swallow France, *both* Germanys, Italy, England, Scotland, Wales and still have room left over. Its rugged coastline is longer than the entire continental U.S. coastline, including Atlantic, Pacific and Gulf of Mexico put together. It contains the highest peak in North America (McKinley) and the only one to exceed 20,000 feet.

Its more than 20,000 square miles of fresh water constitute a bit over one-fourth of the U.S. total, and that's a goodly drink when you realize that the southern 48 total is bolstered by the Great Lakes, among the largest in the world. Its largest county, Upper Yukon, is bigger than Idaho! Yet only slightly more than 300,000 people reside in the whole vast state. That makes for a population density less than half that of

Alaskan hunting is far northern hunting, and the weather can turn suddenly sour without warning at almost any time. Be prepared with the right clothing and gear.

Typical brown bear hunting country on the Alaska Peninsula.

outer Mongolia or less than one-fourth that of Australia or Iceland — none of which are exactly what you would call densely populated.

This is truly a land of superlatives and of contrasts. It is brutal at times and yet ecologically very fragile. It is still, along with western Canada and Africa, one of the three greatest game fields left on earth. Home to the snow white Dall sheep, the magnificent grizzly bear, and coastal dwelling brown bear, the gigantic Alaskan moose, the spectacularly antlered caribou, the sleek black bear and the stratosphere-loving mountain goat, Alaska is truly a big game hunter's dream come true.

### How to Get There

**By Auto:** One can drive up via the Alaska Highway which stretches some 1,520 miles from its inception (Mile 0) at Dawson Creek, British Columbia, to Fairbanks, Alaska, or 1,640 miles from Dawson to Anchorage. Although you would probably be driving up during the best time of year to traverse this highway (May 30 to October 1), remember that about 1,200 miles of the road is still gravel surfaced, and this calls for certain prudent but rather easy-to-handle precautions. Although road widths are ample, 26 to 40 feet, and traffic is generally light, it pays to go slow. High speed travel on gravel builds up enormous heat through friction, and this is very hard on your tires. Also, it pays to slow *way* down when passing anyone in order to minimize danger from flying gravel. Take your time and enjoy the scenery. If you're in a hurry, don't drive — fly up via scheduled air carrier.

Custom bug and gravel screens made of wire mesh help to protect you from losing your headlights due to flying gravel and also help avoid plugging your radiator during the heavy bug season. There is no foolproof way to protect your windshield from flying gravel, but these screens, generally at a cost of $15 to $35, help some. You can also fashion your own homemade screens rather easily.

Protecting exposed gas tanks by installing rubber

matting is a good idea as are the elementary precautions of having your car thoroughly serviced, checked and tightened before leaving and then of lubricating it every 1,000 miles or so and checking tire pressures constantly and carefully. Although service stations are available along the road, it's not a bad idea to carry a nominal assortment of spare parts — say an extra fan belt, points and condenser, plugs, tire chains, and a couple of good spare tires.

Here's a rough estimate of driving costs, assuming that two adults, driving at reasonable speeds, are traveling from the northern part of the southern 48 (say Seattle, Washington, or Great Falls, Montana) to either Anchorage or Fairbanks and further assuming that they do no camping along the way. This situation also assumes that the trip will take 8 days, at an average of 300 miles per day. (Of course all of the below figures can vary depending upon the cost of gas at a given time and the mileage that your vehicle gets — however this will at least provide you with a broad-gauge expense yardstick for driving.)

1. Three meals per day/8 days for
   2 adults ............................................. $150
2. 8 nights lodging for 2 adults ..................... $140
3. 8 days driving, 300 miles
   per day/gas & oil ................................ $150
   $440

This comes to a bit over $200 per traveler, one way. Not really exorbitant when considering the length and nature of this very unique drive. Camping out some and preparing some of your own meals would trim these costs a bit as would carrying another traveler with you to split the expenses three ways, rather than two.

Some sample driving mileages from various major southern U. S. cities to Anchorage may be of value in helping to visualize this trip:

1. Seattle— 2,288        5. Houston— 4,249
2. San Diego— 3,547      6. New York— 4,450
3. Minneapolis— 3,239    7. Atlanta— 4,317
4. Kansas City— 3,596    8. Miami— 4,971

If you do decide to drive, the first thing you should do is to order a copy of the invaluable little paperback book called *The Milepost*. Updated annually so that it is always current, this little book, as the name implies, covers the whole highway and adjacent feeder roads literally in mile-by-mile fashion. In fact, it's a good idea to order this book and scan it even if you aren't traveling by auto because it offers so much good general information for the traveler new to Alaska. It's available for $5.95 plus 75¢ for postage. Add $2.50 for airmail:

Alaska Northwest Publishing Company
Box 4EEE — Dept. HD
Anchorage, Alaska 99509

**By Airplane:** Several domestic and international carriers service Alaska, and all sorts of routings and fares are available. It pays to take your time and check out the many options carefully, perhaps using the services (no charge) of a professional travel agent or booking agent to help insure that you pay the cheapest rates among the many excursion fares, seasonal specials and other cut-rate options.

When traveling by air and carrying expensive guns and cameras, I always try to get special dispensation to have them carried in the passenger compartment rather than subjected to the often rough handling in the baggage compartment. A ticket agent, security guard, or pilot may require that you unlock the case and show them the contents (even though it may have already been inspected), and they may then seal it themselves when you re-lock the case/s. Usually they will require that the case be carried up front in the pilot's compartment or in some other area where you can not reach it. Incidentally, always carry your guns with the bolts or magazines out. Sometimes it is possible to get this special handling and sometimes not. Usually it depends upon how crowded the flight is and the disposition of the individual captain (pilot) who must ultimately make the decision.

If your precious guns and optics must go into the Siberia of the baggage compartment, then check with the baggage master to insure that they receive special handling. I often go downstairs into the bowels of the baggage processing areas of major airports with my equipment and explain the situation personally to the crew chief and then watch while the gear (worth thousands of dollars in my case) is packed and put in the baggage compartment of the plane. With a bit of patience and good humor on your part, you'll be surprised at how helpful these people invariably are when handling your precious gear. The problems come in when they don't *know* it's precious.

I always hand carry all unexposed or exposed film onto the airplane to avoid the various X-ray type security checks. If you must ship film via the baggage compartment, or if the particular security person insists on use of an X-ray type check of your carry-on baggage, it is your right to *insist* upon a "hand check." Do *not* expose precious, irreplaceable film to these various X-ray type scans even though you are assured religiously by the personnel that they are "perfectly safe" or "too low level" to ruin film. Maybe. And maybe not. Either way, play it safe and insist on the hand check.

**By Boat:** You may elect to go by cruise ship or possibly go up via ship and return by airplane (since cruise ships are generally operated only during the summer visitor season). Further information on cruise ship sailings to Alaska can be obtained from the following people:
(Departing from Vancouver, British Columbia)
    Canadian National Railways
    1150 Station Street
    Vancouver, British Columbia, Canada

(Departing from Los Angeles or San Francisco)
   Pacific Far East Cruises
   1 Embarcadero Center
   San Francisco, California 94111

Again, it's a good idea to use a professional travel agent to help you through booking complexities that may arise.

The state of Alaska maintains a year-around combination passenger and auto ferry service. The *Alaska Marine Highway System* connects Seattle, Washington, with Prince Rupert, British Columbia, and a number of southeastern Alaska towns. This unique approach of driving one way and returning the other way via the marine highway makes for an unusual and idyllic trip. The scenery in many spots when traveling via the marine highway is nothing short of spectacular rivaling the fjords of Norway in splendor. Further information on this auto/ferry service may be obtained from:

Alaska Marine Highway System
Division of Marine Transportation
Pouch R
Juneau, Alaska 99801

*Warning:* Many times these spaces are booked months in advance, so don't wait until the last minute to check into this method of transportation.

### General Tips on Alaskan Hunting

Though subject to periodic change, the current rule is that nonresident hunters in Alaska are not required to have a guide to hunt moose, caribou, black bear or mountain goat, but they must be accompanied by a licensed guide or resident 19 years of age or older when hunting Dall sheep or grizzly or brown bear.

Take adequate cold weather and foul weather gear to Alaska no matter when you go. This "high latitude" weather is subject to instant change at any time of the year, and chill winds or rain are an ever present possibility.

Bring more money than you think you will need. Everything in Alaska is fearsomely expensive, and especially when hunting or traveling in the bush, things don't always go according to plan. An unexpected bush plane flight or a couple of extra days in Anchorage can really run those costs up.

Take both rubber boots and leather boots for wet and dry going. Hip boots are often necessary for slogging through marshy areas in many parts of the state, or for constant crossing and recrossing of the twisting rivers that often snake through the glacier gouged valleys and usually run calf to hip deep depending upon the time of year and the amount of runoff.

This is rugged wilderness hunting. Get your weight down and your physical condition up. This isn't like playing an extra nine holes of golf before hitting the clubhouse.

Take plenty of film and, if possible, an extra camera. Any hunting trip to Alaska, no matter how many times you may have been before or how many times you may go again, is truly a "trip of a lifetime." Take a lot of pictures. They'll be priceless in the years to come.

In Alaska as elsewhere in North America, most really good hunting means mountain hunting.

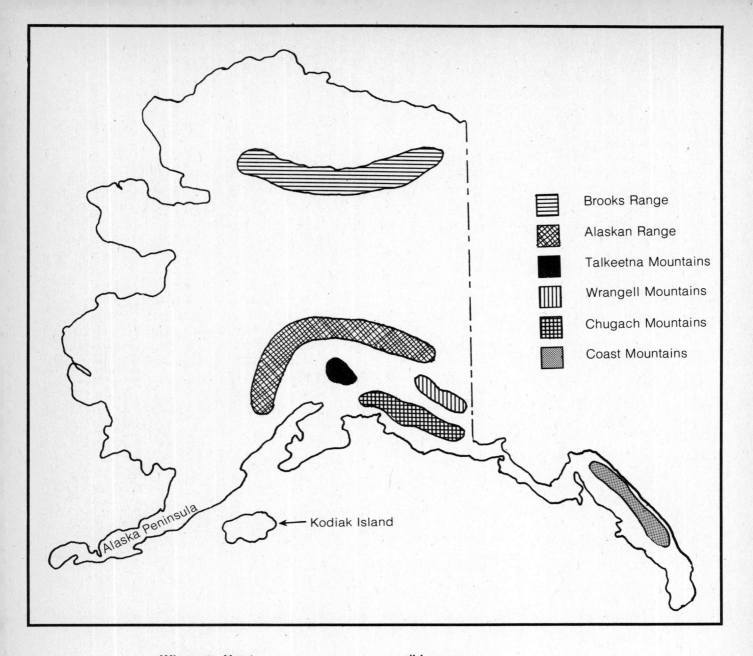

Legend:
- Brooks Range
- Alaskan Range
- Talkeetna Mountains
- Wrangell Mountains
- Chugach Mountains
- Coast Mountains

Alaska Peninsula

← Kodiak Island

### Where to Hunt

Alaska's very immensity can work against the sportsman unfamiliar with this vast state. Where to go for which species? Which type of hunting (horseback, vehicular or on foot) is available where? Where are the largest trophies? Where are the largest concentrations of game? As is the case with any other game field, there is no single "best" place. Some areas are better for some species than others, while still different areas are better for different types of hunts. Here's a broad brush look at the state:

*1. The Talkeetna Mountains:* The Talkeetnas are the smallest of the mountain ranges which we'll scan, covering only about 50 by 80 miles according to my rough reckoning. Since the southern edge of this range lies only 75 miles north of Anchorage, via a good road through the Matanuska Valley, it is also the most ac-

cessible range.

The Talkeetnas aren't particularly high, ranging from 5,500 to 8,000 feet with the highest peak slightly exceeding 8,800. The terrain isn't bad at all, and always bearing in mind that mountain climbing is never *easy,* I would rank them as the easiest of the eight mountainous areas that we'll cover in this survey. Thus, they are a good bet for the older hunter or the hunter with a health problem, either of which should have their physician's blessing before departing on any mountain hunt.

Probably more horseback hunting is done in the Talkeetnas than anywhere else in Alaska since Alaskan hunting is, by and large, a fly-in and walk proposition. Even here, including both resident and nonresident hunters, horses are probably used in no more than 15 percent - 20 percent of the big game hunting.

Hunts that, to one degree or another, use mechanical means such as jeeps, tracked vehicles or highway vehi-

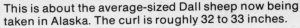
This is about the average-sized Dall sheep now being taken in Alaska. The curl is roughly 32 to 33 inches.

The Alaska brown bear is, with the possible exception of the polar bear, the largest carnivore on earth and a magnificent trophy.

cle plus walk-in probably account for 40 percent - 50 percent of the resident and nonresident hunting here. (*Note:* This is not to imply that any of these hunts is totally mechanized, just that vehicular travel may play some part in the general hunt.) The balance of the hunting, about 40 percent, is accounted for by the standard bush plane fly-in and walking approach that is most prevalent throughout Alaska.

Dall sheep are holding up reasonably well throughout most of Alaska despite increasingly heavy hunting pressure. However, the larger heads are becoming much harder to get. (The *average* Dall sheep now being shot in Alaska runs 32 inches to 33 inches — all stories to the contrary notwithstanding.) The Talkeetna sheep hunting reflects this fact of life. Even though these mountains are located very close to the major city of Anchorage and the total range (as I am defining it) only amounts to about 4,000 square miles, sheep inhabit a

good 50 percent of that range. That's not a bad ratio of sheep ground to total ground in any mountain range. There are probably some 1,600 to 1,700 in the Talkeetnas out of a statewide total of 30,000 to 35,000 Dalls. Figuring that the trophy percentage of any animal herd generally runs around 5 percent to 6 percent means that there are, each year, about 80 to 100 harvestable rams here. In recent years the harvest has varied from 75 to 88 sheep per year.

Although these aren't the largest sheep in Alaska, you have an excellent chance of taking a good trophy if you employ a first rate outfitter and guide and then do your part during the hunt. The hunter success ratio for nonresidents employing guides runs a very respectable 68 percent which is rather healthy for most any kind of sheep hunting.

Grizzly bear are regarded by many sportsmen as the premier Alaskan trophy, even upstaging the Dall. This

Alaska has more airplanes per capita than any place on earth. The ubiquitous 5-gallon gas can is used for about everything imaginable. This pair have been rigged into a 10-gallon water carrying appliance to minimize the number of trips to the river.

Alaska has some 25,000 or so snow white Dall sheep, the largest herd of these magnificent animals anywhere on earth.

school of opinion has increased greatly in the last few years as inland mountain grizzly have become far harder to take than Dalls. The outlook for mountain grizzly throughout much of the state is, as elsewhere, not too bright. Although only 10 to 12 of the big bear are taken here each year, relative to the small size of the range, the amount of hunting pressure it receives and the trend of grizzly hunting in general, that isn't too bad.

The gigantic Alaskan moose is the largest deer that has ever trod the earth and a highly desirable trophy. Probably 300 to 400 are taken here each year. Although some of the very largest heads have historically come from a bit farther south on the Alaska and Kenai Peninsulas, the Talkeetnas feature very large trophy moose and are probably exceeded only by the Chugach Mountains in percentage of BIG moose taken by hunters.

Caribou are among the most beautiful large animals in the world. Carrying huge racks that sprout in an almost infinite variety of shapes and forms, they add elegance and a dash of the exotic to anyone's trophy room. The caribou kill for the Talkeetnas is difficult to formulate because, of Alaska's 13 separately recognized caribou herds, the Nelchina herd migrates between three of the mountain ranges we are considering here: the Talkeetna, the Chugach and the Wrangell.

However, some broad conclusions are possible. Caribou are cyclical animals with populations showing sharp peaks and/or declines within relatively short time periods. Although the Nelchina herd grew from approximately 30,000 in 1948 to over 60,000 in 1970 and as late as 1971 was still considered to be a "major" herd, it is now probably less than 15,000 in strength. Thus caribou hunting is not at its best right now in this area, and probably no more than 100 to 200 animals have been taken in recent years.

Black bear do not rate as highly as the other four trophies with many hunters, but they are a fine trophy that a man hunting in Alaska should try for, especially if he has little or no black bear hunting on his home ground. While the best black bear hunting in the state is undoubtedly found down on the coastal southeastern area of the panhandle, probably 30 to 40 of them are taken each year in the Talkeetnas which makes this a reasonably good inland ground for this animal. There is no mountain goat hunting in the Talkeetnas.

The Talkeetnas are close by Cook Inlet which, in turn, is warmed by the Japanese current. They are, along with the southeastern islands and the coastal range, among the "warmest" of the ranges, thus, the best times for a mixed general game hunt may fall a little later than in some of the other areas. Although this could vary by year and by season limits for various species, I would suggest August 20 to September 15 as the best times to hunt in this area. The caribou and moose should be out of the velvet during much of this period, or if not, close enough to it so that your taxidermist can easily strip the velvet and stain the antlers for you (at an additional charge). The sheep should be nicely filled out and not have that skinny-necked look that they often have in early August. The grizzly should be in relatively good pelage by mid-September in most years.

2. *The Alaska Range:* This is, by most reckoning, the largest mountain range in Alaska. There's more here: more area, more mountains, more sheep, more moose, and more hunters than in any of the other ranges. In fact, there's probably more of everything here except the goat, black bear (southeastern Alaska) and the caribou (Brooks Range).

Arcing south and west in a huge sickle-shaped parabola from the Yukon border to the mouth of the Alaska Peninsula, this giant range covers an area of about 650 miles by 70 miles in average width. That amounts to some 45,000 square miles of mountains or something more than the area of the state of Tennessee. That's a lot of hunting ground!

Sheep, in huntable numbers, populate just about half this total area. For such a giant swath of country, that's a creditable ratio of sheep ground, indeed. There are probably about 12,000 sheep here or almost half of Alaska's total herd. Chances of bagging a sheep, using the nonresident hunter success ratio as a reference, are

Most Alaskan hunting can legally be done without paid guides. As of this writing only Dall sheep and the big bears require guides and that is also subject to change.

Good mixed bag of sheep, caribou and moose from a successful Alaskan hunt.

tied with the Wrangells for second among the various hunting areas. Most of the sheep are in the western part of the range, west of McKinley Park. Sheep hunting in this westerly section is second only to the Brooks Range in success ratio with nonresident hunters scoring at the rates of 69 percent and 67 percent in two recent hunting seasons.

The average Dall sheep now being shot as a trophy in Alaska runs 32 inches to 33 inches around the horns, and that's about what you'll get here. In the eastern part of the range there are less sheep, 622 hunters took 187 sheep in 1973 for a hunter-success ratio of 30 percent in the eastern half of the Alaska Range. Further west that same year, 211 hunters took 119 sheep for a 56 percent success ratio — both of these figures include both non-resident *and* resident hunters. However, the eastern half does produce heads a bit larger than the western section. In fact, as a general rule, the further north and west you go on Alaska's various sheep grounds, the more sheep you'll see, while the further east and south you hunt, the less sheep you'll see in numbers but the larger the individual heads will run.

In 2 recent years the total number of rams harvested from the entire Alaska Range were 388 and 301 respectively. When you consider that the yield from the far smaller (and historically overhunted) Wrangells was 332 and 357 rams for the same two seasons, then the Alaska Range does not appear to be overhunted at the present time.

There is a considerable amount of vehicle assisted hunting throughout this vast area. That is, there are some expensive fully outfitted and guided nonresident hunts that make varying use of different types of tracked and 4WD vehicles. Many outside fringe hunts by residents involve parking and hoofing it in on their own two feet. As elsewhere throughout Alaska there is also considerable fly-in and walk hunting, and there is some limited horseback hunting here.

More grizzly (about 60 to 70) are taken here than on

any of the other inland ranges. That doesn't mean that this is the richest bear ground. There are far more brown bear in southeastern Alaska, and some other inland areas field a higher density of bear in certain spots. This large total (by grizzly standards) primarily reflects the huge overall size of the mountain range and also the large number of hunters rather than the thicker concentrations of the big bear. In fact, I would say there is somewhat less chance of taking a grizzly here relative to man-hours spent in the field after them than there is in most of the other inland ranges.

Some 700 to 800 moose are taken here and they run about average in size for Alaska, which is GIGANTIC by most any other yardstick! They are somewhat smaller than the giants down on the two peninsulas and over in the Talkeetnas and the Chugachs. However, moose hunting is good here, and you should have little trouble filling your tag. If you are willing to walk some and don't take the first nice bull that you see, your chances for meeting or exceeding the fabled 60-inch spread ar excellent. A fair number of 65-inch racks come in and a few in the 70-inch class are taken each year. However, a nonresident unfamiliar with the area needs a guide and more than a dollop of luck to stumble onto one of these record book heads.

Although nothing like the enormous Brooks Range herds, caribou populations are good here. Around 800 to 1,200 are taken each year with the heads running in the average class for Alaska (similar to the situation for moose). They are somewhat smaller than the giant caribou down on the Alaska Peninsula and over in the Chugachs and the Talkeetnas. However, many fine heads are taken, and with a bit of patience and persistence on your part, you should be able to collect a creditable trophy with main beams in the 45-inch to 50-inch class. That head would make a striking addition to any trophy room. Although he didn't come easy, I picked up a nice bull running a bit over 51 inches and just shy of the record book in this area. (I also picked up a moose slightly over 60 inches.)

There's good black bear hunting here with around 150 to 200 being taken each year. This probably equals the total of the other inland ranges put together. This is, outside of southeastern Alaska, the best black bear ground in the state. Since much of this giant range lies well inland, it is "cooler" than most of the other areas, and depending upon the variable weather of the individual year, the most comfortable hunting time is often to be found between August 1 and September 1. However, bear are in far better coat in September and grizzly season doesn't open up until then.

Although this range includes the highest peak on the North American continent (McKinley which towers to over 20,000 feet), it is not the most difficult terrain in the state. Though it's always tough to generalize about such a huge area, much of this ground is not nearly as tough to walk in and climb in as the farther south Wrangells and Chugachs. Many of the more westerly areas in this range are actually quite easy hunting and thus are good choices for some older hunters.

Most Alaskan hunting is via combination of bush plane fly-in and camping and walking with far less reliance on horses than in British Columbia or the Yukon.

More caribou are taken in Alaska each year than all other big game species combined. The other chief trophies are: moose, Dall sheep, black bear, brown and grizzly bear and — down on the panhandle up near Anchorage — some mountain goat.

*3. The Brooks Range:* Lying entirely north of the fabled Arctic Circle, this fragile and lovely land is, to me, the most romantic of the lot. Second only to the Alaska Range in size, this huge area covers some 450 by 80 miles (average width) or about 36,000 square miles. A bit over half of this territory is good sheep ground, and although the sheep don't run as large as those in some other areas, hunter success ratios are very high. In 2 recent years for nonresidents (only) it ran a whopping 90 percent and 76 percent, respectively. The comparable figures for statewide nonresident (only) sheep hunters ran 71 percent and 69 percent for the same 2 years, respectively. However, the Brooks are now being combed rather hard for sheep, and it will probably be scrutinized rather carefully by the Game and Fish Department officials in the next few years in order to avoid over harvesting.

The sheep harvest in the Brooks Range steadily climbed in recent years, primarily due both to the ease of hunting and to the fact that this was the last major sheep ground to "open up" and therefore there was less competition. Considering only terrain, this is probably the easiest area in Alaska to hunt. However, it is so far north that the weather can be treacherous at times, even very early in the season.

This is the most fragile ecological area of those we are considering and one of the most fragile in the world. The north slope of the Brooks is most threatened by man's encroachments right now, and no one truly knows what the effect will be on the game once man has rammed his highways and pipelines through and begun heavy-duty exploitation of the area. Sheep are probably safer from these incursions than most animals since they are basically nonmigratory high country animals. Grizzly and caribou, due to the antisocial habits of the one and the free ranging migratory pattern of the other, are probably the two most threatened.

This is not the best area to take a big sheep head though some nice rams have been taken here. Even when the curl is long, the horns are generally not particularly large based or massive in this short growing season area. Actually, sheep ratios are probably lower here than most other areas, but this game field is so large and has been less intensively hunted (until recently) that hunter success ratios have been misleadingly high. There are probably about 7,500 sheep here or barely more than half the estimated total in the Alaska Range which has only about 15 percent more sheep ground.

A tremendous portion of the hunting here is by bush plane fly-in and walking. Sadly, the amount of vehicular assisted hunting will inevitably increase as man further expands his road network into this pristine wilderness. This isn't the best bear ground around. Some black bear are taken on the south slope, but none on the north slope. Only about 20 to 30 grizzly are taken each year.

Due again to short growing seasons, the moose don't run as large as they do in some southerly portions of the state. However, if the nonresident sportsman is willing to work for his trophy and to bide his time until a nice one comes along, he should be able to take an animal in the 55-inch to 60-inch class and, with luck, even break the 60-inch barrier. Probably 200 to 300 of the big deer are taken here each year. The same general comments apply for caribou hunting, and probably 400 to 500 of the latter animals are harvested each year. However, there are so many caribou here that some very large bulls are occasionally taken due to the sheer abundance of the animal. The two largest caribou herds in Alaska, totaling approximately half a million animals, reside in this area throughout much of the year.

It's a good idea to hunt this high arctic area early, especially if the hunter has a low tolerance for cold weather. Also, bad weather can cost many hunting days here (as may be said for most of the other areas, also). Though nice trophies may be taken here, this is not the area to try for record book heads. Rather, it's an unusual hunt with chances to view some of the most pristine country left in the world and some interesting native peoples, especially the Eskimo hunters around Anaktuvuk Pass, and excellent opportunities to take a decent Dall sheep. Hunting here is rather expensive, even by Alaskan standards, due to the extended transportation requirements for hunters, duffle and supplies.

4. *The Chugach Mountains:* This mountain range lies immediately east of metropolitan Anchorage, within plain sight of the city center. It encompasses about a 300 by 60 mile area and perhaps 10,000 square miles of this 18,000-square-mile total is decent sheep ground. Mountain goat are also available in the Chugachs. Much of the area in this range falls within the boundaries of a newly formed reserve.

The Chugachs are tough hunting by and large and they vie with the nearby Wrangells for the "toughest climbing" honors. Depending upon whom you're talking to, opinions are about equally divided as to which ground furnishes the hardest going. For myself, I'd bet on the Chugachs. There are around 5,000 sheep in here with recent annual yields of 80 to 100 or so, which is below general Alaskan averages. When you consider that the nonresident hunter success ratio ran barely 50 percent in 1973 and the all hunter (residents and nonresidents lumped together) ratio was only 19 percent, the difficulty of the sheep hunting in here becomes more obvious.

More moose, around 1,000 to 1,500, are taken here than in any other mountain range. These monsters are

(Above) Happy young hunters show sheep and caribou from a successful Alaskan Hunt.

(Below) By good Alaskan standards, this is only a fair to middling caribou head at best.

huge, rivaling even the behemoths further south on the peninsulas. Moose hunting is rather good here with the animals being relatively plentiful and large in size. The same comments for caribou hunting in the Talkeetnas apply here. The heads run large, if anything larger even than in the Talkeetnas, but the same general herd migrating through both areas is at a rather low ebb right now, and the hunting is none too good for this spectacular trophy.

This is excellent black bear range. Although less of the smaller bruins come in here than in the Alaska Range, 75 vs. 100, in relation to the size of the total area and the number of hunters hunting both ranges, I would have to rank this the best black bear ground in the state after the southeastern coastal area, that is.

Alaskan hunting offers some unique opportunities. Here noted big game hunter, Elgin Gates, surveys a batch of floats that have washed ashore from Japanese and Russian fishing nets. These are highly prized momentos and many collect them. Gates picked these up while hunting walrus in Alaska some years ago.

Grizzly hunting isn't too bad here, either. Probably 30 to 40 of these larger bear are taken each year and some are very large indeed considering that this is an inland mountain grizzly and not a fish eating coastal bear.

The Chugachs are even closer to Anchorage than the

Alaska has the biggest caribou racks on earth and some of the best caribou hunting.

Talkeetnas and, as such, are very heavily hunted. The saving grace that has helped to partially offset some of this pressure is the roughness and steepness of certain parts of the range. Also, the weather can sour up pretty rapidly here, as it often does, even by far north standards.

5. *The Wrangell Mountains:* This is tough hunting. Many rank the climbing here roughest of all, and when you include the fact that this has historically been the most intensively hunted sheep ground in Alaska and that the animals have become very wary, this just may be the toughest white sheep hunting anywhere. (Special new "trophy" regulations and restrictions being designed as this is written may affect the sheep hunting considerably here in the future, though.) There are big sheep in here, and if a man is after a record book head, the Wrangells and the Chugachs are still, if he is willing to chance complete disappointment, among the better spots to look.

The Wrangell Range, as I'm defining it, encompasses an area of about 8,400 square miles, and there are probably about 3,000 to 3,500 sheep in the less than 4,000 square miles of sheep ground here. The country has been combed hard, which is the main reason for the newly revised sheep management orientation and regulations. Some 350 sheep were taken back in 1972 and 363 in 1973. That's over harvesting by most any yardstick, especially in certain pockets. Many of the outfitters who now operate up in the Brooks fled from the mounting pressure in the Wrangells for this very reason. However, interestingly enough, nonresident hunting success ratios were generally holding up very well, running 82 percent in 1972 and 76 percent in 1973. The success ratio for all sheep hunters (residents and visitors) also ran high — 51 percent and 43 percent for the same 2 years, and were exceeded only by those of the Brooks and the western half of the Alaska Range.

The Wrangells are not the best place to hunt either of the 2 bears. Only about 15 to 20 grizzly come in each year and around 40 black bear. Although the Wrangells aren't a particularly large mountain range by Alaskan standards, they are intensively hunted and that's not many bear to be harvesting for so many hunters. There are probably twice as many folks hunting the Wrangells as the Chugachs (especially the "serious" nonresident trophy hunters) and yet only half as many grizzly are taken here and less than half as many blacks.

Nor is this a good area for caribou. Probably no more than 50 to 100 per year were taken in recent years, and the caribou hunting here, as long as the herd stays so low, is now in serious jeopardy. Moose hunting isn't tops either. Some nice bulls are taken, but the density is not high right now (a statement which can be made for moose hunting throughout much of Alaska right now). About 200 to 300 bulls have been taken each year in recent seasons. This is beautiful country though. Its very ruggedness lends it a drama and beauty reminiscent of the Rockies which is missing in some Alaskan mountains. There is, by Alaskan standards, a fair amount of horse hunting here.

**Wrap-up of General Game Hunting Areas**

This pretty well covers the five "basic" areas that have historically played the largest role in general mixed game hunting in Alaska. The three areas we'll scan later are more special purpose, and when most folks refer to the "classic" Alaskan general game hunt, they are talking about the five inland ranges we have just covered. Also, bear in mind that I am comparing all of these ranges with each other and what is "not so good" by Alaskan standards would still probably make the average eastern whitetail hunter swoon with rapture and even give the western Rocky Mountain hunter pause for thought.

*1. The Talkeetnas:* Easy hunting; big moose; good weather; average sheep; poor caribou prospects; and decent grizzly hunting.

*2. The Alaska Range:* Good hunting for smaller to medium sheep; variable hunting conditions running from medium hard to easy; good moose and caribou hunting; only fair hunting for grizzly but good black bear prospects.

*3. The Brooks:* Good hunting for smaller sheep; easy walking; highly variable weather; smaller moose and caribou but excellent caribou hunting due to large herds; limited grizzly and black bear hunting; unusual and unique locale.

*4. The Chugachs:* Tough hunting; BIG moose and good moose hunting; poor caribou hunting; big sheep heads but not abundant; decent grizzly hunting and good black bear hunting.

*5. The Wrangells:* Tough walking and climbing for wary animals; good sheep heads but not overabundant and hunted hard in past; poorest caribou hunting of all and not good moose prospects; grizzly only fair and black bear about the same; currently undergoing a general change due to revised hunting regulations and game management objectives for this area.

The three other hunting areas we'll consider are all of a more specialized character than the preceding.

*6. Kodiak Island:* Lying south/southwest of Anchorage and hard by the Alaska Peninsula, Kodiak is the largest of Alaska's many islands. At 103 miles in length and slightly over half that width, Kodiak encompasses some 3,465 square miles. Considering the fact that it supports more than 3,500 brown bear or more than one bear per square mile, this may well be the richest bear ground anywhere on earth. It is a wild untamed land, shrouded for much of the year in fog and rain. The terrain is rugged and thickly covered with sitka spruce and cottonwood as well as many less desirable botanical citizens like devil's club and damnably thick alder thickets. The climate is rather temperate for much of the year, thus yielding a northern rain forest that is easy to get lost in and can be very difficult to hunt.

Kodiak's brown bear are justly famed the world over as being among the largest — perhaps the largest bear on earth. Rivaled only by the giants to the west of them on the Alaska Peninsula, these huge island bear occasionally square out around 11 feet and weigh, at the right time of year, as much as 1,600 pounds.

Hunting is generally from permanent or semipermanent camps rather than the boat hunts seen farther east and south off the panhandle, and the prices are high. Plan on paying $300 and more per day for a first rate outfitted hunt lasting 10 to 15 days in a prime area. There is a possibility that Kodiak has been over harvested in sections in the past so the game management is extremely closely monitored here. Bear in mind when planning to hunt Kodiak that a nonresident sportsman is only allowed to take one inland grizzly *or* brown bear (not one of each) during a 5-year period. A grizzly harvested on a mixed game hunt further north on the mainland means that you won't be able to hunt Kodiak (or any other brown bear ground) for 5 years. Conversely, if you harvest a giant Kodiak brownie, you'll have to pass up any grizzly that you see on a mixed game hunt in Alaska within a 5-year period.

Though the bear on Kodiak are historically among the largest, the area has been combed hard for the really big trophies for so long that the average bear being shot nowadays is actually no larger than the genetically smaller browns of the southeastern offshore islands. The days of the 10-foot bear are about gone, and any sportsman should be ecstatic to take a well furred, prime bear that squares out anywhere around 9 feet. Eight-foot bear are taken regularly now, and bear this size can generally be taken on the southeastern islands.

*7. The Alaska Peninsula:* This rugged thumb of land jutting out into the Pacific Ocean to the west of Kodiak is also a rugged, storm swept area with its terminus at the Aleutian Islands featuring some of the most forbidding weather on this planet. The brown bear are also very large here, rivaling the biggest on Kodiak, and some feel that no matter which of the two areas *theoretically* fielded the largest genetic bear, that in practical terms there are larger bear available now on the rougher eastern side of the peninsula than on Kodiak due to more intensive harvesting in years gone by on the island.

The largest moose and caribou in the world also live here, though the moose will never again equal those being taken here in the mid 1960's due to increased harvesting and changing conditions. This is still a good place to look for record book moose. The caribou taken here are still the largest in the world, and the annual migrations around Ugashik Lake (where the current world's record was shot) and Lake Iliamna are the best places to look for trophy heads. Thus, the peninsula offers a more mixed hunting menu than Kodiak. This is rough country, be in good physical condition and hunt with someone who knows the area intimately.

*8. Southeastern Islands/Panhandle (Coastal Range):* This umbrella category covers several different kinds of hunts, all relatively recently "discovered" by southern 48 hunters. Though Kodiak and, to a lesser

Though caribou numbers have dropped dramatically in Alaska in the last few years (due to discontinuation of all wolf control programs and unlimited native killing in the far north), most any hunter going to Alaska should count on taking one if he goes to a good caribou area.

degree, the Alaska Peninsula, have been meccas for big bear hunters ever since World War II, hunters just began flocking to the southeastern coastal islands of Admiralty, Baranof and Chichagof islands in numbers to hunt brown bear in recent years.

Though the bear run a bit smaller in theory here, in today's practical hunting terms, the sportsman can often shoot as large a trophy here as on Kodiak or on the Peninsula. With a bit of work 8-foot bears can usually be taken and the occasional bruin running upwards of 9 feet is harvested. The hunting is cheaper here, usually running about two-thirds the cost of Kodiak hunts. Boat hunts are the mode of the day here, cruising the shorelines and tidal bays of these large islands in big, comfortable 50-foot and larger boats scouting for game. The average hunt runs about 14 days and the success ratios run high. Brown bear, large black bear and wolves may be taken on the spring hunts. In the fall, mountain goat, sitka deer and waterfowl may be added to the menu.

The coastal range of mountains on Alaska's narrow panhandle coast immediately to the east of these islands is rugged indeed. This is the home of what may be the largest concentration of mountain goats in the world and certainly some of the largest billys anywhere live here. For many years they went almost unharvested by nonresident sportsmen as practically everyone journeyed to British Columbia for their goat shooting. Though the generous two-goat limit has recently been reduced here, there are still plenty of goat to go around and the sportsman in good physical condition who is willing to work for his billy can almost be assured of getting a trophy goat within 3 to 4 days, assuming no weather problems.

This is also the home of the dainty Sitka blacktail deer. An elfin cousin to the mule deer and Columbian blacktails farther to the south, these small deer are among our most beautiful animals, and they abound in good numbers here in the rugged coastal range. The generous game allowances usually permit the sportsman to take several if he so desires.

Southeastern Alaska is a good bet for the hunter making his first trip to Alaska and trying to economize a bit in the process. More information about the hunting in this and all the other areas mentioned can be obtained by writing to:

    State of Alaska
    Dept. of Fish & Game
    Subport Building
    Juneau, Alaska 99801

An Alaskan hunt, even if the hunter has been there before, is truly a "hunt of a lifetime." Not for the beginner though, the hunter should be in good condition physically and know how to shoot his gun and how to hunt so that he can get the maximum amount of benefit out of these tremendously expensive and often demanding hunts.

# CHAPTER 19

# Recommended First Big Hunt: Late Season Moose/Caribou

**THE FROZEN WOOD** cracked and boomed like incoming howitzer shells as the bonfire struggled against the brutal minus 30-degree chill of northern British Columbia in late November. My stepbrother John McCartt, a warm weather flower from Alabama, promenaded endlessly around the flames, turning every 10 seconds or so to alternately toast one frozen side and then the other. Frequently he had to wipe the tears from his eyes before they froze as the biting cold periodically triggered his involuntary tear reflex.

It was midmorning, and he and his guide had stopped to build their fire and thaw out a bit. Strange things had begun to happen perched high up on those frozen saddles: hands became unfeeling sticks that ceased to work right, bottoms froze to saddles and legs became numbed stumps that wouldn't support the hunters when they dismounted. The fire also enabled them to toast their lunches of frozen sandwiches into near edibility.

"Nonstop from a slab of icy granite to instant charcoal," as John ruefully described the results of these necessary lunchtime cookouts.

Suddenly the guide motioned to John as a big bull moose lumbered out of the fringe of ice-white spruce

Here the author shows nice Canadian moose taken on late season hunt with outfitter John Holmes in the Cassiar Mountains of northern British Columbia.

Gary Larsen, a happy young Washington State hunter, shows moose and caribou trophies collected on late season hunt with Johnny Holmes in northern British Columbia.

trees several hundred yards across the vast frozen flat. They glassed the beast intently for several excited moments, trying to determine through their teary eyes if the big deer would meet John's minimum goal of a 55-inch spread. This was the third day of a 7-day moose/caribou late season combination hunt (with big moose as the main target), and John had already passed up several large bulls in the process of looking over nearly a hundred animals. The game, including the big trophy bulls, were down off the mountains and moving around out on the open flats as they constantly searched for food to ward off the brutal cold. There are occasional problems of one sort or another on some of these late season, cold weather hunts but finding game usually isn't one of them.

After several more moments of glassing the bull and some whispered discussion, John finally decided to take him. He was sure that the spread was well over 55-inches, possibly even approaching the highly coveted 60-inch mark. The paddles didn't appear to be extremely wide, though, and it was a toss-up as to whether the animal might qualify for the record book. Plenty good enough for any man's first moose, however!

Hardly 10 breathless minutes later John had collected his huge, shaggy trophy with two well placed Nosler 130-grain slugs, sped along by a healthy handload of 60 grains of 4831 from his pre-64 Model 70 Winchester. The shaking steel tape showed him that the antlers swept out to an impressive width of 60½ inches, and the rack green-scored enough to make the Boone &

Crockett record book at the time. (Alas, *sic gloria transit,* Boone & Crockett shortly thereafter raised the minimum score for the Canada moose category and knocked his bull back out.) A fine trophy in any man's book though, especially at the bargain basement cost of barely $40 per day!

Two days later he had also collected a decent caribou. He and his friend Herman dropped two nice bulls standing almost side by side in a small band of animals trooping through the next valley. He had the added thrill of doing it with his heavy barreled .243 Browning varmint rifle which he had carried along just for that purpose. (A feasible rifle to carry around on this all-horseback hunt.) With a single well placed shot, just as he had promised me, too.

Those two fine trophies plus several hundred beautiful pictures and scores of unforgettable memories of the far north, draped in its winter mantle of white, added up to a trip that would have been a bargain at any price. But it was doubly sweet coming at a price comparable to that of a trophy mule deer hunt in the western U. S.

That was some 10 years ago and the $40 per day rates for these hunts have more than doubled to run from $75 to $125 per day (depending upon the area, accommodations and length of stay). But the prices of other hunts (and most everything else!) have increased at least as much, and the same tasty relationship exists. *Late season moose/caribou combo hunts can be made with top outfitters in best hunting areas at barely half, sometimes even less, the cost of a general all-species mixed game hunt in the same country during the balmier days*

This caribou bull, shown here still in velvet with antlers not fully developed in the early season, will offer much easier hunting later on a winter hunt.

*of August and September.*

Thus, two of the world's largest and most impressive trophies can be hunted, with a very high chance of success for both, for about the same cost as a quality pronghorn or mule deer hunt or a first rate bird shoot. And, if you select the right area and outfitter, your chances of bagging good trophies on both of these animals runs from about 95 percent up on these late season specials. Not bad odds, eh?

### Defining the Late Season
### Moose/Caribou Hunt

These hunts are usually available from early October through November, sometimes on into December. The timing varies a bit. They may be available a bit earlier if the outfitter's general mixed game hunt bookings run out and he's trying to fill holes, if the season dates on some species have changed so that they are not available and thus bollix up the all-species hunts, or if winter comes early and cancellations roll in due to that.

These hunts may be available a bit later than mid-November if that particular winter permits (the cold won't stop the hunting, but ground fog and snowstorms sure will) and if the season dates for either or both trophies still allow hunting that late that particular year.

Figure on mid-October to mid-November as being the heart of the availability for this bargain hunt.

Though these hunts usually, as the name implies, are limited to moose and caribou, there are a few instances in north central British Columbia where goat might also be available (usually at an extra fee if a trophy is taken) on an "early-late" season hunt of this type. These moose/caribou combo hunts almost always mean two hunters to the guide whereas the more expensive earlier season mixed game hunts with the same outfitter would probably feature one guide for each hunter. Some of these hunts try to run three, four or even more hunters to the guide. Stay away from these "bargains." With this gaggle of nimrods following him around, the guide is at best a tour guide, not a hunting guide even on a strict meat hunt (*vs.* trophy hunt).

If you are interested in trophies of respectable size, you usually must look over a large number of heads. Seldom ever are you fortunate to spot "the big one" in the first animal or two that you see. For this hunt I strongly recommend that you not share a guide with more than one other hunter. Remember: Just field dressing a moose for meat and trophies is a monumental job, usually taking up the major portion of a day. If the bull was felled some distance from your camp and you must transport all that bulk back over rough terrain, it can pretty well kill 2 days for you to fully "process" a downed moose. Figure that each downed moose will mean at least a full day lost out of your 7- to 10-day hunt.

Where are these hunts available? By and large the British Columbian outfitters pioneered this type of hunt, but it is also available to varying degrees in Alaska and Alberta. To date the Yukon's 22 licensed outfitters have stuck exclusively to the mixed game all-species hunt and have not offered the moose/caribou combo hunt, but I look for this to change in the near future. These hunts are not available in the two districts of the Northwest Territories that are currently open to nonresident big game hunting nor do I look for them to be in the foreseeable future.

### Advantages of the Late Season Moose/Caribou Combo Hunt

There are quite a few other attractions offered by these late season bargain hunts other than the obvious one of far lower costs. Actually, your odds on taking a nice trophy in both species are usually better on this hunt than they are on the costlier early season all-species hunts in the same area. The cold has forced the animals down from the heights where they had fled earlier in the year to escape the heat and insect pests of

(Above) Though late season caribou and moose hunts are often conducted from hard roof base camps, these hunters have been working out of canvas out-camps. Now they're roping on the antlers from a successful hunt and getting ready to get out before the high passes get snowed in.

(Below) Coming back in from a successful late season moose/caribou combo hunt with antlers securely roped aboard. These hunts, though sometimes conducted in severe weather, give the hunter a chance to see the far north in its true colors and character and are an interesting change of pace from the late summer-early fall hunts.

(Above) Late season hunts sometimes offer extreme, almost bizarre weather swings with a hunter experiencing temperatures varying as much as 30 to 50 degrees within a 10- to 14-day period.

(Right) When the snow gets deep on some of these late season winter hunts, it is almost impossible to move around through thick cover without the use of horses.

(Below) Most of these late season moose/caribou combo hunts are conducted from hard roof base camps or lodges such as this one of outfitter John Holmes deep within the Cassiars of northern British Columbia (Holmes seated on far left).

summer.

Not only is less food available during the late season hunts than during the earlier "green" period, the colder weather has also increased the animal's energy consumption. Even though they may have stored up a lot of summer fat to help carry them through this period, nature's computer is telling them not to "cut into capital" and use this built-in safety factor until they have to. Take my word for it, other things being anywhere near equal, you'll see far more moose and caribou in a given area in November than in August. Especially the big ones. This is the main reason why that, if you've done a good job of selecting the right kind of outfitter and area, there's no real problem in sharing a guide with another hunter.

Another big plus that these late season jaunts offer is that they let you see the harsh yet fragile north country in its true character. August and September hunts have their advantages, but they don't present the great northwestern game fields of North America in anything like their true colors. You simply are not *experiencing* the far north during that lovely and all too brief Indian summer period.

Still another advantage of the later hunt is that your chances for those highly prized bonus trophies, wolf and wolverine, are far better. These predators are also hungrier and moving around more to find food. If you do luck out and take one of these marvelous trophies, your rug will be at its magnificent best in both color and length since the animals are in finest fur now. Earlier in August their pelage is, by comparison, a bit mousey and straggly and they remain so on into September in most years.

### Why Are These Hunts So Much Cheaper?

Several reasons. First, and most obviously, the "expensive" trophies such as sheep and grizzly, aren't being offered. The season is usually already closed on them, and even if not, it's usually impossible to get up to either since climbing is out of the question due to the snow and ice. The bear are usually already denned up, anyway. In fact, the outfitter probably couldn't even get his hunters through the high passes to get up into the high backcountry where these two animals are usually found.

A second reason they are cheaper is that they are usually conducted from the outfitter's lowland, hard roof base camp or lodge. That's another big cost cutter. It simply doesn't cost the outfitter as much since one cook can cook for more hunters and less wrangling help is needed. Also, less horseflesh is used since the hunters aren't moving around from out-camp to out-camp with all their gear as well as hunting. Incidentally, another big advantage of this type hunt is that if you want to bring your wife and/or children along to share this unique experience with you, they'll find it far easier and more comfortable (if they don't spend extended periods of time out in extreme cold) than moving around from camp to camp and living under canvas in the higher, more rugged backcountry.

Still a third reason for the lowered costs is that the outfitter often has trouble booking hunts during this period. This is partly because the cold weather scares some folks off, but mostly because so many hunters just aren't aware of these hunt's very existence, much less how much money they can save. Outfitters must be businessmen, and the larger ones must generate astonishingly large amounts of income just to stay afloat in this highly-capital-intensive little "industry." Horses, tack and gear, airplanes and all the other expensive machines are investment costs that must be, to the degree possible, amortized by year-around use. The longer the outfitter can stretch his paying hunting season, the better he can do this. Reduced rates are his bait to help him to accomplish this.

Probably the main reason for the reduced price tag on these hunts is the fact they are less expensive for the outfitter to provide. His guide costs are cut in half if he is only providing one guide for each pair of hunters rather than a guide for each hunter. If he's running the hunts out of his permanent hard roof base camp, he's not incurring the wear and tear on his tentage and other gear, and he can get by with less staff (cooks, assistant guides, wranglers, etc.) than would be required if he needed to keep several roving packstrings operating at peak efficiency back in the high country.

Another point is that much of this game is shot rather close to home, and it's easy for the outfitter to salvage all of the meat (and trophies). The meat is often donated to him by the hunters (except in specific meat hunt situations, of course), and it keeps him and many of his relatives in meat for the rest of the year. Incidentally, it's also far easier for the sportsman to salvage this meat and take it out as compared with most of the earlier, high country hunts. And, with meat prices skyrocketing, it is often possible to take out several hundred pounds of tasty protein at some real savings. For instance, 500 pounds of fatless, boned out meat worth about $1.50 per pound on the average will pay a lot of shipping costs to get this meat back home safely and still probably help defray several hundred dollars of the base cost of the hunt itself.

### How to Set-up Your Late Season Bargain Hunt

Everything starts with one simple decision: are you more interested in moose or caribou? Though you will almost always be able to take both animals on a good hunt of this type, invariably a given area will boast better trophies of one species than the other. Also, you should decide *realistically* what size trophy head you want. A "good" or "big" trophy isn't very exact, either in defining your goals to yourself or in communicating them to others. Try to decide what size moose you want in either spread (55 inches) or in Boone & Crockett points (e.g. 180 points). With caribou, try to decide whether you want one that scores a certain amount of B & C points (e.g. 350) or has 46-inch mainbeams or a 40-inch spread.

If you are interested in the extra large head for one species or the other or in a large head for both trophies, then the 12- or 14-day trip is indicated rather than the 7- or 10-day hunt. Another point to remember is that an area that harbors extra large trophy-sized animals (old bulls), usually does not have nearly the same density of the game as an "incubator" type area that features a heavy population of small to medium animals. This fact also tends to encourage the longer hunt for the hunter after real trophy-sized animals of both species.

Chances are you will encounter the coldest weather of your life sometime during this hunt. Make sure that you carry plenty of warm, best quality clothing. Though the weather can vary greatly and sometimes in freakish situations can be almost mild, you must be prepared for severe cold. And you must be able to not only survive this cold but to be able to function and function vigorously in it, perhaps for many hours on end. Take extra socks, good raingear and high (10-inch) insulated rubber pacs as well as the standard 8-inch high leather hunting boots.

You can't carry too many pairs of good heavyweight socks. These thick, absorbent socks are spongy and help absorb the moisture as your feet inevitably perspire in the waterproof rubber (and nonbreathing) boots or pacs that you will often have to wear to stay dry in the snow or while crossing partially frozen streams. Two pairs of socks should be worn so that much of the perspiration will be "wicked" out to the outer pair leaving the feet and inner pair relatively dry.

REMEMBER: If your feet go out on you, your hunt is over. The *moment* you become conscious of your feet bothering you when you're out in the field stop *right then* and do something about it. Straighten your socks out to get rid of that blister-causing wrinkle. Change socks right then and there if the ones you are wearing are wet and beginning to chafe. Do something! Knowledgeable hunters carry an extra pair of socks afield, sometimes a bit of talcum powder too, for just such emergencies. The minute you become aware of some seemingly minor foot irritation — you are already in trouble!

Take several pairs of warm mittens along with you. Although everyone's personal thermostat varies, extended exposure below the temperature range of 15-20 degrees above zero (Fahrenheit) usually makes most people uncomfortable in coldfingered gloves. I prefer the double-mitten set for this type of extreme cold weather work — leather outers and soft wool liners. The leather helps to cut the wind, and the wool is soft and stays warm and (mostly) unfrozen even when wet.

Two sets of raingear are also a good idea. One set can

(Above) Though a hunter may be used to what he considers "cold weather" deer hunting in the eastern U.S., these late season hunts in the near arctic call for much more care in the selection of gear and clothing.

(Below) Since most late season moose/caribou hunts are conducted from snug, weathertight base camps with many of the comforts such as this one, these are often good type hunts to take your wife on. She can relax in comfort in camp while you hunt.

easily get torn or lost. Extreme cold weather alters the properties of most materials, and raingear can become brittle so that it rips or tears more readily than usual. Raingear is invaluable both to help knock the frigid wind off on gusty days as well as to keep you dry during snow or rain. Helping to cut the wind chill is especially important when you are sitting high up in the saddle and most of these late season combo hunts are largely horseback affairs.

Though this may be considered as sacrilege by some, it's a good idea to leave the lever, pump and autoloading rifles at home on these cold weather expeditions. Though all three actions have been perfected to the degree hardly dreamed of a generation or so ago and most are amazingly tough and durable, the hardy bolt action still gets the nod for heavy-duty use in extreme cold weather conditons. Most outfitters get the vapors when they see a hunter show up with one of the faster talking actions for a sub-zero hunt.

All late season hunts aren't always conducted under heavy snow and extreme cold conditions. The far northern weather is capricious, and though usually cold during these hunts, the weather may actually be relatively decent.

"Winterize" your gun by removing all the grease and oil and be sure that you sight it in *after* doing this. Not only can your action freeze up, but severe cold weather can also cause problems with that most fragile link in the whole shooting chain — the brass cartridge case. A jammed case calls for the heavy-duty camming power inherent in a good bolt actioned rifle.

Chapstick and sunglasses are also musts for these hunts. A good stocking cap of wool or Orlon and a wide brimmed western hat for the windy days are both good bets. Ditto for a little turtleneck dickey which takes up practically no room to carry and weighs next to nothing and yet can be almost as warm as an extra heavy wool shirt by helping to seal off the chill hole around your neck. Be sure to see your dentist before taking off on one of these trips. Very cold weather can unearth all sorts of toothaches and dental problems that you were just thinking about having fixed back in the city. And if there's a hell on earth, it's being stuck with a severe toothache many miles from the nearest dentist.

### Sources of More Information On These Type Hunts

For more information on which outfitters to contact and where to contact them, write to:

Alaska Dept. of Fish & Game
Subport Building
Juneau, Alaska 99801

Gov. of the Province of British Columbia
Dept. of Recreation and Conservation
Fish and Wildlife Branch
Victoria, British Columbia
Canada

Gov. of the Yukon Territory
Box 2703
Whitehorse, Yukon Territory
Canada

Gov. of the Province of Alberta
Dept. of Lands & Forests
Natural Resources Building
109th Street and 99th Avenue
Edmonton, Alberta
Canada

It's always a good idea to boldly letter on the front of your envelope: REQUEST FOR BIG GAME HUNTING INFORMATION.

It's also a good idea to check with a reputable professional hunting consultant or booking agent. He can often save you extra money and put you in touch with the best outfitter for your particular wants. I have had especially good results booking these type hunts over the years from:

Jack Atcheson & Sons, Inc.
Dept. HD
3210 Ottawa Street
Butte, Montana 59701
(Tel. 406/792-3498)

# Chapter 20

# Using A Hunting Consultant Or Booking Agent

**A HAPLESS FELLOW** I know recently indulged himself in a trip of a lifetime — a 3-week all-species hunt in several areas of Alaska. Four years of scrimping and saving went into financing this sabbatical since our friend, like most of us, is not rich by any means. A lot of sweat and strain were in there too, as he cut and sold Christmas trees and firewood during that time as well as hiring out to do some journeyman house painting and carpentry. He had "earned" this trip in the most direct sense of that word, and it was a dream come true for him.

He was going to hunt only prime areas with a first class outfitter who was to furnish nothing but the best in guides, tentage and other camp gear. It cost a bit more, but our friend had taken the commendably prudent stand of deciding to save his money for an extra year and do things right rather than trying to slide by by paying less money but perhaps getting only a second-rate hunt in the process. "I'll only do this once in my life," he told me before he left, "and I want to do it right."

Unfortunately, though our friend had the right basic idea, and in spite of all the money he spent and all the

A good booking agent, such as Jack Atcheson of Butte, Montana, usually spends many weeks a year in the field and is personally acquainted with the *current* situation of most of the outfitters he books hunts into.

Good outfitting involves several basic skills ranging from the ability to be a good hunter and employ guides who are good hunters to the ability to organize considerable amounts of provisions, money and equipment so that everything needed is at hand. Also, equally important, the really good outfitter should know how to make his hunters feel relaxed and at home during their trip. This "host" ability is something the booking agent is often aware of in the case of any given outfitter.

work he did, he made several key mistakes that ended up spelling disaster on his big hunt. What were these mistakes? Well, first he automatically assumed that if he spent a lot of money he would get a good hunt. Not so! Though you usually do get what you pay for in big game hunting as in most other things, it's certainly possible to over pay and get swindled here as in other types of purchases.

His second mistake was in assuming that since he was going to Alaska, no matter what the circumstances of his specific hunt, he simply could not have a bad hunt due to the general quality of that great game field. Of course, that was completely erroneous. There were and are many places in Alaska's giant vastness that do not provide good hunting or only do so at certain limited times.

Furthermore (and perhaps this is even more important), it is quite possible to be right in the midst of good game country on a deep wilderness hunt and not be able to have a good hunt if the logistics of the hunt are badly organized and the camps and staff are underequipped. A deep wilderness hunt is an entirely different thing than a local tramp in the woods for nearby whitetail. To get around in wilderness country properly, and stay warm, dry and well fed while doing it for days or weeks on end is no small undertaking.

His final, and by far most severe, mistake was to believe everything that his "professional" hunting consultant told him without bothering to perform the least bit of verification himself. If he had been buying a car or house or making practically any other purchase of substantial proportions, undoubtedly he would have at least attempted to verify what the salesman told him.

A good outfitter, such as Johnny Holmes, is constantly out checking his camps during the season to make sure all is going according to plan and that his hunters are being taken care of. Often he'll personally guide each hunter for a day or so just to keep his hand in.

A good outfitter employs a good staff, even if he has to spend a few bucks extra to do it. The good guide works hard for his hunter while the indifferent one loafs along. Good booking agents try to keep up with the changing situation in each outfitter's camp every season.

This "checking out" phase doesn't mean that you don't trust your salesman or other authority, nor does it mean that you want to intrude so far into the process as to be disruptive. It's just good business to avoid communication problems that can arise under the best of circumstances, and I've seen this same fellow do it and do it quite tactfully and effectively on other purchases involving hardly a tenth the cost of his safari to the far North.

After our man had arrived in camp and paid the balance due on his hunt (which brought the total up to that of the price of a nice, medium-sized car), what did he actually get for his money? Well, he did hunt three different areas, but the areas weren't selected in order to give him a *balanced* hunt but rather were selected so that the outfitter would have at least one hunter in each camp at all times to help amortize the cost of the camps. The area had obviously been rather heavily shot over in recent years, and near the end of the hunt our pilgrim found that the outfitter was in the process of selling out so that he had obviously been stripping the area rather than "farming" it on his more recent hunts.

To make matters still worse, the outfitter had been letting his maintenance go on the tentage and other camp gear, and he was providing second-rate food. About the third time our hunter had leftover breakfast pancakes with peanut butter and jelly between them as his lunchtime "sandwiches," he began to rebel. Worst of all, the outfitter had obviously scrimped in the most

valuable thing that an outfitter provides — staff. The cooks were second-rate and not clean, and the guides were young and untested and not even familiar with the areas they were asked to guide in. All in all, it was quite a debacle. Yes, that outfitter had been one of the best and had hunted in some of the best areas of the state.

But all that had changed and changed drastically. And this is an all-too-common occurrence. Outfitting is a risky and unstable business. The man who is providing excellent hunts may, just about the time he gets a good general reputation with the lay hunting public, be turning out second-rate excursions that bear little resemblance to his hunts of a few years back. These dramatic changes can occur for many reasons. Perhaps the man has had personal or financial problems that force him into a temporary expedient of "mass producing" hunts. Or, perhaps he is getting a bit old for this arduous business and figures he'd better "get his" by stripping the area and then selling out and getting out.

And keeping up with the *current* state of hunting is one of the major reasons why you should consider utilizing a hunting consultant or booking agent to help you in your hunt planning and booking. Though it certainly is not the only reason. Good hunting consultants can be an invaluable help and cost you nothing. Or, a bad one can — knowingly or unknowingly — be almost the sole cause of your having a bad trip. He can do this by booking you with a bad outfitter, or even by booking you with a good one who doesn't provide the services and game that meet *your* requirements. Either foul-up is ruinous.

## How Did Consultants And Agents Come About?

Who is this new face on the big game hunting scene — this hunting consultant or specialized booking agent? Where did he come from, and how did he come about? How does he operate and what can he do for you?

Modern big game hunting has, alas, come of age as a business. It is now a *big* business, offering its "consumers" a highly rationalized, well processed product. It's trite but still ever so true to say that exploding human populations, teamed with increased disposable

intensively harvest the game. The equipment caused, in its own right, all sorts of new complications and changes. Now the outfitter had to know: what to buy; how to run it; how to use it *year-around* (not even Dan'l Boone would let a capital investment of $100,000 to $200,000 lie around unused most of the time!); how to trade it; how to maintain it; how to play the tax and accounting angles; and so on. It literally became, in many cases, too expensive for him to deal directly and continuously with all prospective new clients. There are just too many window shoppers — as any outfitter or booking agent will hasten to agree — and the outfitter had too many demands on his limited time to be able to deal with each and every one of them personally.

Big trophies, such as this nice caribou bull, often come from entirely different areas than those fields producing the most heads of game. If *you* know your own priorities, a good hunting consultant can be invaluable in helping you to select and set up the right hunt in the right area.

income and leisure time, plus rapid travel and access to ready credit have all conspired to create a truly enormous demand (relative to the dwindling supply in many areas) for quality big game hunting.

This rising demand created the big-time outfitter. No longer was he a simple rancher or trapper who "knew the country" and was "a good hunter." He became a sizable small entrepreneur who had to buy, operate, and maintain substantial capital equipment such as airplanes with both wheels and floats, other vehicles of both tracked and wheeled persuasions or large strings of horses with all the associated (and expensive) tack and rigging required.

This equipment was necessary to more rapidly and

Ironies of ironies!

Thus arose the need for a new middleman — the hunting consultant. Many of the biggest outfitters fly in from northern Canada or Alaska once or twice a year and hit the chopped-chicken banquet circuit like any other "star" or pop celebrity. The booking agent has been handling the ongoing nitty-gritty, and he only exposes his "star" to small, well selected and intimate gatherings of the most promising prospects. Thus the outfitter's time is managed most efficiently. Many tales of derring-do are traded over good sipping whisky and fine cigars, and finally, after dinner, the soft but satisfying rustle of large checks trading hands is heard throughout the room.

## Pros And Cons of Working
## Through a Hunting Consultant

In simpler times and climes, say until about 8 or 10 years ago, the vast majority of hunters dealt with and negotiated more or less directly with the outfitters. This was true even in the case of many African safaris. Nowadays a great portion of hunts costing over $1,000 and an even greater portion of those costing over $2,000 are booked solely through these specialized booking agents with little or no contact with the outfitter himself. When there is outfitter contact, it is usually of the most limited and artificial type such as that just portrayed.

This is okay. There is certainly nothing inherently wrong with dealing through these booking agents. They are the logical product of the way trophy hunting and more expensive general big game hunting is inescapably evolving. The fact is, they can and many times do offer significant advantages over the old way of doing business *if* properly worked with by the hunter himself.

(CAUTIONARY NOTE: As in many other fields, some of the fast buck artists, have scented the sweet smell of easy pickings. Although overstatement of both the hunting consultant's field experience and knowledge and of the outfitter's game and gear is by far the more common problem, I am constrained to say that there are a few people operating who make *outright misrepresentation* a way of life.

There aren't too many hunting consultants of this stripe around but the few do a lot of damage. Some of these charlatans would make bunco artists of the pave-your-driveway or fix-your furnace stripe blush with shame, they indulge in such outrageous practices.)

Now let's talk about the advantages of using a good booking agent. For one thing, he should represent many different types of outfitters in different geographical areas, and thus, he should be able to tailor a hunt objectively to the specific wants and means of his individual clients. Obviously, the individual outfitter

Setting up a successful all-family hunt, such as hunting consultant Jack Jonas, Jr. did for his own family here, takes a special knack. The hunt should produce nice game and also be *enjoyable* to *all* members of the family. A good consultant can be invaluable in helping you to work out these kinds of details.

A good hunting consultant can help you set up the hunt of your choice as long as you are relatively clear and realistic in your own thinking. These hunters have taken a yearling bull elk on a meat hunt. Don't expect trophy hunting at meat hunt prices!

may be something less than totally objective about his own area and outfit.

Another potential advantage is recourse. If an individual hunter has booked his own hunt and then is badly treated by an outfitter, he often has little or no recourse for recovery of some of his fee or reduction of price for another, better organized hunt the following year. If this same hunter were booked by a sizable booking agent who books a number of hunters with the outfitter each year, obviously his leverage is potentially much greater. Bad service here could be translated into numerous cancellations and lost hunts — not just one.

Another advantage is that the booking agent can often be a big help in smoothing out all the normal kinks and problems built into any major trip like this. The adroit hunting consultant should have both the know-how and business connections to help out on everything from lost baggage and misrouted trophies to passport, visa or hunting license confusion on complicated trips. A good agent can be a jewel of the highest luster and not cost the hunter one cent extra!

### How Much Money Do They Cost?

These fellows operate on a standard 15 percent commission basis (at times it may be 10 percent or 12.5 percent). Thus, a $3,000 hunt would net the agent some $450 in commission fees. It is standard practice for the hunter to deposit between 25 percent and 50 percent of the hunt when he first books it, and when a booking agent is used, this deposit is tendered to him rather than

to the outfitter. This deposit is made when the hunt is booked, usually about 8 months to a year before the hunt is to begin, and the agent pockets his fee, there and then, out of the initial deposit. Thus the agent gets his dough even if the hunter should later cancel out on his hunt (forfeiting his deposit by doing so).

Incidentally, speaking of canceled hunts, this brings up another thing that these fellows can occasionally do for their clients. If you must cancel a hunt, sometimes they can find someone else to take the booking (if you let them know in time about the cancellation) thus saving you part of your precious deposit that you would otherwise forfeit in its entirety.

Conversely, at times they can put you onto a real bargain hunt wherein some hunter has canceled at the last moment, and you can save most of the cost of their deposit by booking the hunt yourself. This requires some luck and flexibility on your part, and it is not what I would call a "basic" selling point for using a hunting consultant. These bargains only come up occasionally and at random. But they do occur, and you would practically never, on your own, have a chance at one of these opportunities.

Hunting consultants and booking agents say that their services are entirely "free" in that their commission comes out of the basic hunt cost and is not an added cost. In some situations this is a theoretically arguable contention, but in many instances, the outfitter would (and does) charge the same rate whether a booking agent was employed or not. Either way you look at it, the proper use of an ethical consultant is well worth whatever money comes out of whichever pocket.

## Types of Consultants or Agents

Who are these fellows? Broadly they fall into three categories:

**1. Taxidermists who branched out into booking trips:** This is by far the most influential group, and with only a few exceptions, the largest operators are in this group. There are about 25 or 30 of these fellows scattered around the country, and they probably account for about 60 percent to 75 percent of the hunting trip volume written by booking agents of all types. (I do look for this dominance to decrease a bit in coming years as more broad line and general travel firms become aware of an interest in the outdoor/leisure travel field.)

**2. Major Independents:** These fellows do nothing but book outdoor trips, and they tend to concentrate on either foreign safaris (with both gun and camera) or the most expensive of North American hunts. They work on the biggest trips because that's where the biggest dollars are, and since they have no taxidermy volume to fall back on, they must look for the big buck. There are about 12 guys in this group.

**3. Small Operators:** These fellows only represent one or two outfitters and are often just captive agents ("house shills" as a vinegar-tongued buddy of mine once put it) who do this part-time just to pick up a free hunt themselves.

Anybody's guess is good on how many of these types are around, but it must be at least 50 or so.

Group #1 claims that their taxidermy business enables them to see where the actual trophies are coming in from and thus stay more on top of who the best outfitters are and where the best areas are. They also say that being in taxidermy as well as hunt booking better enables them to spread their overhead, and thus they can afford to give better service. Group #2 rebuts this by saying that their *only* business is booking hunts, so they are not distracted by other considerations and complications. They also hint that there is less chance of them getting into some of the subtler conflict-of-interest situations that the taxidermy boys might occasionally face. Group #3 should generally not be used by the average sportsman unless he happens to have particular personal knowledge of the journeyman "booking agent" or the outfitter involved or unless some other special circumstances exist.

## How to Deal With Bad Booking Practices

What are some of the more flagrant abuses? Well, the most common one is the hunting consultant's overstatement of his own *recent, first hand* knowledge of areas and outfitters. I know of numerous cases where clients were booked into various African countries that were downright unsafe. In some instances this was done knowingly, and thus was the most corrupt breach of ethics imaginable. In other instances when the agent

Many booking agents are also taxidermists, and this double exposure helps them keep attuned as to the areas where the best trophies are coming from season by season.

There are many, many factors, some not so obvious to the inexperienced hunter, that determines whether one outfitter is better than another. What kind of horses he has and how well he maintains them is one factor. A good booking agent may be personally acquainted with the situation in many instances.

Trophies like the wolverine are marvelous additions to any hunt, but they should be considered (in most cases) as secondary or bonus trophies on a pick-them-up-as-they-come basis. Don't let a misplaced attempt to shoot "one of everything" on a single trip unbalance your planning with a booking agent.

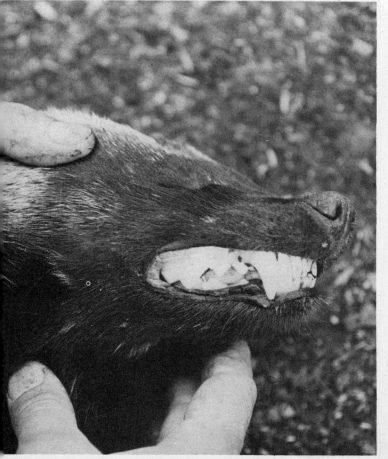

indicated that he "wouldn't hesitate to go there with my own family," he was simply indicating that he didn't know what he was talking about.

Another all too common failing is that uninformed agents have been known to book older or out-of-condition hunters into rugged areas on hunts that they simply couldn't handle. (This can also be the fault of the client and often is. More on this later.) Also, there are certain areas or times of the year when specific animals are harder to get, and this may directly conflict with the client's primary objectives. When a consultant is rhapsodizing and rising to new heights of poetic eloquence about an outfitter or an area, check his sources. Ask him how long it's been since he himself has been in that area or with that outfitter or at least how long it's been since he's talked directly with several people who were.

When the consultant is giving you references on an outfitter, ask him for more than one or two and make sure they don't all fall in the same party who hunted together at the same time and thus only constitute one reference. Make sure that these different references are recent. Then *call* as many of these references as possible rather than writing to them. It's more convenient for them to talk to you over the phone, and they'll often be franker. And, if the hunt isn't worth a few long-distance phone calls, ask yourself if you're really serious about the whole thing. You can keep the costs of these calls down by calling during low rate periods, outlining your questions in advance to keep the conversations as brief and meaningful as possible and noting down all answers on paper so that they don't become blurred in your mind.

Ask the references for the names of other hunters who hunted with that outfit. That way you are not confining yourself solely to the names of handpicked references selected by the outfitter or booking agent. Every outfit runs a few good hunts by accident if not by design. The question is: how did the *majority* of the hunters do? (NOTE: Question unhappy hunters carefully and with an open mind because it is at least as easy for a hunter to be biased and unethical as it is for an outfitter or booking agent. All too many hunters want to blame their own shortcomings on the outfitter or the area when perhaps they themselves weren't in the physical condition that they should have been, or couldn't hit the game, or just expected too much out of the hunt for the time and money involved.)

There is another area of problems beyond this semi-innocent area of overstatement and overselling that we have just been discussing. This second group of potential problems includes various "sharp" practices that border on but do not fall into the category of outright fraud. For instance, I know of one booking agent stable (and a big one at that) that was booking hunters into "guaranteed" hunts for California bighorn sheep in northern British Columbia. The demand for these highly prized trophies being what it is, they had a lot of takers.

The regular, nonguaranteed hunt for these animals costs $900. The "guaranteed" hunt ran $1,750, with a $1,000 "credit" if the "guarantee" didn't work out. The guaranteed hunt was exactly the same as the nonguaranteed hunt (same length of time; same area; same outfitter; same time). All that was different was the cost of the hunt and the existence of the "guarantee."

Okay, so the hunter has a guarantee. Now things really get complicated. First, the "guarantee" was for a "good shot" *not* for a kill. (Most anyone would be a fool to guarantee outright kills since this leaves them vulnerable to ridiculous marksmanship whereby the hunter might miss his standing game at 50 yards and still want his guarantee. Or even, in some cases, the hunter might miss on purpose because he wanted to try for a larger head and felt safe in doing so because of the cushion of the "guarantee." For any business featuring ethical sport hunts to protect themselves from these kinds of vagaries, they would have to charge such stratospheric rates for guaranteed kills that no one in their right mind would pay the cost.)

So the guarantee is for a "good shot." What's a good shot? A standing animal at 300 yards? A walking or partially obscured animal at 200 yards? A running jumpshot at 100 yards or less? You can readily see how many different permutations that there might be in the definition of a "good shot."

Even if client and outfitter/booking agent agree more or less on what constitutes a "good shot," who determines if the shot meets that criterion? If the shot was supposed to be within 300 yards, what happens if guide and hunter disagree on the estimate of the distance or other specifications? I could go on and on, but it should be obvious that defining and determining what a "good shot" is and if a "guarantee" has been met begins to approach the futility of medieval theologians learnedly discussing how many angels could dance on the head of a pin!

The worth of the "guarantee" becomes even foggier when analyzed dispassionately and rationally. If the client got his ram then the outfit pocketed an extra $850 for nothing (the difference between the $900 non-guaranteed and the $1,750 guaranteed hunt), since the guaranteed hunt didn't cost them any more to run. If the client never even saw anything (thus under no condition could he not collect on his guarantee), the outfit gave him a "credit" of $1,000 against another hunt, which must be booked within 2 years — not an outright cash refund which the hunter thought he would get. Thus the booking agent and outfitter still pocketed more *cash* even if the client "collected" on his guarantee. All it cost them was $150 on paper if the client booked again through them. If the client didn't (or couldn't) book another hunt through them within the 2-year period, then they still came out $850 ahead, in cold cash.

Of course, if the client did "collect" on his guarantee and was intrepid enough to book another hunt with this bunch of shysters within the 2-year period, it doesn't take a genius to see that it would be very easy for the booking agency to merely raise the cost of the next hunt an additional $150 (or more) to cover their paper "loss." The whole thing smells to high heaven!

Then there's the old bromide about signing, as part of your booking agreement, a commitment to let the same firm (or some designated firm) do all your taxidermy from that hunt. I regard this practice as being very unethical. If you have a bad trip, you may not want to give this firm any more business of any type. Also, the firm might be lagging far behind in delivery, and yet the hunter would not have any flexibility to go elsewhere since he had already signed a commitment a year or so ago when he first booked the hunt itself. Even if the hunt is a good one, the outfit could be a good booking agency but a not-so-good taxidermist. Basically, the two services are just that — two different services. And each should stand or fall on its own merits.

Then there are the more fraudulent cases that are far worse than the "sharp practice" instances. I know of situations where deer hunters have been booked into northern areas to hunt a month after the bucks had dropped their antlers.

People have been booked into areas for animals that were not legally huntable there or that, in some horrible cases, did not even exist there. Unscrupulous "hunting

Though pronghorn are a good "do-it-yourself" hunt animal, a good hunting consultant is of great value in wetting up a specialized hunt tailored for a youngster this small to insure that he gets not only his game but that the hunt is organized in such a fashion that he'll *enjoy* it.

consultants" have been known to go to small-time outfitters who were mass manufacturing meat hunts for elk by hunting 10 or 12 men out of the same camp with little or no guide service for $300 a throw and arranged to book hunters in for $600 to $750 for the same hunts but calling them "trophy hunts." This cost the unethical outfitter nothing, he just picked up more $300 hunters without having to bother with dealing with them before the hunt, and the booking agency picked up a 100 percent to 150 percent commission — and the poor unsuspecting, overtrusting hunter got it in the neck on his "trophy" hunt!

People have even been booked into outfits that no longer existed or that had changed hands and thus radically changed character.

### Basic Practices for Hunter to Follow

How could such horrible examples as these happen?

Basically because the hunters let it happen. They didn't do their all-important desk work, especially their reference checking. Here's what a hunter should do whenever booking a hunt through one of these middlemen:

1. Deal only with established consultants or booking agents who have a proven track record that can be checked.

2. BE HONEST! Don't vastly overstate your own hunting experience, marksmanship and physical condition and then get mad at the lack of honesty in others. (You *know* that being able to play 18 holes of golf down at sea level doesn't qualify as "good" condition to a guy who can start out a mile high and then climb a 4,000-foot mountain in 2 hours! You *know* that two or three deer and a cow elk don't qualify you as a seasoned sheep or big bear hunter!).

3. BE REALISTIC. Decide on the one animal that

you want and don't go into mixed game country expecting to shoot one of everything there. Tell your consultant what you are mainly after and be specific about the size trophy you are talking about. When and if the agent offers you a miracle hunt with all sorts of "guarantees" at a low, low price — beware! Most hunters get into trouble because of their own greed. They hear what they want to. Sure, there are good bargains around, and careful shopping and checking will help you to find and verify them but, if a deal sounds "too good to be true" — chances are that it is!

**4.** Deposit early. This way the agent knows you are serious about the hunt, and he can and will get the best arrangements possible for you. About 98 percent of the folks that a booking agent talks to are "just looking" and will not end up booking a hunt with him. And he knows that. Since he does know this and he's a businessman, he can't spend an unlimited amount of time on any one client planning and working up the best deal for him without knowing if that client is serious.

*Remember:* Two of the most important things you buy on any hunt are time and access to game. A 10-day sheep hunt is not and never will be the equivalent of an 18- or 21-day sheep hunt in comparable country. You should never try to trophy hunt out of a camp with more than four hunters in it. To dump a dozen hunters, six or seven guides and a couple of cooks and wranglers into one camp and call it "trophy elk hunting" is a joke. Elk are wary animals and with 18 or 20 people stumbling around over the same three or four mountains, they'll leave that country overnight, with the big bulls leading the way.

The hunting consultant/booking agent is here to stay. There are some extremely good ones around, and the vast majority of them are ethical, helpful people. Most of them don't wear either white or black hats but, rather, are about as honest as the hunter/client will let them be. If the hunter expects, even demands, miraculous "deals" and "guarantees" galore, he usually gets about what he deserves.

On the other hand if the hunter realizes that he is not buying dead animals like so many canned goods but instead is buying an experience — an honest, sporting hunt — then there are a lot of good people around in this middleman category who can save him time, trouble and money and who can help insure that he books the hunt that best serves his needs and resources.

Good staff, guides, cooks, and wranglers are the biggest single problem of any outfitter. A booking agent or hunting consultant usually knows the situation of most leading outfitters in this respect.

# CHAPTER 21

# Take Care Of Those Leather Goods!

**IN THIS AGE** of synthetics, some things still haven't been equaled or bettered in their natural state. For the big game hunter leather is one of these. There's something inherently *right* about the use of fine leather goods outdoors whether we're talking about hunting boots, hiking or camp shoes, rifle scabbards, saddle bags, camera, binocular or spotting scope cases, or all sorts of other interesting pouches, carrying cases, holders and other oddments that can be custom crafted to make your life outdoors more comfortable and productive. From the warmth of a lightweight, wear-forever buckskin shirt to the convenience of the small, belt type, leather ammunition holder, the hunter has found how to make leather work for him as few other natural materials can.

However, it's amazing how many sportsmen buy top quality (which means expensive) leather goods and then never do anything to maintain them except perhaps turn a hose on them to wash them off. Then, more times than not, they set them next to direct, dry heat to dry them off. This is the WORST thing to do. The forced, quick drying robs the leather of its vital natural oils and preservatives, causing it to become dry and brittle and begin to crack.

The field life of an expensive boot like this can literally be doubled with proper care. (Photo courtesy Browning Company)

Quality leather hunting boots such as these various weights and types sold by Browning are expensive, and they should receive the proper care to extend their life and make them more comfortable. (Photo courtesy Browning Company)

Yet these very same neglectful hunters religiously clean and shine their dress shoes to make them look better and last longer. Chances are their heavy-duty hunting boots cost twice as much as those street shoes — so how do you figure it?

We're talking some real money for best quality heavy-duty boots. A pair of top quality 8-inch mountain boots with Vibram soles comes dear. They should have strongly reinforced counters, box toes and heels. For hard work in mountain and rough rock country they are — quite simply — worth their weight (which is considerable) in avoided blisters, ankle sprains and broken legs. Any of these occurrences, even a bad set of blisters, can be a not-so-minor tragedy when they lay a fellow up on a hunt costing a $100 a day and more. To get the best boots, figure $50 and more — sometimes considerably more.

Then the well equipped hunter should have a good pair of leather topped, rubber bottomed "Pacs" for the lighter, wetter walking often encountered after a snow, in marshy lowlands or in much of our southern or eastern deer hunting. These boots cost $25 to $30 and considerably more if you want them with Vibram soles (which I highly recommend). The well equipped hunter should also have a pair of lightweight 6-inch "walking shoes" for dry land work that doesn't demand the real heavyweights. These shoes are cooler, less tiring to wear and, where maximum protection isn't necessary, a joy to climb and walk in. They go for $35 and up.

A pair of comfortable leather fleece-lined camp shoes of the Chukka boot variety or similar type will ring the cash register for another $25 or $30. By the time a fellow adds in his tax and freight (if they were ordered from a mail-order firm), chances are this little array of foot savers is going to cost him upwards of $200 or more. Bearing in mind that boots and footwear are the big game hunter's single most important piece of equipment, that $200 or so makes good sense and is an investment more than an expense. Remember, if you can't walk, you can't hunt.

Now let's take a look at some of the hunter's other leather items. A good pair of saddlebags, cunningly contrived for both good looks and extra heavy-duty protection of your cameras and other precious "breakables," will last a lifetime with proper care and be worth several times their original cost. After seeing some of the canvas or burlap horrors that some outfitters have furnished clients on a "make-do" basis to serve as saddlebags protecting breakables worth hundreds of dollars, the $50 to $100 price tag on good leather bags looks reasonable indeed.

A well designed and crafted rifle scabbard should have a fully detachable hood that comes well down over the bottom part of the case, thus fully enclosing and protecting the rifle inside. This zone of overlapping leather, leaving none of the gun or scope exposed, is the key to adequate protection of the rifle inside which is expensive in and of itself and which the hunter is relying on to make the even more expensive hunt a success. To get one that is made of the best grade leather, with buckles and hardware that won't rust or break under heavy use and one that is put together with the best thread and lining (made of glove leather and *not* fleece which holds moisture) will cost better than $100 these days.

Again, considering that this case will be protecting a

The amount of leather items, from boots, belts, knives and camera cases to gun scabbards and saddle bags, carried by three typical hunters such as these is amazing. Yet how many give any thought to the care of these items?

rifle that probably costs two or three times as much, the scabbard is an investment and not an expense. These scabbards can also be used as regular carrying cases to shuffle guns to and from the range or protect them in the back seat of the car during off-season varmint outings or other nearby shoots.

And, good rifle scabbards are, as is the case with any fine handmade item, a treasure to have and use. A single instance where a scabbard saves your gun from being knocked out of zero (or worse) on a big hunt could make the difference in whether you get that trophy of a lifetime or not. Considered that way, the extra initial cost for lifetime use of one of these cases begins to look very reasonable.

Then there are all manner of miscellaneous binocular cases, camera cases, ammunition pouches, leather shirts or vests, gun slings, leather over-mittens or gloves, special custom crafted cases for extra camera equipment or other goodies and many other leather items which should be cared for and maintained with the same pride and attention that the hunter lavishes on his guns. All of these miscellaneous items run into sizable chunks of money in their own right, some are awkward to replace and all protect valuable items.

And yet most of these leather items receive little or no care. The hunter who scrupulously maintains his guns and other gear seldom ever spends any time on his leather goods. In fact, it usually doesn't even occur to him that he should. What makes all this lack of "leather lovin' " doubly perplexing and puzzling is that it's so darn easy and inexpensive to take good care of these valuable items!

I usually work my own leather goods over twice a year; first in general cleaning and policing I do on all my gear before hunting season opens, and secondly, after hunting season closes when I check everything over before putting it away. What's the "secret" to all this leather maintenance? Couldn't be simpler! About $3 or $4 worth of saddle soap and neat's-foot oil (or another very important but lesser known product we'll talk about in a minute) can put you into business for several years!

Here's how to go about it. Remove any caked on mud and grit by dry brushing with brush or broom. Dampen the leather item to be cleaned with lukewarm water and likewise dampen your bar of saddle soap. Rub the soap lightly with a *clean* rag to produce a lather. Then pour the elbow grease onto it. Scrub those dirty boots hard, by the old hand-and-rag method, not by using stiff wire brushes that may harm the leather.

Wash until clean, making several applications of saddle soap if necessary. Then remove any excess soap with a damp cloth, and while the leather is still damp (not wet), apply either neat's-foot oil or Lexol. Neat's-foot oil is actually made from horses' hooves and various other animal parts, almost "made from the leather itself," as they saying goes. It will penetrate dry and cracked leather and do an amazing job of "bringing back" seemingly ruined leather.

However, there's still another product that I think does an even better job of leather protection and restoring. It's been on the market a number of years but is surprisingly unknown except among horsemen and saddlery experts. This off-white liquid has a *vegetable* base, and it's called Lexol. It's available at any good saddle shop, and I use it exclusively in preference to neat's-foot oil.

Neat's-foot oil generally leaves a slight oily residue,

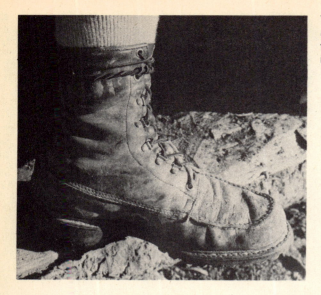

These dry, cracked hunting boots have been too long without a good treatment of oil or similar dressing. However, note how the hunter does correctly have the rawhide laces wrapped rather than bow-tied for a sturdier yet more flexible binding.

about some leather items that will be enclosing and completely surrounding such optical items as rifle-scopes, binoculars and cameras, one doesn't have to be a genius to see why oil and grease residue are big NO-NO's.

Both products have simply amazing penetrating and regenerative powers where leather is concerned if the leather isn't already too deeply cracked and dried out. A friend of mine actually used Lexol to "bring back" some civil war era relics that he picked up in Georgia. Another buddy used the same magic elixir to restore an Eskimo dog harness, of vintage years to say the least, that had been used for many years in the harsh northern Yukon.

After you apply either the neat's-foot oil or Lexol, just let your boots or other items sit, at ROOM TEMPERATURE in a dry place, while the solution penetrates the leather. Don't over apply. Either solution can, if used over generously, make the leather too soft and supple on some items. You don't want the ankles of those mountain boots or the spine of that rifle scabbard to lose all their body. Better to apply it in several sessions, if need be, to avoid this.

no matter how carefully it is applied. Not so slight if you overdo things when applying it as is the tendency with beginners. Lexol, due to its vegetable base, is not oily or greasy in the least and never leaves this residue.

In years gone by, the Hollywood studios used Lexol with almost religious fervor on those baroque, silver-mounted and highly bejeweled saddles that the leading horse opera cowboy stars used to sport so proudly in the '30's and '40's. Some of these "saddles" were valued at up to $35,000 — back then! Since neat's-foot oil also generally causes a bit of discoloration if enough of this residue is left, the studio prop men wouldn't let a can of the stuff in the same room as one of those valuable saddles.

Yet, for some completely unknown reason, neat's-foot oil is always extolled to the skies in articles of this type with nary a mention of Lexol. Since we are talking

After your leather items have soaked up the solution for a full day or so, wipe off any excess and polish them with a dry, clean cloth. You'll be amazed at your "new" boots, gun cases, and camera bags. They'll last longer, look better and save you money in the long run.

So, on a rainy day sometime — take the time to do a little "leather lovin'."

Center items are all custom made. (Left to right: case for movie camera; saddlebags; case for 400mm telephoto camera lens; scabbard for custom knife.) These are expensive leather items in their own right, and they protect far more valuable gear. They deserve the best of care.

# CHAPTER 22

# A Planning Primer For Your Hunt Of A Lifetime!

*Nearly 36 major hunts — covering all major big game species, all important hunting areas on the North American continent and at all price levels — for you to choose from in setting up your own "dream hunt!"*

**MOST ALL** hunters yearn to make at least one "Hunt Of A Lifetime" to the far places for strange and exotic game or outsized trophies. Once a sportsman has made that big hunt, he's always twice as anxious to make the next one! And why not? At their best these memorable major hunts become life happenings that far transcend the mere stalking and taking of trophy game. They furnish us with marvelous memories of cold mountain streams and warm campfires, clear nights and cold snowy days and — most of all — good comrades who share the same feelings about what is important in life.

I know of no other experience that can quite match an extended big game hunt back into the remaining wild places of our continent for sheer excitement and for the opportunity to get to know some fascinating characters (among them, ourselves!). And, most fortunately, North America is still rich enough in wild places and

Caribou can often be hunted at less expense than most other deep wilderness species.

Mountain sheep are expensive trophies to take, no matter how many corners one cuts.

different animal species to afford us these opportunities in an almost bewildering variety of options for differing kinds of game taken on differing kinds of hunts and at vastly differing prices. There are so many possibilities that any serious hunter can afford at least several of the options, no matter what his financial status.

This awesomely confusing variety of possibilities is the very reason why we are surveying the situation in the most concise, unconfusing manner possible — with current costs included as well as background remarks in these charts. First, a few points should be made so that you can derive the maximum benefit from these accompanying charts:

1. Obviously I haven't covered every single hunt possibility and sub-possibility in every single locale on these charts. Fortunately we do still have such a mix of options that it is still impossible to completely cover every variation on every theme within the compass of this chapter. However, all the *basic* hunts are included. Those that are left out are either what might be called secondary hunts (cougar hunts with dogs, winter wolf hunts) or are actually slight refinements only of the basic hunts covered here.

2. Some of the hunts do, of necessity, overlap my arbitrary price ranges in some cases. Professional hunting outfitting in North America is now an old and accepted profession going into its third generation of existence. In that time, ingenious outfitters have thought of

about every conceivable version or gradation of the basic hunts and have offered them to the public at varying costs. In this chapter I have indicated the general price range for certain hunts and then assigned them to the correct price range that they will fall into most of the time when considering good hunts from reputable outfitters.

Legitimate bargains will occasionally be available (due to special circumstances such as last minute hunt cancellations by other sportsmen or because the outfitter is especially anxious to "fill out" his bookings for the hunt or the season), but beware of the unbelievably "good deal." Often this low, low price means a second-rate hunt in an area where the game is sparse to nonexistent and the services and accomodations being provided are even worse. A hunt which is not enjoyable is no bargain no matter what the price!

3. I have not included any of the so-called "guaranteed" hunts for numerous reasons. Most of them are shady operations that camouflage "set up" hunts rather than ethical, fair chase hunts, and practically all of them actually cost the hunter more, not less, money. Perhaps the primary thing I have against them is the feeling that a "guarantee" is contrary to the very essence of sport hunting. For more detail, see Chapter 20.

4. You will notice that a dollar sometimes seems to be worth more or less on some of these hunts. Part of that is due to the fact that certain areas or types of hunts

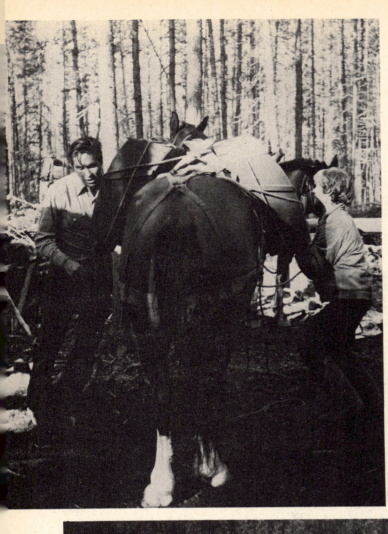

(Left) Guiding and wrangling is a skilled profession that is demanding and, at times, downright dangerous. Good ones are always in short supply. Expect to pay for their services.

(Below) Some horseback hunts, for more common game species located in semi-wilderness rather than deep wilderness areas when large outsized trophies aren't demanded, are surprisingly modest in cost. The *experience* is as exciting and unique as that of the more expensive horse hunts, even if the bag isn't as full.

Well constructed, comfortable hunting quarters such as this, located in deep wilderness many miles from the nearest road, are expensive to build and maintain. The hunters have to pay for it.

may offer a generally better possibility of getting the game being hunted and/or the game (such as Alaskan moose) may be the largest trophy size for that particular species thus you pay more. But, aside from these various legitimate factors that appear to distort the price picture, there are some literal bargains available to the calculating big game hunter trying to stretch his recreation dollar as far as possible without giving up quality.

Some examples? Well, if I were interested in a top quality far north mixed game hunt for the premier trophies (including sheep and grizzly), I'd check out the Yukon first and Alaska second. Changing license costs, political and game management considerations and other factors have made the classic horseback hunt in British Columbia and Alberta somewhat less attractive as this is being written.

In recent months, (this being written in the summer of 1977), the Canadian dollar has been discounted about 7 percent — meaning that the U.S. dollar is worth that much more than the Canadian dollar. Naturally, this does not mean that it is cheaper to hunt in Canada, but keep it in mind when booking a hunt in Canada. It's probable that prices have gone up a similar amount in Canada, to offset the approximate 7 percent loss to the outfitter.

Elk are one of the most in-demand trophies for the eastern whitetail deer hunter out after his first larger-than-deer trophy. My recommendation would be to try Montana and Wyoming in that order, both for better chances and for bigger trophies. The Canadian elk hunts suffer from the exchange rate problems just discussed, and the elk populations in Alberta are down significantly due to changing objectives in game management. They are trying to improve their bighorn sheep herds by doing away with the marginal competition from some of the elk herds.

This priority management consideration that the sheep are receiving is highly laudable, and I agree wholeheartedly with the approach. Pity is that it isn't followed in similar fashion in parts of several other provinces and states. However, it is affecting the elk outlook to a degree. Look to those special "call" late

Professional guides who can help the hunter to locate and kill rare trophies such as this wolverine, are expensive but well worth the cost!

Well constructed camps
such as this one make a lot
of difference in the hunter's
efficiency afield

season hunts in Montana for your best chance at a big trophy bull. (They are "called" on a somewhat last minute basis depending upon whether the herd didn't get adequate cropping from the normal early hunting season or if the winter has been particularly severe and more elk than usual need to be cropped due to the decreased carrying capacity of the range.) These late hunts usually begin after the first of the year and may, in some cases, be available into March.

To take proper advantage of one of these late hunts, you'll need to be in a position to pick up and go on rather short notice because these hunts are usually scheduled, with the limited number of permits on a last minute basis. The services of a good hunting consultant or booking agent would probably come in handy on setting up this type of hunt.

Looking further east, one of the better bargains now available to the big game hunter is the Quebec-Labrador caribou hunts costing around $500 to $1,000 plus license and travel cost. Very few people return without their bull, and chances for a really large trophy are quite good if the sportsman hunts with a good outfitter and allows enough time for the hunt so that he can look over a goodly number of heads.

This herd has only been hunted for sport for a few years, and a good number of people, including myself, believe that the largest caribou of all the four trophy types currently recognized by the Boone & Crockett Club will eventually come from this herd. Actually, the highest scoring trophy caribou head of all time currently comes from this area but, with increased sport hunting here (and the herds can stand much more hunting than they are getting at the hands of sportsmen), this head should eventually be bettered even though it has outranked all other known heads for over 40 years now.

One of the biggest bargains of all still remains the semi-do-it-yourselfer hunt for mule deer, pronghorn or — where regulations allow — a combo hunt for both.

Write to the Fish and Game Departments of Montana and Wyoming and get a list of the ranchers who allow nonresident hunting on their ranches for a fee and write to these ranchers for more information.

Also, get the name of the local game warden or wildlife biologist stationed in the area you are interested in hunting and contact him *by phone* in order to get the best information (off the record) on hunting prospects for that general area and the best ranchers to hunt with.

One of the biggest *non*-bargains is the Newfoundland trek for moose and/or caribou. The animals are not of the largest size relative to their respective species, and when you add in the stratospherically high license costs for either or both, this hunt is anything but a bargain. Based on your chances for success, your chances for a larger than average trophy and the general opportunities for scenic grandeur and picture taking, this hunt doesn't rate up with the other "basics."

5. License costs. These were not included as they change so rapidly. **CHECK THEM CAREFULLY.** They are rising even faster than the other hunting costs and have come to play a very substantial part in the overall cost of the hunt for the nonresident hunter. It is not uncommon now to pay over $1,000 in some areas for a complete array of licenses. That's hardly less than what some southern African countries charge for their safari licenses for three times the amount of game! Careful checking of current license costs could even, by themselves, cause you to select another locale for your hunt where the license costs for nonresidents aren't quite so nosebleedingly high.

The main thing is to know what you're after, what you can spend and what your physical condition is. If you have these factors clearly and unemotionally in mind, the following charts can start you off well ahead of the game in planning your own hunt of a lifetime! *NOTE: The following charts are based on 1975 prices. Inflation being what it is has probably added 15% to 20% to the prices given.*

# North American Hunts Costing Up To $500*

| HUNT/GAME AVAILABLE | HUNT LOCALE | HUNTING METHOD | HUNT DURATION | TOTAL HUNT COSTS (EXCL. LICENSES, TRAVEL TO & FROM, AND INCIDENTALS.) | AVG. HUNT COST PER DAY | SPECIAL EQUIPMENT OR GEAR REQUIRED. | GENERAL REMARKS |
|---|---|---|---|---|---|---|---|
| Pronghorn. | Wyo., Mont. | Afoot and from jeep from ranch house or motel. | 3 days | $200-$450 depending on accommodations and whether 1, 2 or 3 hunters per guide. Averages around $350-$450 (in '75) for good hunt on good ground. | $75-$150 | Flat shooting rifle and special permit. | This hunt is more and more replacing the mule deer/pronghorn combo hunt as the eastern sportsman's first western hunt. Advise getting there a couple of days early and scouting around; the first morning is very important on this type of hunt. Be sure to apply for permit in time. Usually around June. |
| Basic mule deer-only meat hunt. Occasional good trophies taken. | Wyo. or Mont., Colo., Ida. | Afoot, from horse or jeep out of ranchhouse, established camp or motel. | 3-5 days 3 days avg. 5 days advisable if possible. | $250-$500 depending on length of stay, number of hunters per guide and hunters per camp and type of camp or accommodations. | $75-$150 | General hunting gear. | This basic hunt can net you a good trophy or a bad time. Check the Fish & Game Dept. carefully and also other hunters who've *recently* hunted with the outfitter-guide in that area. |
| A "semi-do-it-yourself" hunt for pronghorn, and/or mule deer. | Wyo. or Mont. | Afoot or from vehicles from motel or ranchhouse or ranch cabins. Even from your tent on the ranch! | 5-10 days | $100-$200. Depends on length of hunt, whether rancher furnishes place to stay, some or all of the meals, limited use of his 4WD vehicle and "orientation" tour of hunting ground on his place. | Not Applicable | Basic hunting gear and any necessary food or camping gear. | Write to Fish & Game Depts. for list of ranchers who allow hunting on their lands and what services they provide, if any, in addition to basic access for hunting. You must then pay rancher the "accommodation fee" for being allowed to hunt on his place plus costs of any other services that you secure from him. A good hunt and a terrific bargain, *if* carefully worked out by the visiting hunter. Do your homework, check references, select a good area to hunt, have clear understanding of services he will furnish and take the necessary gear. |
| Do-it-yourself bighorn sheep hunt. (Only unlimited area not requiring special permit for bighorn left on continent.) | Southwestern Montana; areas 301 and 501. | You'll hike in carrying your camp on your back and establish camp at about 8,000 ft. with most of your hunting being done between 8,500 and 10,500, on foot. This is rough, tough country and this hunt, if done right, is probably the ROUGHEST HUNT IN NORTH AMERICA. (There's a reason why sheep are still unlimited here with no permit required!) | 3-5 days (That's all that 99% of us will be able to take of this kind of hunting.) | Variable. Food and any added lightweight camping and survival gear that you have to buy. Not much money but a lot of work! | Not Applicable | Freeze dried food. Finest quality, lightweight camping gear, expedition quality pack frame and bag, warm clothing, lightweight rain gear, GOOD MAPS, survival gear, compass. | This is one of the biggest bargains left *for the right man* or men. Write Montana Fish & Game Dept. for maps, info on access points and season dates and game populations. Carry a compass and know how to use it. Season is long, from Sept. thru Oct. well into Nov. Earlier in season is more comfortable but, if you want to hunt elk and mule deer at the same time, you must go late. Goat and moose also available here, but only by special permit. |

| | | | | | | | |
|---|---|---|---|---|---|---|---|
| Semi-do-it-yourself moose hunt for meat. | Ontario; Quebec | Afoot from camp or cabin | 5-7 days. | $200-$300 depending on guide services accommodations and length of stay. | $40-$75 depending on extent of guide services and quality of camp accommodations. | Food and general camp and hunting gear. | Usually stay back-in in rustic "house keeping" cabins and utilize little or no serious guide services aside from orientation tour or briefing and help getting meat out. Not the highest probability of success here but then again you may do well. |

*NOTE: The following charts are based on 1975 prices. Inflation being what it is has probably added 15% to 20% to the prices given.*

## North American Hunts Costing $500-$1000*

| GAME AVAILABLE | HUNT LOCALE | HUNTING METHOD | HUNT DURATION | TOTAL HUNT COSTS (EXCL. LICENSES, TRAVEL TO & FROM, AND INCIDENTALS). | AVG. HUNT COST PER DAY | SPECIAL EQUIPMENT OR GEAR REQUIRED | GENERAL REMARKS |
|---|---|---|---|---|---|---|---|
| Basic elk hunt, sometimes mule deer or black bear also available. | Wyo., Mont., Colo., New Mex., Ida. | Usually from horseback out of established camps. This hunt varies tremendously depending on services furnished. | 7-14 days | $500-$1200 depending on how many hunters to the guide (2, 3 or 4) and how many hunters to the camp (4 to 10). This is basically a meat hunt with chances of taking a big 6-pt. bull usually rather slim. A good hunt of this type lasts about 10 days and costs $800 to $1000 (in '75). | $50-$100 | General mountain hunt gear; good binoculars and powerful elk rifle. | A man has to be pretty lucky to even see, much less take a trophy bull on one of these hunts. However, it is quite possible to have a good time, see some grand country and take a good young bull for meat. With the grocery store prices running what they are today, that's no small dividend! |
| Non-guided moose and caribou meat hunt. | Alaska | Either fly in from Anchorage or Fairbanks to established camps and hunt from there afoot (several operators provide these services) or take or rent your own camp gear in Alaska and charter bush plane to fly you and your buddies in and pick you up a week or 10 days later and set up your own camp. | 7-10 days. | $500-$1000. The operators flying you to their camp can provide a variety of services. They may furnish the food or not, they may leave a cook-"guide" to oversee camp and they may or may not fly out a certain quantity of meat for you. This hunt is a good bet for four hunting buddies who have hunted together before. | Not applicable | General camping and hunting gear plus pack bags, chain saw and butchering implements. | For 4 experienced hunters and woodsmen who thoroughly check out where and when to go through the Alaska F & G Dept. and other local sources, this can be an unforgettable experience that nets them *tons* of good boned-out meat and probably at least 1 or 2 good trophies. For greenhorns who blunder into this without bothering to do their homework, it can be expensive, dull and downright dangerous not to mention wasting the precious vacation! |

## Hunts costing $500 — $1,000 (continued)

| | | | | | | |
|---|---|---|---|---|---|---|
| Early or late season trophy mule deer hunt. | Colo., Wyo., Mont., Ida. | Combination of afoot, by vehicle and on horseback, depending on exact nature of hunt. | 5-10 days. | $500-$1000 depending on whether 1 or 2 hunters to the guide, length of hunt, desirability of hunting ground and comfort of camps and/or ranch house accommodations. This hunt averages about $750 (in '75). | General hunting gear and clothing. | A good hunt for the eastern sportsman to take after his first mule deer and pronghorn combo hunt. |
| Mule deer/pronghorn combo hunt — for meat or trophy. | Wyo., Mont. | Combination of on foot, by vehicle, and from horseback. | 3-7 days. 5 days most common. | $350-$700. This hunt averages about $500 (in '75) depending on whether 1 or 2 hunters to the guide and how many horses and vehicles are used. | Flat shooting rifle and good binoculars. | For more than a generation this has been the classic "first western hunt" for eastern whitetail hunters. And for good reason; an outstanding chance at 2 fine heads of game for a relatively reasonable price. Changing game seasons have generally restricted the availability of this hunt in recent years but it is still possible in some areas and still a good bet! Sometimes whitetail may also be possible. |
| Trophy Caribou hunt. (Salmon fishing also available at some camps and always secondary chance at northern gray wolf.) | Ungava Peninsula, Northern Quebec | Afoot from established camps. | 5-7 days. | $600-$1000 depending on length of hunt, whether good salmon fishing is also on the menu and number of camps available to hunt and their general proximity to the best points on the normal migration routes. Mid-Sept. during the migrations is the time to go. | General hunting gear and rubber boots. | This hunt is growing in popularity and it's a good idea to fork out for the extra 2 days as weather insurance. Excellent chance of taking a good bull and it's easy enough to bring that 150 lbs. of boned out, tasty meat back with you. A short drive from the crowded eastern seaboard. |
| Meat hunt for moose. Secondary chance at black bear and (sometimes) whitetail. | Ontario, Quebec. | Afoot from canoe or boat. Occasional vehicle use. | 5-10 days. 7 days avg. | $350-$750. This hunt averages about $500 (in '75) depending on length of hunt, type of accommodations, guide arrangements and success of outfitter previous year. An occasional good trophy bull is taken. | General hunting gear. Way to bring back meat. | This isn't my own personal favorite type of hunt but it does have its share of excitement and, if the hunter does score, he can bring home 500 or 600 lbs. of the tastiest meat around. |
| Moose. Only chance left in N.A. for woodland caribou if you're lucky enough to draw a permit. | Newfoundland. | Afoot from established camps. | 7-10 days. | $400-$800 depending on length of stay, camps, whether caribou are included. | General hunting gear. | Hunter beware! While a number of fine outfitters operate here, in years gone by some haven't had the most enviable of reputations for professionalism or client comfort. Licenses, at $350 for moose and $500 for caribou, are verging on the ridiculous. |

| HUNT/GAME AVAILABLE | HUNT LOCALE | HUNTING METHOD | HUNT DURATION | TOTAL HUNT COSTS (EXCL. LICENSES, TRAVEL TO & FROM AND INCIDENTALS). | AVG. HUNT COST PER DAY | SPECIAL EQUIPMENT OR GEAR REQUIRED | GENERAL REMARKS |
|---|---|---|---|---|---|---|---|
| Trophy whitetail hunts. | Sundance, Wyo.; Rapid City, S.D.; Laredo, Tex. (Check with Chamber of Commerces, State F & G Depts.) | Afoot; by horseback or from jeeps and 4WD's. Can be from ranches or established camps or even motels. | 5-10 days. 7 most common. | $300-$700 with $500 being most common depending on length of hunt, chance of success, whether 1, 2 or 3 hunters to the guide and type of accommodations. | $75-$150 | General hunt gear. | Trophy whitetail are never easy to come by but these three areas seem to produce their share year in and year out. Also, big whitetails from various areas in Missouri (check F & G Dept.) and Saskatchewan (check Provincial F & G Dept. to see if non-resident deer hunting allowed.) |

## North American Hunts Costing $1,000 - $2,000*

| HUNT/GAME AVAILABLE | HUNT LOCALE | HUNTING METHOD | HUNT DURATION | TOTAL HUNT COSTS (EXCL. LICENSES, TRAVEL TO & FROM AND INCIDENTALS). | AVG. HUNT COST PER DAY | SPECIAL EQUIPMENT OR GEAR REQUIRED | GENERAL REMARKS |
|---|---|---|---|---|---|---|---|
| Trophy elk hunt. Sometimes mule deer or black bear also available. | Mont., Colo., Wyo., New Mex., Ida. | All of these premium level elk hunts are, to my knowledge, horseback hunts. Usually conducted from established out-camps but can be from a ranch, base camp or moving packstring, depending on the locale, season and situation. | 10-15 days. 14 days avg. and advisable | $1000-$2000 (in '75). Will average about $1800 for good 12- or 14-day trip with a good expectation of getting a true trophy bull. | $125-$175 on these 1-hunter-per-guide trophy hunts. | General mountain and horseback hunting gear. Many of these are late season hunts requiring cold weather clothing and gear. | Big bull elk are getting harder to come by every year because of hunting pressure (tho general elk hunting is in its heyday as management for quantity like eastern whitetail hunting, hits its stride). It's harder to make the record book with elk than any other species except mule deer and whitetail and a big bull is worth an expensive hunt. My own first choice would be Montana. |
| Moose and caribou meat hunt. | Cen. & no. British Columbia; Alberta. | Varies widely. Can be from horse out of base camp, afoot, even from boat. | 10-15 days. | $1000-$1500 depending on length of hunt and desirability of hunting ground. Almost a 100% cinch to get both animals barring accidents and weather, in good country. Occasionally there are legitimate bargains here for hunts only costing $600-$750. Check father-son special hunts in B. C. for good prices. | $100-$150 on this 2-hunters-per guide hunt. | Cold weather gear for this late hunt. | The wife can go along on this one if you'll be hunting out of a snug, weather-tight base camp. Some few 7-day hunts still available and not a bad deal if you're truly not concerned with trophy size and don't mind added chance of weather doing you out of second animal. 7-day hunt can go for only $700-$1000. |
| Goat and black bear. Marginal chances at elk, mule deer moose or whitetail in some areas. | So. and cen. British Columbia | Can be from horse but more often it is afoot from small, temporary camps. | 10-15 days. 10 days still common. | $750-$1500 depending on duration, hunting method and hunting ground. Some good bargains here for under a $1000 if you're in good shape and don't mind roughing it. | $75-$125 depending on how many hunters to the guide. | Mountain hunting gear, flat shooting rifle. | Years ago this was one of my first north-of-the-border hunts and it's still a good bet for the whitetail hunter after he's made that first trip out West for mule deer and pronghorn. |

279

## Hunts costing $1,000 — $2,000 (continued)

| HUNT/GAME AVAILABLE | HUNT LOCALE | HUNTING METHOD | HUNT DURATION | TOTAL HUNT COSTS (EXCL. LICENSES, TRAVEL TO & FROM, AND INCIDENTALS) | AVG. HUNT COST PER DAY | SPECIAL EQUIPMENT OR GEAR REQUIRED | GENERAL REMARKS |
|---|---|---|---|---|---|---|---|
| Spring grizzly hunt. Some black bear. | Cen. and so. British Columbia; western Alberta | Usually on horseback. | 10-14 days. | $1000-$2000 depending on how many hunters to the guide and the hunting area. Averages around $1250-$1500 (in '75) for a hunt in a good area (which means you'll have about a 50-50 chance of connecting, maybe a little more). | $100-$150 | Mountain hunt gear. | Not only are the bear hunting odds better in the spring as you glass the bare hillsides for bear coming out of their dens and digging for marmots and skunk cabbages, but the hides are in better shape than the fall. Usually a comfortable hunt in good weather. |
| Dall sheep. (Sometimes other species available at extra cost.) | Alaska | Sometimes afoot from established camps but, more often, fly in to remote areas and live off the pack on your back. | 7-14 days. 10 days avg. | $1500-$2000. Hunt is over when the sheep is taken. Sometimes moose or caribou available at an extra agreed upon fee. I look for this type of hunt (living off the pack on your back) to play an even larger role in Alaskan sheep hunting, especially for *trophy* sheep. A TOUGH HUNT. | $150-$175 depending on length of hunt, type of camp, area hunted, size of sheep sought. | A mountain hunt strictly afoot. Guide-outfitter furnishes camp gear, dried food, etc. You need top quality expedition grade backpack. | This type hunt usually run by small, 1-man operator who is not a full-time outfitter or guide. This can either be a fabulous experience and a real bargain or a swindle. Check carefully before signing agreement. This is the way to try for that outsized trophy Dall but a tough hunt; about 5 days avg. is all the avg. hunter can take of this strenuous spike camp living if weather is good; less in bad weather. Be in good condition and ready to "hurt" a bit! |

# North American Hunts Costing $2,000 - $3,000*

| HUNT/GAME AVAILABLE | HUNT LOCALE | HUNTING METHOD | HUNT DURATION | TOTAL HUNT COSTS (EXCL. LICENSES, TRAVEL TO & FROM, AND INCIDENTALS) | AVG. HUNT COST PER DAY | SPECIAL EQUIPMENT OR GEAR REQUIRED | GENERAL REMARKS |
|---|---|---|---|---|---|---|---|
| Moose/Caribou hunt. Sometimes includes chance at elk, too. (In no. B.C. elk limited to a few areas in the *east*.) | Cen. & no. B.C.; Alberta. | Fly in and then by horseback. Most of these hunts in B.C. (not Alberta, tho) are late season hunts in late Oct. and Nov. when it's *cold* and the outfitters have completed their earlier general game hunts for bear and mountain game. | 10-15 days. 15 days minimum if elk also included and becoming more common than 10 days even for moose and caribou only. | $1,500-$2,500. Averages about $2,000 for a good hunt in a prime area (in 1975). Price rises as length of hunt increases, desirability of area for trophy game improves and if elk are also included. Sometimes legitimate bargains are available on this type hunt when outfitter is trying to round out his season with fully booked hunts. Savings can run to $500 if you hit it right (and negotiate a bit). | $125-$175. Per diem price increases for better areas and shorter hunts. | WARM CLOTHING! Both wool (warm when wet) and down types. Sturdy rain gear and comfortable long johns. | These hunts are often conducted from the outfitter's more luxurious, lower elevation base camps rather than his high elevation outcamps. Thus, though *you* may get very cold hunting all day, this hunt is often a good bet to bring your wife or children on if they want to see the winter wonderland of the far north in late fall, sample some exotic game meats and cooking and generally lounge around the snug base camp and meet some fascinating folks they'd never get to rub elbows with back home. Depending upon the outfitter's set-up, much lower "non-hunter" daily rates can often be negotiated for these family affairs. A good hunt to check into! |

| Game | Location | Method | Duration | Price | Per Day | Gear | Comments |
|---|---|---|---|---|---|---|---|
| Elk, mule deer, black bear and (if you've been lucky enough to draw the permit) possibly sheep, goat, moose or grizzly. | Rocky Mtn. states of western U.S. | Fly or drive in to base camp and then by packstring to out-camps. Often this hunt will be in country 2,000 to 4,000 feet higher and in rougher mountains than the equivalent far north hunt — so be thin and in good physical condition! | 14-15 days. Possibly longer if exceptional trophies of several species are desired. | $2,250-$3,500. This basic Rocky Mtn. mixed game hunt is available in an infinite number of versions (at an infinite number of prices!) but this example is the top-of-the-heap deluxe hunt with one guide to the hunt in a prime area. This hunt averages around $2,500 to $3,000 (in 1975). | $150-$200 | Heavy-duty boots, good binoculars and spotting scope and clothing appropriate for high country hunting. | The deluxe Rocky Mountain trophy hunt is usually more expensive than its equivalent northern Canadian hunt particularly due to the currently favorable U.S./Canadian currency exchange rate. |
| Mixed game hunt with less emphasis on size of sheep or availability of other game such as moose, caribou and (especially) grizzly. | Yukon | Fly in and then hunt by horse. Similar to more expensive version of this hunt mentioned in the "$3000-$4000" category. | 14-15 days. (Practically no 10-day mixed game hunts now available.) | $2100-$2750. This is more of a general hunt than a true mixed game trophy hunt since this one is often a few days shorter in duration and in country less remote or with less outsized trophy game. Often (tho not always by any means) the sheep hunting is only mediocre on this hunt. | $150-$175 | Clothing and gear necessary for high country, hunt by horse. | If carefully checked out by the hunter, this expensive but not astronomical hunt can be a good "compromise" hunt. |
| Spring brown bear hunt. Black bear also usually available. | Southeastern Alaska | Hunt afoot from boat. Cruise islands and coast until bear or bear sign spotted then hunt afoot. This also can be a good hunt to take the wife on as some of these boats are quite comfortable, if not luxurious and this area is beautiful, especially at this time of year. | 10-15 days. (The longer the better; weather very unpredictable here even in spring.) | $1750-$3500. Varies by length of hunt, how many hunters per guide, luxuriousness of boat accommodations. A good hunt of this type averages $2500-$3000 (in '75) with one guide per hunter and $1750-$2500 with two hunters per guide. | $175-$225 | This is wet country. Good raingear, hip-boots for slogging across tidal beaches and marshes and climbing boots are necessities. | There are actually more bear here than in the fabled grounds of Kodiak and the Alaska Peninsula and you will probably get a bear just as large here (8'-9') as you will further north and west tho the bear here do not get as large at their largest as they do elsewhere. A good hunt for the money. Since the boat is a fixed cost for the outfitter, often you can work out very attractive savings if you bring 3 other hunters for a 4 hunter/2 guide hunt. |

## Hunts costing $2,000 — $3,000 (continued)

| HUNT/GAME AVAILABLE | HUNT LOCALE | HUNTING METHOD | HUNT DURATION | TOTAL HUNT COSTS | AVG. HUNT COST PER DAY | SPECIAL EQUIPMENT OR GEAR REQUIRED | GENERAL REMARKS |
|---|---|---|---|---|---|---|---|
| Canadian brown bear hunt; spring or fall. (Huge mountain goat also possible in fall.) | The Coast Ranges of northwestern British Columbia | Hunt afoot, checking river sandbars and salmon pools, from established camps. Though they are practically never hunted on this hunt; the world's largest mountain goats live high above these same bear grounds in the rugged coastal mountains. The enterprising hunter could well take one as a "bonus." | 14-21 days. 15 days most common | $2,000-$3,500. Varies by length of hunt, luxuriousness of camps, desirability of hunting grounds. A good hunt of this type averages $2500-$3000 (in 1975). | $175-$225 | Wet weather gear and hip boots. | This area literally teems with bear, including many fine trophies in the 8½'-9' class. If you want a record book goat this is the hunt for you tho you'll probably have to talk your outfitter into it as most don't fool with them on this hunt. This is NOT a good hunt for the wife or family. Most of the camps on these hunts are very Spartan and at least 1 major outfitter specializing in this hunt (who has some of the very best bear ground) has a less than glowing reputation for client comfort! |
| Elk. Often one or more of moose, caribou, mule deer, goat, black bear also available as secondary possibilities. Also chance at bighorn sheep if you luck out and draw one of the nonresident sheep permits. | So. & cen. B.C.; western Alberta | Usually by horse tho some cheaper hunts are afoot from camps reached by vehicle or hike-in. | 10-21 days. 14-15 days most common unless sheep are also on the agenda. | $1200-$3000 depending on length of hunt, whether horses used and whether one or two hunters to the guide. This hunt averages $2,000 to $2,500 (in '75) tho some two hunter per guide hunts will run $1500-$1800. | $100-$200 | General mountain hunting gear. | Chances for elk are somewhat better in some B.C. areas than in Alberta. But if trophy elk were my goal, I'd check Montana or Wyoming. Getting a legal bighorn ram either place is somewhat chancey and true trophy rams are about as common as unicorns. |

# North American Hunts Costing $3,000 - $4,000*

| HUNT/GAME AVAILABLE | HUNT LOCALE | HUNTING METHOD | HUNT DURATION | TOTAL HUNT COSTS (EXCL. LICENSES, TRAVEL TO & FROM, AND INCIDENTALS) | AVG. HUNT COST PER DAY | SPECIAL EQUIPMENT OR GEAR REQUIRED | GENERAL REMARKS |
|---|---|---|---|---|---|---|---|
| Mixed game hunt for Dall sheep (sometimes Stone or Fannin-intergrades also available), moose, caribou, grizzly. Few or no goat or black bear available in the Yukon. | Yukon Territory, Canada | The 22 outfitters operating up here universally rely on horses after a fly-in. Sometimes by moving packstring but most often out of established camps with brief spike-out for sheep, if necessary. | 14-21 days with 18 being most common | $2,750-$3,500. Averages about $3,500 for a good 18-day hunt (in '75). Varies by desirability of hunting area, esp. sheep and grizzly availability. (NOTE: limited Stone sheep hunting also available in Yukon in southern portion around Pelly mountains.) With British Columbia putting sheep on limited quota system, this factor will influence prices from outfitters having black as well as white sheep. | $150-$225 | Good saddlebags & rifle scabbard. Extra rain pants and long john pants to serve as light duty chaps when needed. Binoculars & spotting scope as in any other mountain hunting. | This huge, game-rich area has less people now than it did in 1900 and historically it has been a "bargain" as compared to comparable hunts in B. C. and Alaska. Though prices are rapidly escalating, this is still true (relatively) and the sheep hunting here can't be beat! This is the only area other than B.C. where Stone sheep can be taken and the license costs also generally run well below Alaska & B.C. A good prospect to check. |

| | | | | | | | |
|---|---|---|---|---|---|---|---|
| *BIG* Brown bear (best chance at 9' and about only chance at 10' trophy. Spring and fall hunts; moose and/or caribou usually available at extra cost on fall trips. | Alaska. Mostly limited to Alaska Peninsula and Kodiak Island. | Fly-in to *established* camps (required by law) and hunt afoot. (NOTE: Alaska law now limits a hunter to 1 brown bear *or* grizzly every 5 years so bear in mind that this hunt and a "5-animal" hunt aren't worthwhile in same 5 years.) USUALLY A ROUGH HUNT. BRING A BIG GUN YOU CAN SHOOT AND BE READY TO WORK. | 10-15 days. Hunt is over when you get your bear. Spring hides far better than fall and hunt is often easier. | $2,750-$4,500. Prices vary all over the lot depending on length of hunt, and various factors but mostly on outfitter-guide's reputation and how good his season was the preceding year. $3,500 about average (in '75). Good bear populations but 10' giants are very hard to come by. | $225-$350 | Two sets rain gear, at least one to be heavy-duty. Hip boots. Two rifles, both dependable non-jamming and authoritative calibers. Wet weather a nemesis so bring enough clothes and socks to insure that you always have a dry change. | Since wet or inclement weather is even more of a factor here than in the normal "big country" mountain hunt, a 12- or 15-day hunt is far preferable to 10 days. Practice your shooting. Though it doesn't often happen, brown bear *can* shoot back! All your optics should be high quality, water resistant types. Wool clothing in both heavy and light weights, more desirable than cold-when-wet cotton jeans, shirts and underwear. |
| Stone sheep *only* | Northern B. C. | By horseback out of established out-camp to spartan spike camp up high for trophy sheep. | 14-21 days. 15-18 most common | $3,000-$4,000. By today's hunting realities an "average" Stone sheep usually ends up costing about $3,000. Some outfitters levy a surcharge on larger trophies with sheep over 40" coming very dear. | $200-$275 depending on availability and size of area and duration of hunt. | Top quality high power binoculars (9x or 10x) and spotting scope, either zoom type of with several eyepieces to carry you from 20x through 30x to 45x or 60x. | If you're at all serious about this type trophy hunt, it most always involves spiking out with just you and the guide to do all cooking and chores in a high camp. Several days of that kind of living is far rougher than it sounds in a magazine story, especially if the weather is rotten. (NOTE: British Columbia's new quota-permit system may significantly affect the availability and/or cost of this hunt, depending upon the final provisions of the system.) |
| Mixed game hunt for several animals including some or all of moose, caribou, goat, elk, black bear and fair to good chance at grizzly. Also, may include outside chance at bighorn sheep (again, depending on upcoming quota-permit system). NO STONE SHEEP. | Cen. & no. B.C.; Alberta. (NOTE: No grizzly or goat mixed game hunts in Alberta. Goat closed there and grizzly is spring season only.) | Runs the gamut depending on exact nature of this widely variable hunt. Can be horseback, fly-in and walk, fly-in and horse, vehicle (to end of road) and walk or horseback. More expensive hunts in better areas involve horse and planes, usually. | 10-21 days. 14-18 average | $1,000-$3,500. Various grades of this hunt are available at many prices. One guide to the hunter, good camps in a wilderness area and a better than avg. chance at grizzly and bighorn (B.C.) or bighorn only (Alberta) runs this hunt to around $2,500-$3,500. Prices drop as these 2 "premium" animals are no longer available, as two-hunters-to-the-guide hunts show up and as lesser numbers of the other animals are realistically available and horses not used. | $100-$200. Good grizzly and/or bighorn hunt usually $175-$200 (in '75). | Equipment necessary for wilderness hunt. Specifics determined by exact nature of particular hunt. | This is a widely variable hunt which usually straddles the $3,000 and $2,000 classifications if grizzly and sheep included in well run trophy camps. Outfitters have made every conceivable variation of this hunt available with "savings" accumulating as quality of game and hunt decreases. Some good bargains available here, though. |

## Hunts costing $3,000 — $4,000 (continued)

| | | | | | | | |
|---|---|---|---|---|---|---|---|
| Record book or at least outsized moose and caribou (only). | Alaska. Primarily Alaska Peninsula but also in southern Alaska Range and Talkeetna Mountains. | Mostly fly-in and walk. Some vehicle usage on more expensive hunts, especially on Peninsula. Some horses used in Talkeetnas. | 10-15 days. 14 or 15 days far more preferable for weather safety and to allow more selectivity. | $2,500-$3,750 depending on amount of flying, number of camps hunted, size of heads desired, duration of hunt, luxury of accommodations. For best quality trophies of record book or near record size, this hunt averages $3,000-$3,200 (in '75). | $200-$250 | General; plus adequate foul weather gear. | Moose and caribou are available considerably cheaper elsewhere but not this size and not this comfortably (most B.C. moose-caribou only hunts are late season, cold weather propositions.) This Alaska hunt is usually a Sept. or October situation. |
| "3-animal" hunt with your choice of Dall sheep, moose, caribou, black bear and sometimes goat. Sheep usually included but not always; grizzly practically never included. | Alaska. Often several different areas hunted. Generally larger heads (and heavier hunting pressure) ound further south and east you go in state. | Mostly fly-in and walk. Some limited use of horses and vehicles. | 10-16 days. 10 very risky, 12 most common | $3,000-$4,500. Varies by use of plane and vehicle, no. of areas hunted, whether sheep included and how good the sheep area is and duration of the hunt. Less than 14 days is risky if good heads desired, and sheep important. Averages $3,500-$4,000 (in '75) for good hunt. | $250-$300 | Foul weather gear; pack bag or day pack; hip boots; etc. | This is an interesting hunt and, in many ways, more attractive than the enormously expensive "5-animal" hunt. Of the two animals you're foregoing, you can let one be the black bear, a trophy available for much less money elsewhere, and your chances at a mountain grizzly in Alaska realistically run from about 30% to 50%. Also, if there's any chance you might make a brown bear hunt within the same 5 years, remember that only one bear of either grizzly or brown type (they're actually the same species, Ursus arctos) is legal in a 5 year period. |

# North American Hunts Costing $4,000 And More*

| HUNT/GAME AVAILABLE | HUNT LOCALE | HUNTING METHOD | HUNT DURATION | TOTAL HUNT COSTS (EXCL. LICENSES, TRAVEL TO & FROM, AND INCIDENTALS). | AVG. HUNT COST PER DAY | SPECIAL EQUIPMENT OR GEAR REQUIRED | GENERAL REMARKS |
|---|---|---|---|---|---|---|---|
| "5-Animal" hunt for Dall sheep, grizzly, moose, caribou & black bear. Mountain Goat also available on some hunts. | Alaska. Often 2 or more widely separated locales. | Bush plane fly-in to well established comfortable camps and then hunt afoot. Sometimes tracked or big-tired A.T.V.'s also utilized. One guide per hunter. | 18-21 days. | $4,000 - $6,000. Varies depending on how many camps you hunt and how much flying you do, use of other expensive bush vehicles, plushness of camps, desirability of hunting areas for both quantity and quality of game, whether basic in and out by bush plane from jumping off point included, etc. | $200-$300. Shorter hunts cost more per day. | Hip boots usually needed both for boggy areas and for constant fording of shallow rivers in most valleys. | As the prices imply, these are "Country Club" hunts with all the trimmings in the better game areas. Horses not available except with a few outfitters in the Wrangell's and one in the Brooks Range — plan to walk a lot! Most mountains not particularly tough by Rockies standards though the Wrangell's and the Chugach in S. E. Alaska can be rough. Bring daypack to carry lunch, down vest, etc. Full size packframe & bag desirable if you will spike camp out any. |

| Type of Hunt | Location | Method | Duration | Cost | Fee | Equipment | Comments |
|---|---|---|---|---|---|---|---|
| Largest Brown bear: record book moose and caribou | Alaska Peninsula, Alaska | Bush-plane fly-in and walk; A.T.V.'s frequently used. | 15 days. | $3,750-$4,500. Varies depending on amount of flying done, sophistication of other ATV transportation available and plushness of camps. THIS IS ROUGH COUNTRY but the world's biggest moose and caribou live here, especially around Ugashik Lakes and Lake Iliamna. Biggest bear now on eastern (roughest) side. | $250-$300. Sometimes "trophy fee add-on" charged by outfitter for record book trophy or trophies over a certain size. | Hip boots and day pack. | This is the hunt for record book moose and caribou and the brown bear rival (many would say exceed) those on Kodiak. Bear not in as good coat as spring. If caribou are especially important, reserve the Sept. 15-30 period which is usually the height of the migration. Much thick cover here so face-to-face meetings with bear aren't uncommon. Bring the biggest gun you can accurately shoot with .338's and .375's getting the nod. Recommend caliber with no less than 3500 lbs. muzzle energy. |
| General mixed game hunt for Dall sheep, grizzly, moose, caribou. Few or no black bear or goat available. | MacKenzie Mts. Northwest Territories, Canada | Bush plane fly-in and walk. Some limited use of jet boats and pack dogs. No horse hunting to my knowledge. | 18-21 days. A few 15-day hunts available but not generally advisable. | $3,600-$5,000. Varies by number of camps hunted, luxuriousness of camps, amount of bush plane service furnished, number of hunters per camp (important when hunting limited radius afoot), etc. One guide per hunter. Check cost of bush plane in and out; some outfitters include it and others don't. | $200-$250 per day. | Hip boots (sometimes) and day pack or packboard. | Good game availability but trophies generally don't run as large as for same species further west in Yukon or Alaska. Only hunted for sport since 1964 by about 130-150 sportsmen per year, this is some of the wildest, least known ground left on earth. |
| Mixed game hunt for Stone sheep, grizzly, moose, caribou. Black bear and/or goat may or may not be included. | Northern British Columbia. Biggest moose gen. in N.E. part of Prov.; biggest caribou in N.W. Cassiar Mtns. and area probably has most big sheep right now. Atlin area also good. | This is the classic packstring hunt. Fly in by bush plane then hunt by horse either out of established camps or by moving packstring or combination of both. May also spike camp for sheep. | 18 to 35 days. 21 days most common and usually minimum necessary to realistically count on good all-around bag. | $3,750 to whatever you want to spend. Avg. cost for good hunt (in '75) probably around $4,500. Costs vary by factors mentioned but especially by how many sheep and grizzly in area and how many big sheep. Some of these are basically big sheep only hunts with the other game there if you want it. | $225-$275 | Your own well-made saddlebags and gun scabbard with boot that fits over gun butt to protect entire gun. Rainpants and long johns to cushion legs when necessary. | This is THE classic mountain hunt but proceed with care; some well-known areas overharvested in last few years. (NOTE: in early 1975 the B.C. Gov't installed a quota hunting system. CHECK CAREFULLY. Grizzly and sheep are almost certainly limited; other species in question.) Hunt costs may be greatly affected if permits are given to outfitters (rather than drawn for directly by hunters) who then charge what trade will bear. |

# APPENDIX

# Where To Get Your Deer

THIS INFORMATION-packed chart portrays the basics of whitetail, mule deer and blacktail deer hunting throughout the nation in a recent year. Though the exact figures may vary a bit from season to season, the patterns portrayed here are valid and are expected to remain so for the foreseeable future. As one might expect on any set of figures this comprehensive, there are a few instances when all figures aren't directly comparable to each other. Some states lump their bowhunters in with the gun hunters in a single figure while others break them down separately. Thus, in calculating the various "Hunter Success Ratios" I had to make an arbitary decision on whether to base the figure on all hunters or gun hunters only. I chose the latter, feeling it more accurately portrayed the basic situation for the vast majority of us.

This information should be handy in helping you to assess how your state's deer hunting stacks up with the rest of the country in both quantity and quality and also in helping you to plan more productive out-of-state deer hunting trips.

A quick glance at the chart immediately highlights several points of interest. The states currently harvesting the *largest whitetails* are: Minnesota (133 pounds average field dressed weight), Kansas (129 pounds), West Virginia (127 pounds), Wyoming and Nebraska (125 pounds) and Arkansas (120 pounds).

States yielding the *largest mule deer* are: Wyoming (145 pounds) California (140 pounds), Arizona (135 pounds), North Dakota (130 pounds), and Colorado (126 pounds).

States with the *best whitetail hunter success ratios* are: Texas (65.4 percent), Alabama (51.2 percent), North Dakota (46.2 percent), Louisiana (44.9 percent) and South Dakota (44.3 percent). All of these states have respectable sized herds, and if you're planning an out-of-state whitetail hunt, these are the best bets to score. However, bear in mind that the deer are very small in Texas (73 pounds), Alabama (75 pounds) and Louisiana (82 pounds) while they run considerably larger than the national average in North Dakota (118

pounds) and South Dakota (115 pounds). The southern states offer the added advantage of running longer seasons and later seasons so that you can often schedule a southern deer hunting jaunt without missing deer season in your own home state.

States with the *best mule deer/blacktail deer hunter success ratios* are: Alaska (with a whopping 106.8 percent blacktail ratio for its tiny little Sitka blacktails, indicating that some hunters scored on more than one deer), Colorado (50.4 percent-mule deer), Utah (43.4-percent mule deer) and Nevada (41.7 percent-mule deer). All of these states have medium to large herds and are good prospects for the visiting out-of-state hunter.

Montana is rather difficult to place because its tremendous 81.7 percent success ratio, which certainly makes it an attractive option for the out-of-state hunter, isn't broken down between mule deer and whitetails. Another thing to bear in mind while digesting these figures is that a state featuring two or three species of deer actually has a better *overall* deer success ratio than may be implied by looking at each species individually. For instance Washington, with all three deer species, actually has an overall statewide all-deer success ratio of 26 percent which is respectable. South Dakota, with two species of deer, has an extremely impressive 67.5 percent overall ratio when combining the two. Oregon's all-deer success ratio is an attractive 33.9 percent when you add its two species together to evaluate the statewide prospects.

Some of the *most underhunted states for whitetails* (i. e. low ratio of all hunters to deer herd size) are: Texas 17.7 percent), Alabama (21.6 percent), Florida (30.1 percent, South Dakota (36.8 percent). In other words, counting both gun hunters and archers, there are only 17.7 hunters per hundred deer in the state.

Some of the *most under hunted states for mule deer and blacktails* are: Alaska (6.6 percent), Nevada (38.8 percent), Wyoming (39.3 percent), California (40.0 percent). Montana would undoubtedly fall in this group if herd estimates of its mule deer were available upon which to base these calculations.

## Deer Hunting at a Glance
### Nationwide statistics to show you how your state stacks up and to help you better plan any out-of-state deer hunting expeditions!
(W = Whitetail; M = Mule deer; B = Blacktail)

| State | Type of Deer | Est. herd size (in 000's) | No. of Hunters (000's) (Bowhunters incl. with gunhunters some states) | | Kill (000's) Both sexes | Hunter success ratio (Cal. on gunhunters only) | Avg. Wt. Field Dressed |
|---|---|---|---|---|---|---|---|
| | | | Bow | Gun | | | |
| Alabama | W | 750.0 | 2.2 | 160.0 | 82.0 | 51.2% | 75 |
| Alaska | B | 90.0 | | 5.9 | 6.3 | 106.8 | 110 |
| Arkansas | W | 425.0 | 10.0 | 210.0 | 35.0 | 16.7 | 120 |
| Arizona | M | 128.5 | 7.0 | 64.5 | 11.8 | 18.3 | 135 |
| | W | 25.5 | | | 2.2 | 3.4 | 80 |
| California | M | 1,000.0 | | 400.1 | 11.1 | 2.8 | 140 |
| | B | | | | 20.3 | 5.1 | 80 |
| Colorado | M | 315.1 | 14.9 | 149.5 | 75.4 | 50.4 | 126 |
| | W | 5.0 | | | .1 | — | — |
| Connecticut | W | 19.0 | 4.5 | 6.8 | .8 | 11.8 | 90 |
| Delaware | W | 8.0 | 3.0 | 10.0 | 1.5 | 15.0 | 106 |
| Florida | W | 570.0 | | 171.4 | 57.2 | 33.4 | 85 |
| Georgia | W | 165.0 | 22.9 | 176.0 | 44.6 | 25.3 | 80 |
| Hawaii | B | .7 | | .4 | (10) | — | 110 |
| Idaho | M | 329.4 | | 157.5 | 44.3 | 28.1 | 125 |
| | W | 70.6 | | | 9.5 | 6.0 | 100 |
| Illinois | W | ? | 13.0 | 62.5 | 14.7 | 23.5 | 100 |
| Indiana | W | 60.0 | 21.4 | 57.7 | 7.2 | 12.5 | 100 |
| Iowa | W | 35.8 | 10.0 | 34.3 | 14.0 | 43.7 | 117 |
| Kansas | M | 4.6 | 4.7 | 8.3 | .9 | 10.8 | 125 |
| | W | 18.4 | | | 3.2 | 38.5 | 129 |
| Kentucky | W | 60.0 | 13.7 | 50.0 | 10.3 | 20.6 | 95 |
| Louisiana | W | 300.0 | 167.9 | 166.7 | 74.8 | 44.9 | 82 |
| Maine | W | 225.0 | 1.8 | 196.1 | 24.8 | 12.6 | 126 |
| Maryland | W | 60.0 | 5.0 | 90.0 | 9.7 | 10.1 | 100 |
| Massachusetts | W | 12.0 | .1 | 5.3 | 2.1 | 39.9 | 95 |
| Michigan | W | 700.0 | 158.7 | 616.0 | 70.7 | 11.5 | 110 |
| Minnesota | W | 400.0 | 29.2 | 294.3 | 69.0 | 23.4 | 133 |
| Mississippi | W | 400.0 | 9.6 | 168.7 | 35.0 | 20.7 | 100 |
| Missouri | W | ? | 25.3 | 210.8 | 34.8 | 16.5 | 85 |
| Montana | W | ? | 7.2 | 150.0 | | | |
| | M | ? | | | 122.6 | 81.7 | 120 |
| Nebraska | M | 45.0 | 8.8 | 24.2 | 7.9 | 32.6 | 105 |
| | W | 55.0 | | | 8.0 | 32.6 | 125 |
| Nevada | M | 125.0 | 2.0 | 46.5 | 19.4 | 41.7 | 108 |
| New Hampshire | W | 40.0 | 2.6 | 80.0 | 5.5 | 6.9 | 108 |
| New Jersey | W | 75.0 | 30.0 | 126.0 | 11.3 | 9.0 | 90 |
| New Mexico | W M | 250.0 | 2.0 | 111.0 | 30.5 | 27.5 | 125 |
| New York | W | 389.7 | 73.9 | 630.3 | 75.4 | 12.0 | 120 |
| North Carolina | W | 400.0 | 25.0 | 145.0 | 45.0 | 31.0 | 80 |
| North Dakota | M | 20.0 | 6.0 | 56.0 | 2.2 | 3.7 | 130 |
| | W | 80.0 | | | 27.5 | 46.2 | 118 |
| Ohio | W | 70.0 | 6.0 | 100.0 | 7.6 | 7.6 | 120 |
| Oklahoma | W | 85.0 | 15.0 | 93.0 | 7.6 | 8.2 | 108 |
| Oregon | M | 403.8 | 16.8 | 296.3 | 41.3 | 13.9 | 107 |
| | B | 685.9 | | | 62.1 | 20.0 | 95 |

| State | Type of Deer | Est. herd size (in 000's) | No. of Hunters (000's) Bowhunters incl. with gunhunters some states) | | Kill (000's) Both sexes | Hunter success ratio (Cal. on gunhunters only) | Avg. Wt. Field Dressed |
|---|---|---|---|---|---|---|---|
| | | | Bow | Gun | | | |
| Pennsylvania | W | 570.0 | 195.0 | 800.0 | 126.9 | 15.9 | 95 |
| Rhode Island | W | 2.0 | .6 | 2.4 | .1 | 4.1 | 90 |
| South Carolina | W | 210.0 | 5.0 | 100.0 | 46.0 | 46.0 | 100 |
| South Dakota | M | 90.0 | 5.7 | 52.1 | 12.1 | 23.2 | 115 |
| | W | 157.0 | | | 23.1 | 44.3 | 115 |
| Tennessee | W | 120.0 | 16.0 | 120.0 | 11.4 | 9.0 | 119 |
| Texas | M | 168.3 | 50.0 | 560.0 | 10.3 | 1.8 | 90 |
| | W | 3,453.6 | | | 366.0 | 65.4 | 73 |
| Utah | M | 200.0 | 25.2 | 200.6 | 86.8 | 43.4 | 97 |
| Vermont | W | 150.0 | 26.7 | 137.0 | 9.6 | 7.0 | 100 |
| Virginia | W | 303.4 | 28.7 | 250.0 | 60.8 | 24.3 | 82 |
| Washington | M | 150.0 | 10.0 | 224.3 | 18.8 | 8.4 | 120 |
| | W | 80.0 | | | 8.6 | 3.8 | 100 |
| | B | 240.0 | | | 31.0 | 13.8 | 100 |
| West Virginia | W | 185.0 | 21.0 | 150.0 | 25.9 | 17.3 | 127 |
| Wisconsin | W | 600.0 | 106.0 | 514.6 | 90.6 | 17.6 | 100 |
| Wyoming | M | | 2.1 | 121.9 | 57.1 | 46.8 | 145 |
| | W | 315.8 | | | 4.3 | 3.5 | 125 |
| 1971 Totals Note: Various Totals Adj. to Incl. Est. for Missing Data in Table . . . | M | 3,314.4 | 806.2 | 7,358.1 | 511.8 | (Not valid— all hunters not hunting all species . . . ) | 117.2 |
| | W | 9,793.0 | | | 1,248.7 | | 100.8 |
| | B | 939.7 | | | 105.3 | | 103.4 |
| TOTAL | | 14,047.1 | | | 1,865.8 | | |
| 1972 Totals Adj. to Incl. Est. for Missing Data | M | 3,013.4 | 877.2 | 7,673.4 | 501.2 | (Not valid — all hunters not hunting all species . . .) | 119.0 |
| | W | 10,769.3 | | | 1,504.9 | | 103.5 |
| | B | 1,004.0 | | | 98.5 | | 102.0 |
| TOTAL | | 14,786.7 | | | 2,104.6 | | |
| 1973 Totals Adj. to Incl. Est. for Missing Data | M | 3,447.2 | 1,205.0 | 8,410.3 | 525.4 | (Not valid— all hunters not hunting all species . . .) | 119.6 |
| | W | 11,584.9 | | | 1,564.0 | | 103.0 |
| | B | 1,059.7 | | | 119.7 | | 96.2 |
| TOTAL | | 16,091.8 | | | 2,209.1 | | |